Also by Souad Mekhennet

The Eternal Nazi: From Mauthausen to Cairo,
the Relentless Pursuit of SS Doctor Aribert Heim
(with Nicholas Kulish)

Die Kinder des Dschihad: Die neue Generation des islamistischen Terrors in Europa
[*The Children of Jihad: The New Generation of Islamic Terror in Europe*]
(with Claudia Sautter and Michael Hanfeld)

Islam
(with Michael Hanfeld)

I WAS TOLD TO COME ALONE

I WAS TOLD TO COME ALONE

My Journey Behind the Lines of Jihad

Souad Mekhennet

Henry Holt and Company | New York

Henry Holt and Company
Publishers since 1866
175 Fifth Avenue
New York, New York 10010

www.henryholt.com

Henry Holt® and ▥® are registered trademarks of
Macmillan Publishing Group, LLC.

Distributed in Canada by Raincoast Book Distribution Limited

Library of Congress Cataloging-in-Publication Data

Names: Mekhennet, Souad, author.
Title: I was told to come alone : my journey behind the lines of jihad / Souad Mekhennet.
Description: New York : Henry Holt and Co., 2017.
Identifiers: LCCN 2016054740| ISBN 9781627798976 (hardback) | ISBN 9781627798969
  (electronic book)
Subjects: LCSH: Emwazi, Mohammed, –2015. | IS (Organization) | Jihad. | Terrorism—Middle
  East. | Mekhennet, Souad. | BISAC: BIOGRAPHY & AUTOBIOGRAPHY / Personal
  Memoirs. | POLITICAL SCIENCE / Political Freedom & Security / Terrorism. | RELIGION /
  Islam / General.
Classification: LCC HV6433.I722 I8562 2017 | DDC 363.3250956—dc23
LC record available at https://lccn.loc.gov/2016054740

Our books may be purchased in bulk for promotional, educational, or business use. Please contact
your local bookseller or the Macmillan Corporate and Premium Sales Department at (800) 221-7945,
extension 5442, or by e-mail at MacmillanSpecialMarkets@macmillan.com.

First Edition 2017

Designed by Kelly S. Too

Printed in the United States of America

1 3 5 7 9 10 8 6 4 2

To my grandparents, parents, and siblings

CONTENTS

I WAS TOLD TO COME ALONE

Meeting ISIS

Turkey, 2014

I was told to come alone. I was not to carry any identification and would have to leave my cell phone, audio recorder, watch, and purse at my hotel in Antakya, Turkey. All I could bring were a notebook and a pen.

In return, I wanted to speak to someone in authority, someone who could explain the long-term strategy of the Islamic State of Iraq and al-Sham, or ISIS. It was the summer of 2014, three weeks before the group became a household name by releasing a video of the beheading of the American journalist James Foley. Even then, I suspected that ISIS would become an important player in the world of global jihad. As a journalist covering Islamic militancy across Europe and the Middle East for the *New York Times*, major German news outlets, and now the *Washington Post*, I had watched the group take shape in the world created by the September 11 attacks, two U.S.-led wars, and the upheaval known as the Arab Spring. I had been talking to some of its future members for years.

I told my contacts with ISIS that I would ask whatever questions I wanted and that I wouldn't clear quotes or show them the article before it was published. I also needed their guarantee that I wouldn't be kidnapped. And since I'd been told not to bring anyone else from the *Post*,

I asked that the trusted contact who had helped arrange the interview be allowed to accompany me.

"I'm not married," I told the ISIS leaders. "I cannot be alone with you."

As a Muslim woman of Moroccan-Turkish descent, born and raised in Germany, I am an outlier among the journalists covering global jihad. But in the years since I started reporting on the September 11 hijackers as a college student, my background has given me unique access to underground militant leaders such as the man I was to meet that July day in Turkey.

I knew that ISIS was holding journalists hostage. What I didn't know was that the leader I would meet oversaw the group's hostage program, supervising the British-accented killer who would appear on the videos and become known to the world as Jihadi John. I would learn later that the man I met that summer, who was known as Abu Yusaf, had taken a leading role in torturing the hostages, including waterboarding them.

I had asked to meet Abu Yusaf during the day in a public place but was told that wouldn't be possible. The meeting would be at night, and in private. A few hours beforehand, my contact moved the time back to 11:30 p.m. This was not a comforting development. A year earlier, members of the German antiterrorism police unit had knocked on my door at home to tell me they had learned of an Islamist plot to lure me to the Middle East with the promise of an exclusive interview, then kidnap me and force me to marry a militant. Those threats came back to me now, as I wondered if I was crazy to be doing this. Despite my nerves, I pressed on. If everything worked out, I would be the first Western journalist to interview a senior ISIS commander and live to tell the story.

It was a hot day toward the end of Ramadan, and I wore jeans and a T-shirt as I prepared my questions at the hotel in Antakya. Before leaving, I put on a black *abaya*, a traditional Middle Eastern garment that covers the whole body except for the face, hands, and feet. One of Abu Musab al-Zarqawi's associates had chosen it for me years earlier, when I'd visited the late Al Qaeda leader's hometown of Zarqa, Jordan. The Zarqawi associate had bragged that this *abaya*, which had pink embroidery, was one of the nicest styles in the shop, and the fabric was thin enough to be comfortable even in hot weather. Since then, it has become a sort of good luck charm. I always wear it on difficult assignments.

We were to meet Abu Yusaf along the Turkish-Syrian border, not far from the border crossing at Reyhanli. I knew the area well: my mother had grown up nearby, and I had visited often as a child.

I said good-bye to my *Post* colleague Anthony Faiola, who would stay behind at the hotel, leaving phone numbers he could use to reach my family in case anything went wrong. At about 10:15 p.m., the man who had helped arrange this interview, whom I'll call Akram, picked me up at the hotel. After a forty-minute drive, we pulled into the parking lot of a hotel restaurant near the border and waited. Two cars soon appeared out of the darkness. The driver of the lead car, a white Honda, got out; Akram and I got in. Akram sat behind the wheel and I climbed into the passenger seat.

I twisted around to look at the man I had come to interview, who sat in the back. Abu Yusaf looked to be twenty-seven or twenty-eight and wore a white baseball cap and tinted glasses that masked his eyes. He was tall and well built, with a short beard and curly, shoulder-length hair. Dressed in a polo shirt and khaki cargo pants, he would have blended in seamlessly on any European street.

Three older Nokia or Samsung cell phones lay on the seat beside him. For security reasons, he explained, no one in his position would use an iPhone, which could make him especially vulnerable to surveillance. He wore a digital watch similar to those I'd seen on American soldiers in Iraq and Afghanistan. His right pocket bulged; I assumed he was carrying a gun. I wondered what would happen if the Turkish police stopped us.

Akram turned the key in the ignition, and the car began to move in darkness along the Turkish side of the border, sometimes passing through small villages. I could hear the wind against the car windows. I tried to keep track of where we were, but my conversation with Abu Yusaf drew me in.

He spoke softly and calmly. He tried to hide that he was of Moroccan descent and where exactly in Europe he came from, but I noticed his North African features, and when I switched from classical Arabic to Moroccan Arabic he understood and answered in kind. It turned out he had been born in Morocco but had lived in the Netherlands since his teens. "If you want to check my French as well, just tell me," he said, smiling. He also spoke Dutch. I would learn later that he had been trained as an engineer.

As we drove, he explained his vision: ISIS would free Muslims from Palestine to Morocco and Spain and then go farther, spreading Islam all over the world. Anyone who resisted would be treated as an enemy. "If the U.S. hits us with flowers, we will hit them back with flowers," Abu Yusaf said. "But if they hit us with fire, we will hit them back with fire, also inside their homeland. This will be the same with any other Western country."

ISIS had plenty of resources and expertise, he told me. In fact, the group had begun quietly establishing itself long before it appeared on the world stage. Its members included educated people from Western countries, highly trained security officers from Saddam Hussein's presidential guard, and former Al Qaeda acolytes. "You just think we have nutcases coming to join us?" he asked. "No. We have people from all over the world. We have brothers from Britain with university degrees and of various descents: Pakistani, Somali, Yemeni, and even Kuwaiti." Later, I would realize that he was also talking about the guards that several ISIS hostages would dub "the Beatles": Jihadi John and three others with English accents.

I asked what had pushed him to join the group. Abu Yusaf said that he'd grown fed up with the hypocrisy of Western governments, which were always talking about the importance of human rights and religious freedoms, while relegating their Muslim residents to a kind of second-class citizenship. "In Europe, look how we have been treated," he told me. "I wanted to be in the society I grew up with, but I felt, 'You're just the Muslim, you're just the Moroccan, you will never be accepted.'"

The U.S. invasion of Iraq in 2003 had been unjust, he said: there were no weapons of mass destruction, Iraqis were tortured in Abu Ghraib, and the Americans faced no consequences. "Then they're pointing at us and saying how barbaric we are."

"You say you're against the killing of innocent people," I said. "So why are you killing and kidnapping innocent people?"

He was silent for a few seconds. "Every country has a chance to get their people free," he said. "If they don't, that's their problem. We didn't attack them; they attacked us."

"When you take people hostage, what do you expect?" I responded.

He then started talking about his Moroccan grandfather, who had fought the French colonialists for freedom, drawing a parallel between that jihad and this one. "This is all the outcome of the Americans colonizing Iraq," he said. "Now we're fighting the jihad to free the Muslim world."

But my grandfather had been a freedom fighter in Morocco, too. When I was a little girl, he'd talked to me about that "jihad," about how Muslims and their "Jewish brothers" had fought to expel the French who had seized control of their ancestral lands. "We did not kill any women and children, and no civilians," my grandfather had told me. "That's not allowed in jihad." His rebellion was nothing like the horrors perpetrated by ISIS.

"But he was in his country," I said. "This is not your country."

"This is Muslim land. This is the country of all Muslims."

"I grew up in Europe like you," I told him. "I studied like you in Europe."

"Why do you still believe the European system is fair and just?" he asked.

"What is the alternative?"

"The alternative is the caliphate."

Our debate had grown heated, personal. There seemed to be so many parallels between his background and mine. Yet we had chosen different paths, and mine wasn't what he would call the "right way" for a Muslim woman, not the Islamic way.

"Why are you doing this to yourself?" he asked. "You really believe that the West respects us? Treats us Muslims equally? The only right way is our way," by which he meant the way of the so-called Islamic State.

"I've read your stuff," he told me. "You interviewed the head of Al Qaeda in the Islamic Maghreb. Why are you just a reporter? Why don't you have your own TV show in Germany? Why are you not making a career in Germany, with all the awards you've won?"

I couldn't pretend I didn't know what he was talking about. Coming of age and making my way professionally as a Muslim in Europe had at times been trying. I don't wear a head scarf; I'm considered a liberal and a feminist; I've cowritten a book about finding one of the last living Nazis in Cairo and won prestigious fellowships in America. But Abu Yusaf was right: I don't have a TV show in Germany. To rise in my home country as a Muslim migrant, or even as the child of migrants, you have to toe the line and praise Europe's progressiveness. If you criticize the government too loudly or raise serious questions about anything from foreign policy to Islamophobia, the backlash can be intense.

I obviously didn't agree with Abu Yusaf that the caliphate was the solution. But I couldn't help thinking that Western societies and politicians have made little progress toward addressing the policies that radicalize young men like him. More intelligence services putting more restrictions on people is not the solution, nor are global surveillance networks that compromise the privacy of the innocent along with the guilty. Abu Yusaf was part of a generation of young Muslims who were radicalized by the invasion of Iraq, much as the generation before him had been radicalized by the Soviet invasion of Afghanistan in 1979. In some ways, he reminded me of my younger brother, and I felt a big sister's responsibility to protect him. But I knew it was too late for that.

"You may be right that we face discrimination and the world is unfair," I told him. "But this is not the jihad, what you're fighting. Jihad would have been if you'd stayed in Europe and made your career. It would have been a lot harder. You have taken the easiest way out."

For a few seconds, no one said anything.

Abu Yusaf had insisted on taking me back to Antakya rather than returning to our original meeting point, and by this time we were close to my hotel. I thanked him and climbed out of the car. Even at this hour, the coffee shops were busy with people eating before dawn, as is common in Ramadan, when Muslims fast during the day. I felt glad to have gotten the interview, but I was also worried. Abu Yusaf had spoken with such confidence and fury. "Whoever attacks us will be attacked in the heart of their countries," he had said, "no matter if it's the USA, France, Britain, or any Arab country."

We're losing one after the other, I thought. *This guy could have been somebody different. He could have had a different life.*

1

Stranger in a Strange Land

Germany and Morocco, 1978–93

I was born with thick, curly black hair and big brown eyes. My parents were more or less the only immigrants in our Frankfurt neighborhood, and I became something of a local curiosity. Even then, I had a particularly expressive face, but I also drew attention because I didn't look German. In the park, parents would leave their children and come to look at me. Many U.S. soldiers and their families were stationed in Frankfurt, not far from Klettenbergstrasse, where our apartment was, and they would greet us kindly.

"You looked so different from all these kids," the woman I would come to call my German godmother, Antje Ehrt, told me later. "You looked so critical when you were pissed about something. People could see, she's angry. They would fall in love with you, this funny, beautiful baby."

I was born in the spring of 1978, on the eve of a period of dramatic change in the Muslim world. In the months after my birth, events in Iran, Saudi Arabia, and Afghanistan sent the Muslim world into turmoil and started what would become decades of coups, invasions, and war.

In Iran in January 1979, the shah abdicated and fled with his family. On February 1, Ayatollah Khomeini returned from his years of exile and declared an Islamic republic, turning against his former allies the intellectuals and liberals. Instead, he instituted a return to conservative religious and social values, curtailing women's rights and enforcing Islamic dress codes. On November 4, student revolutionaries took over the U.S. embassy in Tehran, seizing sixty-six American hostages, fifty-two of whom would be held for more than a year.

Sixteen days later, on the first day of the Islamic year 1400, a group of armed religious extremists took over the holiest sites in Islam, the Grand Mosque in Mecca and, within its courtyard, the Kaaba. Their sharpshooters climbed the minarets and took aim at pilgrims, worshippers, and police, all in an attempt to destabilize the Saudi monarchy and establish a regime based on fundamentalist Islamic ideology.

The Siege of Mecca lasted fourteen days and resulted in an estimated one thousand deaths and major damage to the holy structures before it was put down by Saudi troops with the help of foreign special forces teams. The reverberations were felt around the world, and forward in time. Osama bin Laden often recalled the defilement of the shrine by Saudi forces, laying blame on the Saudi royals and praising the "true Muslims" who had brought havoc to the holy place. A few weeks after that, the Soviet invasion of Afghanistan ushered in nine years of guerrilla warfare, as bin Laden and other Muslim fighters flocked to Afghanistan, giving rise to the era of global jihad.

My parents' lives were much more mundane. My mother, Aydanur, was from Turkey; my father, Boujema, was Moroccan. They'd come to West Germany in the early 1970s, within a few months of each other. They were guest workers, part of a tide of migrants from across southern Europe, Turkey, and North Africa seeking work and an opportunity to build more prosperous lives. At the time, West Germany was still recovering from the devastation of World War II and trying to turn itself into a prosperous industrialized nation. The country needed workers: young, healthy people who could do hard labor and take on the unpleasant jobs that many Germans didn't want to do. German companies were recruiting workers from Greece, Italy, Turkey, Yugoslavia, Spain, and Morocco. My parents were among them.

My mother had come to West Germany alone, at nineteen, on a trainful of Turks. Working in Hildesheim, not far from the East German border, she wrapped and packed radios and TVs for shipping and lived in a house full of other migrants, sharing a room with three other women. She later moved to Frankfurt to be closer to one of her brothers, who lived and worked there. She had long hair that she didn't cover with a scarf, and she liked to wear skirts that showed off her legs.

She met my father in 1972, through an older Moroccan gentleman who saw her waiting tables at a Frankfurt shopping mall café and decided to set them up. Back then, my father was working as a cook at a place called Dippegucker, which was known for international fare and Frankfurt specialties such as the city's trademark green sauce, made with herbs and sour cream, and served with boiled eggs and cooked potatoes. This was all new to my father, who had trained in the French cooking more popular in Morocco, but he had long dreamed of coming to Europe. Since his arrival in Germany a year earlier, he'd worked hard and made himself an asset in the kitchen.

My mother liked him immediately, but she was skeptical. The girls she knew were always saying that you had to be careful about these Moroccan guys, that they were good-looking but fickle, second only to the Algerians when it came to caddishness. Out of curiosity, she stopped by the restaurant and saw that he really was cooking, not just washing dishes, as she'd suspected. He was tall and muscular with thick, dark, wavy hair, and he looked impressive in his sparkling chef's whites and toque. She noticed that he went out of his way to smile and speak courteously to others, not just to her. They drank coffee together, and he asked when he could see her again. When she arrived home from work the following day, she found him waiting with flowers and chocolates.

"If you think you're coming upstairs, you're mistaken," she told him. Then she invited him up, and they drank more coffee.

The romance moved fast, and they married in a civil ceremony at Frankfurt's City Hall a few weeks later. My father's boss was his best man, and my mother's Japanese roommate was her maid of honor.

My mother got pregnant quickly. But life changed dramatically for Muslims and Arabs in West Germany during the 1972 Olympic Games in Munich, when a group of eight Palestinian terrorists entered the Israeli team's quarters, killed a coach and a weight lifter, and took nine other athletes hostage. The militants belonged to a group called Black September. They vowed to kill the hostages unless Israel agreed to release two hundred Arab prisoners and guaranteed the hostage takers safe passage out of West Germany. Israel, following a long-held policy, refused to negotiate. The Germans, however, promised to fly the militants and their hostages to Tunisia. At the airport, German snipers opened fire on the Palestinians. But the terrorists were well trained; they killed the hostages. The raid ended in disaster, with all the hostages, five of the hostage takers, and a police officer dead.

Years later, it emerged that Black September was an offshoot of Fatah, Yasser Arafat's wing of the Palestine Liberation Organization. But in the immediate aftermath of the Munich attack, Muslims and Arabs faced new scrutiny. My parents felt the change, especially my father. Police would stop him often and ask for his papers. The homes of Arab students were searched because police suspected them of supporting militant groups or sheltering their members. "Some people would even say, 'Arabs should leave,'" my father told me. It didn't bother him because something bad had happened, and the Germans were trying to figure out who was behind it. He understood why they were suspicious.

The pressure continued throughout the 1970s, as terrorism became a daily reality in West Germany. Groups such as Black September and the Baader-Meinhof Gang, which called itself the Red Army Faction, were motivated by hostility toward Israel and what they dubbed Western imperialism, but ideologically they were left-wing and secular. The Red Army Faction included the children of German intellectuals; they saw West German leaders as fascists and compared them to Nazis. This wasn't entirely wrong; at the time some influential posts in West Germany were held by people with connections to the Nazis. The Red Army Faction undertook bank robberies, bombings, hijackings, kidnappings, and assassinations. The group had connections to the Middle East. In the late 1960s, Baader-Meinhof members traveled to a Palestinian training camp in Lebanon for instruction in bomb making and other guerrilla skills, and some members took part in joint operations with the Popular Front for the Liberation of Palestine and other groups. The Red Army Faction kidnapped West German politicians and industry leaders, including Hanns-Martin Schleyer, an influential businessman and former SS member, whom they also killed.

In 1973 my mother gave birth to my oldest sister, Fatma. A year later, my sister Hannan arrived. Then, in 1977, my mother learned that she was pregnant for the third time. The doctors advised her to have an abortion. They thought I would be born with a congenital defect that could leave me without arms or hands. My mother was distraught.

"It's all in the hands of God," my father told her. "Let's have the child and whatever happens, happens. We'll deal with it."

In those days, some Turkish migrants were known to cause scenes at German hospitals when women gave birth to girls. They wanted sons.

When I was born, the doctor looked apologetic. "I'm sorry," he said. "It's a girl."

"Is she okay?" my mother asked. "Does she have arms and legs?"

"Not only is she okay," the doctor said, "she just peed on me!"

Because I was born healthy, against all the doctors' predictions, my parents named me "Souad," which means "the happy fortunate one" in Arabic. And in many ways I was a very lucky child. Klettenbergstrasse, where we lived then, is one of the nicest streets in Frankfurt. My father's boss, who owned the restaurant where he worked, rented an apartment at number 8, and he found us an apartment in the same building, at the very top, in a sort of attic. The building was old and had six flats. Most of the other residents in the building and the neighborhood were bankers, managers, or business owners. A stewardess for Lufthansa lived in the other top-floor apartment, across from ours. We were the only guest worker family.

While the area was beautiful, our apartment was not. The roof leaked so badly that sometimes my mother had to set up buckets to catch the rain. Both of my parents had to work, and not only to support us. They also felt responsible for their families back in Morocco and Turkey and sent their parents money every month. A German woman cared for my two older sisters during the day in her apartment. When my mother's younger sister came to visit her and their brothers in Germany, she took care of me during the day.

When I was eight weeks old, my parents learned that my mother's father was very ill. They couldn't afford to buy airline tickets on such short notice; the bus was more affordable, but it meant at least four days of travel. My parents worried that the trip would be too much for me.

Antje Ehrt and her husband, Robert, who lived in our building, offered to take care of me for the four weeks that my parents would be gone. My parents accepted but insisted on paying for my expenses. But my parents' return was delayed because my grandfather's health worsened, so they stayed longer. There were no telephones. The Ehrts started to worry about how they would explain to the authorities where this baby had come from.

After my parents came back, the Ehrts became like godparents to me. The couple had two children of their own and were more open-minded and inviting than some others in the neighborhood. Robert Ehrt was a manager at a big German company. I was told later that when I was a baby, he would come home from work and play with me and give me a bottle.

The family used to eat in their kitchen, and when I stayed with them as a baby they would leave me in the bedroom. But I didn't like that. I wanted to be where the action was. I would scream until they came and got "madam" in her bassinet. They would put the bassinet on the kitchen counter so I could be close to them as they ate.

On the ground floor lived another couple who would influence me. Ruth and Alfred Weiss were Holocaust survivors. My father would sometimes buy them bread from the bakery, and my mother would send them cookies or food she had cooked.

"Many of my teachers were Jewish," my father always told us. "I am very grateful for what they have taught me."

When I was just a few months old, my mother's sister, the one who had come to Germany to visit and had been babysitting for me, decided to return to Turkey to help care for my grandfather. My parents discussed sending me to Morocco, to stay with my father's mother. There, I would be with someone who would really take care of me; I would also learn Arabic and get my early Islamic education.

It seemed the right choice. I was still breast-feeding, and since my mother wouldn't be with me, my Moroccan grandmother found a Berber woman in her neighborhood to nurse me. Back in Germany, my mother mourned. She knew that I would make my first memories far away from her.

My Moroccan grandmother, Ruqqaya, had been named after one of the Prophet's daughters. She and her relatives bore the surname Sadiqqi; they were known to be descendants of Moulay Ali Al-Cherif, a Moroccan nobleman whose family came from what is today Saudi Arabia and helped unite Morocco in the seventeenth century, establishing the dynasty of the Alaouites, who are still in power today. They were a dynasty of *sharifs*, a title that only the descendants of Muhammad's grandson Hasan are allowed to carry.

My grandmother had been born into a wealthy family in the province of Tafilalt, in the city of Er-Rachidia, in the early years of the twentieth century. In those days, birthdays weren't always carefully recorded, but she remembered the French marching into Morocco in 1912. Her family owned land in the region, and she used to tell me about the date palms there, and the cows, sheep, goats, and horses they kept. Her relatives were considered nobility because of their connection to the Prophet. Such people are sometimes called by honorifics—*moulay* and *sharif* for the men and *sharifa* or *lalla* for the women—but my grandmother never used her formal title.

She was married young, at thirteen or fourteen, to the son of a close friend of her father's, a prosperous and wellborn boy a bit older than she. She gave birth to a baby boy about a year later. Over the next few years, they had another son and a daughter, but her husband grew violent, hitting her and their children. She told her parents she wanted a divorce. This was discussed in the family, but the friendship and business ties between her father and her father-in-law proved too strong. Have patience, her family told her, these things sometimes pass. My grandmother refused. She divorced her husband and left, taking her three children with her.

It was a radical move in those days, and my grandmother became an outcast. She was a young woman on her own who couldn't read or write, and she had never learned to work because she'd never had to. She fled with her children to Meknes, one of Morocco's four royal cities, where she married again. She never talked about her second husband, except to say that the union was brief: he left her while she was pregnant with another child, a girl named Zahra. Now she was alone again, with children from two different men. She swore never to marry again, vowing instead to work and support her family alone. In those years, she made her living mainly as a nurse and midwife, and she also mixed and sold healing oils.

My grandmother took risks but she always knew who she was—and she never forgot her roots. She told me that some of her most crucial role models had been the wives of the Prophet. His first wife, Khadija, had been a successful businesswoman who was older and had supported Muhammad financially and emotionally when his own tribe turned against him. She is honored by Sunnis and Shia as the first convert to Islam and as Muhammad's most loving and faithful confidante. Another of his wives, Aisha, was known for her intellect and extensive knowledge of the *Sunnah*, the tradition of sayings and activities of Muhammad, which is the second most important theological and legal source for many Muslims after the Koran. While Sunnis revere her as one of the Prophet's sources of inspiration, some Shia see Aisha more critically, suspecting her of having been unfaithful to the Prophet and arguing that her opposition to Muhammad's son-in-law Ali was an unforgivable sin. "Don't think women have to be weak in Islam," my grandmother told me.

She met the man who would become my grandfather in Meknes. His name was Abdelkader, and he, too, came from a wealthy background. But by the time they met, prison and torture had broken his body and his fortune was gone.

My grandfather came from a province known as al-Haouz and its outskirts, not far from Marrakech, which was known to have one of the strongest opposition movements against the French. In al-Haouz and other parts of Morocco, Muslims and Jews fought side by side for independence. My grandfather had been a tribal chief and a local leader in the independence movement, developing strategy and helping to funnel weapons and supplies to fighters trying to force out the French. They called it a jihad, but my grandfather and his comrades had strict rules: they could target only French soldiers and known torturers who worked on behalf of the French, not women or civilians.

One day in the late 1940s, the French arrested my grandfather and asked him to give up the names of those belonging to the resistance in his area. "You will get even more land and privileges," the French interrogator told him. "If you don't work with us, we will throw you in jail and take away your lands."

Grandfather believed in the rebellion. He believed that even if the French took away his property, one day his country would get independence and he would get his land back. They threw him in jail, where he was beaten. They made my grandfather and other prisoners stand naked in contorted positions, urinated on them, and doused them with cold or hot water; some were raped with bottles. They seized his olive trees, his almond and orange groves, and his horses. They gave many of his possessions to collaborators.

He spent a few months in prison. When he was released, the French banned him from returning to his lands; he had lost everything but his pride and hope. He went to Meknes, where he found work as a laborer, building houses. He didn't know the trade, but he had to survive. Meknes was booming, and people needed places to live.

This man who had once owned horses and many acres of land decided to settle in Sidi Masoud, a ragged community that resembled a shantytown. Sidi Masoud was home to Moroccans who had come to the city from different regions and for different reasons; they built their dwellings hurriedly and poorly from wood, sheet metal, and whatever else they could find or get cheaply.

One day, a woman of noble lineage moved into Sidi Masoud with her children. One of Abdelkader's friends, who knew of his past as a tribal chief, told him laughingly that his status in the neighborhood would now be topped by that of a true *sharifa*.

Abdelkader knew that this woman had children, so he went to welcome her and brought along some sweets. Instantly suspicious, she told him she didn't need candy or gifts. He was impressed. Within a few weeks, he'd asked her to marry him. Abdelkader was in his midtwenties, younger than my grandmother, and while he still felt strongly about Moroccan independence, the jail and torture had weakened and scarred him. As a child, when I asked about the marks on his hands and arms, he said they were from lit cigarettes that the French had pressed into his skin; he bore the marks of a horse whip on his back. I think he was drawn to my grandmother in part because of her strength, and because she was a healer. He undertook to provide for her and her children, even adopting her youngest daughter, who had been born fatherless and had only her mother's name on her birth certificate.

In 1950, less than a year after their marriage, my grandmother gave birth to my father; he was her youngest, and her favorite. The family lived in a small, simple dwelling made of iron and wood. The walls were roughly nailed together, leaving gaps where you could see the sky. There were two small rooms and no running water or kitchen. The washroom was a partitioned corner with a hole in the ground for a toilet and a bucket of water for washing.

"There was one well with drinking water," my father told me. "You had to walk two kilometers and carry the filled buckets back the whole way."

The French still occasionally summoned my grandfather or came to the house to arrest him. They told him that he could still get his lands back if he would only cooperate with them. But my grandfather refused. He worried for his family, especially that the French would take my grandmother to hurt him even more. There were rumors of French soldiers and those who worked with them raping women. My father remembered my grandfather used to have a pistol that he kept hidden in the house. Once, when my father was four or five, my grandparents got into an argument and my grandmother threatened to tell the French about my grandfather's gun. "They'll lock you up, and I'll get rid of you," she said, only half joking. My grandfather didn't want to go back to prison. He took the pistol to the mosque and threw it in the latrine.

My grandparents were both still active in the Resistance, particularly in motivating neighbors to take part in protest marches against French rule. In 1956, Morocco finally got its independence, but my grandfather never got his land back. Instead the local mayor offered him two kilograms of sugar. My grandparents refused to accept it. Both were deeply disappointed, and my grandfather fell into a depression.

When my father turned seven, my grandparents divorced. Grandfather Abdelkader moved to a different part of Meknes, and my grandmother and her children were on their own again.

"She would wake up in the morning, pray, make breakfast for us, wake my oldest sister to take care of the rest, and then leave in the early morning and come back just before it turned dark," my father recalled. They had a primitive gas oven, which they used for cooking, or roasted their food over hot coals. They had one small radio that worked only when my grandmother had the money to buy batteries, and they relied on candles and oil lamps for light.

By the time I arrived in Morocco as an infant, to live with my grandmother, she had left the shantytown. Working in Frankfurt, my father had earned enough not just to support us but also to send his mother money to buy a house in the middle of Meknes with three rooms, a kitchen, and an indoor bathroom with a traditional squat toilet and a faucet in the wall.

My grandfather used to visit and would tell me stories of fighting the French colonialists. He also once told me that the most powerful people were those who could read and write, because they would be the ones to explain to the world, and to write history. He feared that people would hear only the account of the French colonizers and that the stories of people like him would be forgotten.

A Jewish family lived three houses down from my grandmother. The mother would often come over on Fridays and bring homemade bread, which she said had been baked specially for that day. I now know that it was challah, prepared for the Jewish Sabbath. In exchange, my grandmother would bring over plates of couscous or cookies. Their daughter, Miriam, became a close friend of mine. She was two years older than I, and fluent in French; we called her "Meriem," the Moroccan version of the name. Before I turned four, she and her family left for France.

My grandmother had deep, dark eyes and white hair that was sometimes dyed red with henna. She was probably five foot six with very strong hands and a firm, muscular body, shaped by hard physical labor and toned by the medicinal oils she made and rubbed into her skin. She had an irresistible, contagious laugh.

She lived in the city, but her home had the feeling of a farm. She had no land to speak of, but she kept chickens, rabbits, and pigeons in a sliver of open ground between the living room and kitchen. She didn't trust the local butchers, so she slaughtered her own chickens and we always had fresh eggs. She also fed and cared for a couple of neighborhood cats. She always told me that the Prophet Muhammad took care of cats, so we should treat them well. She would never let a beggar leave our doorstep without giving him something to eat, and when a beggar came, I would often end up sitting on the stoop and talking to him, asking why he was poor and other impertinent questions. My grandmother was so embarrassed. "Why don't you let the man eat?" she'd say. But I was curious. She didn't just feed the beggars and send them off. She'd have something to say to them, a good word, something to give them hope. "You're going through tough times, but God is great, and you're going to get better," she'd say. As a sign of respect, they called her *hajja*, a title usually reserved for people who had completed the *hajj*, the annual pilgrimage to Mecca, where my grandmother had never been.

Although she had been born into comfortable circumstances, she had a natural head for home economics. Having her own chickens meant that even when money was tight we never went hungry. She cooked or baked with the eggs, or gave them to neighbors as gifts. Her pigeons were trained to deliver letters, a lucrative side business. She worked on a farm sometimes, milking cows. (When she took me with her, I would pull their tails.) She also still worked as a nurse and midwife and made medicinal oils.

She kept her coins—what she called "small money"—in a handkerchief hidden in her traditional long Moroccan dresses, but she hid her "big money"—bills—in her bra. "Make sure you don't keep all your money in one place," she told me. "You have to hide it so the sons of sin don't see how much money you have." "Sons of sin" was my grandmother's term for anyone who behaved badly, from a neighborhood tough to a serious criminal. I thought her bra trick funny at the time but, later, I found myself emulating her. In dicey reporting situations, a bra can be a good hiding place for memory chips and money. Especially in the Muslim world, few people will dare to check there.

My grandmother was stern but immensely lovable. When my grandfather visited her, he'd say, "Why don't we get married again?" But she wouldn't let people mess around with her. That was what made her different from other women. She wasn't afraid to take risks; that's something I learned from her.

My grandmother explained to me that no matter what position a person had, if he or she was in the wrong, one shouldn't keep silent. I remember once on a crowded bus in Meknes, a lot of young men were sitting while we stood. "Which one of you is going to stand up and make space for an older woman and a child?" she asked. When nobody paid attention, she grew irate. "You sons of sin!" she yelled. "You should be ashamed. In Germany, they would all get up and make space for an older woman and young child." The bus driver was laughing and telling her to take it easy, but finally one of the men grew so ashamed that he got up and gave her his seat.

At the time, the political situation in Morocco was sensitive. Anyone who criticized the police or the government could face trouble. My grandmother didn't care. Once, a policeman asked her for a "donation" after he saw her coming out of the bank. She asked him what charity organization the police were running now. When the cop made clear the money was for him, my grandmother began to berate him. Wasn't he ashamed, not only of being corrupt, but of taking money from a poor old woman who had to feed her granddaughter? "Why don't you go ask the guys in ties if they'll give you a private donation?" she asked him. "Because you don't dare. Instead, you take it from those who are weakest." The policeman shushed her but she yelled even louder, so that all of the people around us would hear what she had to say. And it worked: he finally went away without his bribe.

She spoke up on my behalf in ways I'll never forget. My grandmother couldn't read, but she had mastered most of the Koran. When I was almost four, she decided I should learn to read the holy book, so she started sending me to Koran school a few mornings a week. I'd sit on the floor with other kids, learning to read and memorize the suras, and on

Friday I'd recite what I'd learned in front of my grandmother. Our teacher, known as a *fqih*, would read out the lines, and we would repeat them, following along in the text. But the teacher was an aggressive young man, and when a student did something he didn't like, he'd strike the child's hands with an iron ruler.

My grandmother was very protective of me. She took seriously the responsibility my parents had given her when they left their baby daughter in her care. When I started at the Koran school, she had a talk with the *fqih*, Si Abdullah. "Don't ever touch this girl," she told him. "Don't ever beat her." One afternoon, Si Abdullah caught me speaking with another child, and the ruler came out. He told me to hold out my hands, palms up, and struck them with the metal. Then he asked me to turn them over and brought the iron down hard on my knuckles. I yelped in pain, burst into tears, and ran out of the classroom and down the street to my grandmother's house.

I cried and told her that Si Abdullah had beaten me. When she saw the marks on my hands, she was furious. She grabbed me and dragged me back to the school. We crashed into the classroom, where my grandmother took off her leather sandal and started beating Si Abdullah in front of everyone, shouting that she wouldn't let anyone touch her granddaughter. "Why did you beat her?!" she yelled. I was still crying, but all the other kids laughed as Si Abdullah cringed and ducked to avoid her blows.

She was so inspiring that I picked up her appetite for arguments and would eagerly debate with her. Once, when a friend of my father's named Mahmoud was visiting, she made me one of my standard meals: two- or three-day-old bread with warm milk, honey, and cinnamon. "I don't want to eat this again," I told her. "I've been eating this every second day."

"You'll eat what I make for you," she answered.

"But why are you always making this bread with milk? My parents send you enough money that we could afford other food."

"You should say *Alhamdulillah* that you have something to eat, you little devil," she told me, invoking a common Arabic phrase meaning "praise be to God." "There are so many poor people who would be happy to have something to eat."

She and Mahmoud were astonished by the sharpness and strength of my arguments, given that I was only four years old. Mahmoud burst into laughter when he heard my answer: "Well, Grandmother, if you are so worried about the poor people who have no food, then why don't you invite them to our house and let them eat this?"

My grandmother kept herself very clean. We had a faucet in our washroom, which we used for daily washing, but twice a week she would drag me to the *hammam*. I dreaded those bathhouses, with their heat and darkness, the stink of olive oil soap, and the loud voices of the naked women, who sounded to me like they were screaming. The women who worked there washed me with hot water and soap, roughly scrubbing my skin. My grandmother told me to close my eyes and keep quiet, but it felt like torture.

Meknes was very hot in the summer. The smell of the sandy ground hung in the air. When it rained, which wasn't often, everyone would open their doors and welcome the drops. I used to dance in the rain, while my grandmother screamed at me to come back in before I got sick. "But if the rain is washing me, we don't need to go to the *hammam* this week," I told her.

My father and mother understood that my grandmother would have loved to keep me in Morocco, but after three years they wanted to bring me back to Germany. It was a shock for my grandmother, who was hoping that I would stay with her.

For the first time, I saw her crying while speaking to my parents. But she also understood that it was time for me to be reunited with my mother, father, and sisters.

Three months later, my father came to take me back to Germany. I still remember how I hugged my grandparents and we all cried. My grandparents asked me not to forget where I came from. "I will go to school there and come back to you," I told them. "I promise I will not forget who we are. Never."

———

BACK IN FRANKFURT, I met my two sisters. It was December, and I saw snow for the first time in my life. I learned that my eldest sister, Fatma, now nine, had suffered brain damage because of complications when she was born. She needed a lot of extra help and support and went to a special day care. Hannan was just a year younger than Fatma, and we became fast friends.

I missed my grandparents deeply, and it took time to get used to my parents. My mother spoke Arabic, but I barely understood her when she didn't speak *darija*, the Moroccan dialect, which she had learned but spoke with a funny accent. Then there was the weird language everyone else around me spoke. I couldn't understand a word of German.

One evening, I saw Fatma and Hannan each cleaning one of their boots and putting it in front of our bedroom. They told me I should do the same because "Nikolaus" would come. I had no idea what they were talking about. I asked if this was a friend of our parents. I didn't know that Germans celebrate the coming of Saint Nikolaus early in December, several weeks before Christmas. They told me that Nikolaus would bring chocolates, and if the boot was cleaned well, there would be more sweets in it.

I began to clean my boots, too, and thought that if I cleaned both of them, Nikolaus would fill both up with sweets. When my parents sent us to bed, I kept thinking about this Nikolaus who would come with chocolates. I heard some noise and then I heard my parents switch off the lights.

I climbed out of bed, carefully opened the door, and looked for my boots. One was empty, but the other was filled with chocolates and candy. I couldn't believe that a stranger would bring in one evening as much chocolate as I had ever gotten in almost three years in Morocco. I began to eat the candy and chocolates in the dark, until the boot was nearly empty. Then I began to worry about my sisters. It would be unfair, I thought, if they saw their boots filled and mine empty, and they felt bad for me. So I took candy and chocolate from each of their boots and dumped them into mine.

The next morning when we all woke up and saw what Nikolaus had brought for us, my sisters wondered why their boots hadn't been filled up to the top.

"You should be happy that he came," I told them. "In the past he has always forgotten me, when I was in Morocco."

Both my parents were laughing. "You'd better go and wash away the chocolate around your mouth," my mother told me.

Our observance of Nikolaus's yearly visit was one way in which my parents tried to help us fit in in Germany. My mother worked for a church, and I went to a Christian kindergarten and later to day care on the premises. My parents told us that the three monotheistic world religions had a lot in common. There were Adam and Eve, who were banned from paradise, a story that was not only told in Judaism and Christianity but also found its way into the Koran and Islamic traditions. There was Abraham, the "father of believers," who is mentioned in the Koran, the Torah, and the Bible. There was Jesus, who was a prophet in Islam, but also important for Christians, since they believed he was the son of God. There was Moses, a prophet to Jews, Christians, and Muslims. All three faiths shared traditions of fasting, the belief in one God, and the importance of the holy scriptures. My parents explained that, as Muslims, we honored all prophets; the main difference was that we believed Muhammad was the last prophet of God.

Along with the Muslim holidays, we celebrated Christmas with a plastic tree and electric lights—my parents were too afraid of fire to get a real tree and decorate it with candles—as well as wrapped gifts. They would take us to the Christmas market, where we'd ride the carousel and eat traditional heart-shaped cookies, roasted chestnuts (a favorite of my mother's), and popcorn with salt and sugar, followed by dinner at McDonald's, Burger King, or North Sea, where we ordered fish and chips.

My mother worked as a laundress for nuns in a church community. A nun ran my kindergarten, where the teachers included a mean-spirited woman who would read us fairy tales. "You see, all the nice princesses are blond, and all the bad people are dark-haired," she'd tell me. I was the only dark-haired girl in the class, so this really hit me. "Wasn't Snow White also dark-haired?" I asked. This didn't seem to matter to this teacher, who sometimes took the opportunity to smack me when no one was looking, until Hannan caught her and told her to stop.

In the church laundry and dry cleaning service, my mother worked with a nun named Sister Helma and two women from Yugoslavia, whom we knew as Aunt Zora and Aunt Dschuka. They would wash and iron the nuns' habits and white head coverings. We called the place where they worked the "washing kitchen." There were several washing machines, including one for sheets and another for head coverings, and one big dryer. Each woman had an ironing table. My mother's iron was so heavy that it strained her back, giving her aches that still troubled her decades later. At break time, they drank coffee and ate bread or *borek*, a pastry stuffed with sheep cheese, brought by one of the Yugoslavian women. The nuns' head coverings reminded me of the head scarves worn by my grandmother and other elderly women in Morocco.

The kindergarten playground was visible from the window where my mother stood ironing. I would look up from playing to wave and wink at her, or she would come and bring me something to eat or drink. Aunt Zora's husband was a gardener in the same compound. He was always drunk, but he had a good heart. Whenever my sisters and I saw him drinking beer from the stall across the street, he'd tell us not to tell his wife, and he'd buy us ice cream.

At the restaurant, my father worked with several Germans, an Indian we called Uncle Baggi, Uncle Latif from Pakistan, and a gay Scotsman named Tom, whom we called Uncle Tommy and whose partner sometimes picked him up from work. All the men wore tight trousers and shirts and listened to rock music, and they became my father's friends. They would come over for lunch or dinner, and Latif or Tommy would bring bottles of beer and get funny after a while. I remember Uncle Tommy sometimes staying overnight in our guest room when he worked too late to catch the train home.

Latif was a sort of handyman for Willy Berger, my dad's boss, doing electrical and maintenance work at the restaurant and in Mr. Berger's and our home when it was needed. In the mid-1980s, Latif went to visit his family in Pakistan. He returned a changed man.

Shortly after he got back to Germany, my father called him because the lights in our house weren't working. When I opened the door, I saw Latif, who used to wear tight jeans and shirts unbuttoned halfway down his chest, clad in wide white trousers and a traditional tunic. His hair had grown since I'd last seen him, and he had a long beard.

Before, he'd always greeted my mother with a handshake, but now he refused to touch or look at her. He started looking into the problem with the lights. When my father got back from the grocery store, I could see surprise in his eyes.

My mother had prepared coffee and cake. But she told my father she sensed that Latif was no longer comfortable sitting with her. My sisters and I joined my dad and his old friend. Latif looked intently at my father and spoke to him. I was only about seven years old, but I remember hearing him say something about the need for hijab, a head scarf, for my mother and us girls, and that my father should think about the "jihad that Muslims were waging in Afghanistan." He also said that my father had to stop being friends with Uncle Tommy because he was gay.

We later learned that Latif had been in touch with groups in Pakistan that were supporting the war against the Soviets. He ultimately became part of the mujahideen movement, though we never learned the exact details. While the Arabic term *mujahid* refers to someone performing jihad, it was commonly used to describe the fragmented Islamist movement against the Soviet Union in Afghanistan. When I asked my father later which groups Latif was linked to, he said he'd never asked because he didn't want to know.

Latif's presumptuousness enraged my father. He told his old friend that he had no right to come to our house and tell him what Islam was, how his daughters and wife should dress, or whom he should be friends with.

My mother heard my father's voice rise and came to see if everything was all right.

"Tommy is our friend, and if you don't like it, then you can stop coming over here," I heard my father say. Latif took his things and left.

Some weeks later, my father came home and said that he had seen Latif in the city center with other bearded men. They had set up a table and chairs under a tent, and they were handing out books, trying to convert people to their interpretation of Islam and telling them about the war in Afghanistan. They were speaking to migrants but also to Germans, many of whom remained bitter about the division of Germany and hated the "godless" Soviets.

"There were men from Algeria, Morocco, Pakistan. They all were calling for support of the 'jihad' in Afghanistan," my father said. He told my mother never to let Latif into our house again. "I don't want you or our daughters to have anything to do with people like him," he said.

There was something else happening in Europe at about this time. In Britain, France, and Germany, some men who had returned from the fighting in Afghanistan began to tell other Muslim immigrants that it was their duty to protect oppressed Muslims around the world. Back then, these men weren't seen as threats. Western Europe was proud of its freedom of thought and expression, and these former fighters were allies of a sort, helping defeat the Soviets. Political leaders didn't suspect that the people fighting the Soviets would one day turn against them and their allies in the Middle East. They didn't realize that a quiet battle was beginning between secular, individualistic ideals and radical religious ideologies coupled with the will to rise up and fight injustice.

In our family, my parents wanted us to integrate as much as possible into German society while not forgetting our own culture. Two afternoons a week, we attended Arabic school with a Moroccan teacher, a school organized and financed by the Moroccan consulate, but most days we played with the kids in our class after school. Unlike some Muslim girls in Europe today, who don't take part in swim lessons or other athletic activities, we played sports. I played field hockey for six or seven years, which my parents encouraged. One of my sisters even joined a church youth group for a while.

Still, some of the families in our neighborhood would not allow their children to play with us. This was partly because my parents were blue-collar workers, and there were also those who made fun of my oldest sister, who was disabled; others said that we came from a backward culture.

More than once, neighborhood parents spoke to my sister Hannan's primary-school teacher and asked that she be removed from the class because she didn't "fit in." Often the children of immigrants were asked to repeat classes, in some cases because they had problems writing German but also because of racism. Sometimes, after the first four years of primary school, they would be sent to Förderstufe or Hauptschule, vocational schools for children who weren't planning to go to university. Even though my sisters and I were all fluent in German, Hannan's teacher and some of the parents decided that she should go to the Förderstufe. Luckily she performed so well that after a year her teachers sent her back to the regular secondary school, which we call gymnasium. I was lucky with my teacher Mrs. Schumann. She supported my hopes to go straight to gymnasium when I was eleven.

Our neighbors the Ehrts are one of the reasons I speak German as well as I do. Antje would keep an eye on what I was doing in school, and she was always very particular, especially about my writing. She wanted me to learn the best form of German. When I was a small child, she would read with me and often gave my sisters and me books of fairy tales and cassette tapes of Mickey Mouse stories that her children had outgrown. We were thrilled. My parents couldn't afford to buy us many books or tapes.

Around the time I started gymnasium in 1989, I began to see changes among the Yugoslavs who worked with my mother in the church community, including Aunt Zora and Aunt Dschuka. Their children had been in the after-school day care, like me. We had all been close friends, especially because our mothers were unskilled workers, which set us apart from German children, many of whose parents had been to university. Their children had names like Leika, Zoran, Ivica, and Ivan. They would always say proudly that they came from Yugoslavia. Suddenly, they refused to play with each other. Instead of sharing Yugoslavian heritage, they began to say, "I am Croatian," "I am Serbian." Others called themselves "Bosnians" or "Muslims." Their mothers stopped joking with each other and drinking coffee and eating *borek* together in the break room.

While we could clearly see a divide between Yugoslavs at my mother's workplace, my parents asked us not to generalize. Aunt Zora and Aunt Dschuka were Serbs. They and their families came to visit and eat with us. Like us, they were horrified by what they heard and saw in the news but would always say that the country's schism hadn't come from within. "We used to be one people," Aunt Zora told us. "We never asked if someone was Serb, Slovene, Croatian, or Muslim." She believed that the war was a Western plot to weaken socialist Yugoslavia.

We heard about massacres on the news or heard in school about someone's uncle having been killed fighting in the former Yugoslavia. But this was all far away from my family and me. We had often felt like outsiders in Germany, but we didn't feel directly threatened until September 1991. Almost two years after the fall of the Berlin Wall, xenophobic riots broke out in Hoyerswerda, a town in the northeast of Saxony. Right-wing groups attacked workers from Vietnam and Mozambique and threw stones and gasoline bombs at an apartment block that housed asylum seekers.

My parents and I watched on TV as Germans applauded when a building burst into flames. Some even raised their hands in a Hitlergruss, the infamous straight-armed Nazi salute, and screamed, "Germany for the Germans! Foreigners out!"

My parents said not to worry, that this was in the former East Germany and that people in the West would never do something like this. "The people here know that without people like us, their economy would not be where it is today," my father said.

I was angry with my parents during that period, especially with my father. While my grandmother in Morocco was very strong-willed and never let anybody boss her around, I felt that my father did whatever his bosses or other Germans told him. As a chef, he worked long hours, and we barely saw him. But very often when he had a day off, his supervisors would call and ask him to come to work, and my father would immediately go. It didn't help that he lived upstairs from the restaurant owner, Mr. Berger, who always knew when my father was home. When we went to the German authorities to renew our residency documents, I noticed that my father never asked questions or talked back, even when the people on the other side of the table treated him shabbily.

In our apartment building, Mrs. Weiss, who had survived the Holocaust with her husband, invited me into her apartment for a cocoa the same week that the news was full of the riots. She and her husband had told me about the concentration camps and their dead family members. The old lady seemed in distress; her face was pale. She told me that she hadn't slept in days. The images from Hoyerswerda haunted her. "Please, child, take care of yourself and your family. I worry for you," she said. "These people, these thoughts, they are ugly and dangerous."

I told her not to worry, and that this all was happening in East Germany and would never reach us in Frankfurt, but Mrs. Weiss shook her head. "No, no, you don't understand," she said. "If the Germans had learned, what has happened in Hoyerswerda could not have happened."

A year later, in November 1992, my parents' argument lay in tatters, as members of a right-wing gang set fire to two houses occupied by Turkish families in the city of Mölln, in the western part of Germany. A Turkish grandmother and two girls were killed and seven others were injured. The attackers called the fire department themselves to report the attacks, ending their calls with the words "Heil Hitler!"

It was the Jews who spoke most forcefully against this terrifying attack. While most German politicians chose to stay away, the head of the German Jewish community, Ignatz Bubis, and his deputy Michel Friedman went to pay their respects to the victims and their families. On May 29, 1993, the house of another Turkish guest worker, Durmus Genc, was burned in Solingen, also in the former West Germany. Genc's two daughters and two granddaughters, aged four to twenty-seven, were killed, along with a twelve-year-old visitor from Turkey. Again, members of Jewish organizations spoke up the loudest.

That summer, my parents took us to Morocco on vacation. By now there were four of us children, my brother Hicham having been born in 1986. We flew to Casablanca, drove to Meknes, and spent three or four weeks at my grandmother's house visiting and receiving family and friends.

My father's half sister Zahra also lived in Meknes, about ten minutes from my grandmother. She was married and had seven children, and one day my sister Hannan and I went to visit. One of Zahra's sons, who was about nineteen at the time, had some friends over from the neighborhood. They were all watching TV.

I saw a mountainous region and cars with bearded men carrying guns. They said, "*Allah hu-Akbar,*" meaning "God is great." The screen showed women crying and screaming. A voice said that these women had been raped and their families killed by Serbs. My cousin and his friends began to look angry. The next scene showed men with long beards standing behind two kneeling men. One of the bearded men said something in a language I couldn't understand. A different voice, apparently of the cameraman, said "*Allah hu-Akbar.*" Next, I saw one of the bearded men holding the heads of the kneeling men in his hands. My cousin and his friends applauded.

"What movie are you watching?" my sister asked.

My cousin and his friends stared at us. It wasn't a movie, they said.

"This is the truth about what is happening in Bosnia," one of my cousin's friends said. "It shows how the mujahideen fight in Bosnia against the Serbs who massacre Muslims." He continued: "All Serbs should be killed. They rape our sisters and kill our brothers."

Hannan and I told them that not all Serbs were bad and that in fact my mother had two Serbian coworkers who were very kind.

"You can't be friends with these people," my cousin's friend said. "You will see. Soon they will try to kill all the Muslims in Europe. Without the mujahideen, you will all be slaughtered."

My sister told me in German not to listen to him and that we should leave soon.

"How come you don't know about this?" my cousin asked. "These videos come from Germany. The man who films them is a German of Egyptian descent."

This man's name was Reda Seyam, and his videos from Bosnia were some of the earliest examples of jihadist propaganda that has since ballooned into today's use of violence as a recruiting tool. Many jihadists of my generation would later describe Bosnia and especially the massacre at Srebrenica as their "wake-up call." The Dutch UN soldiers who stood by and watched as Muslim men and boys were seized and killed in Srebrenica convinced some Muslims that the West would do nothing as Muslims got slaughtered.

Back in Germany, things got worse. Later that summer, Hicham and I went out for ice cream one afternoon not far from the Holzhausenpark near our house in Frankfurt.

As we walked home, a car packed with four German men pulled up next to us. "Gypsies! We will kill you, Gypsies!" they yelled. With their shaved heads and tattoos, the men stood out as skinheads. It was rare to see people like this in our neighborhood. I looked around to see if they were talking to somebody else, but the street was empty. "We mean you two Gypsies!" one of them shouted. "We will kill you. We will take you to the gas chambers!"

My brother started crying. I threw our ice cream away, grabbed Hicham's hand, and screamed for him to run. The car was following us. I knew I couldn't run fast enough—my brother was too slow, so I lifted him and turned onto a one-way street. The car was about to follow when other cars showed up and honked. One of the other drivers screamed that he would call the police, and the car full of skinheads drove away. My brother and I ran home sobbing.

I told my parents we had to leave Germany. I begged them, "First they burned the Jews, and now they'll burn us." I thought back about what my cousin's friend had said in Meknes, about people going after Muslims in the middle of Europe. Was he right?

I started having nightmares about the car with the shouting skinheads, from which I'd wake up crying and screaming. I began to read extensively about the Third Reich, the Holocaust, and how it all began. I was filled with fear as strong as anything I'd ever felt, not just for me but also for my whole family. Reading about what the Nazis did to handicapped people, I couldn't help thinking about my sister Fatma. I felt we were no longer safe or accepted in Germany. For days, I begged my parents to pack and leave. "These people don't want us here," I told them.

That week, I heard a radio interview with Michel Friedman, one of the Jewish leaders who had been so responsive to the attacks on Muslim immigrants. He spoke about the Holocaust, how it felt to be the child of survivors and to live in Germany. Yet Friedman didn't want to abandon the country he'd grown up in. "Leaving Germany and settling somewhere else would have been the easiest option," he told the host. "We—and I am talking about whoever has a sense of humanity, no matter if Jewish, Muslim, or Christian—cannot let these right-wing groups win by allowing them to shut us up or by packing our bags."

That was the moment I stopped asking my parents to leave. Instead of giving in to my fear and alienation, I took them as a challenge, one that continues to this day. I decided to work as hard as I could and do my best to prevail over the forces that so frightened me. That was what I meant all those years later, when I told the ISIS leader on the Turkish-Syrian border that he'd taken the easiest way out. I believed my way was harder.

My parents are partly responsible for saving me. I wasn't able to say that all Germans were bad because I lived among some good ones who supported and cared for me. It all sounds obvious now, but back then I was a teenager, and I was very angry.

I sometimes wonder what would have happened if an Islamic State recruiter had found me in those dark moments. I'm not sure how I would have responded, or whether I would have been strong enough to resist.

2

The Hamburg Cell

Germany, 1994–2003

When I was a teenager, politics and current events captured my imagination. I asked my German godparents to keep their magazines and copies of *Frankfurter Allgemeine Zeitung*, one of Germany's big daily newspapers, so I could read them. One day, I saw an article about an old movie focusing on two journalists whose reporting led to the resignation of the American president Richard Nixon. "Based on a true story," the article said. There was a large black-and-white photograph of Robert Redford and Dustin Hoffman in the newsroom.

Like all kids, I'd thought about what I wanted to be when I grew up. I had considered becoming an actress or a politician, but *All the President's Men* tipped the balance in favor of journalism. I was thrilled by the notion that these two reporters, Bob Woodward and Carl Bernstein, were taking on people in power, that they were so persistent in finding the truth, and that their articles had such impact. *Look at this*, I thought. *Journalism can change things*. It reminded me of what my grandfather in Morocco had said years earlier: the people with power are the ones who write history. I could see that journalists didn't simply write what happened; what they wrote could change lives.

My parents weren't especially excited about my career plans. My mother said that the prisons in Turkey were filled with journalists. My father delivered the opinion of one of his coworkers, who told him that there were already many "German Germans" who wanted to become journalists and couldn't get a job. "She said this profession is more for German Germans and that you are better off doing something else," my dad relayed. "For example, you could become a nurse."

I understood my mother's argument. She was worried about my safety. But when it came to my father, I was just disappointed. Why would he let other people decide what was right or wrong for me? And what did it mean that many "German Germans" wanted to become journalists? Hadn't I been born in Germany?

Redford and Hoffman were stronger than my parents' concerns. After seeing the movie, I cut out the photo of the actors standing in the newsroom and hung it on my bedroom door. I was determined to become a journalist. I also knew that I'd have to pay for my education because my parents wouldn't be able to.

When I was fourteen, I took on two jobs, working Saturdays in a bakery and babysitting twice a week. At sixteen, I added two more: tutoring kids in math and German and working at a home for elderly people in the evenings. I cleaned floors, washed dishes, and fed the old ladies.

In the meantime, I established a magazine at my high school called *Phantom*. The first contributors and editors were some of my closest friends. We interviewed politicians and personalities, including Michel Friedman, the Jewish leader who had so inspired me after the killings of Turkish migrants and who was also a politician in the Christian Democratic Union, and Gerhard Schröder, then prime minister of the state of Lower Saxony, whom I met at a political event in Frankfurt before he became the Social Democratic Party (SPD) candidate for the chancellery. Ignoring all the media and bodyguards surrounding him, I tapped on his shoulder, introduced myself, and asked for an interview for my school paper. I told him how important I thought it was that politicians talk to young people. He turned to his assistant. "Sigrid, can you give this young lady your business card?" he said.

In return, I proudly presented my own homemade business card, which was white with my name in blue. I'd decorated the cards with silver sparkles because I didn't want people to forget me.

Schröder smiled. "When we get questions from *Phantom*, just forward them to me," he told his assistant. We chatted for a few minutes, and he asked what grade I was in.

I didn't realize that other reporters had gathered nearby, and some were taking pictures. The next day, my mom got a phone call from one of her friends: "Your daughter is in the newspaper with Gerhard Schröder!" I bought the paper and tore it open, but then I saw the caption: "Gerhard Schröder explains politics to a young Frankfurt party member." I was outraged. I called the paper and asked for a correction. "You can't just write that I'm a member of the SPD," I told them. "I'm not." But the people in the newsroom just laughed and told me it was a great picture.

At about this time, I also began writing letters to the editor in response to news coverage or issues of the day; one of them, about Islam and women, was even published in the *Frankfurter Allgemeine Zeitung*. After it ran, somebody from the neighborhood called my mother. "Tell your daughter to stay out of politics," she said. But I was adamant that as a young woman and the daughter of guest workers I had a voice, too.

I didn't identify primarily as a Muslim in those days. I felt that my siblings and I had more in common with our friends whose parents had come from Greece, Italy, or Spain than we did with other Muslim kids. What mattered was that we were the children of immigrants, that we weren't "German Germans" but outsiders.

In Germany, it is usual for high school students to do brief internships in fields that interest them. When I was sixteen, I began calling local newspapers and asking if I could do an internship, even unpaid. I got one at the *Frankfurter Rundschau*, a daily paper that was more liberal than the *Allgemeine Zeitung*. I worked on the local desk, writing about elementary school students growing flowers in their school gardens and about disputes between neighbors over garbage pickup or where their dogs had peed. I did whatever came along, on top of schoolwork and my other part-time jobs.

Soon after, I was invited to be a guest on a public radio talk show for immigrants called *Rendezvous in Germany*. I seized the opportunity to ask the editor to let me intern there for two weeks. It was the beginning of my radio career. The show had guests who spoke Greek, Turkish, Spanish, and other languages, and they always needed two moderators, one an immigrant, the other a child of migrants like me. My Turkish wasn't good enough to host a program. I can order food in that language but not more, and at the time they didn't have Arabic programs. Ironically, I was useful on the show because I spoke fluent German, even if most Germans considered me a foreigner.

The shows were very political. We talked about integration, the role of women, and racism within migrant communities. Some people of Turkish descent wouldn't let their children marry Moroccans, and some migrants discriminated against blacks. These people craved respect but, at the same time, they didn't respect others. We talked about racism in soccer, about gay rights, and about hypocrisy in general.

After I'd been working part-time at the station for about a year, the head of a pop music program offered me a job moderating a call-in request show called *The Wish Island*. Sometimes I couldn't even pronounce the names of the songs, which were mostly in English. I was taking English at school, but my teacher preferred casual conversation in German to teaching. Nevertheless, the head of the show told me I had a great voice. He wanted me to work on other programs as well. I felt that moderating a pop music show was fun and surely the best-paid job I'd ever had—it paid twice what I made hosting the migrant program. But it wasn't what I was aiming for. The photograph from *All the President's Men* still hung on my bedroom door. I gave up the music show after two months.

I was still freelancing for *Frankfurter Rundschau*, covering local neighborhood stories. One afternoon, a very nice assistant to one of the editors told me about a journalism school in Hamburg. "The Henri-Nannen School is one of the best in Europe," she said. "You should look into it after your studies." I still had half a year of high school to go, but she had planted a seed. *There's no harm in trying*, I thought.

I learned that most of the people who went to Henri-Nannen already had careers in journalism; they had finished their university degrees and wanted to get access to big outlets such as *Der Spiegel*, *Stern*, or *Die Zeit*, all of which funded the school. Competition to get in was brutal. Applicants had to research and write a narrative and an editorial; we also had to select one of five topics chosen by the school and report and write a story about it. The year I applied, narrative topics included following a young athlete, spending a night at a gas station, or spending the day at a home for elderly people. I tried the gas station but didn't like it, so I ended up spending a couple of days with a woman my mother knew who lived in a home for the elderly. For the editorial, I wrote about whether the private lives of politicians should be covered by the press. It was the height of the Bill Clinton–Monica Lewinsky scandal. I don't remember exactly what I wrote, but I do recall suggesting that if Bill Clinton had engaged in sexual activities with Monica Lewinsky somewhere other than in the Oval Office, the act would have been less publicly important. Because he did it on official turf, it was an abuse of power, and thus fair game for journalism. The topic was risqué for a nineteen-year-old. It got the school's attention.

A few months after I applied, someone from the Henri-Nannen School called to tell me I had been accepted. I was overjoyed, but there was a problem. Sometimes the news organizations that funded the school would insist that a doctor or lawyer get preferential treatment over a high school graduate. I was asked to try again the following year. *No*, I thought. *I'll never do that.*

Instead, I graduated from high school and started at Johann Wolfgang Goethe University in Frankfurt, working at the radio station when I could and living at home. I kept building my journalism skills and making contacts. While interning at a weekly paper in Hamburg, I traveled to the Netherlands to interview the primary European leader of the PKK, a Kurdish separatist militant organization that the United States and the European Union had labeled a terrorist group. I lied to my parents for the first time, telling them that I was going to interview a Kurdish painter.

The following winter, when I was caught up in my studies, I got another call from Henri-Nannen. Apparently someone in the class had received a job offer. "We want to offer you the spot," the woman from the school said. "Can you be here in ten days?"

I put my university studies on hold and started at the Henri-Nannen School in Hamburg, nearly four hours by train from Frankfurt. Luckily I knew the city a little and had one close friend there, who had interned with me at the Hamburg weekly, working in the paper's arts and style section. He had grown up in a conservative town and had been forced to leave after he came out as gay. He moved to Hamburg and, like me, he understood what it meant to be an outsider.

I even felt like an outsider in my journalism classes. Unlike most of my fellow students, my parents hadn't been educated at universities. There was a lot of talk in my presence about oppressed Muslim women, and some of my fellow students asked ridiculous questions like "Will your parents choose your husband?" or "Are you going to marry one of your cousins?" I think if I had been the daughter of rich Arabs or if my parents had been doctors, things would have been different. The people who ran the school told me that I was one of the youngest students they'd ever admitted, and the first child of Muslim guest workers.

My classmates were the children of German parents, what my father's coworker had called "German Germans." They were older; some had studied in Britain, the United States, or France, and many had been journalists for a while. To make matters more difficult, I wasn't interested in partying, nor was I afraid to question some of the established journalists who came to talk to our class. When a journalist who was considered one of the country's top investigative reporters described his research on Iran, I couldn't contain myself.

"Have you been there?" I asked.

"No," he said. "I do my interviews by phone."

I was incredulous. "Aren't you worried about your sources? If you talk on the phone, don't you think the intelligence services might listen, and your sources might get in trouble?"

The reporter gave me a dim look. Such threats were overestimated, he said. But I remembered how Woodward and Bernstein would make a point of meeting people in out-of-the-way places so as not to be overheard. I told him that I'd interviewed the European leader of the PKK in person for just this reason. Later, some of my classmates criticized me for speaking to their idol this way, but compared to Woodward and Bernstein, my fellow students seemed frustratingly uncritical.

In early 2001, shortly before graduation, our class organized a five-day trip to New York. Besides being excited to see the country I'd admired for its great movies and investigative journalism, I longed to eat a typical hamburger in a typical diner. The school gave us some money, but only enough for airfare and some of our accommodations. I used the money I'd put aside from working weekends at the radio station to cover the rest.

In New York, I wandered alone around the city. People were different than in Germany, busy but smiling. I went to the World Trade Center and stood in front of the Twin Towers. At a class visit to the *New York Times*, we looked at the Pulitzers on the wall and visited the newsroom, which was similar to the one I had seen in *All the President's Men*. It was like a dream. I wondered what might have happened if things had been different, if my parents had settled in the United States instead of Germany, or if they'd been rich enough to send me to America or Britain for a year to learn better English. Might I have had a shot at working for the *New York Times* or the *Washington Post*?

I graduated from the journalism school in May and returned to Frankfurt, where I wanted to finish my university degree in political science and international relations and eventually apply for a correspondent's job with a German radio station or write for a magazine based in the Middle East or North Africa.

That was the plan, but it all seemed very far away. I divided my time between studying and freelancing for local newspapers and the radio station. I was living with my parents to avoid paying rent, but I didn't end up saving much. After years of punishing labor in a poorly ventilated kitchen, my father suffered from asthma, and back injuries had left him unable to stand for long periods. By the time I moved back home, he was working reduced hours and would soon retire. My mother had also retired early because of the pain in her back and shoulders from years operating the heavy clothing irons at the church laundry. My parents also suffered from depression, though they didn't talk about it. Immigrants of their generation, the cleaners and cooks, worked hard and kept their heads down, never challenging the authority of the "German Germans." For years, my mother visited a doctor who gave her painful injections for a ringing in her ears that never went away. She meekly accepted that the doctor knew what he was doing until the day I accompanied her to his office and asked why her condition hadn't improved. The doctor was genuinely surprised. "Usually, people like your mother don't ask me questions," he said.

"We didn't understand that we also had rights," my mother told me later. "We never dared to question anything."

My parents had left their homes and families, and they worked tirelessly to build better, easier lives for their children, yet we still struggled. When my father's boss had died several years earlier, the owners of our building in the beautiful, affluent neighborhood where I'd grown up decided to sell, and we were asked to leave. We moved to a different part of the city and into a former U.S. military housing development where all the buildings looked the same. The barracks had been bought and turned into affordable housing, mostly for immigrants. In our new apartment, the door opened right into the living room, as is common in American homes, rather than the typical German layout with a foyer and hallway leading to a more private living space. The building managers extolled the apartments' built-in shelves and cabinets, but we later learned that some of them contained poison from disinfectants that had been used to clean them.

My sister Fatma worked, but she didn't get paid much, and because of her disability she needed support. My brother was still in high school. With my parents unable to work much, supporting the family fell to my sister Hannan and me. I still kept the photograph of Redford and Hoffman on my bedroom door, but I knew where my responsibilities lay: not in the glamorous world of American journalism, but here at home.

Shortly after I returned to Frankfurt, I learned that the radio station where I'd worked on the migrant and music shows was looking for a backup correspondent in Rabat, the capital of Morocco. During journalism school, I'd interned for six weeks with the station's previous Rabat correspondent, Claudia Sautter, who had become a friend. Now she was leaving, and the station had chosen her replacement, but it needed someone else who would cover North and West Africa when the new correspondent went on vacation. I'd worked on a range of shows at the station, including political programs, and my internship and visits to my grandmother had made Morocco a kind of second home to me. I spoke Moroccan Arabic. Claudia encouraged me to apply.

I met with the editor, but things didn't go as I'd hoped. The editor explained that he wouldn't send someone who came from a particular country to be a correspondent there. I told him that I didn't understand this logic, but that it didn't matter, because I was from Frankfurt.

He was clearly uncomfortable. My roots were in Morocco, he said, and therefore he couldn't nominate me for the post. My insides started to ache, and I felt tears coming. *Don't you dare cry*, I told myself.

I repeated that I had been born in Germany and explained that my parents had actually come from two different countries, Morocco and Turkey. By his logic, I said, he would have to immediately fire all the "German Germans" who were covering Germany and bring in foreigners. He turned pale and said that we had nothing more to discuss. I stood up and dashed out of his office just as the tears began to slide down my cheeks. *You will never be accepted as a full German*, I thought. *You don't stand a chance in journalism.*

Three months later, on a Tuesday in September, I was listening to my favorite international relations professor, Lothar Brock, lecture on . . . something. I don't remember, because in truth I wasn't really listening. At the beginning of the talk, I had turned off the ringer of my mobile phone, but for the past hour I'd felt it vibrating through my backpack. Something was terribly wrong; the only reason someone would be calling me over and over was that something had happened to my family.

When Professor Brock called a break, I rushed outside. The messages on my phone confirmed my fears: "Souad, where are you?" "Souad, you must come home." "Souad, come home now!"

Yes, something was definitely wrong at home. I ran back into the lecture hall and spoke with Dr. Brock. "Go home," he said. "I hope everything is okay. You'll let me know, won't you?"

I ran for the bus, for the twenty-minute ride to my family's apartment. When I burst through the doorway, everyone but my father, still at work, was seated around the television.

Wordlessly, I sat down and stared at the scenes of carnage from New York City. My thoughts immediately turned to my visit six months earlier. I had gone to lower Manhattan specifically to see the World Trade Center, the towers that stood so heroically, icons of American money and power.

Now they were gone. And all those lives.

"Maybe it was the Russians," my mother said hopefully. And unconvincingly.

I glanced at Hannan, who was staring at me. "I hope no Arabs were involved," she said. "If so, the backlash is going to be huge."

But she and I already knew. Here in Germany, Muslims would suffer. We stared with horror and incomprehension at the televised scenes coming now not just from New York, but also from Washington, DC, and a small town in the state of Pennsylvania. How did this happen? What could drive men to such violence, such hatred, such extremism?

Very quickly, a German angle emerged. We learned that the plot's ringleader, Mohamed Atta, two other hijackers, and several other key players in the attacks had lived and plotted in Hamburg, making up what would become known as the Hamburg cell.

I told my professors I had to go there to find out more. I called my former landlady, and it turned out my room was still empty. I took the next train to Hamburg and moved back in.

I had no newspaper to work for, so I started freelancing. The German papers were filled with reports about possible connections between Mohamed Atta's group and the al-Quds mosque in Hamburg. A Moroccan student who had known Atta told me that he was brilliant but intense when it came to Islam. "If you want to know more, go to Steindamm," the student told me, referring to a busy street in Hamburg's red-light district. Atta and his friends used to eat at a chicken shop there, he said, and gave me the address.

So I put on my standard student uniform of jeans and a sweater, along with some lipstick and kohl, the thick black eyeliner favored by Moroccan women, and went to Steindamm. In this neighborhood, which I'd never visited during my time in Hamburg, sex shops, sex cinemas, and hookers coexist with small Turkish, Arab, and Persian groceries and informal mosques. I hadn't anticipated the scene and felt a bit out of place. I noticed people on the street looking at me.

I went into a little restaurant the student had told me about and sat down near a window, just watching the activity on the street. I ordered bread with honey and listened as people at nearby tables talked in Arabic.

They were saying that they were afraid their businesses would suffer, and they were warning one another not to talk to reporters.

"How is life, brother?" I heard one man ask, and I thought he and his companion must be relatives. Later, I came to understand that something like brotherhood and sisterhood knitted Muslims together, no matter where in the world they were.

The other man answered that he knew some of the men on the planes. "Oh, God, these journalists. They are asking a lot of questions. They think we are all terrorists."

I sat there for a bit, drinking tea. The restaurant had a separate room for families and children, but I had chosen the main dining room, where the men sat. The people at nearby tables must have thought me strange, sitting there all alone.

A group of men sat at an adjacent table. One was obviously a respected personality. The others listened intently when he talked, and nodded in agreement. He spoke a Moroccan dialect of Arabic. "How should we have known that?" he said. "They used to be such nice guys."

I knew that if I listened quietly I might learn something. I found that these men were affiliated with the al-Quds mosque. I discovered that the man to whom the others deferred was called al Hajj and was the head of the Mosque Council. Sometimes a reporter is simply lucky enough to pick the right restaurant for tea.

I went back to my apartment and looked for the number of the mosque. It was not in the phone book, and there was no Internet connection, so I went to an Internet café to get the number and called.

"*As'salam alaikum,*" a man's voice said. Peace be upon you.

In my excitement I didn't say "*wa'alaikum as'salam,*" the traditional response. After hearing the complaints about reporters, I didn't identify the purpose of my call. I just asked for al Hajj.

"Just tell him it's Souad," I said.

"There's someone called Souad who wants to talk with you," the man called out.

When al Hajj came to the phone, I said, "My name is Souad. I'm Moroccan. I'm just trying to find out the truth about what is going on."

He was a clever man. "I don't want to talk with journalists," he said.

"They don't honor and respect our rules in the mosque. Who are you working for?"

"I'm Muslim. I will respect the rules. Could we just have a cup of tea?"

He agreed to meet me for tea at a shop near the mosque the following afternoon, provided I did not tape the conversation. I was about to take the first tentative steps into a world I haven't left since.

I had so many questions, not least how I was going to talk to him. Again, I wore the typical clothes of a German university student: jeans, sneakers, a shirt, and a jacket. He arrived wearing Arab trousers and a tunic. He had a long beard and looked solemn.

"Are you Souad?" he asked before sitting down. "We didn't do anything. We had nothing to do with this. We cannot prevent people from going to the mosque. They came sometimes, they prayed, they ate."

I showed al Hajj photographs of the men who had participated in the attacks. He studied them carefully. "That's el-Amir," he said, pointing to Atta, whose full given name was Mohamed el-Amir Atta. Al Hajj said he knew that people were going to say it was our religion that inspired the attacks.

We talked pleasantly for a while, and somehow he took a liking to me. He told me about a place nearby, a bookstore, where Atta and his group sometimes met.

I felt I was making some progress and was relieved that the task of gathering information wasn't insurmountable. In fact, it seemed pretty straightforward. But I also worried that I was being given a bad lead. Ten minutes after al Hajj left, I went to the bookstore, which stood around the corner from the mosque.

The bookstore was one big room with wooden floors and wooden bookshelves. Books for women and children were kept in a small area in back, separated from the main room by a curtain. There were books in Arabic, German, and English. Two men greeted me. I introduced myself to the younger one, who looked to be in his early thirties, and told him I was a freelance journalist trying to figure out what had happened. It helped that, like him, I spoke a Moroccan dialect of Arabic.

"No journalists have come to us here," he said. "I'm wondering why you came."

I asked if he knew Atta and the others.

"They came in sometimes. They were normal people."

"Why did they do this?"

"They became political. Ask the Americans why they have killed people in Iraq and Palestine."

The man told me that he was from Casablanca and that he hadn't been religious before. "My brother was a bartender," he said, as if to drive home his secular credentials. At some point, while he was on vacation with his German wife, he had a strong feeling that his life wasn't proceeding as it should. Both he and his brother became religious, and they invested all their money in the bookstore. Over time, they and other young men their age became Atta's acolytes, praying and studying together and moving in the same circles.

On the day I visited, a bunch of students were sitting in the bookstore talking politics and criticizing Israel. They told me they weren't speaking against the American people, because "we know the people are good," but against America's involvement in the Middle East.

"If Israel's the country you have a problem with, why are you attacking the United States?" I asked.

"The Americans are supporting the Israelis," one of the men said.

It seemed that they blamed the United States reflexively for everything that was wrong in the world. And one word kept coming up: jihad.

"What exactly do you mean by jihad?" I finally asked.

"You have the right to defend yourself," a Moroccan student told me.

"Who attacked you personally?" I asked. "What are you talking about?"

"They attacked us."

"Morocco was not attacked."

"We don't think as Moroccans," he said. "We think as Muslims."

I began to understand that I was entering a world from which my parents had always tried to protect me. As a journalist, it was my job to report what was going on in these men's minds and to explain it to others. This was just the beginning.

Another man, an Egyptian, seemed suspicious of my questions. "Why do you want to know these things?" he asked. "Who really wants to know the truth? Didn't people see the truth all these years, and they did nothing? These men took a decision, based on the truth."

I knew after talking with these men that I wanted to know the truth and that I hadn't found it yet. Days passed, and I continued to explore and talk to people. The Steindamm neighborhood was only the first of many surprises. I'll never forget my first interview with the father of Mounir el-Motassadeq, an alleged September 11 collaborator, in Hamburg that fall. I wore a suit, thinking I would look professional. But when I met the man who'd set up the interview, he eyed me dismissively.

"Don't you have something to wear on top?" he asked. "You can see everything from the back. Where's your head scarf?"

I went to a Pakistani shop and bought a very long shirt and some scarves.

At another mosque where Atta and his comrades had prayed, I heard about the wars in Bosnia and the Arabian Gulf from an entirely new perspective. I had thought the United States was protecting Muslims in those wars. But for the first time, I was talking to people who hated America, and they saw Western intervention differently. They believed that the United States and its European allies were only interested in economic gain and were forcing their "system" and "way of life" upon others. Some mentioned what the United States had done in South America, specifically that "they killed Che Guevara and others because they didn't like U.S. imperialism." These men also accused America of supporting a "genocide against the Palestinians" for decades. To them, the United States was "the big Satan."

I also began hearing a narrative about the meaning and spirit of Islam that was very different from what I'd grown up with. Like my parents, I believed that religion should be separated from politics. Suddenly I found myself among people whose religion and political views were hopelessly intertwined. At first, the Hamburg connection to the September 11 attacks had baffled me. But the more time I spent there, the more certain I grew that Mohamed Atta and the others had been radicalized and recruited in Germany.

People on Steindamm described Atta as an austere man, strict in his thinking and quick to point out religious lapses in others. He chastised

Muslims for their love of music and for smoking cigarettes. He and his cell were not sleeper agents. Atta was known in the city, as were some of his friends. But he'd operated out of sight of German authorities in this parallel world. I found it extraordinary that no one in the security or intelligence services had noticed such extremism.

Despite my naïveté, I did have some advantages, even then. The al-Quds mosque in Hamburg, where Atta and his circle had prayed often, was run by Moroccans. They had long beards, unlike anyone in my family, but the fact that I spoke Moroccan Arabic helped a lot—and not just with the Moroccans.

That fall in Hamburg, I was out for a walk when I happened to meet the head of *Der Spiegel*'s investigative unit, who had spoken at my journalism school the previous year. He asked who I was working for.

"Nobody now," I said.

"But you speak Arabic," he responded.

Der Spiegel was Germany's most famous weekly magazine, with a reputation for integrity and courage. It was one of the media outlets I most respected. In 1962, its editors had been accused of treason for printing a story that criticized the country's military readiness. The magazine's founder had been imprisoned along with several top editors and reporters. It ultimately emerged that the defense minister had lied about his role in the affair, and he was forced to resign.

The magazine had a staff of top-notch reporters but needed someone with access to the Arab communities in Germany. The editor passed my name along, and I became a stringer for the magazine—contributing stories but not yet on staff. It was a huge break, the kind of lucky happenstance that can make a young reporter's career.

What I didn't know at the time was that someone from the magazine had called the German security services and asked if I had "a clean sheet." Did my family have links to any terrorist groups? How religious were my parents? Was I attending mosque, hanging out with the wrong people? Was I part of a sleeper cell, another Mohamed Atta in the making? As a Muslim and the daughter of migrants, I was automatically suspect in Germany, the country of my birth.

I threw myself into my work for *Der Spiegel*'s investigative team.

I soon grew interested in a nineteen-year-old German convert to Islam named Dennis Justen, an ordinary teenager from a Frankfurt suburb. Justen had become an observant Muslim seemingly overnight, fasting for Ramadan and breaking up with his girlfriend. His parents didn't think much of the changes until one day he disappeared. In September 2001, he was arrested trying to illegally cross the border from Afghanistan to Pakistan and interrogated by the FBI. I called an editor and told him I wanted to interview Justen's parents. The magazine had tried several times to talk to them, but they had refused. I wasn't sure I could convince them either, but I was deeply curious and felt obligated to try.

This editor wanted the interview with Justen's parents, but he wasn't keen on my involvement. "It's better you stay away from this," he answered. "If this involved a mosque or Islamic bookstore, you could do it. But these are German parents."

"I don't understand what you're trying to tell me here," I answered.

"Well, if I imagine myself in their shoes and see someone like you knocking on my door, I would think you might be a spy for the Taliban," he said.

Once more, I felt a sharp pain in my stomach. I wanted to throw up. It seemed that my own colleagues and editors didn't trust me. I knew this editor wouldn't support the extension of my contract and that it was just a matter of time before I would have to leave the magazine. So I decided to prove him wrong. That evening, on my own, I drove to Dennis Justen's parents' home. I found his grandfather there, who spoke with the parents on my behalf. I met with them that same night. The next day, they agreed to the interview. I wrote the story with a colleague in the Frankfurt office.

I called the editor. "See, they didn't think that I was a spy for the Taliban," I told him.

My hope was that he would understand how much his comment had hurt me and that the next reporter of Muslim descent to work for the magazine wouldn't face the same prejudices.

MY EARLY EXPERIENCES with journalism devastated me and gave me a sense of the alienation and rejection that so many Muslims in Europe were feeling. But I didn't let my feelings deter me from my search for what was really happening on the streets. I remained interested in understanding how young Arab men could be brainwashed in the country of my birth—and often their birth as well. Sometime that fall, I called al Hajj again.

"I would like to see the mosque," I said.

"Don't let anyone know you are a journalist," he advised. "Do you have a hijab? You know, Sister Souad, you will have to wear one."

I told him not to worry. As I entered the mosque, it felt strange to be walking in the literal footsteps of Mohamed Atta. My heart started to beat faster. I couldn't look into the faces of the people who were there to pray. I thought they would be able to see that I was a reporter.

To me, a mosque was an imposing building with a minaret. Here was a mosque on the same street as sex shops, with prostitutes standing outside. The nondescript building occupied a seedy area near the Hamburg train station, right across from a police station. The men's prayer room was a study in color, with brightly colored carpets and turquoise walls in a sprawling room built for hundreds. By comparison, the women's prayer room was plain and cramped.

After praying, I ducked into the mosque's library. In it were videotapes of Imam Mohamad Fizazi, a fiery preacher from Tangier and one of the biggest influences on Atta. "The Jews and Crusaders must have their throats slit," the imam said in a sermon videotaped at al-Quds. At the mosque I spoke to an Egyptian and a Moroccan who had known Atta and the others. I asked why their friends became radicalized and why they ended up killing all those people. The Egyptian told me that I'd been "brainwashed by the Western media, which isn't surprising because you ended up working with them. Look at all these tens of thousands of Muslims who have died for years now, and they are not even mentioned in the media." Atta and the other hijackers, he said, had "paid America back for what they and the Jews have done to us all these years."

I was a bit shocked, but also very young. If that's how they think, I thought, I'll just need to spend more time with them to understand.

Soon I moved back to Frankfurt, balancing my freelance journalistic work with my studies. I also started attending a major terrorism trial there. The case involved five Algerians who had been accused of plotting to blow up the Notre Dame Cathedral and the Christmas market in Strasbourg, France, in December 2000, nine months before September 11. Most of these men had spent time in training camps in Afghanistan, and I wanted to understand who they were and why they'd made the choices they did. Sometimes I wrote articles for one of the Frankfurt papers or reported for the radio station, but it was really my own curiosity that made me keep showing up.

During a break in the proceedings, at a nearby coffee shop, I ran into some American journalists. One of them was Shannon Smiley, an American who worked in the *Washington Post*'s Berlin bureau as an assistant to the correspondent and stringer. She spoke German, and I'd talked to her before at the courthouse. There was also a guy from the Associated Press, someone from the *Chicago Tribune*, and a woman from Reuters. And there was another reporter I hadn't met before: Peter Finn, the *Post*'s Berlin bureau chief and an important contributor to its global terrorism coverage.

"The Watergate *Washington Post*?" I asked when I was introduced to Peter. He smiled. I couldn't believe that I was sitting with a senior correspondent from that paper. I asked if Woodward and Bernstein were as good-looking in real life as the actors in the movie. Peter and Shannon laughed.

Back then I barely spoke English. But with Shannon's help, we chatted about Hamburg, and I told them about some of the people I had gotten to know there.

"Interesting," Peter said.

A week later, Shannon called me and said that Peter had a proposal and wanted to meet me. My heart was beating very fast when I walked into the breakfast room of the Steigenberger airport hotel that day in May 2002. Peter stood up to greet me. He said that he was working on a piece for the *Washington Post* about the Hamburg cell. It was supposed to be the main story in the paper one year after the September 11 attacks.

"Would you work with me on this?" he asked.

I was close to tears. After all I'd been through with the German media, here was a *Washington Post* reporter asking if I would work with him on a story. I'd been burned before. During my time in Hamburg, I'd seen how some reporters would press Arab students, using incriminating photos of them with the September 11 hijackers and telling them the photos would be printed if they didn't agree to an interview. I was cautious about working with Peter. "Would it include blackmailing Arab students?" I asked.

"We don't do that," he told me. "You have to follow the ethical principles of the paper." He explained that we always told people who we were working for. We couldn't blackmail sources. This was the beginning of a new path into the world of journalism, one I'd always dreamed about.

For this new assignment I had to go back to al-Quds. I wanted to know if this was a place people could go into and come out as terrorists. I wanted to know what was taught there. Where in my religion did it say that Muslims had a right to kill innocent people?

I returned to Hamburg, speaking with young men who had known the September 11 pilots, going to the places they had gone, reading the same strict interpretations of the Koran and books about how a Muslim should behave in the West that they had read. I no longer felt nervous or out of place on Steindamm.

I learned how Atta and his group operated and how they were influenced by Bosnian and Afghan war veterans who were affiliated with Al Qaeda. I learned how their plot had unfolded here in plain view.

On September 11, 2002, I entered the world of American journalism as a named contributor on a long piece in the *Washington Post* headlined "Hamburg's Cauldron of Terror." After what felt like a long journey, I had, in a sense, arrived. But I had much farther to go.

———

ONE COLD FALL day later that year, I joined a crowd of journalists from around the world standing in line outside a courthouse in Hamburg. We had been told to arrive four hours early for the chance to score a press pass to cover the trial of the first man accused of direct involvement in the September 11 attacks: Mounir el-Motassadeq, a twenty-eight-year-old Moroccan student in Hamburg who had been a friend of Mohamed Atta's and a signatory to his will. Prosecutors said that Motassadeq was a moneyman for the Hamburg cell, paying rent and utility bills for a hijacker named Marwan al-Shehhi, and sending money to him in America. Motassadeq was charged with more than three thousand counts of being an accessory to murder and belonging to a terrorist organization. He said he had no prior knowledge of the plot. If convicted, he could spend up to fifteen years in prison.

After the September 11 anniversary story, the *Washington Post* had put me on contract. I also began to take intensive English-language classes, so I could contribute not only as a researcher but also as a writer. As one of my first tasks for the *Post*, Peter Finn sent me to get our accreditation to the Motassadeq trial. But as I stood freezing alongside correspondents, cameramen, and producers from Asia, the Arab world, and all the big American news organizations, I had no inkling that covering the Motassadeq trial would change my life. It would propel me into a war zone, and from there into the heart of jihadi networks, including the Islamic State.

The trial was supposed to last several months. Peter and I attended the first few sessions, then moved on to other stories. We returned to Hamburg some weeks later, when the relatives of several September 11 victims arrived to testify. Among the most impressive was Maureen Fanning, whose husband was a firefighter who had died at the World Trade Center. Fanning struck me as strong and determined. She had two autistic sons, and with her husband gone, she'd had to send the fourteen-year-old to live in a group home while she cared for the six-year-old, who could not read, write, or speak. Like the other victims' relatives, she was still waiting to see what kind of support she would get from the U.S. government. It was her first time in Hamburg, and after hearing her testimony, some of us invited her out to dinner.

It was a cold, dark night in early winter. We chose a steak restaurant in the center of the city, a short walk from our hotel. I sat next to Peter and across from Fanning. Some of the reporters ordered beers, while I had my usual: apple juice and sparkling water. We ate and talked about the trial. After dinner, we ordered espresso, and Fanning began to open up. She said that while she blamed the terrorists for the attacks that had killed her husband, she also blamed the U.S. government, and even us, the press. "Nobody told us there were people out there who hated us so much," she said. "Why didn't we know this? Politicians didn't tell us. You're journalists, but you never told us."

Then she looked straight at me. She knew from our previous conversations that I was of Arab descent. "Why do they hate us so much?" she asked. I stammered something about Western foreign policy being unpopular in the Arab world. It was an imprecise answer, and I think she sensed that I felt terribly awkward, but the moment was also meaningful for me. She was questioning whether we were doing our jobs, and I found her criticism legitimate. *Why aren't we doing a better job of telling people like Maureen Fanning what the jihadis think of them?* I wondered. Back at the hotel after dinner, I asked Peter what he thought of the terrorism coverage in the United States before September 11. Of course people had written about Afghanistan when the Russians were there in the 1980s, he told me. Some even reported from the country when it was under Taliban rule. But few Western reporters had talked to members of Al Qaeda and other terrorist groups or understood their views.

"But don't you think it's interesting?" I asked. "And isn't it our job?"

"Of course. But who has access to these people? It's very hard to get them to talk to us."

I didn't say anything, but I was thinking: *Maybe we should try.*

In the coming days and months, Fanning's question played over and over in my head. Even with my background, I had no idea why Mohamed Atta and his cohorts had felt the way they did. I hadn't grown up hating the United States. The attacks had been a surprise to me, too. I felt compelled to learn what had driven those men and what drove others like them.

We were already hearing about the possibility of an American war in Iraq. Through the fall of 2002 and into early 2003, I closely followed the coverage of the UN inspectors, who were searching for the weapons of mass destruction that U.S. officials said made Saddam Hussein a global threat. I was still a university student, but because I was of Arab descent and working part-time for the *Post*, a local radio station in Frankfurt asked me to join a debate about the war. The other panelists supported the invasion, but I couldn't contain myself. The weapons inspectors should be allowed to finish their job, I told the audience. If the United

States invaded Iraq and it turned out there were no weapons of mass destruction, there would be more terrorism. My sister and a friend were in the audience and clapped, but this wasn't what German intellectuals and diplomats wanted to hear. Afterward, some of the other panelists refused to shake my hand.

Instead, people argued in op-ed pieces and on TV that even if Saddam Hussein had no weapons of mass destruction, he was a bad person, a despot who was killing his own people, a monster who had gassed the Kurds. I couldn't argue with any of this, but these things had been known for many years. But where was the evidence that Saddam still had weapons of mass destruction or that he planned to use them? An important source for the Americans was Rafid Ahmed Alwan al-Janabi, an Iraqi asylum seeker who came to Germany in 1999. He told the German intelligence agency that he had worked at an agricultural facility in Iraq that served as a cover for a secret biological weapons program. Al-Janabi's alarming claims were shared with the U.S. Defense Intelligence Agency, and while the Germans later warned the Americans about the possible unreliability of the source (who was given the code name Curveball by U.S. intelligence agencies), the Bush administration ignored the warnings and treated the allegations as fact.

At the United Nations, Secretary of State Colin Powell argued that Saddam Hussein was linked to the September 11 attacks through his support of an Al Qaeda offshoot in Iraq. Powell spoke of the "sinister nexus between Iraq and the Al Qaeda terrorist network, a nexus that combines classic terrorist organizations and modern methods of murder." Hussein's Iraq was now home, he said, to "a deadly terrorist network headed by Abu Musab al-Zarqawi," a Jordanian who had fought in Afghanistan more than a decade earlier and was a close collaborator of Osama bin Laden. According to Powell, Zarqawi had returned to Afghanistan in 2000 and had overseen a terrorist training camp there that specialized in poisons.

Powell's words, and their implications, were terrifying. Today we know that Saddam Hussein hated Al Qaeda as much as the Americans did and that Iraq possessed no weapons of mass destruction. But at the time, public opinion was divided. Some of my professors said that a U.S.

invasion of Iraq would violate international law, while others seemed eager for a war. "Saddam Hussein is a dangerous man," one of my professors argued. "If he has these weapons, the world is in danger."

"Whatever happened to presenting evidence and proving someone's guilt?" I responded.

He didn't want to hear it. He was certain Iraq would be a better place with Saddam gone. All this speculation made me angry. I felt that I needed to be in Iraq, to see with my own eyes what was happening there. I didn't want to be like those foreign affairs "experts" who lived comfortably in Germany but went on TV day and night to talk about global hot spots they never dared to visit. I thought back to the famous foreign correspondent who spoke to my journalism school class about reporting on Iran by telephone.

I asked Peter about the possibility of going to Iraq for the *Post*. "Are you really sure you want to go there now and end up in the war?" he asked. "What about your parents? What do they say?"

"I haven't told them yet."

After a few hours, Peter called back. "Okay," he said. "If you can get a visa, there is one story we should try to do as soon as possible. We need to find the diplomat who allegedly met with Mohamed Atta in Prague. We need to find al-Ani."

Ahmad Khalil Ibrahim Samir al-Ani was an Iraqi intelligence officer who had been working as a diplomat in Prague in 2001, and who was accused of having met with Atta in April of that year, five months before the attacks on New York and Washington. A senior Czech official had mentioned the meeting at a press conference in October 2001, and it became a key piece of evidence tying Al Qaeda to Saddam Hussein.

I asked for a meeting at the Iraqi embassy in Berlin to request a visa. When I arrived, the consular official stared at me. "You want to go to Iraq? Now?"

"Yes," I answered.

"You want to go there at a time when people are trying to find a way to leave?" he asked me. "To watch the war?"

"No. I want to go there and see if the reasons for a possible war are true or not."

He looked at me, his dark brown eyes widening. "Who cares if the reasons are true?" he asked. "Do you think anyone cares about the truth? You are so naïve. You think the Americans care about Iraqi lives? About the fact that we had nothing to do with 9/11 or weapons of mass destruction?"

"I want to go and find out what the truth is," I told him. "My colleague and I are really interested in finding the truth."

He laughed out loud. "Let's see what Baghdad thinks about this, and if they'll give you a visa." He stood up and reached out to shake my hand.

"How will I know if I get the visa?"

"You will be called."

I got ready to go. "Wait," he told me. He was scribbling something on a piece of paper. "This is my number in Iraq. I'm sure the Germans will soon throw us out. In case you make it to Iraq, call."

I took his contact information and left.

———

EVEN THOUGH I was still living at home, my parents didn't know about my plans. My bedroom doubled as my office, but I had my own phone line, and when I made phone calls about Iraq, I spoke in whispers. I didn't think there was any point in telling them until I got a visa.

And I was right. The call from the embassy never came. Instead, as the diplomat had predicted, he and his colleagues were asked to leave Germany. It was clear that the war was coming.

None of this deterred me. I nagged Peter, asking him to help me get approval from the *Post* to look for al-Ani, even if I didn't get an official visa. Maybe I could go in after the invasion, if the Americans or someone else took control.

As it turned out, that was exactly what happened. A week after the fall of Baghdad, Peter sent a message telling me to book a flight to Jordan through the *Post*'s office in Berlin. I would stay overnight at the Four Seasons Hotel and then drive to Baghdad. "Call Ranya in Jordan," he told me. "She will arrange everything."

I called Ranya, who was a stringer for the *Post* and the *New York Times* in Jordan. Glamorous, brassy, and descended from a well-educated and affluent Jordanian family, Ranya is the only Arab woman I know who dares to wear tight jeans and high heels to interview Islamists. We've become friends over the years, but on that day in 2003, I was a nervous twenty-five-year-old novice reporter heading into a war zone for the first time. "You'll have a couple of hours' honeymoon in a five-star hotel," she told me, laughing, "before they send you on a drive to hell."

I told my parents over dinner that evening, leaving out the part about hell.

"Of all places, you need to go there?" my father asked. "It is very dangerous. How will we know where you are?"

My mother burst into tears. "Where will you sleep? Who will take care of your safety?" she asked, then shook her head. "If only I'd let you become an actress."

I explained that I was going for one specific story and that I would be staying at a house with other *Washington Post* journalists. I also promised that I would stay away from places where we knew there was fighting going on. Back then, few could have predicted how quickly the war would spread from traditional battlefields to city streets.

Finally, my father asked what I needed for the trip. I'd learned my lesson about making sure to wear long shirts and clothes that didn't show the shape of my body. My father had always helped me by going to Pakistani and Afghan import-export shops in Frankfurt and finding the largest, ugliest tunics. His choices guaranteed that I wouldn't look feminine at all. I asked if he would help by getting me more clothes.

I called Peter, who was already in Baghdad. He told me not to carry lots of cash and to try to blend in as much as possible on the road from Jordan.

"There have been robberies between Amman and Baghdad," he explained.

I didn't tell my parents that, either. The next day, I boarded a flight to Jordan.

3

A Country with a Divided Soul

Iraq, 2003–4

When I landed later that night, I called Ranya. She had arranged for a car to pick me up and take me to the hotel. We would leave early the next morning. "You have to be ready by three a.m. It's safer for you to drive then," Ranya said. If she was nervous, her voice didn't betray it. She sounded as if she were reading a manual about how to turn on a TV. She also said there had been a change of plans: instead of traveling to Baghdad alone, I would now be sharing a car with a correspondent from the *New York Times*. This rattled me. How was I supposed to blend in if there was an American, who might have blue eyes and blond hair, in the car with me? And not just any American, but a guy from the *Times*? "Come on, darling, it's not that difficult," Ranya told me. "You're sharing a car, not a bed." After hanging up with her, I called Peter Finn in Baghdad. "It's okay," he said. "Just make him sit in back, and you sit in front."

At the hotel, I phoned my parents to let them know I'd arrived safely. "Everything is super," I told them, trying to sound casual. I managed to sleep for a couple of hours, then showered and dressed. When I tipped the waiter who brought my croissant and coffee, he couldn't stop grinning. I later realized I'd messed up the exchange rate and given him more than twice the cost of the breakfast.

It turned out that the other reporter was also young and nervous. When I met him in the lobby, I informed him that I'd sit in the front seat. Ranya had also urged me to do this, saying it would lower our chances of being robbed. "Yes, sure," he said. "Ranya knows best."

We climbed into a black SUV. It was nothing special—the kind of rugged car that Iraqis often used to travel back and forth across the Jordanian border. The driver, Munther, was a Jordanian of Palestinian descent and a real sweetheart. He'd brought along small, freshly baked pizzas, drinks, and cookies for the road, but neither the *Times* reporter nor I felt like eating much.

The trip from Amman to the border took about four hours. Then, if nothing went wrong, it would be another six hours to Baghdad. Munther and I chatted in Arabic. In the backseat, my fellow reporter listened to music on his headphones. At one point, Munther offered to plug the music into the car stereo, and heavy metal blared. "If we listen to this the rest of the way, I'm going to need aspirin," Munther told me in Arabic. "Tell him that if people hear it, they might know there's a foreigner here."

I handed the music back to the *Times* reporter. "It's a security thing," I said. But he was smiling. "Yeah, yeah," he said. "You don't like my music." I told him that '80s pop was more my speed.

At the border, we saw Jordanian soldiers but no Iraqis. I was the only woman there, but I couldn't tell if the men were staring at me because I was female or because I was wearing one of the ugly long shirts my father had bought. Once across, we drove through the desert on a smooth, empty road. Iraq's infrastructure was much more advanced than I'd expected. Judging by the roads and buildings, this wasn't a Third World country. It looked civilized, even prosperous. There was pride in the way people walked, in the way they looked at each other, but I also saw anger and disappointment in their faces.

After a while, Munther stopped the car. "Okay, look, guys, we are going to pass by a region where there are lots of robberies," he told us. "If you've got money, give it to me and I will hide it for you."

I told Munther that I had three hundred dollars with me, but it was already in a safe place. I had taken my Moroccan grandmother's long-ago advice and hidden it in my bra. "Child, the world is full of sons of sin," she told me then. "If they stick their hands in my dress pockets, they will get some coins, but not the large notes." I'd kept twenty dollars in my wallet, so that if thieves stopped us, they wouldn't be suspicious.

But the *Times* reporter had more money—a lot more. He hadn't expected Munther to ask for it and wasn't sure whether to hand it over. "The bureau will freak out," he said.

"What is it?" I asked. "Ten thousand dollars?"

It was much more than that and in cash, he told me, strapped to his body in one of those money belts.

When Munther saw the big stack of American dollars, he blanched. "This is very dangerous for all of us," he said. "They might think we're agents or spies for some foreign country." He hid the money in a special compartment under the floor of the car.

We started driving and soon passed through the first bad area, a nondescript little town in the middle of nowhere. About an hour and a half later, Munther turned to us. "The last problematic area is Fallujah," he said. "They've been shooting Americans there lately." Then he asked me in Arabic, "Can you tell your colleague it might be safer for us if he would stay away from the windows? It's best if he stays out of sight as we pass through here."

The *Times* reporter understood and immediately got down on the floor in the back. I stayed where I was and looked straight ahead. In my black hijab, I could have passed for an Iraqi. "They have the best kebabs here," Munther told me as we passed through Fallujah, "but these people feel their country was taken from them by the Americans and Iranians, so they are very aggressive. If you are in Fallujah, hold your breath and pray."

———

I'D TOLD MY parents that I'd be gone for two weeks, but I ended up spending several months in Iraq. There was so much happening, and it felt vitally important to be there. My interest was also personal. The longer I stayed in Iraq, the more often people asked me whether I was Sunni or Shia. Sometimes the question came from people I was interviewing, sometimes from curious Iraqis who worked with us in the *Washington*

Post bureau in Baghdad. My answers depended on the situation, but the real answer was: *both.*

My mother is Shia and my father Sunni, both descendants of the Prophet's family. The distinction had never been made in our house, but when I arrived in Iraq in the late spring of 2003, tension between the Sunni and Shia communities was building.

The historic roots of the religious Sunni-Shia conflict lie in the question of the righteous succession of the Prophet Muhammad. His followers divided over the question of whether Ali, his son-in-law and cousin, or Abu Bakr, his father-in-law, should follow him as the leader of the Islamic *ummah*, or community. Abu Bakr prevailed and became the first caliph. The Shia, however, believe that only Ali had the right to succeed Muhammad. A minority in the worldwide Muslim community, the Shia developed their own religious practices and sources. And while the conflict between the sects has not always been violent, the Shia have suffered from oppression throughout their history. Some Iraqi Shia scholars had fled to Iran or Bahrain, where they could practice their religious traditions freely. In Saddam's Iraq, anyone who opposed the Ba'ath Party became an enemy.

Under Islamic law, sectarian allegiance is patrilineal. When I was in Fallujah or speaking to conservative Sunnis, I would tell them that my father was Moroccan. There are no Shia in Morocco, so the implication was clear. But I also played with it. In Shia neighborhoods, I would tell people that my mother was *Ahl al-Bayt*, a member of the Prophet's family, and they would nod knowingly. In Shia Islam, this term, which can be translated "people of the house," traditionally includes only Muhammad; Muhammad's daughter Fatima; her husband, Ali; their two sons; and their direct descendants, the imams. In Sunni areas, people also liked to hear about my heritage. While some share the common Shia interpretation, others also count the Prophet's wives as members of the holy family. But both sects agree on the honorableness of *Ahl al-Bayt*.

The fact that both my parents are descendants opened doors, but it also showed me something terrifying: there were people who would refuse to talk to or associate with those who came from a different sect. For the first time, I was experiencing a dividing line within Islam that my parents, and especially my mother, had confronted years earlier, before I was born. I sensed that covering Iraq would be a turning point in my life, but I didn't yet realize how much the war would teach me about my own family history.

I spent the first few months at a house in the Jadriya district with Peter Finn and other colleagues from the *Post*. I quickly grew friendly with the brilliant and humble Lebanese-American journalist Anthony Shadid. We talked about the Sunni-Shia divide, and I told him that it shocked me. "It's been going on for hundreds of years," he told me, and he predicted that things would get worse.

My task was still to find Ahmad al-Ani, the diplomat who had allegedly met with Mohamed Atta in Prague. I had phone numbers for two Iraqi diplomats in Baghdad—one that a contact in Germany had given me, the other from the man I'd met at the embassy in Berlin. I met with each of them separately at the Hamra Hotel, where the *Post* had booked a room to be used for interviews. For security, we never brought any of our sources to the house without discussing it with the bureau chief first.

The Iraqi diplomat from the embassy, the one who had laughed at my naïveté, found al-Ani for me. "This is his number," he told me. "I've been to his house and told him he can trust you. But don't waste too much time. I'm sure you're not the only one who's looking for him."

I called the number the diplomat had given me. A woman answered. "Who are you?" she asked.

I knew that the phones might be tapped, so I tried to be careful.

"I'm Souad," I told her. "I think your family member has heard about me."

"Wait," she said in Arabic, and then I heard her whisper, "Souad?"

"Yes, yes, give me the phone," I heard a man say. "Yes, this is al-Ani. I'm the diplomat you're looking for."

I wanted to stop him from saying too much over the phone, but he went on. "I know they will try to make me disappear, but I want you to know, it is all a lie. What they said about me is a lie. I never met any of these terrorists, nor have we had anything to do with these attacks."

"Please don't say these things here," I broke in. "Somebody might be listening."

"I want you to know, it is all a lie. They will come for me anyway, I know. But at least now you know and the world has to know."

He agreed to meet the next day, saying, "The person who gave you my number will bring you here."

I called the man from the embassy. His friend had invited us for tea the next day, I said. "Could we meet at the Hamra and go together?" He agreed.

The next day, in a *Washington Post* car with an Iraqi driver, we reached al-Ani's house to find the door broken. A man came outside. His gray hair still had some black in it, and his skin looked pale. He wore dark blue trousers and a mint-colored shirt. My diplomat friend got out of the car, introduced himself, and asked to speak to Mr. al-Ani.

"You mean my brother?" the man answered. "He's gone. They took him last night."

"Who took him?" I asked.

The man looked at me. "Are you Souad the journalist? He told me about you."

He said that the previous night, six or seven men had stormed the house. They wore masks and carried guns, and they shouted al-Ani's name. "They handcuffed my brother with plastic ties, blindfolded him, and took him away," the brother reported. "We don't know where he is."

"Who are 'they'?" I asked.

"We don't know for sure, but we think the Americans. You know they used him as a scapegoat to create a reason for attacking Iraq."

With al-Ani gone, I knew that the story would be difficult to write. I asked if I could talk to his wife. Al-Ani's brother told me that she and her sister had been at the house the previous night and were in shock; they had gone to stay with their parents.

"I can understand that she might be in shock, but it is important I talk to her," I said. "Can I talk to her tomorrow or the day after?"

He shook his head.

"You can't. The men who took my brother told her not to talk to the media."

I was speechless. Why had this man and his family been silenced? Didn't they have as much right as anyone to tell their story? I had his denial over the phone, but it wasn't good enough. I'd never met al-Ani before that call, so I didn't know his voice and couldn't be sure it was really him I'd spoken to. If I'd met him, I would have asked for proof of his identity.

We tried to locate al-Ani by calling military spokespeople; some colleagues tried to find him through sources in other agencies, but no one wanted to say anything on the record. Finally, we confirmed that the Americans had arrested him.

Al-Ani was gone, but I stayed in Iraq. I got to know the *Post*'s Iraqi staff. One of the two older women who cooked for us said she had worked in one of Saddam Hussein's palaces and boasted that he loved her white beans and rice. One of our Iraqi stringers, Naseer, teased her: "Maybe because that's the only dish you can truly cook."

I learned a lot from the staff, who included Shia, Sunnis, and Kurds. Their ethnicities and religious beliefs didn't matter, they said, and they told me that these hadn't mattered before, either. Most of the local stringers were highly educated. Some had been businessmen or engineers, while Naseer, whom we called Abu Sayf, had been a pilot for Iraqi Airways. He worked as a translator and stringer, and his son was a *Post* driver.

I became part of the fast-paced metabolism of the bureau, chasing stories about what life in Iraq had been under Saddam as well as the continuing search for weapons of mass destruction. Paul Bremer, the head of the Coalition Provisional Authority that was running Iraq, had recently announced that the Iraqi army and police forces would be disbanded. During one press conference, Ahmad Chalabi, the Shia politician who led the Iraqi National Congress and had helped persuade the U.S. government to invade, said that honorable men in his organization would take care of security, but that the new Iraq could function only if those who had belonged to the Ba'ath Party were held responsible for their crimes. But de-Ba'athification would have serious consequences; the dissolution of the army and police left crowds of mostly Sunni men with security experience unemployed, armed, and angry. It turned into a recruitment bonanza for Al Qaeda in Iraq.

From what I could gather, Chalabi had a questionable reputation. Why would Bremer hold press conferences with such a man? Why would someone like Chalabi—who had spent many years outside Iraq—have more say in the future of this country than those who had lived here their whole lives? Was this really about building a better future for the Iraqis, or was it about the United States putting people in power who would be easy to handle?

"But doesn't the United States think that a guy with such a track record will be more harm than help?" I asked Anthony Shadid one day, during a tea break in our garden.

"Souad, most of the people in the United States don't think that far," he responded. "Chalabi speaks English. He has studied in the United States. He knows how to crack the right jokes. He knows how to play the game in DC. Believe it or not, that's what matters to some of these decision makers."

———

EVERY NIGHT WHEN my colleagues called their loved ones, I dialed my parents in Germany. During those conversations, as I talked about what I was seeing, I began to learn more about the early years of my parents' marriage, and how the Sunni-Shia rift that was deepening in Iraq had been a source of trouble for them, too.

The sectarian divide had been much more problematic on my mother's side. My mother was born and grew up in Antakya, a Turkish city near the Syrian border. During the First World War, my great-grandfather had sheltered Armenians in his house and helped to smuggle them across the border to Syria in horse carriages. My family never talked about it much because even years later they feared the consequences. Some members of the family had been jailed for aiding Armenians. They didn't share a faith, but they had something else in common: both were minorities in the Ottoman Empire and later Turkey.

My mother's relatives are Turkish citizens, but of Arab descent, having come originally from Syria. When she was growing up, people of Arab descent in Turkey were often sent to do their compulsory military service in Kurdish areas, where there was active conflict. My mother's father, a successful tire dealer, and her older brothers told stories about how, in the 1950s and '60s, armed Turkish soldiers would show up and say, "We'll rape all your girls. We'll kill you. You're not really Muslims." As a result, people in the Arab-Turkish border regions began to resist the Turks. They built up their own local security forces and monitored their own neighborhoods, allowing only Christians and people of Arab descent to live there.

My mother told me that when she was a teenager, she had fallen in love with a Turkish policeman. They'd wanted to marry, but her brothers had said they would kill her if she married a Turk. My grandmother was sympathetic, but my mother's brothers were firm: she was not going to marry a Turk or a Sunni.

My mother turned down the policeman's proposal, but her heart was broken, and she was furious with her family. "I pray that God takes me away from you, to where there are seven seas between us," she told them. That was part of the reason she went to work in Germany. When she and my father started seeing each other and decided to marry, she didn't tell her family. She waited until after the wedding to share the news, for fear of what they'd do or say.

And she was right: the old wound hadn't healed. My mother's brothers flew into a rage. They had forbidden their sister to marry a Turk, and now she had gone and married a man who wasn't even from their part of the world—and on top of that, he was a Sunni. Some of her brothers threatened to kill her. When my sister Fatma suffered brain damage at birth, they thought the worst. "You will see, he is going to leave you now that you've had a sick child," one of them told her. My father stuck around, but when my sister Hannan was born a year later, some of my uncles still wouldn't speak to him.

It was then that my grandmother in Morocco went to a "letter writer" and dictated a message to be sent to my grandparents in Turkey. "We are honorable people," she told them in Arabic. "You say you are descendants of the Prophet Muhammad. We are also descendants of the Prophet, and we're not allowed to discriminate. We love your daughter, and we will do our best to make her part of our family."

Perhaps her letter had some effect, because while my uncles remained angry, my grandfather began to soften. When my father, mother, and two sisters traveled to visit my mother's family in Turkey for the first time, some of her brothers refused to shake my father's hand and left the room when he entered. They told my mother they would never accept her marriage.

My grandfather put an end to that. "Enough is enough," he told his sons. "He's part of the family, and you have to accept it." He welcomed my father and ordered my uncles to do the same. "I'm still the head of the family," he said. "If you don't do what I say, you'll no longer be my sons."

In the years that followed, my parents won further favor in the family because they cared for my grandparents so well. They sent money to Turkey every month, and when one of my mother's brothers didn't want to do his mandatory military service, my mother and father helped him pay to get out of it. This brother was part of a political student movement, and he ultimately had to leave the country. My parents helped him get a visa to come to Germany, and he lived with us for a few months. All this proved that my father had fully embraced my mother and her family.

When I was in Iraq, these stories poured out of my mother. As I told her about the growing hatred between Sunnis and Shia in Iraq, she started speaking in a way I'd never heard before.

"There has been a lot of suffering, because they were killing us," she said one night.

"Who're 'they'?"

"The Sunnis."

"Mom, your kids are Sunni!"

I could hear my father in the background, asking what she was talking about. I heard him say, "Don't forget we left all this behind us."

She told me about her upbringing in Turkey and how, when she was a child, Turks would come and say, "We're going to kill you."

"This was because you were Arab, not Shia," I said. "If you'd been Sunni, they would have said the same."

"Yes," she said. "You're right."

I told her that militia fighters loyal to the Iraqi Shia leader Muqtada al-Sadr were going into mixed neighborhoods and telling Sunnis they would be killed if they didn't leave their houses. Sadr wanted to turn these places into pure Shia enclaves. "Why are these Shia doing this?" I asked my mother.

"They have also suffered," she said. "You should look into what happened to them before."

Sunnis and Shia had lived together in the same Baghdad neighborhoods for decades, I told her. The difference now was that fundamentalists were claiming those neighborhoods as their own. "You have no idea," I said. "These people are criminals."

The rise of Iraq's Shia majority was aided by the return of powerful Iraqi exiles, politicians and religious figures alike, who had ties to Iran—and in many cases had lived there for years. One of these was Nouri al-Maliki, who would later become Iraq's prime minister. A dissident under Saddam, he'd lived in Iran and Syria before returning to Iraq in 2003. Another was Ayatollah Mohammad Baqr al-Hakim, an important figure in U.S. efforts to build a new Iraqi government. After more than two decades of exile in Iran, he returned as head of what is now called the Islamic Supreme Council of Iraq, a leading Shia political organization. The group's militia, known as the Badr Brigades, had been recruited, trained, and armed by Iran's Revolutionary Guard. After the fall of Saddam, Iran continued to provide political, financial, and military support to the Supreme Council and the Badr Brigades.

While some of my journalist friends attended pool parties at the Hamra Hotel, I spent my nights reading my politics books for school and writing reports for my professors. I had made a deal with three of them: they would allow me to miss lectures if I sent them weekly reports. It was surreal to be reading Marx or trying to understand the theory of complex interdependence at night after witnessing the collapse of a nation by day.

I wondered how the United States and Britain had allowed Iraq to fall into this trap. While we reporters could clearly see that sectarian tensions were rising and religious figures were gaining influence, no one in authority seemed particularly concerned, certainly not Paul Bremer. There were many things I didn't understand. Why didn't U.S. officials choose Iraqi engineers and architects, who were among the best in the Arab world, to rebuild the country? Instead, they gave the contracts to Jordanian, Lebanese, British, or U.S. firms, which then subcontracted the jobs to Iraqis. It didn't make sense.

As a child in Frankfurt, I'd loved U.S. soldiers, but now I was seeing those troops—and America itself—from a different vantage point. My previous experience with Americans had come from growing up near a U.S. military base. When I was in kindergarten, my mother tells me, I liked to flirt with the soldiers. Whenever I saw them in the streets, they would smile and give me chewing gum or a lollipop. Most important, the Americans spent a lot of time working with the school for handicapped children that Fatma attended. Every year, they organized a Special Olympics. It was held on a grassy field, and there were hot dogs, soft drinks, and ice cream. One soldier would volunteer to take care of each child, and everyone got a medal.

But the American soldiers I saw in Iraq weren't friendly. I began to understand that most American soldiers knew little or nothing about Iraq or about Arab culture. Once, when I wanted to go to a press conference in the Green Zone, I decided on purpose to stand in the line for Iraqis rather than the one for foreigners. As I waited, an American soldier walked past, gun in hand, grimacing and spitting on the ground. I could see that the Iraqis in the line were appalled.

"Excuse me," I said to the soldier, in English. "Don't do that. It's very rude. It's as if you're spitting on their country."

I didn't spend much time with American soldiers in Iraq. But one day in July 2003, I got a call from an Iraqi source who urged me to come to Mosul as fast as I could. "There's a shoot-out going on here," he said. "American soldiers are involved as well. I cannot say more. The phones might be tapped."

We confirmed that there was shooting, and we heard that American soldiers were conducting an operation. But against whom? I called my source back and asked an adviser to drag him out of a meeting.

"Do you know what is going on?"

"Yes," he answered. "The U.S. soldiers are having a heavy battle with people who were hiding in a house."

"Who are these people?"

"I can't give you details now, but you should come. This is big."

I told him it was too risky to come without knowing who was involved. The road to Mosul wasn't safe, and the bureau chief would want to know why we were going.

"They are people from the most wanted list, very important, very big. I can't tell you more now."

At first, I planned to go alone, but given the distance and the curfew, it became clear that I would have to spend the night in Mosul. Another *Post* reporter, Kevin Sullivan, joined me, along with an Iraqi stringer and driver.

When we reached the affluent residential part of Mosul where the shooting had occurred, we saw that U.S. soldiers had closed down the area. A large villa had been destroyed. There was broken glass everywhere and bullets still lodged in the walls; helicopters circled overhead. Passersby told me that the Americans had just carried bodies out of the house.

"Did you see who it was?" I asked.

They nodded. "Uday and Qusay, the president's sons," a bearded Iraqi army veteran in a white ankle-length robe, or *dishdasha*, told me. "May God have mercy on their souls."

On the street nearby, three soldiers who looked to be nineteen or twenty years old stood in front of a tank, trying to keep people away from the ruined house. I wanted to talk to more people, so while Kevin sat in the car making calls, I approached the tank. When the soldiers heard I was from the *Washington Post*, they weren't happy.

"We hate the *Washington Post*, and the fucking *New York Times*," one of them said. "You guys are always writing such shit about us."

I took out my satellite phone and made a call. One of the soldiers watched me closely.

"Can you call the United States on that?" he asked when I got off.

I told him you could call anywhere.

"So can I call Texas?" He hadn't spoken to his pregnant wife in several months. "I just want to tell her I'm okay."

"Take it," I told him.

He looked at the sergeant on top of the tank. "Can I?" The sergeant nodded. The soldier called his wife, and one of the other soldiers called his parents.

"Ma'am, I'm sorry we weren't polite to you in the beginning," one of the soldiers said afterward. "We're under so much pressure. It's not what we expected."

"What did you expect?"

"We thought people would love us here. We thought they'd offer us tea and be happy to see us. Instead, they attack us. We see our friends getting killed. People are angry with us."

The sergeant wouldn't tell me who they'd killed in the villa, but I overheard one of the soldiers say, "There was Uday and then it was just boom, boom, boom." We called the *Post*'s bureau chief back in Baghdad, who got confirmation from the army: Saddam Hussein's sons, Uday and Qusay, two of the most wanted men in Iraq, had been killed.

By then it was getting dark, and we had to find a place to spend the night. Unfortunately, the only decent hotel in the city was already full, so we settled for a grimy motel with no name whose main clientele seemed to be Iraqi truck drivers. It wasn't the kind of place where a respectable woman would stay—in fact, I didn't see any other women on the premises—but it was our only option.

The man at the reception desk told us to wait until his colleague arrived. That man was responsible for the rooms.

Men in long robes occupied four chairs in the reception area. One of them was smoking, and I realized that he was staring at me. He turned to the man next to him and whispered something in his ear. The second man stood up and left the hall.

The man who had been staring took out a pack of Marlboros and offered me one. He had dark skin, a mustache, and very dark eyes.

"Thanks, but I don't smoke," I said in Arabic.

"Where are you from?" he asked.

"Morocco. You?"

"Deir Azzhor. I am the chief of a big tribe there." He took another drag on his cigarette. "So you're staying here, too?"

I told him we weren't sure. Kevin and our Iraqi stringer sat nearby in

the lobby, but our driver was still out in the parking lot, and I was beginning to wonder what was taking him so long. I left the reception area and
went out to look for him. Sure enough, the man who had been sitting with
the tribal chief was talking to our driver. When he saw me, he went back
into the motel.

"What did he want from you?" I asked the driver.

"He said he was working for this tribal chief from Deir Azzhor and
asked me about you, if you were Muslim and if you were married."

"What did you tell him?" I asked.

"I told him you were Muslim and not married."

"Why are you telling him private stuff about me?"

The driver shrugged. "It's normal."

"No, it's not," I said.

When I went back into the reception hall, the men were still sitting
there. The tribal chief followed my every movement with his eyes, still
smoking. Once or twice, he smirked at me lasciviously.

When the receptionist finally came, I gave him twenty dollars and
asked him not to tell anyone which room I was in. He took the money
and smiled. "Of course not. Don't worry."

Our stringer, Naseer, was watching. He told me I shouldn't trust the
receptionist.

"Did you see what kind of watch the tribal chief was wearing? They
might look poor but the guy is rich. You gave the receptionist twenty dollars. That chief will give him two hundred dollars to get your room
number and the extra key."

We had four rooms close to each other. The bedsheets were crumpled
and dirty, and the toilet was a hole in the ground. It reminded me of the
toilet my grandmother had in Meknes when I lived with her as a child,
except that this one was filthy and stank. Brownish water trickled from
the shower head.

My room was on the same floor as the others, but while my three male
colleagues had rooms next to each other, mine was at the far end of the
corridor.

I asked Naseer to switch rooms with me but not to tell anyone. I told
him to come get me in the morning and gave him and Kevin a pass-

word: "apple pie." If I didn't hear those words, I told them, I wouldn't open the door.

Even though I was still a bit worried about the tribal chief and his men, I was exhausted. I put my windbreaker over the pillow and slept with my clothes on. In the middle of the night I heard loud voices and the noise of people running but realized it was happening somewhere else on the floor. I went back to sleep.

The next morning I waited for Naseer to knock on my door and accompany me downstairs. "You know, you're really lucky we switched rooms," he said, laughing. "They came in the middle of the night. It seemed as if they were planning to kidnap you." When they opened the door and saw Naseer, they shouted and ran away.

"They left the hotel, but I told you that bastard receptionist must have given them the room number and key."

We passed the receptionist as we walked through the lobby to our car. His cheeks and left eye looked swollen, and he wasn't smiling. "Instead of the two hundred dollars, he probably received two hundred slaps and punches for not delivering the bride," Naseer said, giggling.

We drove back to the neighborhood where Saddam's sons had been killed. While Kevin and I were standing near the car, making calls on our satellite phones, someone tapped my shoulder.

"Are you a journalist?" he asked in Arabic. "If so, why don't you write about the boy Anas who was killed by U.S. soldiers yesterday?"

I thought I'd misheard him. "What are you talking about? What boy Anas? The only ones killed yesterday were Uday and Qusay. How do you know about this?"

"Anas was my brother."

Kevin and I followed the man to his house, where his family was in mourning. The father was very kind, but the oldest brother was livid, especially when he saw Kevin. "You're American!" he yelled. "Why did you kill my brother? He was just a boy."

"I'm so sorry, but I didn't kill your brother," Kevin said, taken aback. "We want to write about it."

The family told us that American soldiers had closed down some streets in the neighborhood during the raid to get Uday and Qusay. That afternoon, Anas, a twenty-one-year-old student, learned that he'd done well in his classes. He wanted to go to the mosque and give thanks, but the soldiers had blocked the road, and a crowd had begun protesting at the barricade. When some Iraqis started throwing rocks, the soldiers got nervous and a few of them fired on the demonstrators. A bullet struck Anas in the head.

We had the story, but it would be hard to prove. The army denied that any civilians had been killed. We talked to doctors who had treated the wounded, and who described their injuries as being specific to machine-gun fire. We found other victims and interviewed them again and again. "You think we made all this up?" a man who had been shot in the leg asked me incredulously. "Do you think we shot ourselves?" We convinced the doctors to show us the bullets they'd removed from people's bodies, then went back to the neighborhood and got bullets out of the walls to see if they matched. Kevin took the ammunition to the army for confirmation, but the Americans continued to deny what dozens of witnesses had seen.

One moment from those days will always stay with me. When we were talking to Anas's family, his oldest brother, the one who had accused Kevin of killing him, pulled me aside. "If you're Palestinian, go and fight against these Americans and Jews," he said.

"I'm Moroccan."

"You should fight," he told me, looking straight into my eyes.

His father overheard and apologized. "My son was very close to his brother," he said.

I told him I understood. "You lost your son, but we didn't kill your son. Every American is not bad," I said.

But I couldn't help remembering Maureen Fanning's question: *Why do they hate us so much?*

———

IN AUGUST, AFTER more than three months in Iraq, I flew back to Germany, but I kept thinking about Baghdad. Maybe because I spoke Arabic, I felt that I understood the place more fully than others. Like many reporters, I felt responsible to the Iraqis, as if, by staying away, I was letting them down.

I went back to the university, but it felt stupid to be sitting in class when there was a war going on. My classmates talked about the rest of the world with typical Western arrogance, but they'd never seen the suffering or complexity of war up close. What had been tolerable to me before was now unbearable. Once you've wept with someone who's lost a family member because of another country's political decisions, it's hard to view international relations with detachment. At home, I monitored news from Iraq obsessively, constantly flipping on CNN in case I'd missed something. My parents said I seemed nervous, but I didn't notice.

After three weeks, to my parents' dismay, I went back. The land route from Jordan had become too dangerous, so Peter and I, along with Guy Raz, an NPR reporter, flew to Turkey and drove across Iraq's northern border. This time, my working arrangement was a bit different. Guy had asked me to work for him, and Peter had agreed, as long as I could report on breaking news for the *Post*. I also got approval to work on occasional small pieces for German newspapers and to do interviews with German radio in case of breaking news.

The NPR correspondents stayed at a small hotel in central Baghdad. It was quieter than the *Washington Post* house, and my work with Guy moved at a slower pace and allowed me to explore communities that often didn't make the news. Our main translator, Abu Aara, was an Armenian Christian, a community that had for decades lived freely in Iraq. He invited us into his home, and we attended the baptism of one of his relatives' sons. The guests I met there spoke of a different Iraq.

The families of these Armenians had fled the massacres of the Ottoman Empire ninety years before. Under Saddam, they said, they'd lived and worshipped freely. "What people in the West don't seem to understand is that the Ba'ath Party was the force trying to separate religion as much as possible from politics," Abu Aara's pastor told me. "Saddam was fighting the ayatollahs in Iran because they wanted to brainwash Shia in Iraq and fight secularism, but it would be wrong to say that whoever was Shia was deprived of rights." Minorities weren't automatically subject to discrimination, he said. I thought of Tariq Aziz, a Christian who had been Saddam Hussein's longtime foreign minister.

I couldn't stop thinking about the pastor's words. Our politicians and advisers hadn't done their due diligence. They had come with the perspective that our system—democracy—would work for everyone, and they didn't consider the consequences that adopting an entirely new system might have for people living elsewhere. I wondered, not for the first time, whether the West was unintentionally opening the door to a more religious and sectarian Middle East.

SINCE MY ARRIVAL in Iraq, I'd seen neighborhoods changing. In some cases, Shia militias had forced Sunni families to move to other areas. Shia women living in areas that were controlled by militias told me that they had to wear a full body covering known as a *chador* or *abaya* when leaving the house. "It wasn't like that before," a woman named Hannan, who had been in the Iraqi army, told me. "I just wore my uniform; I never put on a veil." But since the fall of Saddam Hussein, things had changed dramatically. "It's increasingly the mullahs and militias who are running the show," she told me. "I can't leave the house uncovered or without my mother anymore."

Meanwhile, Al Qaeda had increased its attacks, striking U.S. soldiers as well as politicians cooperating with the United States and prominent Shia figures. The sectarian violence reached an apex with the assassination of Ayatollah Mohammad Baqr al-Hakim, the head of the group that is now called the Islamic Supreme Council of Iraq, who was killed along with 125 others when a car bomb exploded as he was leaving the Imam Ali mosque in Najaf in late August. The Islamic Supreme Council belonged to the U.S.-appointed Iraqi Governing Council, and his role as a respected religious leader gave the U.S. occupation authority much-needed credibility. Abu Musab al-Zarqawi and his terrorist network later claimed responsibility for the attack.

I realized that if I wanted to understand Iraq's sectarian divide, I had to go to Najaf, one of the holiest places on earth for Shia, where Ali is buried, where Shia clerics revolted against British colonial forces in 1918, and where Ayatollah Ruholla Khomeini prepared the Iranian revolution during his exile there in the 1970s. Najaf was where Khomeini wrote his anticolonial polemic *Islamic Government*, in which he explained the impiety of monarchies and the need for an Islamic republic. In 1978, Khomeini was expelled from Najaf by Saddam Hussein, who was being pressured by the shah of Iran, but he left many supporters behind. A highly symbolic place of Shia resistance and militancy—many members of the founding generation of Hezbollah had also studied there—Najaf was now the site of a major terrorist attack. Security was very tight following Hakim's assassination. Shia militias had made it clear that they wanted to protect their own holy sites, and U.S. and British soldiers stood aside as the militias took over what had once been the job of the Iraqi army and police.

Guy had talked to American and Iraqi officials, and they all said it would be best to visit one of the leading Shia groups before going to Najaf, to ensure that we wouldn't run into problems with the militias there. Abu Aara, our stringer, said that Hizb ul'Dawaa was one of the most influential Shia political groups and that I should go there first. They had an office in Baghdad.

There were metal detectors at the entrance, but women were winked through. *Not good*, I thought.

Hizb ul'Dawaa was a religious party. Many of its members had spent years in Iran and saw no distinction between religion and politics. We were told that one of the leaders of the party was waiting for us. He had visitors but invited us in.

He was in his late fifties or early sixties, with a neatly trimmed beard and striking light brown eyes. He wore an Iranian-style black turban that, along with his title, *sayyid*, indicated he was a descendant of the Prophet.

I introduced Abu Aara and our driver, Abu Ali, who was Shia, and explained that I wanted to go to Najaf to report on the changing relationship between Sunni and Shia and to explore the question of whether there would be some kind of Sunni-Shia war. I also wanted to know how much influence Iran had in that area, but I didn't tell the *sayyid* that.

He listened and smiled. "Where are you from?"

I told him that my father was Moroccan but that I had been born in Germany.

"And who are you?"

I'd just introduced myself, I thought. Why was he asking again? "I am Souad Mekhennet. I am a journalist."

"No, no. I understand what your name is and who you are representing," he said. "What I'm asking is, whose descendant are you?"

"Why?"

"Because I think you and I share some of the same blood lineage."

"How do you know this? How could you know?"

He said he felt it, that it was written in my eyes. He was not only a religious scholar but deeply spiritual. "I think you are a *sayyida*, or how do you say it in Morocco, *sharifa*?" he said with a smile.

I felt unnerved but also intrigued. I suddenly wanted to talk to him about everything that was happening in Iraq, and to Islam in general. I couldn't change who I was and saw no reason to conceal it. I told him about my parents, their intersectarian marriage, and how angry my grandparents had been when they found out. I wondered aloud if the Sunni-Shia divide would cause more bloodshed in Iraq.

He agreed that trouble lay ahead. In his youth, he'd been active in some secular political movements, but he told me that his whole family had come under attack when one of his brothers opposed Saddam Hussein's regime.

"I had no choice but to go to Iran, live there in exile, and study religion."

I cut to the question that was foremost in my mind. "Why are Sunnis and Shia still accusing and killing each other over things that happened hundreds of years ago?" I asked.

"Politics," he whispered, and smiled. "But you must know that you cannot discuss such things with everybody. There are some who could misunderstand your critical and philosophical mind-set and take it personally." He asked me when I planned to go to Najaf; I told him I was leaving in two days.

He took out a piece of paper and wrote something on it. "You will go in the morning and come back the same day, right?" he asked. I nodded. He folded the paper and gave it to me. "Whenever you reach a checkpoint, show them this paper." He then turned to a man who was among the others sitting at the far end of the room. "Hassan, call Najaf, tell them a journalist called Souad Mekhennet will be visiting. She and her team should get any help and support they need."

I was stunned by how easy it had been, and I thanked him.

"You know what you are doing is dangerous?" he asked. "Even going to Najaf now is dangerous. There could be bombs. Why are you doing it?"

"Because it's my work."

"No. You could have become an arts writer, a lawyer, or anything else, but you're going into the most difficult areas in the Islamic world, risking your life." He stopped, and I saw that his eyes were wet. He seemed moved. "You have chosen a very hard life. May Allah bring you a man in your life who will be worth your big heart and searching mind. That's what I am wishing for you."

I felt a mix of sadness and vulnerability. He had raised questions I myself couldn't answer. Most of my colleagues were married or at least had steady partners. I had my parents, but that was different. Lots of people also dated in Baghdad. But I wasn't interested in casual relationships. I felt that I might want to get married to somebody of Arab descent, and I knew that reputation was everything. If my Iraqi translators or drivers got the impression that I was one of these women sneaking around the Hamra Hotel with a man, they would lose all respect for me. I was a German reporter, but in their eyes I was first and foremost an Arab woman.

In the car Abu Aara, Abu Ali, and I read what the *sayyid* had written: "Souad Mekhennet is a journalist and she is a descendant of the Prophet's family. As such, she and those with her should receive full protection and be treated with the highest respect." It was dated and signed and bore his party's seal.

And it was incredible how well the paper worked. While other reporters had to park their cars far from the Imam Ali mosque, we were allowed to park right in front. All the militiamen and mosque personnel who read the paper went out of their way to help us.

I didn't know what to expect in Najaf. There was an immense energy in the city, and the closer we got to the shrine of Imam Ali, the more people I saw who were crying for this man, one of my forefathers. It seemed that they felt deeply pained by Ali's death. Seeing the mourners' devotion, I realized how much they were willing to do for anyone who was preaching about or asking for something in the name of Imam Ali or his son Imam Hussein.

I spoke to some younger men outside the shrine, asking what Imam Ali and Imam Hussein meant to them. "I would die for them and kill whoever insults them," one told me. "I would give my blood."

It would be easy, I thought, for Muslim leaders to use this emotional attachment for their own political benefit. They could justify any action in the name of Ali or Hussein. I also understood in a new way that the descendants of the Prophet's family had a grave responsibility to stop this from happening.

———

IN MY CONTINUING attempts to understand the roots of the Sunni-Shia conflict, one of the people I most wanted to speak to was Aquila al-Hashimi, a prominent Shia politician and one of only three women on the Iraqi Governing Council. Under Saddam, she had been involved in the United Nations' oil-for-food program on behalf of the Iraqi government. She had a doctorate in French literature from the Sorbonne and had sometimes served as Tariq Aziz's French translator. Before coming to Iraq, I'd read many news stories about Shia being treated like second-class citizens under Saddam, and I wondered, if that was true, how a woman like al-Hashimi could have risen to such a powerful position in the government. Ahmad Chalabi and others were saying that everyone in Saddam's party had to be purged, but if al-Hashimi had succeeded under that system, things must have been more nuanced than we were hearing. I wanted to ask her what it had been like to live as a Shia under Saddam and what she thought of the de-Ba'athification plan.

"Please come and visit," she said when I reached her. "There is too much going wrong here." Her voice was friendly, and I could tell by her English that she was highly educated. "I'm worried there will be lots of bloodshed. I fear for the unity of my country."

She invited me to lunch the following afternoon. When I called in the morning to confirm the time, a man picked up. He was crying and his voice sounded broken. I heard women screaming in the background.

"Who are you?" he asked.

I told him I was a journalist and had a meeting with Aquila al-Hashimi that afternoon.

I could hear him breathing fast. "They shot her." A carful of gunmen had attacked al-Hashimi's car, and she'd been severely wounded. I hung up the phone in shock. I later learned that al-Hashimi had been shot in the stomach and leg. For several days, she lay in a coma in an American military hospital. As I waited for her to recover, I worked on other stories, including one for NPR about rising violence in the city. We wanted to gauge the concern of young Iraqis, so I interviewed some of the young men listening to Iraqi pop music around the corner from our hotel. While I chatted with them, a man with light brown hair came and stood near us. He introduced himself as "Mustafa" and said he was Palestinian.

We started talking about music, but the conversation shifted to politics. Mustafa was very angry about what had happened in Iraq. "This country was so good to me and my family," he said. "This is all part of a bigger plan to cut the Middle East into pieces and feed us to the Iranians."

Mustafa said he had worked in the security sector under Saddam, but since the security forces had been dissolved, he and others had nothing to do except meet up and spill out their hatred against America, Iran, and Britain. "We felt sorry for the people who were killed in the 9/11 attacks, but now I think this was all just a plot by the Americans so they could have an excuse to invade Iraq," he said.

He asked me where I was staying. Given the lack of security and my experience with the tribal chief in Mosul, I didn't tell anyone where I lived. I apologized to Mustafa, telling him that my parents had taught me not to share such private information with strangers.

"Fine, fine. Just tell me, are you staying at this hotel?" he pointed to a nearby hotel where the NBC crews stayed.

I told him I wasn't.

Afterward, when I got into my car, I told Abu Ali to drive around in case someone was following us.

The next morning I was awakened by a giant explosion. My room was on the first floor, and my bed wasn't far from a window. The impact forced the window open, and I fell out of bed. Whether it was some instinctive reaction or an effect of the blast, I don't know.

I lay on the floor wondering if someone was going to burst in and drag me away. Kidnappings in Iraq sometimes worked that way: attackers would use explosives to blast open the gates before coming inside. I could hear my heart beating and my own deep breathing. Shaking, I stood up, put on my clothes, and grabbed my satellite phone and notebook. I shouted Guy's name and heard him shouting mine. Out in the hall, we saw the hotel workers with shocked, white faces. "Are you okay?" I screamed. "Is everything okay?"

They told me there had been an explosion at the hotel where the NBC crews stayed. We ran outside and around the corner and saw broken windows and lots of smoke. People poured out into the streets, and soon all the reporters got on their phones. I stared in amazement at the burning hotel. Then I turned and saw the man from the night before, Mustafa, standing nearby. He was watching the scene, and when he saw me, he nodded and smiled. I suddenly remembered him asking me where I was staying and mentioning the hotel that had just been bombed. I walked toward him, but he stopped smiling and shook his head as if to say, *don't*.

A white car stopped in front of him. He got in, and the car drove away.

I talked to people from NBC and learned that at least one man, a Somali guard, had been killed. After finishing my report for NPR, I did a quick interview with a German radio station. Back in Germany, my professor Lothar Brock heard it and emailed to say that he was worried about me. My voice had been trembling, he wrote, and I seemed to be in shock. I hadn't realized how traumatized I was.

That afternoon, I learned more bad news: Aquila al-Hashimi was dead. I had already missed the funeral, but I wanted to visit her family and offer my condolences. When I arrived at the house, a young boy pointed me toward a room.

I saw women beating themselves and crying—al-Hashimi's cousins, aunts, and other relatives, wearing *abayas*. In the center of the room sat an old woman with long gray hair who seemed to be in a trance. She cried and screamed, pulled her hair, and beat her chest. Her undershirt had fallen off, and her skin was red from the impact of her fists. It was as if she were trying to beat out the pain. I knew that this mourning ritual was part of Shia tradition, but I'd never seen it up close before. "That is Aquila's mother," a young woman told me. Then she asked who I was. "You can't be here," she said after I told her. "This is only for the family." I apologized and left quickly.

As I climbed numbly into the car, it occurred to me that for the second time in Iraq, I'd come too late. When they'd taken the former diplomat al-Ani, I'd been convinced that someone wanted to stop me from getting the truth. I'd also felt responsible: maybe someone had been listening to our conversation, and that was why he'd disappeared. Either way, I'd never been able to write about what he told me. The people who wanted to silence him had won.

With al-Hashimi's death, they had won again, but this time it felt even worse. As we drove back to the hotel, I began to tremble. I had a very bad feeling that we in the West were destroying the structure of a country that had not been a democracy but that had offered a place to a woman like al-Hashimi, a Shia, who was able to study and enter politics. Maybe it wasn't a system we liked, but we, the decision makers, were now destroying it and destroying all those people, intelligent people like her who came from diverse backgrounds and who should have had a role in the future of their country. I felt that her killing was another step toward disaster.

I couldn't get the image of al-Hashimi's mother out of my head. She reminded me of my grandmother in Morocco. The noise of the beating, of the moment when her fists hit her chest, echoed in my head. I couldn't feel her pain, but I could feel anger that we had let this happen. In the car, the sound of the beating stayed in my head, and the anger knotted my stomach. I leaned my head against the car window and cried.

4

A Call from Khaled el-Masri

Germany and Algeria, 2004–6

Iraq changed me. When I returned home to Frankfurt toward the end of 2003, I carried with me the sound of bombings, the smell of burned flesh, and the screaming of men and women looking for their relatives. On New Year's Eve, I refused to join my family and visiting friends on the balcony to watch fireworks because the sound reminded me too much of exploding bombs.

I didn't feel like celebrating what had happened the previous year or what lay ahead. The lines of hatred between Sunni and Shia were deepening, the war and the occupation of Iraq had become a great public relations opportunity for Al Qaeda, and the murderous behavior of some of the Shia militias in Iraq depressed me. Within a few months, the world would learn of U.S. soldiers torturing and humiliating Iraqi prisoners in Abu Ghraib and elsewhere through a trove of terrifyingly casual snapshots captured by soldiers who seemed to think they were on vacation in an exotic land where morality and human decency didn't exist. These scandals reinforced my sense that the West, particularly the United States, had ceded the moral high ground it had once so proudly occupied and was now operating with impunity in what its leaders called "the shadows."

"People must know, they must understand, that the war in Iraq will result in more hatred, more threats against Americans and Europeans," I told Lothar Brock, my international relations professor, during lunch at the university canteen.

"You must heal," he said, with concern in his eyes. "Don't go back to war zones. I'm sure there are enough stories to follow outside of Iraq." He urged me to devote more time to my studies.

In 2004, I left the *Washington Post* to work for the *New York Times*'s investigative unit. Again, I was on contract, and I was also allowed to work for ZDF, a German public broadcaster that was one of the biggest TV channels in Europe. I was entering an important phase at the university, and my professors were putting extra emphasis on homework and finals. Soon I would begin work on my thesis, the final step before receiving my degree.

Brock, who was also my thesis adviser, insisted that I focus on a topic unrelated to terrorism. He wanted me to write about the water shortage in the Middle East. He suggested I focus on Jordan, where Prince Hassan bin Talal, the brother of the late King Hussein, was deeply involved in water security issues.

I tried to concentrate on my classes and research, but I was still closely following the news from Iraq and becoming increasingly interested in Abu Musab al-Zarqawi, the leader of Al Qaeda in Iraq, and his network. Between reading chapters in my academic books, I monitored the news from the Middle East, switching among Al Jazeera, CNN, and the BBC.

One afternoon I received a call on my cell from a number I didn't recognize. I picked up and heard a low, shaky voice speaking in Arabic: "Are you the journalist Souad Mekhennet?"

"Who are you?" I asked.

"My name is Khaled el-Masri, and I was kidnapped by the CIA."

I moved the phone away from my ear and looked at the number again. It must be some crank, I thought. "Excuse me? I don't understand. Who gave you my number?"

He named a source of mine in Germany, an older man who was under investigation for ties to terrorism. Then his story tumbled out, incoherently at first: "I was on my way to Macedonia. They arrested me. They took me on a flight to Afghanistan. I was tortured."

"Don't say these things on the phone," I told him. "Listen, Mr. el-Masri, where are you? Can I call you back? I think it's better if we meet in person."

I told him to buy a new phone, along with a prepaid SIM card, and call me back so we could set an appointment. In those days, you could still buy a prepaid SIM card in Germany without having to register it under your name. "They" had taken everything he had, he said, but he would find a way to get a new phone and a prepaid card so that we could set an appointment. He began to cry. "My family's gone," he said between sobs. "Did they do something to my family?"

I had no idea if el-Masri was for real, but I wanted to meet with him in person. I called my editor in New York, Matthew Purdy. He was skeptical. "These are big accusations," he said.

I agreed, but I convinced him to send me to Ulm, a city of about 120,000 in southern Germany, where el-Masri lived. Perhaps because I was still relatively new and untested at the *Times*, Matt sent another reporter along with me. We met el-Masri at a train station coffee shop. His dark shoulder-length hair was streaked with gray, and his hazel eyes were bloodshot and ringed with dark circles. We sat down and ordered coffee.

He asked if we would mind him smoking. "I'm a little nervous," he said.

He told us that he was forty-one years old and of Lebanese descent. He was married with four young sons, and he had worked as a used car salesman. In late December 2003, after an argument with his wife, he'd boarded a tourist bus to the Macedonian capital, Skopje, where he planned to take a weeklong vacation. When the bus reached the Serbia-Macedonia border, guards confiscated his passport and prevented him from reboarding the bus. He said he was taken to a small, dark room and accused of being a terrorist.

"They asked a lot of questions—if I have relations with Al Qaeda, al-Haramain, the Islamic Brotherhood," el-Masri told us, pausing between sentences. "I kept saying no, but they did not believe me." Al-Haramain was an Islamic charity suspected of funneling money to terrorist causes, and it was said to be affiliated with Al Qaeda, Osama bin Laden, and the Taliban.

After twenty-three days, the Macedonian authorities turned him over to officials he believed were from the United States. His captors hauled him onto a plane bound for Kabul, Afghanistan, he said. Once there, he was chained and subjected to a series of beatings. He was stripped and photographed naked, then plied with drugs as his interrogators repeated a barrage of questions about his alleged ties to Al Qaeda. After a month-long hunger strike, he was blindfolded and flown to northern Albania, where he was allowed to walk across the border into Macedonia, reclaim his passport and possessions, and fly back to Germany. Altogether, he said he had spent five months in captivity. He had not been charged with any crime.

It was a stunning tale, and el-Masri trembled as he told it. I'd seen people in Iraq who were in shock after they'd witnessed bombings or been released from prison. El-Masri's demeanor reminded me of theirs. I wasn't sure if his story was true, but I was convinced that something bad had happened to him. However, my American colleague, another *Times* reporter, didn't buy it.

El-Masri called me later that evening. "I think your colleague didn't believe me," he said.

I told him that we were just doing our jobs. These accusations were very stark, and we would need evidence. I said I needed time to find more leads, and I asked about his plans. He would contact a lawyer, he said. "I want the people who did this to me to be brought to justice. I want them to acknowledge what they have done to me and others."

I still had doubts. What interest would the CIA have in kidnapping el-Masri? He mentioned that he had prayed at the Multikulturhaus, an Islamic center in Neu-Ulm that was frequented by radicals and closely monitored by the German security services. He also was friendly with Reda Seyam, the creator of the video of mujahideen beheading Serbs that I'd watched as a teenager at my cousin's house in Morocco.

El-Masri's connection with the Multikulturhaus and Seyam were my first clues as to why the CIA might have taken him. Seyam, a German of Egyptian descent, had been radicalized while living in Neu-Ulm as a young man. Later, he had spent time in Indonesia, and the U.S. intelligence services believed he was linked to the terrorist bombings in Bali in 2002. He is now believed to have become a high-ranking figure in the Islamic State.

I knew it sounded crazy, but the more I thought about it, the more I felt that el-Masri was telling the truth. There was something about the way he told the story, and how traumatized he seemed, that stuck with me. I called Matt Purdy again and convinced him to let me dig into the story in my spare time. "Okay, keep me posted," he said. "But remember these are very tough accusations. You'll need a lot of proof."

I understood that a story in the *New York Times* would be seen as a direct attack against the CIA and its practices in the so-called War on Terror, but it wasn't the first story we'd heard about the CIA's extraordinary rendition program, which secretly extradited terror suspects from one foreign country to another "outside of the legal process." Since September 11, this clandestine practice had become widespread, with "snatches" of more than one hundred alleged terrorists, who were transported for interrogation to prisons in other countries and to U.S.-run secret facilities in Afghanistan, Poland, Thailand, Guantánamo Bay, Romania, and Lithuania. Among the kidnap victims was Maher Arar, a Canadian born in Syria who was suspected of being an Al Qaeda operative. Arar said that after he was detained in New York in 2002, the United States had sent him to Syria, where he was held for ten months and tortured. Another detainee, an Australian national named Mamdouh Habib, claimed in a federal lawsuit that he was shipped to Guantánamo Bay, Cuba, after enduring six months of torture in an Egyptian prison. Human rights organizations estimated that dozens of "high value" detainees were being held in secret locations, known as black sites, all over the world.

I went over my notes from the interview again. The next day, I began calling sources in the German security services. Officially, people said they had never heard anything like el-Masri's story. "Have you started believing in fairy tales?" one official asked me. I wondered how many days I should give myself to find out whether el-Masri was telling the truth.

My next best hope were the sources I called the "pay-phone" people, because I called them only from old-fashioned phone booths to make sure no one was listening. Later, I would use old Nokia phones I bought in a shop near a German train station for the same purpose. The shopkeeper there knew how to get unregistered SIM cards, which I used to call sources who I suspected were being monitored. Most of these sources were officials I'd gotten to know during and after my time in Iraq, from Germany, the United States, and various countries in the Middle East and North Africa, people who had access to sensitive information.

I went to a pay phone in my neighborhood and reached out to a senior German security official. He had given me an "emergency number" that wasn't his regular cell.

"Is this a good time?" I asked.

"I can't talk very long, but I was expecting your call."

I told him that I needed his guidance and described el-Masri's case, without giving his name or many details. "I need to know, could this story be true, or am I wasting my time? I appreciate any help you can give me. Also, why did you say you had been expecting my call?"

"No, I don't think you are wasting your time," he answered calmly. "You are on the right track. This is a big thing."

I pushed the receiver closer to my ear, so as not to miss a word.

"The answer to your second question: the German authorities were officially informed around the same day this man made his call to you."

"What authorities? And how did they know he called me?"

"It means either one or both of you were watched. You might want to check with the minister of the interior, but there were others informed as well. I have to go."

I hung up. My head was spinning. I was still looking for a motive, but now at least I knew I was on to something. My next call was to the spokesperson at the Ministry of the Interior. "No comment" was all he would tell me.

I called Matt Purdy at the *Times* from a pay phone, as I wasn't sure if my mobile and home phones were being monitored. I told him what my source had said.

This changed things. My editors said that from now on I would be working on the story with a London-based colleague, Don Van Natta. I called el-Masri and asked for the phone number of his lawyer, Manfred Gnjidic. Gnjidic was a German of Croatian descent who had practiced immigration law and represented people accused of belonging to terrorist groups; he had been involved in other cases linked to the mosque in Neu-Ulm. He told me he'd sent letters to the Ministries of Interior and Justice, to the chief of staff of the chancellery, and to Chancellor Gerhard Schröder and that he had filed a case against unknown individuals on el-Masri's behalf. I filled Don in on everything I learned.

Don was very different from the reporter who had accompanied me to the first el-Masri interview. Big and bearish, he was a veteran investigative journalist, and he quickly understood the significance of what el-Masri had told me and analyzed it in light of other things he knew about U.S. antiterror tactics. Don was bighearted and good-natured, and he cared deeply about getting the story right. I learned a lot from working with him.

"Let's meet him together and also let's meet the authorities who are investigating the case," Don said. "This is a big case, if true. And Souad, if you feel that something weird is going on with your phone or you feel people are watching you, let me know. You work for the *New York Times*. They can't mess with us."

I began to pay closer attention to my surroundings. I would scan the cars parked in front of our house and try to see who was in them. And when I left home each day, I glanced over my shoulder to see if anybody was following me. After the September 11 attacks, German authorities had become more vigilant about political and extremist activities on college campuses, and I knew they had informants at my university. I kept going to classes, but I didn't share anything that was happening with my friends and professors. Don told me to make sure I didn't leave my notes exposed in obvious places, so I started hiding my notebooks outside the apartment.

Some days later, Don flew in from London, and we took the train to

Ulm to meet with el-Masri and his lawyer. El-Masri repeated the whole story. Don asked for more details about how he'd been kidnapped and tortured.

"I do believe him," Don said when we got to our hotel that night. "The details he described about the torture and how the whole situation was handled are similar to other cases."

At a hotel in Munich, we met with the prosecutor and police officials investigating the case. They said that based on the evidence they'd collected, they too believed el-Masri's story.

"We've done some tests based on a sample of Mr. el-Masri's hair," a senior police official in Ulm told us. "The result shows that he must have been in a very stressful situation." They were able to determine that el-Masri had undergone a rapid change in his diet consistent with a hunger strike and that he had been in a climate similar to Afghanistan's.

The next day, I visited el-Masri at home. His wife, Aischa, and their children had returned to Germany to live with him, and I wanted to meet them. Aischa was twenty-nine and soft-spoken. She wore a black dress and a pale blue head scarf; their sons were dressed in matching outfits with elephants on them. When el-Masri left and didn't return, she was deeply worried. Weeks passed with no word, so she went back to Lebanon to stay with relatives, thinking that he might have left her for another woman. Her children often asked, "Why are we here, Mom, and where is Daddy?" she told me, starting to cry. "From time to time, I called his friends in Germany and asked them if they heard anything from him or about him. But no one knew anything."

Her husband had changed since his return, she said. "He is very nervous. Sometimes he wakes up in the middle of the night and screams."

My intelligence sources had confirmed that el-Masri had been in touch with people like Reda Seyam, who were being watched. But el-Masri himself had not been involved in spreading jihadist propaganda, nor was he known to be a member of jihadist movements.

When I got home, I grabbed my copy of the 9/11 Commission report and started paging through it. After some searching, I found a paragraph that said that Ramzi bin al-Shibh and a future September 11 hijacker, Marwan al-Shehhi, had met a man named Khalid al-Masri on a train in

Germany and that this al-Masri had talked to them about joining the jihad in Chechnya. Al-Masri later put them in touch with an Al Qaeda member in Germany, who told them to go to Afghanistan, where al-Shehhi and Ziad Jarrah, another core member of the Hamburg cell and a future hijacker, met Osama bin Laden and were recruited to commit the September 11 attacks.

El-Masri had told us that one of his interrogators in Afghanistan had accused him of being a senior Al Qaeda operative who was trained in Jalalabad, Afghanistan, and an associate of Atta and bin al-Shibh. "I denied everything," el-Masri told us. "I kept saying, 'No, no, no.'"

The names were spelled differently, but were Khalid al-Masri and Khaled el-Masri the same man, or were the Americans confusing the two? Gnjidic, el-Masri's lawyer, believed the latter, and so, increasingly, did we. The similar names, combined with the mosque el-Masri had attended and some of the characters he had known, could have been enough to incriminate him. If so, it was a case of mistaken identity with terrifying consequences.

Our editors made it clear that a lot was at stake. "If anything in this article is wrong, you might not only lose your job, you might be burned forever," a colleague told me. Don and I double- and triple-checked all our facts, a process that took weeks.

The day before the story was supposed to run, I spent hours in my room, going through all my notes, every single piece of paper. *Is there a mistake anywhere?* I asked myself. *Is anything missing?* For days, I'd been unable to eat; I was surviving on coffee.

Don sensed my nervousness. "It is what it is now, Souad. We worked for months on this. Have you told el-Masri that the story is running tomorrow?"

I hadn't. I decided to go for a walk and call him from a pay phone. I walked fast, listening to my favorite '80s pop songs on my iPod as I ran through the story in my head. "I just wanted to let you know that the story will run tomorrow," I said when I reached him. "There might be some reactions. That's why I'm calling."

"Tomorrow?"

"Yes, tomorrow." Silence. "Khaled?"

"Yes, I am here," he said, and his voice sounded deeper. He was crying.

I stayed silent, too.

"Thank you, Souad, and thank your colleague Don. Thank you for believing me."

"We just did our job." I felt a wave of exhaustion wash over me.

On my way home, I thought about how el-Masri, after all that had happened to him, was able to distinguish between Americans. He had thanked Don. He had never shown any hatred against Americans in all the times I'd talked to him.

When I saw the story online, I read every word. We wrote several follow-up stories, one of which focused on what German authorities knew about the case and when. One of our *Times* colleagues had sources in Macedonia who told him that at least one member of Germany's external intelligence service, the BND, knew about el-Masri's arrest immediately after it happened. This midlevel intelligence officer said that a stranger approached him in a government cafeteria in Macedonia in January 2004 and told him that a German citizen had been arrested in Skopje and handed over to the Americans. This was nearly a year before our story ran.

When Don and I confronted German authorities with our findings, a spokesperson for Foreign Minister Joschka Fischer warned us that if we printed this information, there would be consequences. We printed it anyway. It was not until June 2006 that the Germans publicly admitted that they had mishandled el-Masri's case.

A year and a half after Don and I broke the el-Masri story, el-Masri and Gnjidic called and asked for a meeting. I took a train to Ulm and met them at a restaurant not far from the lawyer's office. El-Masri was surprisingly upbeat. "I would never have thought that the world would listen to me and that people even in the United States would be interested in my case," he said with a smile. He added that he had received many messages of sympathy from people in the United States who had been touched by his story, but so far he had received neither an apology nor any real explanation from the U.S. and German governments. He seemed very bitter about it. "I don't understand. How can they call themselves countries with rule of law and human rights when they kidnap and torture people like this?"

I told him that many journalists had written about his case, including a team of *New York Times* reporters who uncovered flight data indicating that a jet operated by a CIA-linked shell company had flown from Skopje to Baghdad to Kabul on January 24, 2004, the day after el-Masri's passport was stamped showing his departure from Macedonia. Coverage like that might eventually help get him the answers he craved, I told him.

"There is something we wanted to discuss with you," Gnjidic said. "There is another prisoner who had been in jail with Khaled, and who got out. He was in touch with him just recently." The man, Laid Saidi, was back in his native country, Algeria.

"How did he get your phone number?" I asked el-Masri.

"We communicated with each other through the cell walls," he replied. "We memorized each other's names and phone numbers, so in case one got out, he would call the other's family."

Speaking to a man who had been in the same prison as el-Masri could shed more light on the whole renditions practice, I thought. I didn't know if Saidi had been involved in terrorism, but he might be able to tell me more about the prisons used for such renditions. I also thought that if there were ever a trial in the el-Masri case, Saidi might be called as a witness.

I excused myself and called my editors, who said that if Saidi would speak to us, I should travel to Algeria and meet with him. I went back into the restaurant. "Would he be willing to speak to me?" I asked the lawyer and el-Masri.

"Yes, that's why we called you. He actually asked if he could speak to you," Gnjidic answered.

I handed my phone across the table to el-Masri. "Please call him now and let him know I will come, I hope by mid–next week at the latest if the visas come through fast."

El-Masri took out his wallet, which was filled with ID cards and scraps of paper. He unfolded a piece of blue paper, laid it on the table, and dialed the number with one hand. "*Salam*, it's me, Khaled," he said. He asked if he could put me on the line, then handed over the phone.

Saidi said he would meet with me, but his voice sounded a bit tentative. "My lawyer has to be there as well, please," he said.

I told him that I would get in touch with him once I got a visa.

"Please don't come without the permission of the Algerian authorities," he said, with a note of fear in his voice. "I don't want to get in trouble. My family and I have been through a lot. Please."

I reassured him that I would come only with a valid journalist's visa and that I would contact his lawyer and make every effort to see that no harm would come to him.

"Please forgive me," he said, "but I have been in hell in the last few years, and I can't go through it again."

After we said good-bye, I asked el-Masri how he knew this was the same man with whom he'd been in prison.

"I know him from his voice," he said. "I recognized his voice from the first time we spoke on the phone after his release."

A short time later, I flew to Algiers and met Saidi's lawyer, Mostefa Bouchachi, for coffee. He told me that his client was nervous and traumatized. "He has endured torture, and whenever he speaks about it, it's as if he's reliving it."

A *Times* colleague from the Paris bureau, Craig Smith, met me in Algiers, and together we went to speak to Saidi at Bouchachi's law office. When I got there, the former prisoner was seated in a corner and wearing a long white tunic and a white skullcap. His right hand covered his left, and he looked shyly at us. As I explained our interest in his case and that we'd found him through el-Masri, he glanced often at his lawyer. When I was finished, he asked Bouchachi how he should proceed.

"You must be honest in what you tell them," Bouchachi said. "Nothing will help you more now than telling the truth."

Saidi took a deep breath. He told us he'd left Algeria in the early 1990s, when the country was in the midst of a civil war. He went to Yemen to study, moved to Kenya, and in early 1997 to Tanzania, where he began working for the al-Haramain Foundation, the charity suspected of funneling money to Al Qaeda. Saidi eventually became the head of the foundation's branch in the city of Tanga.

I knew from the research I'd done that U.S. and European security services had long been interested in the financial activities of members of the foundation and their connections to terrorist plots. Some suspected that the foundation had financed the bombings of the U.S. embassies in Tanzania and Kenya in 1998. The September 11 attacks raised further suspicions among U.S. and Saudi security authorities that the foundation had been infiltrated by people with links to terrorist groups and that some money had been diverted to them.

"Have you ever been involved with any members of terrorist organizations?" I asked Saidi. "I'm speaking about Al Qaeda, the Taliban, or others." I mentioned these groups by name because I knew that people with backgrounds like Saidi's sometimes didn't see Al Qaeda or the Taliban as terrorist organizations but as "freedom fighters."

"No. I never had anything to do with such groups."

"Was there anything you did that was against the law when you lived in Tanzania?"

Saidi looked at me and then at his lawyer.

"Go on, tell them," Bouchachi said.

Saidi said that at some point he'd lost his Algerian passport and began using fake Tunisian identity documents. He showed us a document bearing the name Ramzi ben Mizauni ben Fraj.

"Why did you use a fake passport?" Craig asked him.

Saidi said he had been afraid of going to the Algerian embassy while the country was at war with Islamists. He denied that he had been active in any of the groups declared terrorist organizations by the Algerian government, but he explained that his religiosity would have been enough to make people at the embassy suspicious. That, he said, was the sole reason he'd adopted a false identity.

On May 10, 2003, shortly after he left his home in Tanga, Tanzanian police surrounded his car and brought him to a jail in Dar es Salaam. At first he thought they were arresting him for using a false passport, but three days later, he was taken to the border with Malawi and handed over to a group of Malawians in plainclothes and two middle-aged "white men, like your colleague," he told me in Arabic. "They were also wearing jeans like him and T-shirts."

I could hear the anxiety in his voice. "Please don't worry," I told him. "You can trust us, as Khaled el-Masri already has done."

"The white men, they spoke English to the Malawians," he said. "I was handed over, and I understood that something very bad was going to happen."

Saidi told us how the Malawians held him for a week before handing him over to five men and a woman. What happened then was similar to what el-Masri had described: His eyes were covered with cotton and tape, his feet and hands shackled. His clothes were cut off, and he heard the clicks of what he believes were cameras. They drove him to an airport and loaded him onto a plane.

After a long flight, they took him to a dark prison. "The lights were almost never turned on, and there was awfully loud and deafening Western music," he said. One of his masked interrogators told him through a translator, "You are in a place that is out of the world. No one knows where you are. No one is going to defend you." He described being chained by one hand to the wall in his cell.

After a week, he was taken to another prison. "There, they put me in a room, suspended me by my arms, and attached my feet to the floor," he told us in a low voice. "They cut off my clothes very fast and took off my blindfold." A young woman with shoulder-length blond hair and an older man entered the room and interrogated him for two hours, using a Moroccan translator. It was then that Saidi learned why he was there.

The interrogators asked him about a phone conversation he'd had with his wife's family in Kenya. "They said, you were talking about airplanes, and I said I never talked about airplanes." He was left chained up, without clothes or food, for five days, he said. "They beat me and threw cold water on me, spat at me, and sometimes gave me dirty water to drink. The American man told me I would die there."

He described how extended, forced standing, with his wrists bound to the ceiling, had caused his legs and feet to swell. After his return to the "dark" prison, a doctor used a syringe to pump a liquid into his legs. He spent a night there before being moved to another holding area, where the Afghan guards told him he was outside Kabul. The basement area consisted of two rows of six cells, each of which had a small opening in the door through which prisoners could glimpse one another as they were taken into and out of their cells.

They could also talk sometimes, mainly at night. It was there that he'd met el-Masri. He was later handed over to the Algerian government, which released him without charges. He later learned that the phone conversation for which he'd been jailed was in fact about car tires. He had used the English word "tire," which sounds like the North African Arabic slang word for "planes," and whoever had listened to his conversation had thought he was talking about airliners.

Like el-Masri, Saidi wanted to bring to justice those responsible for what happened to him. "I know I didn't do anything wrong," he told me. "What right did those people have to take me or Khaled el-Masri? What they did to us will haunt us for the rest of our lives."

We asked the U.S. intelligence services about Saidi, but they refused to comment.

I thought that now there was a witness who could play an important role in el-Masri's case against his tormentors, someone who had actually seen him in a prison in Afghanistan. After our stories and all the other media attention el-Masri had received, I was certain that the courts would listen to him, and now to Saidi, and investigate the miscarriage of justice that had indelibly marked their lives.

But I was mistaken. As we learned from documents declassified much later, the CIA informed the Senate Intelligence Committee in 2007 that it "lacked sufficient basis to render and detain al-Masri," still misspelling el-Masri's name in the way that had led to his detention. According to the executive summary of the committee's declassified report, the CIA director decided that no further action was warranted against the officer who advocated for el-Masri's rendition: "The Director strongly believes that mistakes should be expected in a business filled with uncertainty and that, when they result from performance that meets reasonable standard, CIA leadership must stand behind the officers who make them."

However, a 2007 CIA inspector general's report on el-Masri paints a darker picture. "This Report concludes that there was an insufficient

basis to render and detain al-Masri and the Agency's prolonged detention of al-Masri was unjustified," it notes. "His rendition and detention
resulted from a series of breakdowns in tradecraft, process, management,
and oversight."

The CIA's inspector general referred el-Masri's case to the Department
of Justice for prosecution, but in May 2007 the Office of the U.S. Attor-
ney for the Eastern District of Virginia declined to pursue the case.
Apart from an "oral admonition" given to three CIA attorneys, the ACLU
would later note, no one has been held accountable for el-Masri's ordeal.

I wondered what cases like Saidi's or el-Masri's said about Western
society and its commitment to human rights and the rule of law. How
could we, and especially our political leaders, still point fingers at other
countries, when U.S. government agencies behaved like this? Was there
a rule of law for some and the rule of the jungle for others?

The unanswered questions were frustrating for us, but they were
devastating for el-Masri and Saidi, both of whom told me they needed
answers and an apology so they could move forward with their lives.
They are still waiting.

In the years that followed his ordeal, el-Masri would be arrested and
jailed for arson and assault. "I have asked several times from the beginning
for psychological help, but without any luck," his lawyer, Gnjidic, told
me after el-Masri set fire to a department store in his hometown. "The
very ironic thing is that he will get psychological help now, after he committed a crime, and as a torture victim didn't get it before, when he
asked for it."

El-Masri tried to find work but couldn't. His wife and children moved
back to Lebanon. In 2012, the European Court of Human Rights ruled
that he had been a victim of rendition and torture because security officials mistook him for someone else. He was awarded €60,000 in compen-
sation, but the money didn't reach him until several years later. By that
time, he had moved to Vienna. Still unable to find work, he lived in a
homeless shelter for a time and sometimes stayed with friends and
acquaintances.

In September 2015, I met him at a hotel in Vienna. His hair was
shorter and whiter, and he had bags under his eyes. I asked if he had

considered joining the Islamic State, as some German papers had recently reported. He smiled sarcastically.

"That's something I will keep to myself," he told me. "I don't want to talk about this now. I will talk about it when the time is right. I don't allow anyone to tell me what I can or can't do or where to go or not. Not after what they have done to me."

He said something else that stuck with me: "People in the West are the last ones in the world that should talk about human rights," he told me. "Look what they have done to me and others. There have been no consequences for those responsible. On one hand, they are great at pointing at others and criticizing them, but then they don't want to look inside and have accountability for violations of human rights."

El-Masri's case was a landmark in our understanding of U.S. rendition policy and the War on Terror; it was the first time we could prove that an innocent man had been kidnapped and tortured by a Western government in the name of fighting terrorism. It was also one of those cases that put the values we say we all stand for on trial. If we are to be true to those values, our political leaders must be willing to acknowledge mistakes, and there must be consequences. Otherwise our systems lose their legitimacy.

In the years since I first spoke to him, I've often wondered how the West might win back the trust of a man like el-Masri. What will his children think of the United States and Germany when they're old enough to understand what happened to him? These questions haunt me. I fear we haven't heard the end of his story or those of many others like him.

5

Even If I Die Today or Tomorrow

Lebanon, 2007

I did not return to Iraq, but the war was never far away. Like the searing memories and feeling of dread I brought home from Baghdad, the war's characters and wicked problems stayed with me. I seemed unable to escape them.

The invasion of Iraq and the abuses committed at Abu Ghraib and elsewhere, as well as the jihadists' growing facility with the Internet as a means of spreading their message, had given Al Qaeda a foothold in places where it had previously lacked a presence. In March 2004, a group of North African Islamists and criminals orchestrated the bombings in Madrid that killed nearly two hundred people and wounded more than eighteen hundred. In July 2005, bombs exploded on three underground trains and a bus in London. The perpetrators lived in and around the gritty English mill town of Leeds and were all Britons, though one had been born in Jamaica.

We saw an increase of potentially moderate Sunnis, who were beginning to embrace Al Qaeda or at least to quietly support its goals. They were outraged by the bogus justification that George W. Bush and Tony Blair had used for the war—the need to destroy Saddam's weapons of mass destruction, which turned out not to exist—along with the lack of accountability for the invasion and the torture and other abuses that occurred. The rise of Shia militias in Iraq and the growing regional influence of Iran also played key roles. Many Muslims I spoke to, whether in Europe, the Middle East, or North Africa, told me they believed the West was at war with Islam.

After the el-Masri story, I visited the *New York Times* headquarters and met my editors and many U.S.-based colleagues in person for the first time. One of the reporters I got to know was Michael Moss, a friendly silver-haired Californian now living in Brooklyn. Michael was in his early fifties, more than twenty years my senior. During the years we worked together, he would become a sort of older brother figure to me and a close friend. He taught me a lot about building stories from different angles and where to dig for information; I appreciated his deep sense of humor and ability to laugh at himself. He was very down to earth—a result of his West Coast upbringing, he claimed.

Michael worked for the investigative unit, to which I was also attached. He was reporting two stories about Sunnis who had been detained and tortured by Shia militias in Iraq—militias that sometimes collaborated with the U.S. military. Michael and I worked on the stories together, traveling to Syria to talk to former detainees who had fled there.

The men we met in Syria had been brutalized. We felt sure that the treatment they had endured would only encourage more hatred against the West and create a larger rift between Sunnis and Shia, not just in Iraq but also throughout the region. And indeed the violence of the Shia militias and the abuse that many Iraqi Sunnis suffered in Iraqi and U.S. military prisons galvanized a new generation of jihadists. Another inspiration for the Sunnis was the Palestinian struggle. Among the new jihadi groups were some that used Al Qaeda's methods and resources to fight for the Palestinian cause.

It was in Syria that we learned about one such militant leader: Shaker al-Abssi. A Palestinian born in the West Bank town of Jericho in 1955, he'd given up his medical studies to become a fighter pilot for Yasser Arafat's Fatah organization. He later staged attacks on Israel from a base he established in a Palestinian camp in Syria. From 2002 to 2005, the Syrians imprisoned him on terrorism charges. When he was released, he crossed over to Lebanon, where he began plotting against Americans in Jordan. Abssi wasn't deeply religious, but he understood that Islamist militancy was the order of the day. His primary area of interest was Palestine, but he used the anger that built in the region after the invasion of Iraq to recruit fighters to his cause.

Abssi also drew our interest because he was a longtime associate of Abu Musab al-Zarqawi, the leader of Al Qaeda in Iraq and a gigantic presence in the jihadi world. Born Ahmad Fadhil Nazzal al-Khalayleh in 1966 in Zarqa, Jordan, Zarqawi was a high school dropout, delinquent, and street thug whose radicalization began when he traveled to Afghanistan to fight the Soviets, returning to Jordan in 1993. With his religious mentor, Sheikh Abu Muhammad al-Maqdisi, who was inspired by the 1979 siege of Mecca, he founded a Salafist group called Bayat al-Imam (Loyalty to the Imam). "Salafism" derives from the Arabic expression *as-salaf as-salih*, generally translated as "the righteous ancestors," which refers to the first three generations of Muslims, who are believed to have practiced a "pure" Islam. In the traditional sense, Salafists are people who recognize only the Koran, the *Sunnah*, and the practices of these ancestors as the correct way to practice Islam. Zarqawi and others in the group were imprisoned for plotting attacks in Jordan in 1994 and gained a following through writings that were smuggled out of prison and published in Salafist media.

Zarqawi was freed in a 1999 general amnesty. After his release, he helped plan the so-called Millennium Plots, a set of Al Qaeda–engineered attacks timed to occur on about January 1, 2000. But the intended attacks in Jordan never got off the ground, and Zarqawi fled to Afghanistan, where he met with Osama bin Laden. The Al Qaeda leader gave Zarqawi support for establishing a training camp for foreign fighters, where he would focus his attention on the "near enemies": Jordan and Israel. Zarqawi also hated the Shia and saw them as rivals.

After the U.S. invasion of Afghanistan in the fall of 2001, Zarqawi was injured in a U.S. bombing in Kandahar and moved his headquarters to northern Iraq. He gained fame in the West when Secretary of State Colin Powell named him in the speech to the United Nations that laid out what was later found to be the flawed American case for war against Saddam

Hussein, claiming that Zarqawi was working in close collaboration with the Iraqi dictator. In fact, he was not. After the United States invaded Iraq, Zarqawi's group, initially called Jama'at al-Tawhid wa'al-Jihad, whose name means Unity and Jihad, emerged in the vanguard of the insurgency, carrying out suicide bombings and assassinations, killing civilians, and inciting sectarian conflict. He was linked to the August 2003 bombs at the Jordanian embassy and the UN office in Baghdad, as well as to an attack on a Shia mosque in Najaf.

In January 2004, Zarqawi wrote to bin Laden proposing a formal alliance. Their negotiations culminated in an October announcement that Zarqawi's faction had sworn allegiance to Al Qaeda, and it came to be known as Al Qaeda in Iraq.

Zarqawi described his espousal of extreme cruelty in a book, *The Management of Savagery*, which was distributed online. His starring role in a horrific video of the beheading of the American businessman Nick Berg established his fame as the "sheikh of the slaughterers."

Zarqawi's assaults escalated in Iraq, and his group continued to operate in Jordan as well. In November 2005, suicide attackers from Al Qaeda in Iraq set off bombs in three Amman hotels, killing more than fifty people, including a wedding party. Although Zarqawi claimed that the intended victims were American intelligence officers, the deaths of so many civilians, including Sunni women and children, angered King Abdullah and sparked protests in Zarqawi's hometown. His own family denounced him, and bin Laden's operational leader, Atiyah Abd al-Rahman, wrote that Zarqawi was required to seek approval for any new major operation.

But just three months later, on February 22, 2006, gunmen loyal to Zarqawi blew up the Askari mosque in Samarra, one of the most important shrines in Shia Islam. Although there were no casualties, the attack set off fighting between Sunnis and Shia that resulted in more than thirteen hundred deaths. Zarqawi celebrated by starring in a video, appearing for the first time in public without a mask.

U.S. and Jordanian intelligence wanted Zarqawi dead. Human sources and drone reconnaissance traced him to a location near Baqubah, Iraq, and on June 7, 2006, a U.S. Delta Force team and F-16 fighter jets were sent in to kill or capture him. The commandos arrived at the site of a building destroyed by two American bombs just in time to watch Zarqawi die. Some politicians and analysts thought that with the ringleader's death his network would disappear. They were wrong.

Shaker al-Abssi was one of the militants who had taken up Zarqawi's mantle. Both men had been sentenced to death in absentia for the 2002 assassination of the American diplomat Laurence Foley, a senior administrator in Jordan for the U.S. Agency for International Development. Foley had been leaving his home in Amman when he was shot at close range by a man who had hidden in his garage. The Jordanian government alleged that Abssi had helped the gunman with money, logistics, and weapons and explosives training, while Zarqawi had contributed ten thousand dollars to fund the assassination, as well as thirty-two thousand dollars for additional attacks.

During the winter of 2006–7, we heard that Abssi was living in Nahr al-Bared, a Palestinian refugee camp in Lebanon, where he ran a new group, called Fatah al-Islam. Declaring himself the restorer of religion to the Palestinian cause, he had taken control of three compounds belonging to a secular Palestinian militant organization and raised Fatah al-Islam's black flag over them. Michael and I wanted to investigate the connection between Fatah al-Islam and the Al Qaeda mother ship.

In February we called Leena Saidi, a stringer in Beirut for the *Times* and other news organizations. Leena was a Lebanese-British mother of two who spoke English with a crisp British accent. We told her that we were looking for somebody who could help us get into the Palestinian camps.

"Yes, there is someone who might be able to help," Leena said. "Let me see if he can meet with you the day you arrive."

A week later, Michael and I boarded a flight to Beirut. The city had always had a nostalgic attraction for me. As a child, my parents listened to famous Lebanese singers like Fairuz, and Beirut played a key role in the classic Arab movies my siblings and I grew up watching on VHS. In these films, Beirut was a beautiful, sunny place filled with unbelievably good-looking people. Lebanese women were chic and powerful; Lebanese men were famous for wooing them with poetry.

The movies were as formulaic as they were romantic: a man falls in love with a gorgeous, alluring woman in a short skirt, black eyeliner, and blue eye shadow, but some obstacle—usually a family conflict—keeps her from marrying him. For people of Arab descent, the movies were culturally familiar, yet they also celebrated Western freedoms. No one wore a head scarf, and the eccentric, demanding Lebanese women always got what they wanted. I wasn't into miniskirts, but I loved the long Marlene Dietrich–style trousers the women wore. When I was eight, I sneaked into my parents' bedroom, climbed onto a chair in front of the mirror, and experimented with my mother's lipsticks and eye shadows. When my mother found me using her makeup, I told her I wanted to be like the Lebanese women in the movies.

But what the movies didn't show were the rifts among the different religious and political factions in Lebanon. Each religious group—Sunnis, Shia, Christians, Druze—essentially had its own political wing, and some areas of Lebanon had been carved up along religious lines. This was the legacy of the country's fifteen-year civil war, which began in 1975 and killed as many as 150,000 people. Groups such as Hezbollah and the PLO had for years operated freely in Lebanon, and the country had increasingly become a haven for international terror suspects. One of the September 11 hijackers came from Lebanon, as did six men accused of planting bombs on German trains in the summer of 2006. Another Lebanese man was among those accused in 2006 of plotting to blow up the train tunnels connecting New York City and New Jersey.

When Michael and I got to Beirut, Leena was waiting for us in the hotel lobby, where she introduced us to a slim, pale, lightly bearded man named Fakhr al-Ayoubi. Fakhr was a local journalist who came from a region outside Tripoli in northern Lebanon, not far from the Nahr al-Bared camp that had become Abssi's base. Fakhr was friendly but quite traditional. Like many conservative Muslim men, he believed that touching a woman who was not his relative was sinful. He declined to shake my hand.

"He knows the group you are interested in," Leena said.

We told Fakhr we wanted to meet Abssi, talk to him and his people, and see how Fatah al-Islam operated and what was happening in the camp. Fakhr listened patiently. When we finished, he sipped his tea and glanced at Leena before looking directly at us. "You really want to go into the camp? You want to meet him in person? No way! Impossible!"

"Why?" I asked.

"Because he won't agree. But even if he did agree, it would be very dangerous. These people are jihadists. They don't trust Westerners, and they don't trust Western newspapers."

I'd heard this before, but in recent years I'd covered terrorist attacks in Casablanca and Spain, and I had developed a network of sources among the militants in North Africa and Europe, including Moroccans and others who had fought in Afghanistan and had links to Al Qaeda. I told him I'd dealt with jihadists who had never wanted to talk to journalists but who for some reason agreed to speak with me.

"I saw your work," Fakhr answered. "That's the only reason I'd even consider working with you. But going in there is very dangerous. These camps are extraterritorial ground. If they kidnap you there or decide to kill you, no one can help you."

"Still, let's try it," I said brightly. "We should try to get his side of the story."

The next day, Fakhr came back to the hotel. "The good news is, Abssi knows your work and didn't say no on principle," Fakhr told us. "The bad news is, Abssi thinks it's not the right time for an interview, and his deputy and other advisers said it's better not to talk to you now."

Anticipating this response, Michael and I had already decided that I should still try to meet Abssi in person to explain our plans. Then at least I would get a sense of the situation inside the camp.

"I would like to speak to Abssi," I told Fakhr. "Tell them I insisted."

Fakhr laughed. "So you don't accept no for an answer?" he asked. "Have you turned into a Lebanese woman?" I smiled at the memory of all those old Lebanese films.

He dialed a number, and I could hear him talking to the group's media man. "I'm here with the sister I spoke to you about from Morocco," he said. "She wants to talk to the sheikh in person." He was told that somebody would call him back in a few minutes.

While we waited, I tried to figure out what I should say to Abssi. How could I convince this man, who knew that various security and intelligence services were hunting him, to meet me?

After a couple of minutes, Fakhr's mobile rang. Abssi was on the line. Fakhr handed me the phone.

"*As'salam alaikum,* Sheikh!"

"*Wa'alaikum as'salam,*" he answered.

I told Abssi that I'd heard he didn't want to grant an interview. "But how about I come for tea?" I said. "It won't be an interview, I give you my word, but I came all this way to get your side of the story, so let's at least meet. I know the custom among us Arabs—you can't let a visitor go home without a cup of tea." I'm not sure where I came up with this idea, except that I was thinking of my grandmother and how she would never let anyone leave her house without a cup of tea.

I heard him laughing on the other end of the line. Fakhr was smiling and shaking his head.

"You want to come for tea?" Abssi finally asked.

"Yes, only for a cup of tea. No interview."

"God willing, you can come tomorrow with Fakhr for tea, but no interview!"

"You have my word, Sheikh. It won't be an interview."

I handed the phone back to Fakhr to arrange the time. "He has refused to see any journalist, and especially from the Western media," Fakhr said when he hung up. "You're lucky. Your family must have prayed a lot for you as a child!"

"You're going to have tea with the devil?" Michael responded when I told him. "Excellent!"

The next day, I put on a head scarf and a long black *abaya* that Leena had loaned me. Before I left, I had handed Michael a piece of paper with phone numbers for the Fatah al-Islam spokesman, who would be at the meeting, and for various Al Qaeda members and their associates from the Middle East, North Africa, and Europe who could put in a good word for me in case anything went wrong. I knew that the Lebanese authorities had limited access to this camp and that Abssi and his people wouldn't listen to them anyway. I needed people with strong reputations in the jihadist world to vouch for me.

Fakhr came to pick me up from the hotel. The camp was about a ninety-minute drive from Beirut. We agreed that I would call Michael before we arrived there and that he would call me back two hours later. If he didn't reach me, he would call again an hour after that. "If you don't hear from me by four hours after our first conversation, call Fakhr," I said. "If he doesn't pick up, call the Fatah spokesperson."

Michael nodded. "Souad, if you feel uncomfortable about this, please don't go," he said. "Because now I'm beginning to feel bad about it."

"No, no, don't worry. I'm just having tea with him. It will be okay."

I was nervous, but also excited. Fakhr and I drove up past Tripoli, a coastal city that is generally more conservative than other parts of Lebanon and is known for its sweets, which are soaked in sugar syrup and stuffed with nuts or cream. After you eat one, you have to fast for two weeks. On this day, we didn't stop. The camp lay a bit farther north. "There's a Lebanese army checkpoint by the entrance," Fakhr said. "But most likely they will check my papers, not yours, since you look like one of the women in the camp."

Fakhr was right. The Lebanese soldiers glanced into the car and seemed to think I was his wife. Once inside, there was another checkpoint, manned by Palestinian guards. They checked Fakhr's papers, but no one checked me.

The Nahr al-Bared camp had the feel of a small city. We passed grocery stores, schools, and car repair shops. Some of the houses were stable and well built, while other areas resembled a slum, the streets lined with open drains. Young men hawked sweets, vegetables, and fruit from carts or stands. We passed a shop that sold pirated DVDs and CDs. The shop displayed religious titles in the window, but Fakhr told me that if you knew the guy in charge, you could get the newest mainstream movies from all over the world. This Lebanon was totally different from some of the glossy neighborhoods in Beirut. Women wore long *abayas* and head scarves, and some even wore the *niqab*, a veil that covers the face, leaving a narrow slit for the eyes.

As we drove deeper into the camp, I lost my sense of direction. "Nearly every man here has a gun," Fakhr told me. We were nearing Abssi's compound. If I wanted to make a phone call, I had to do it now. I dialed Michael.

"Are you okay?" he asked.

"Yes, I'm okay. We're inside the camp and we're about to get to the meeting place."

Even though Abssi was wanted on terrorism charges in Lebanon, Jordan, and Syria, he seemed to have built his current operation with little interference. The camps were like semiautonomous ministates within Lebanon, and as such, they had long been fertile ground for militancy, particularly against Israel, and more recently against U.S. forces in Iraq.

Lebanese intelligence officials feared that, by amassing a growing number of recruits from across the Arab world with experience fighting in Iraq, Abssi was trying to establish himself as a radical leader akin to Zarqawi. Abssi had already tapped into a pool of frustrated young Palestinians and was cultivating their anger against Israel and directing it far more broadly in the service of Islamist goals.

Fakhr stopped the car in front of high walls with a metal gate. A couple of men with automatic rifles stood out front. They asked us to leave our mobile phones and other electronics in the car. Then they led us to what looked like a waiting area. There were a couple of empty chairs at a table, but something about the room was odd. A Kalashnikov leaned against the wall in one corner. On one wall hung a black flag with the shahada, the Muslim declaration of faith, written in white Arabic script: "There is no God but God, and Muhammad is his prophet."

These were the words my parents had whispered in my ears when I was handed over to them in the hospital as a baby: the shahada is one of the five pillars of Islam, along with prayer, fasting, charity, and the pilgrimage to Mecca known as the hajj.

The armed men asked me to sit in a chair facing the wall with the flag. Fakhr and a younger man, who introduced himself as Abu al-Hassan, Abssi's spokesman and communications adviser, sat in two chairs against the wall on my right. Another man sat opposite me a couple of yards away, fiddling with a handgun pointed in my direction. I looked at Fakhr, who had turned pale. I could see that this was not the kind of meeting he'd expected.

I wondered what would come next. Two more men entered the room.

One sat on a chair to my left and took out a notebook and pen. The other, who was carrying an AK-47 and a knife, stood in a corner.

Then I heard a door open behind me. "'*Salam alaikum*," a soft voice said. All the men stood up, so Fakhr and I did, too. A man of medium height with dark skin, graying hair, and moles on either side of his nose entered the room. This was Abssi, who later told me he was fifty-one years old. I hadn't known what he would look like because he didn't allow himself to be photographed. He wore a short-sleeved shirt and dark green trousers, and he sat in a chair near mine, facing me. "You insisted on meeting with me, so welcome," Abssi said.

"Thank you very much, Sheikh," I replied. My eyes wandered from him to the man some yards behind him, who was still pointing his handgun at me. "Actually, I came with respect and in peace to have tea with you."

He smiled. "Yes, the tea is coming, of course, but my deputy and I would also like to ask you some questions." A man entered with a tray, some glasses, tea, and a package of dates. He walked straight to Abssi. "No, no, please serve our guest first," Abssi said.

What came next was a mix of interrogation and discussion about the West's supposed plan to strengthen Iran. "Why else have they allowed the mullahs to take over Iraq?" Abssi asked, referring to the Shia politicians and clerics who now held the upper hand in the new Iraqi government. "We all know this is the long-term plan, to weaken Arabs and Sunnis here."

He and his deputy told me about the humiliation and torture committed by Shia militias in Iraq. "So where are these human rights groups?" he demanded. "Where is America or Britain when these *Rafidah* are killing innocent men and women?" *Rafidah* is a pejorative word jihadists use for Shia Muslims; it means "people who refuse or reject." The term dates back to the schism in Islam after Muhammad's death in the seventh century. Abssi's soft voice was full of anger. "The only solution for us, to protect us, will be a caliphate. And it should be founded here, in the Levant region."

"The caliphate? What caliphate?" I said. "You mean something like the Ottoman Empire?"

"All Muslims should be united, yes." He sipped his tea. "First Palestine was taken from us. Then they gave Iraq to the Shia and Iran. Every Muslim understands that only a caliphate with a strong leader can protect them."

As we talked, the group's spokesman and another man took notes on everything I said. When I asked why, Abssi told me the notes were only for the group's internal records. "We won't publish them," he assured me.

Abssi and his deputy had read many of my stories, from September 11 to Morocco to Iraq and the London transit attacks. The deputy was taller than Abssi and muscular, with a shaved head and dark, serious eyes. Abssi had said that all the fighters at his camp were Palestinian, but I could tell from their features that some of the men we'd seen outside must have come from North Africa or from the Arabian Gulf. I tried to talk to the deputy in Moroccan Arabic, but he told me no, everyone here is Palestinian. He was indeed Palestinian, but some of the others weren't.

"Didn't anybody try to stop you when you worked on the el-Masri case?" the deputy asked.

"No, actually," I answered. "And as you saw, the story was in the paper."

"And what were the consequences for those who kidnapped and tortured him?"

"That's not clear yet. But at least this man had a chance to tell his story."

"Sister Souad, do you think there is a free press?" Abssi asked. "The press is never free." He looked at me as if seeking confirmation.

I thought that his calling me "Sister" might be a sign that he was beginning to trust me. I sipped my tea and thought about how to answer. "Sheikh, I don't know what your definition of a free press is, but I've never been stopped by the *Washington Post* or the *New York Times* from writing things the way they were. In fact, that's why I'm here: to give you a chance to tell your side of the story about all these accusations against you."

He smiled. "That's a smart way of bringing up the interview again," he said and took a date from the package.

I looked at the dates. "It's interesting that you hate the Shia and Iran so much," I said. "But then you eat their dates."

"What?" Abssi asked and glanced at his deputy. The deputy looked furious. I suddenly had the feeling I'd said something I shouldn't have. Fakhr looked at me and raised his eyebrows.

Abssi picked up the package and read the small type: "Made in Iran." He called for the man who'd brought the tea. "Don't ever bring these dates again," Abssi told him.

A little boy, about five years old, entered the room and ran to the deputy. "Baba, can I go and play with the other children?" he asked.

"Yes, *habibi*, go. I need to finish my meeting here," the deputy said. When the boy had left the room, the deputy turned to me. "Tell me, Sister Souad, are you married?"

Here we go again, I thought. Since my first trip to Iraq, during nearly every interview with people from the radical or jihadist scene, the marriage question popped up.

"Why? Are you looking for a second wife?" I asked him.

All the men except him started laughing, even the one who had been pointing the gun at me. That man had been glowering at me since the meeting started.

I looked at Fakhr. He had covered his face with both hands. What was wrong now?

Abssi turned to the deputy. "I'm not sure my daughter would allow you to take a second wife now," he said. He had tears in his eyes from laughing so hard.

Now I got the joke. "Oh, he is your son-in-law, and the boy is your grandson? *Masha'Allah!*" I tried to hide my embarrassment.

The deputy said he had no more questions. Abssi and the other men were still laughing.

"I've answered your questions and endured your tea interrogation," I said, looking at Abssi. "Now I have a question. What about our interview?"

"I will discuss it with my advisers and get back to you," Abssi said. "But I can tell you one thing for sure, we all haven't laughed like this in a long time."

Abssi, his deputy, and the man who had pointed the gun at me left the room through the doorway behind me, while the spokesman and the other man who had been taking notes accompanied us through the same doorway we'd come in.

As soon as we had passed the military checkpoint outside the gate of the refugee camp, Fakhr told me he'd been shocked and worried at the beginning when he saw the setup with the weapons and the black flag. "I swear, I thought they wanted to do something to you," he said. "This looked very alarming." Then he shook his head and started laughing. "You and your colleague, you are crazy, the way you talk to these guys. I will call you Team Crazy."

I called Michael and told him we were on our way back. When we arrived, he was waiting nervously in the hotel lobby. "Is all well? I began to feel bad, but you insisted that I shouldn't go with you," he said upon seeing us.

I told him that this group must indeed have links to a bigger network. The note taker, the spokesperson, the new guns, and the discipline of the guards all suggested a high level of organization and generous funding. I suspected they were linked to Al Qaeda.

Abssi's spokesperson called later and said they were still thinking about the interview. He told us to be patient. He made it clear that they would be very unhappy if anything we'd discussed appeared in print.

"We do monitor the *New York Times*," the spokesman told me. "It's your choice. If you keep your word and don't publish anything before we agree, you might have the chance to get an interview. But if you break our agreement, we will never speak to you, and others won't, either."

I understood that this was a test. We had no guarantee that he would agree to give the interview, and some journalists might still have gone ahead and printed what I'd learned from the tea meeting. But Michael and I suspected that if we broke the agreement, we would be blackballed within the global jihadist network we were trying to understand. We decided we didn't want to risk losing all our contacts.

I flew back to Frankfurt, and Michael returned to New York. We decided to do as much other reporting as we could, talk to our sources in the West, and gather details about Abssi's life. I checked in with Abssi's spokesman, Abu al-Hassan, every few days, in case the interview was granted.

"He actually would like to do it," Abu al-Hassan told me in one of these conversations. "But his deputy is strongly against it. You know, your future husband." He laughed.

I told him that we had gathered all kinds of information about Abssi from documents and Western government officials. "We will keep our promise and not publish anything of what was said during the tea meeting," I told him. "But tell your boss that one day we will do a story, and it would be unfortunate if it were one-sided."

Three days later, my phone rang. I recognized Abu al-Hassan's number. "*As'salam alaikum,*" I said.

"*Wa'alaikum as'salam*, Sister Souad." The voice was Abssi's.

"Sheikh?"

"Yes. I decided to give you the interview. Regarding your security, you will have my word that there will be no harm against you from our side."

"What about my colleague Michael Moss? Can he come to the interview as well?"

"The American? That's his decision."

"Can you also guarantee that he won't be harmed?"

There was a silence on the other end of the phone, a silence I didn't like.

"*Insha'Allah khair,*" he said. The expression means, "God willing, all will be good." It's an optimistic-sounding phrase but not a guarantee. It wasn't good enough.

I called Michael and our editors. They didn't seem too excited about my going back to Abssi's camp alone.

"I know these people are unpredictable, but he gave me his word and a guarantee for my security," I told them. "I am an Arab Muslim woman. For this guy to kidnap me or worse, he would need a very good reason."

"I don't trust their guarantees," Matt Purdy, our editor, said. "What about Michael? Could he go with you?"

"They wouldn't give me a guarantee for Michael."

"So it would be you and the stringer going back alone again?"

"Yes, that would be the plan."

"I'm not comfortable with this," Matt said. "Bill will have to make the final decision."

Matt was the editor of the investigative unit. He was kicking the question upstairs to Bill Keller, the *Times*'s executive editor, the top person in the newsroom. Keller had worked as a foreign correspondent himself for years, and he understood the dangers reporters faced in war and crisis zones.

A short time later, Keller called. I had met him only once before, in 2005, after the el-Masri story ran, and I was very nervous. He asked me to walk him through the security backup plan I had in mind. It was the same as last time: a piece of paper with phone numbers for Michael to call in case something happened to me.

"This man was involved in killings, and he's now affiliated with Zarqawi's network and Al Qaeda," Keller said. "You have to understand, we don't want a Danny Pearl situation."

I explained that it would be difficult for this man to find an excuse for beheading a Muslim woman. "He gave me his word and guarantee of protection. He would lose face if he broke this agreement."

Keller said he would have to think about it. I was impressed. His interest in the story and involvement in security arrangements made me feel safer. It was one of those moments when I felt grateful to be working for the *Times*. I wasn't being treated as an expendable freelancer. The paper really seemed to care about my well-being.

Matt called back two hours later. "Okay, you can go," he said. "Michael will fly in from the United States, not to go inside with you but to be there in case anything happens."

"Thank you."

"That's the least we can do. But Souad, if you or Michael ever think it will be too dangerous or unpredictable, you come back, okay? I don't want you to think you have to do this. Safety first."

My next call was to Abssi's spokesperson. "Tell the sheikh I'm coming for the interview," I said.

IN MARCH, ABOUT a month after our first trip, Michael and I returned to Beirut. It was spring in Lebanon and warm. On the day of our interview, I put on thin khaki trousers I'd worn often in Iraq and a short-sleeved T-shirt. Leena, our Lebanese fixer, again lent me an *abaya*.

The Lebanese government had changed the rules for camp visits since our last trip. Worried about kidnappings, it had forbidden foreigners from going inside. I wore no perfume or makeup and tied my head scarf in the traditional Palestinian fashion, trying to look as much as possible like one of the women who lived in Nahr al-Bared.

My conversation with Bill Keller had comforted me, but it had also made me more conscious of the risks. I wondered if I was missing something. Like last time, I'd reached out to various jihadists to plead my case if anything happened. Again, I wrote down their names and numbers and gave copies to Michael and Leena. But I felt unsettled and apprehensive. This wasn't just small talk over tea. I was there to ask hard questions, and I wasn't sure how Abssi would react.

This time Michael, Leena, Fakhr, our Beirut driver Hussein, and I drove north to Tripoli in two cars. On the way, I ran through the questions and security measures with Michael. The interview was scheduled for 3:00 p.m. We agreed that Michael would call me at five, and that whatever happened, Fakhr and I should be out of the camp before dark.

The closer we got to Tripoli, the more anxious Michael grew. We were supposed to wait for a confirmation call from Abssi's group before Fakhr and I went into the camp, so we stopped at one of the famous sweet shops in the center of Tripoli to kill time. Hussein ordered tea and heavy, sugary pastries.

"Things have changed now," Fakhr said. "There is talk that the army is cracking down on members of Fatah al-Islam when they try to enter or leave the camp, so everyone is very nervous."

Michael turned to me, looking stricken. He said he couldn't sit there eating sweets while I went inside the camp alone.

"But you can't go with me," I told him. "Keller and our editors said there is no way I should allow you to come inside."

"I don't care," he responded. "I can't let you face these people alone."

Fakhr looked at me. "There is no way we will make it in with him," he said in Arabic. "The army will recognize him as a foreigner."

Then Fakhr's phone rang. "Yes, we are coming now, *insha'Allah*," he said. It was time for us to go.

I called the editors in New York and told them that we'd gotten the call. Fakhr and I headed toward the camp.

———

THE SECURITY CHECKPOINT at the camp entrance was bigger than it had been the last time we visited, but the soldiers waved us through. Fakhr called Abssi's spokesman to tell him we were inside.

We drove to the same compound as before. More armed men stood in front of the entrance. They ushered us into the room. Abu al-Hassan was there, and we started chatting.

He began to tell me a bit more about his life. He was twenty-four and of Palestinian descent but had been born in Lebanon. He had a keen interest in journalism and had been studying communications, but the situation in Palestine and the war in Iraq had convinced him to quit school and join Abssi's group.

"When I saw what they had done to Iraq, this unfair war, the oppression against Muslims, I just couldn't keep silent and stand by," he said. By "they" he meant the United States, but also the Shia militias backed by Iran.

He told me about his latest project: an online newsmagazine aimed at attracting jihadi recruits. Al-Hassan was prescient. He and others in Abssi's organization understood the importance of online media outreach long before the creation of *Inspire* and the other online jihadi magazines of today. Al-Hassan felt that the mainstream media didn't fairly portray groups like Abssi's. He wanted the mujahideen to have their own outlet, where they could speak directly to anyone who wanted to listen.

An hour passed. I wondered if Abssi would cancel. There were gunmen in the room, but this time they weren't pointing their weapons at me. Maybe because al-Hassan had spoken so openly, I'd begun to feel more at ease. Al-Hassan told me that he had argued on my behalf and that Abssi's deputy had advised the sheikh against talking to me, but Abssi himself wanted to do the interview.

When the sheikh finally arrived, the men in the room again stood to greet him. He agreed to speak on the record and said that I could also use whatever he'd said in our previous meeting.

I was curious about why Abssi had left Arafat's more secular organization and taken an Islamist approach. He thought about it for a couple of seconds. "My main aim for many years was to free Palestine, and that is still one of my main aims. But many waging that fight turned out to be corrupt and weak, like so many leaders in our region."

This was a fairly common complaint, even among militants and Islamist activists, but I wondered if there wasn't something bigger going on. Had Al Qaeda and its ideology replaced secular groups in the region that had traditionally taken on the Palestinian cause? While Arafat's group had been a local effort, albeit with broad support in the Arab world and beyond, the movement to which Abssi had hitched his wagon was truly global, in both its membership and its ambitions. By attaching a religious motivation to the Palestinian struggle, Abssi and others like him were essentially becoming franchisees of Al Qaeda, while also linking the fight for Palestinian freedom to a much broader and more threatening ideology. His deputy looked a bit annoyed by my question, but Abssi confirmed my suspicion, saying that he would do anything in his power to "free Palestine" and get back his homeland, so he could pass it on to his children and grandchildren.

"Only the caliphate can protect Muslim interests," he told me.

It was a stunning statement, and it showed that the idea of a new kind of Islamic state in the Middle East long predated the arrival of ISIS. In fact, the notion had been gestating for years in the minds of militants fighting first in Afghanistan and later in Iraq and elsewhere. Men like Abssi were now carrying that torch into new communities, gathering more oxygen to feed the flame.

"But after all these decades of war, wouldn't the better option be peace with Israel?" I asked. "Like what Rabin and Arafat started?" I was referring to the 1993 Oslo Accord, in which Arafat and Israeli prime minister Yitzhak Rabin had agreed on a framework for peace—though one that was never fully implemented.

I sensed a growing tension in the room. "And his own people killed Rabin for it," Abssi answered. "They don't want peace and we don't want to be the victims anymore. Arab leaders and rulers are also guilty for all that happened to our nations. That's why we need the caliphate."

He believed that America in particular needed to be punished for its presence in the Islamic world. "The only way to achieve our rights is by force," he said. "This is the way America deals with us. When the Americans feel that their lives and their economy are threatened, they will know that they should leave."

Abssi said that he shared Al Qaeda's fundamentalist interpretation of global politics. He believed that what America and its allies had done in Iraq was a crime and that Muslims should wage a global jihad against the Western "crusaders" who had declared war against Islam. He spoke admiringly of bin Laden, and he clearly saw Zarqawi as a role model.

Killing American soldiers was no longer enough to convince the Americans to get out of Iraq, he believed. But what he had in mind beyond that wasn't entirely clear. He refused to identify his targets. He would only say that his group was training militants to fight Israel and the so-called crusaders.

"We have every legitimate right to do such acts, for isn't it America that comes to our region and kills innocents and children?" he said. "It is our right to hit them in their homes, the same as they hit us in our homes. We are not afraid of being named terrorists. But I want to ask, is someone who detonates one kilogram of explosives [in the West] a terrorist, while someone who detonates tons in Arab and Islamic cities not a terrorist?"

The month before, two commuter buses had been bombed in Lebanon, killing three and wounding more than twenty others. Lebanese law enforcement officials said that they'd arrested four men from Fatah al-Islam in connection with the attacks. But Abssi denied involvement. He said he had no plans to strike within Lebanon, where the Palestinian camps offered ideal locations to grow his organization.

"Today's youth, when they see what is happening in Palestine and Iraq, it encourages them to join the way of jihad," he said. "These people have now started to adopt the right path."

"But isn't the killing of innocents, women, children, and the elderly forbidden?" I asked.

"Originally, the killing of innocents and children was forbidden," he replied. "However, there are situations in which the killing of such is permissible. One of these exceptions is those [who] kill our women and children." In democracies like the United States, he said, each citizen was responsible for the actions of his government. The people in such countries could not be said to be innocent of what was done in their name. Even American antiwar protesters bore some blame, he said. He would be sorry to see them killed, but he viewed attacks in the home territory of countries that had joined the war in Iraq as legitimate.

"Osama bin Laden does make the *fatwas*," Abssi said, using the Arabic word for Islamic legal opinions delivered by a mufti, or religious expert. "Should his *fatwas* follow the *Sunnah*," the second Islamic legal source after the Koran, "we will carry them out."

Abssi acknowledged having worked with Zarqawi, but said he'd had nothing to do with the death of Laurence Foley, the American official shot in Jordan. "I don't know what Foley's role was, but I can say that any person [who] comes to our region with a military, security, or political aim . . . is a legitimate target," he said.

"Do you think you will get enough followers for your idea to establish a caliphate here?" I asked him.

"This is not my idea," Abssi answered. "This is about the new awakening among Muslims here in the region. America has shown that this is a war against Sunni Islam. The idea [of the caliphate] will live and grow, even if I die today or tomorrow."

When we were done talking, I asked for a tour of the camp. Abssi told his military commander to show me a few things. This was the same man who'd pointed a gun at me during our first conversation. I followed him outside, where twelve men, their faces shrouded in scarves, turned their Kalashnikovs on us.

"Oh, shit," I blurted out, ducking behind Fakhr.

"That won't help you much," Fakhr answered. He and the commander laughed. "I'm so thin that every bullet would go through me and hit you."

"Don't worry, this is just training," the commander said. "They don't have bullets in their AKs." Somebody gave an order, and all twelve men turned and lunged in another direction. "*Allah hu-Akbar!*" they shouted, firing their assault rifles into a wall.

"No bullets?" I asked the commander.

"This must be the advanced class," he said, laughing.

The commander told me they had an arsenal of explosives, rockets, even an antiaircraft gun. Fakhr and I were escorted to the gateway we'd come in. A group of fighters, including a handful who'd attended the interview, stood outside. I heard the voices of children.

Four boys with plastic pistols ran toward the men. They must have been about five or six years old. The man who had taken notes through both my meetings with Abssi scooped up one of the boys.

"How was it?" he asked.

"We were at the camp, Baba, and they showed me a real gun," the boy answered. "And then I played jihad and killed the *kuffar*," he added, using the Arabic word for "unbelievers."

The man started laughing. "You killed the *kuffar*?"

"Yes, Baba, with the pistol."

The man kissed his forehead. "I am very proud of you, my son."

It hit me like a knife. In Fakhr's car I put on my sunglasses and didn't speak much the whole way back to Beirut. This didn't end with Zarqawi, I told Michael later, and it won't end with Abssi.

After Michael and I went over my notes and transcribed the interview, I went up to my room. I took off my clothes and got into the shower to wash away the dust. But when I thought of what I'd heard the boy say to his father, I broke down and cried.

6

The Lost Boys of Zarqa

Jordan, 2007

The war in Iraq created a sectarian rift in the Middle East on a scale not seen since the 1979 Iranian Revolution. Iran had always sparred with its neighbors, but those had been conflicts between nations. Now, Sunni militants in Syria and Jordan recruited suicide bombers from around the world, not just to fight the Americans in Iraq but to fight the Iraqi Shia as well.

In Zarqa, Jordan, the hometown of Abu Musab al-Zarqawi, this narrative was unfolding in real time. While I was talking with Shaker al-Abssi in Lebanon, a source in Zarqa got in touch and told me about a group of young men—all friends from the same neighborhood—who had gone to fight in Iraq, where suicide bombings were averaging more than forty a month. "One of them is my cousin's son," the contact told me.

My source was an Islamist community leader in his early fifties whom I'll call Abu Yasmina. He felt that the American invasion of Iraq had opened the door to vast Iranian influence in the region, which was motivating young men in Zarqa and elsewhere to join the jihadi struggle. For many Sunnis, Shia power and Western intervention were equally oppressive. Abu Yasmina didn't support the young men's decision to fight, but he understood it.

"Zarqawi was a terrorist," he told me, but he believed that Iran and the West had turned him into a hero for many young people.

In March 2007, shortly after my visit to Abssi, Michael and I traveled to Zarqa and met with Abu Yasmina in his modest home. He served us small cups of Arabic coffee with cardamom and Jordanian pistachio sweets soaked in honey and sugar water.

"Most of these young people . . . when they see the news and what is going on in the Islamic countries, they themselves feel that they have to go fight jihad," he told us. "Today, you don't need anyone to tell young men that they should go to jihad. They themselves want to be martyrs." Was this what Abssi had meant when he said that this new generation thought the West was at war with Sunni Islam?

Abssi's words and what I would see in Zarqa raised the specter of an epic battle between Sunni and Shia that had already spread far beyond the boundaries of Iraq. The war was a Pandora's box whose contents might transform global Muslim identity. No longer would people ask, are you Arab or Iranian? Instead they would ask, are you Sunni or Shia?

Michael and I wanted to talk to the young men who had left Zarqa to fight in Iraq, at least the ones who were still alive, and their families. I had another source in town, a former close aide to Zarqawi, who offered to help. I met him alone at a coffee shop in the middle of a busy shopping area.

"I talked to the brothers, and they are okay with meeting you for sure, but some of them were nervous about your colleague the American."

I explained that we wanted to understand how these young men had been recruited and how they'd gotten to Iraq. And I asked for guidance. I needed him to tell me when things were getting too dangerous, when it would be possible to take Michael along, and when I would need to work on my own.

"*Insha'Allah* all will be fine," he said. He looked at the long wide trousers and long shirt I was wearing, the same clothes I'd worn in Iraq. "Is this how you wanted to meet them?" he asked.

I nodded.

"Come with me."

I followed him to a nearby shop. Long scarves in all colors were on display in the window, as well as different styles of *abayas*, all black, but made of different kinds of cloth.

He looked around, touching the fabric, and saying things like "This feels like it was made in China," or "This will be too warm." Finally, he held one up. "This one, I think, would be right for you."

I felt my eyes widen. This man with a long beard and traditional Arab clothes, a man who preached the gospel of an Iranian-American war against Sunnis in Iraq, was holding an *abaya* covered with sequins and pink embroidery, the funkiest one in the shop. He even insisted on paying for it.

"Let me pay for this, please, Sheikh," I told him, explaining that as a journalist I couldn't accept a gift from one of my sources.

"You are crazy," he said.

"I have to pay for it, but you chose it, so thank you for that," I told him.

"May this one bring you good luck, and you will always be dressed right for these brothers," he said, laughing.

I still wear that *abaya* for difficult interviews. In some circles, the fact that one of Zarqawi's deputies chose it wins me added respect; in others, it's just a good conversation starter.

Michael and I were staying in Amman, about fifteen miles from Zarqa. On what we hoped would be our first morning of interviews, we met the Islamist community leader Abu Yasmina at his house. He had good news. Some of the families of the young men who'd gone to fight in Iraq had agreed to meet with us.

The six young men had all been between nineteen and twenty-four years old. Some had known each other as small children. Their jihadi adventures were no secret in the neighborhood; everyone knew what they'd done and what had happened to them. Two apparently had died as suicide bombers, and a third by gunfire; one had been arrested by the Americans and was being held in Iraq; two others had been turned back.

Michael and I wanted to talk to as many of those involved as we could: the families of those who had left; the people who'd recruited them; and, if possible, one of the men who had been sent back home.

Abu Yasmina said that two of the families were open to talking, but he added, "I doubt that you'll be able to meet the other ones." He didn't know that my other friend the Zarqawi aide was already working on that.

"*Insha'Allah khair*, God willing, all will be good," I said.

Dressed in my new *abaya*, I drove with Michael and Abu Yasmina to a house nearby. A man who looked to be in his early sixties opened the door and invited us in. Other men stood behind him in the hall. The first thing we saw were two large photographs on the wall showing the faces of two young men who looked a bit alike.

"These were my sons," the older man told us. "They both died in Iraq. Jihad, the older one, in 2005, and Amer just weeks ago."

I looked at the pictures. "I'm sorry for your loss," I said.

"Why sorry?" said one of the men in the hallway. "He has to be happy. His sons are martyrs now." He gave me an angry look.

The forty-day mourning period for Amer was still under way, and the men filling the house were neighbors who had come to pay their respects. People in this neighborhood didn't see young men like Amer and Jihad as terrorists but as heroes who had been forced into a war of self-defense. In front of his neighbors, their father had to pretend he was proud of their sacrifice. But I could see that he was deeply hurt. From time to time, tears filled his eyes. He didn't look proud; he looked broken.

He led us to a different room. I understood that he didn't want to speak to us in front of his visitors. His name was Kasem, and he'd had six sons, including the two he'd lost. "Amer left without even telling us," he said. "He was just nineteen years old."

Amer had been very close to his older brother Jihad, whose name could either mean "struggle" or stand for the Islamic obligation to defend the faith. When Jihad died fighting in Fallujah in 2005, Amer was seventeen years old, a senior in high school, his father said. He started reading religious books.

Shortly thereafter, Amer made his first trip to Iraq. He called his family when he got there. His father sent two of Amer's older brothers to fetch him. "I was thinking and hoping that we lost one son and that was enough. But I could tell Amer was thinking, 'This life doesn't count anymore, and I will follow the way of my brother,'" Kasem told us.

He stood up, left the room, and came back with a tray with sweets, coffee, and tea. When he bent down to pour the coffee into cups, I saw his hands shaking.

"Please allow me," I said. "You've been too kind already to welcome us to your house."

Kasem sat back in the chair. "No, I need to thank you. Please tell the stories of my sons, so other families don't lose theirs," he said. "I lost my sons because of the false politics of America, and thousands of other parents did, too."

He told us about the struggle he and his wife had, trying to hold Amer back from going to Iraq. They even offered to find him a wife.

"No, this is not important to me," Amer told them. "Jihad is."

Amer left again for Iraq the previous October, toward the end of Ramadan, when border security is looser. Shortly afterward, his parents received a letter he'd written before leaving and handed off to a contact in Jordan to send. He was going to fight for the sake of Allah, he wrote. He would reach martyrdom and he would see his parents again in heaven. He asked them to pray for him and not to mourn. As on his first trip, he phoned home three weeks after he'd left to tell them he'd made it to Iraq.

They heard nothing further from Amer until one of his brothers got a call in January. A man told him that Amer had been killed when the bomb in the truck he was driving exploded. There were reports of a truck bombing in Kirkuk on the day Amer is believed to have died, but his family didn't know for sure whether he was the bomber.

I asked the father if he knew who Amer's friends were or where he used to pray.

"Yes, I know some of them, but they didn't come to our home often," he said. "He used to go to the mosque of Sheikh Abu Anas because the sheikh gave good Friday sermons."

We said good-bye, and Michael, Abu Yasmina, and I drove to visit the next family, who lived nearby. This house was smaller, the family less prosperous. The young man's mother showed us into a small room, where we sat on mattresses on the floor.

Her son, a twenty-year-old engineering student, was missing. He was one of seventeen children born into a poor family. His father was old and asthmatic, with a persistent cough and missing teeth. The family had heard that their son had gone to Iraq, but they had no proof. We asked his mother if we could see some of his things, any possessions he'd cared about.

"All he did was read and study," she said. She brought us a physics book, and as she showed it to us she began to cry. She was absolutely sure, she said, that her son had gone to Iraq to study and work. She'd heard about other boys who had gone to fight but was adamant that her son couldn't be one of them, unless someone had tricked him. The family begged us not to print his name for fear of jeopardizing his future, should he return.

The young man's sister sat with us that day, but out of respect for her mother she said little. Later, though, we talked on the phone, and she told me that her brother was being held in an American prison in Iraq. The family had received a letter from him, delivered by the Red Cross. He said that he wanted to let them know he was alive and sent his regards.

About two years before he disappeared, his sister said, she'd noticed a change in him. "He stopped listening to music. He isolated himself from us. At family gatherings, he sat by himself, thinking."

The young man felt pressure to excel but believed he couldn't build a successful career for himself in Zarqa, she said. Wealthier students at his university had their own apartments, while he lived at home to save money. He wanted to study medicine, but he'd failed to win a scholarship to continue his schooling in England. "He wanted to be somebody," his sister told me, "and he couldn't."

He and his sister had talked about the war in Iraq, which he described as a battle against Muslims, particularly Sunnis. He knew his family would oppose his going there.

When we visited the family, I asked the young man's mother the same question I'd put to Amer's father: Had she known her son's friends?

"No. How should I know them?" she asked. "Our home is not large enough for his friends to come here. We are not rich."

She said her son had attended the same mosque that Amer's father had mentioned, and he listened to the same imam.

"The imam is living just here in the neighborhood, not far from us," the young man's father said.

I asked if he could show us the way, but he said he had a better idea.

"Let me get him for you." He stood up and left the house, returning five minutes later with a man in a sparkling white tunic and wide-legged pajama pants.

"*As'salam alaikum*," the imam said. "I heard you were looking for me."

He had glasses and a beard, and his skin was very dark, almost black. He didn't seem the slightest bit aggressive. In fact, he was very friendly. His name was Ahmad Salah, but he went by Abu Anas. We learned that Zarqawi had prayed at his mosque before leaving to fight in Iraq. Michael and I couldn't believe our luck.

Our host invited the imam to sit and offered him coffee. Abu Anas said the young engineering student had prayed at his mosque and tutored youngsters in the Koran. He said that if he had known his plans, he would have tried to talk him out of going to Iraq.

"It's very difficult at the moment," Abu Anas said. "If you do a suicide operation, the Muslims are mixed up with non-Muslims, and maybe you [will] kill Muslims."

But he didn't consider the Shia to be Muslims. Like Abssi, he called them *Rafidah*, an insulting term. In his view, the Shia were killing Sunnis, which made them legitimate targets for retribution. "They hate Sunnis and will do everything to destroy us. That's their mission," he said.

As I translated, I noticed the lanyard around Michael's neck. I knew that he liked to carry important documents and flash drives on a lanyard, and the one he wore today was yellow with green Arabic lettering.

I knew this lanyard. We had bought it together in the Dahia neighborhood in Beirut a month earlier. Lots of fighters and their families from the Shia militia Hezbollah lived in that area, and the neighborhood had its own security service provided by the group.

On one of our visits to the neighborhood, our driver, Hussein, took us to a shop that sold Hezbollah flags, books, and DVDs featuring the speeches of Hezbollah leader Hassan Nasrallah. There were lighters, wallets, and computer cases, all with the yellow flag and green Arabic letters of "Hezbollah"; some even had pictures of Nasrallah's face. The store also sold lanyards that people used to carry keys. "That is very practical for flash drives," Michael said. We bought some, along with a few other souvenirs, as tongue-in-cheek gifts for colleagues back in New York.

Now Michael was speaking to a preacher who had clearly inspired young men to fight in Iraq and who couldn't help showing his hatred against the Shia. I needed to warn Michael before anyone else noticed.

"Sheikh, what do you think about Hezbollah?" I asked the preacher. They had been heroes to many Muslims, both Sunni and Shia, during their war with Israel, so it seemed fair to ask.

"Hezbollah? They are the devil's soldiers. They hate us. They are very bad, and anyone who supports them is an enemy of Islam."

I turned to Michael to translate. I spoke much more slowly and in a louder voice than usual.

"He says, Hezbollah"—I pronounced the word very slowly—"are the devil's soldiers, they hate us, they are very bad and anyone who supports them"—now my eyes opened wider and I put my hands up at my neck while looking at Michael—"is an enemy of Islam."

Michael looked at me questioningly. "Okay," he said and then made small circles next to his head, as if to say, "Are you nuts, or what?"

"He said Hezbollah is very bad, you got that right? Enemies of Islam."

He still didn't get it, so I turned toward him and whispered, "Dude, you are wearing the Hezbollah band around your neck. Go to the bathroom and take it off."

Michael nodded and excused himself.

"So you are working on a story about Zarqa?" the sheikh asked me when Michael was gone.

"In fact, Sheikh, it's about the boys who have left and their families and all who knew them."

"You must come for tea today to my house. I can show you more of what these Shia are doing to us, these *Rafidah*," he said.

"Thank you, Sheikh. We are happy to visit you at home."

"You don't need to call me 'Sheikh,'" he said. "Just call me Abu Anas."

When Michael came back from the bathroom, I saw that the lanyard was gone.

DURING THE TIME we'd worked together, Michael and I had grown close. When I visited the United States, he invited me to his home in

Brooklyn, where I met his wife, Eve, and their two sons. I had promised Eve that Michael's security and safety would be the priority wherever we went.

But the more time we spent in Zarqa, the more unsettled I felt. I watched the faces of residents in Abu Anas's neighborhood when they saw an American man walking with an Arab woman in an *abaya*. I saw anger and hatred in their eyes: *What are those two doing here?*

In his home, Abu Anas showed us a newly released video titled "The True History and Aims of the Shia." It showed Shia clerics in Iraq and Iran apparently insulting Aisha, one of the wives of the Prophet Muhammad, as well as some of the Prophet's companions. It was impossible to tell whether the video had been manipulated, but according to the voice-over the men were calling Aisha a prostitute. Their anger at Aisha had its roots in the old schism between Sunni and Shia Islam.

The video showed scenes of Sunnis tortured and killed by a Shia militia in Iraq. Sunnis from Iraq spoke about the alleged abuses and asked their "Sunni brothers" to come and help. The video clearly enraged Abu Anas. The Shia "have traditions that are un-Islamic and they hate the Sunnis," he told us. "We didn't see the Shia like that before, but now in Iraq, they showed their real face."

When the Shia in the video insulted Sunni caliphs, calling them sons of whores, Abu Anas turned to me. "Did you hear what they said about Abu Bakr and Omar?" he asked.

"Yes, I did, but Sheikh, not every Shia thinks like that, and then there are even Shia from the *Ahl al-Bayt*, descendants of the Prophet, and you said you honor the Prophet, no?" I was thinking of my mother and her family.

"Well, the *Ahl al-Bayt*, that is something different," he said. "They are not like the other Shia."

He turned back to the screen. "See, see how they torture Sunnis in Iraq?" he said. "They hate us and the Americans are helping them. They didn't stop them."

He offered more tea. "Are you not married?" he asked me.

I was still following the screen and taking notes about the video. "No, I'm not," I said.

"Unbelievable," he answered and started reeling off the usual effusive compliments favored by men in Islamist circles, including comparing me to the Prophet's wives. I took a moment to admire the irony: both my parents' forefathers were related to the Prophet's first wife, but I was fairly sure this man wouldn't have appreciated my mother's background much, even if she was from the *Ahl al-Bayt*.

He said that from time to time, he showed these videos to some of the young men who visited his mosque. I asked Abu Anas where he got them.

"Some brothers are distributing them," he said. "If you like, I can help you meet them. But you will need to cover your face."

————

Abu Anas called me that evening to confirm the meeting with the "video brothers." It was supposed to take place at one of their houses in Zarqa. I'd bought a *niqab* for the occasion.

In the car on the way there, Michael read Arabic vocabulary words from orange cards. "Thank you": *shukran*; "good morning": *sabah el hair*.

"No," I answered, "It's *sabah el khair*."

He repeated it the right way. "I think it's nice to be able to say some words in Arabic," Michael said. "It shows them how much respect I have for their culture."

I was apprehensive about this meeting. The night before, I'd called the former close associate of Zarqawi who'd chosen my *abaya* to ask about the "video brothers," and he'd told me that one of the men was potentially dangerous. For safety, Michael and I asked a Jordanian named Marwan to join us. Marwan was a freelance journalist who had researched jihadist networks; he was sometimes quoted as an expert in our stories, and I'd met him a couple of times before. I also asked our driver Abu Dania, who came from a large and well-known family in Jordan, to accompany us inside.

As I had on other trips, I'd listed all the Salafi sheikhs and leaders who could vouch for us in case of any danger. This time, since Michael and I were both going to the interview, I carried the paper with me.

We pulled up to the house, and I drew the *niqab* across my mouth and over my head so only my eyes would show. We got out and knocked at a door in the wall that opened into a small garden. A man with glasses was waiting at the entrance to the house.

"*As'salam alaikum*," we said in greeting.

"*Wa'alaikum as'salam*," he responded.

We followed him inside, stepping into a room furnished with couches and a TV. Another man stood there. He had black hair, a long black beard, and angry blue eyes.

"He is my friend and a sheikh," the man with the glasses said.

Michael and I said hello.

"Is she the Moroccan Muslima?" the angry-eyed man asked in Arabic.

"Yes, Sheikh, that's me," I answered.

"And him?" The angry-looking man glanced at Michael. "He's American?" he said in Arabic.

"Yes, he is American," the man with the glasses answered.

The angry-looking one began to smile. He looked at Michael and then said in Arabic, "Let's kidnap and kill him and make a video out of it."

Next to me, Michael was smiling and nodding. "*Shukran, shukran,*" I heard him say.

We all looked at Michael, and even the angry-looking man's expression changed. "Why is he saying 'thank you'?" he asked us.

I decided not to tell Michael what he had just thanked them for. Instead, I began arguing with the men in Arabic. "Before you kill my colleague, you will have to kill me," I said in as loud and serious a tone as I could manage. I was breathing so hard that the light veil covering my mouth and nose flapped up and down. I told them that we had come as their guests and were under the protection of some figures known in the jihadist circles, whom I named.

"Why are you talking so impolitely to them?" Michael asked me. "They are both here welcoming us and smiling."

The two men whispered to each other, and then the one with the glasses invoked one of the tenets of jihadi etiquette: the host had to consent to killing Michael before it could happen with God's grace. It was his house, the man with glasses said, and he wouldn't allow Michael to be killed there. Marwan also spoke up, saying that Michael was under his protection and that he wouldn't allow him to be slaughtered.

After a few tense moments, we all sat down. I noticed that the host's wife had come around the corner and was standing out of view of the others, where only I could see her. We greeted each other politely.

To be safe, I decided to work as quickly as we could. I asked basic questions, such as where they got their footage and how many DVDs they distributed. Michael kept asking for more details, but I told him we had to hurry, as we had another appointment.

The man with glasses explained that they had received the videos on flash drives from Iraq and burned the footage onto DVDs, which they distributed mainly in Zarqa; from there, they found their way to other cities as well.

"Do you sell them?" I asked.

"No, no, we give them away for free," he said. The effort was financed through private donations, but he refused to tell us who was contributing.

Our host then excused himself, saying that his wife was calling. When he returned, he told me that she wanted to see me.

"It's okay, I already greeted her," I replied.

"No, she wants to welcome you in the other room."

I didn't want to leave Michael alone. "It's fine," I said. "I'm very comfortable here."

"You don't understand," the man with glasses told me. "We have rules in the house, and she insists that you sit with her where the women sit."

Seeing no way around it, I told him I would visit her in a few minutes. We asked if they had given these videos to the young men from the neighborhood who had left for Iraq.

"I knew one of them personally," the host said.

His angry friend grumbled. "They are all mujahideen, *masha'Allah*," he said. "They went to Iraq to kill the evil Americans like your friend, who have sold Iraq to the more evil Shia, who are now torturing our brothers and raping our sisters."

"Sheikh, my colleague is one of the journalists who has reported about the torture that was committed by Shia militias," I told him. "Our paper has published many reports about this and also about the CIA facilities where people were tortured." I wanted him to see that not every American was guilty.

"They are all the same," he answered. "All *kuffar*, and you should not be working with him."

We decided to leave. I asked Abu Dania and Marwan to go to the car with Michael while I said good-bye to the host's wife. She was sitting in the next room watching TV with her four small children. When I stuck my head in, I realized they were watching videos showing attacks on U.S. soldiers in Iraq, and Shia militiamen holding the severed heads of what they said were Sunni men in Iraq.

"You're letting them see all this?" I asked her.

"Yes. They need to see who the enemies of Islam are," she answered. "The earlier, the better."

It reminded me of what I'd seen in the Nahr al-Bared camp in Lebanon, when the Fatah al-Islam fighter had praised his son for "killing" an infidel. A feeling of sadness and disgust swept over me.

In the garden, the angry-eyed man stood near the door that led to the street. I could see Michael and Marwan standing next to the car outside, but as I approached, the man closed the gate. I was trapped in the garden.

"One moment," he said.

I wasn't sure what he was planning to do, but I feared he might try to take out his anger on me. Hadn't he said that I wasn't supposed to work with *kuffar*?

"I need to talk to you alone," he said. "You want to know why I hate the Americans so much?" He was not shouting, but there was aggression in his voice, and his hands were shaking. "You know what they allowed the Shia to do to me in Iraq? I swear by God I had not even been a jihadist then, but after the torture I saw, I became one. These militias, they put electroshocks on every part of my body; they raped me; they pissed on me, spat on me. I need to take medication now because of my nerves."

"Sheikh, I'm really sorry for what happened to you," I said as calmly as I could. "But what happened to you, it's not the responsibility of every American or even every Shia. There are people who are fighting for human rights."

"Human rights?!" he shouted. "Human shit! All these groups, they are just liars, just using human rights for their interests." He clenched his hands into fists.

The host, who had been in the street, opened the door and said, "Please, sister, get into the car."

I looked at the other man one more time. "I am sorry for what happened to you," I whispered.

———

"IT WAS WEIRD what happened there," Michael said as we drove back to Amman. "Those men seemed so nice, and you were so tough with them."

I took off my *niqab* and turned to him. "Do yourself and us a favor: please stop with your Arabic lessons!"

"Why?" he answered.

"You know what *shukran* means, don't you?"

He nodded.

"They were arguing about whether they should behead you and make a video, and you were saying 'thank you' to them."

I explained the whole situation. I also apologized for not telling him what had been said while we were there, and Michael agreed that I had been right not to. "I would have totally freaked out, and then they would have thought I indeed was a spy or something," he said.

"Yes, that's what they would have thought, but you were protected. We three would never have allowed them to harm you in any way."

"*Shukran, shukran,*" Michael said, and we all started laughing.

———

WE FELT WE were making progress, but we wanted to find someone who had been friends with the young men who'd left for Iraq. "You may need to go back to Abu Anas and ask him," Michael said.

I drove up to Zarqa again with my *abaya* and *niqab* in my bag, pulling on the *abaya* before Abu Dania, the driver, and I met Abu Anas at his house.

"There is someone who I think was close to them," he said. "But I'm sure he won't talk to you."

"Why are you so sure?"

He leaned in and whispered: "Because he is only doing what the emir is telling him."

"What emir?" I asked.

"He has the key to everything here in this neighborhood."

He gave me the emir's *kunya*—his nom de guerre—and said he had done all he could. I reached out to another source, the Zarqawi associate, and asked to meet him at a coffee shop in the center of Zarqa.

"Who is this emir?" I asked.

The man was another longtime associate of Zarqawi's, my source told me. They'd fought together, and the emir had spent several years in prison in the 1990s, when Zarqawi was building and strengthening his network from behind bars. When Zarqawi went to Iraq, the emir had helped supply his old friend with fighters. These days, he divided his time between mentoring suicide bombers bound for Iraq and helping to organize militant operations elsewhere.

"He is the key," my source said. "He is a strong man, very strong."

"So you know him?"

He nodded. "Let me talk to him and see what I can do."

I smiled. "Please, can you do it now? We are running out of time. I even wore the *abaya* just for this."

He laughed, stood up, and said I should have another juice or tea. He would be back. About a half hour later he returned, a smile on his face. He told me that he'd told the emir who Michael and I were. They'd looked up our stories on the Internet and discussed the possibility of a meeting.

"He agreed to see you both tomorrow," he said. "See, I told you the *abaya* would bring you good luck."

———

THE NEXT DAY, as Michael and I were about to head to Zarqa, my source called. "You need to come alone, and come now."

I told Michael that I needed to see what was going on, and drove off to Zarqa with Abu Dania, the driver.

I met the source at the coffee shop.

"He canceled the meeting."

"What? Why?"

"He said because of tooth problems, but I think he got nervous. He doesn't seem certain any longer."

This was a setback. We knew that in order to explain to Americans why young Jordanian men were leaving their families and homes to fight in Iraq, we had to have their voices. But without "Abu Jihad"—as some people called the emir—we wouldn't be able to reach them.

"Please, can we visit him with no interview?" I begged, thinking about how well that had worked before with Abssi in Lebanon.

My source shook his head. "Don't you ever give up? Let's go now, but we'll drive in my car. Your driver has to stay here."

It was risky, but two things comforted me: it was the middle of the day and I trusted my source. I told Abu Dania to wait for me at the coffee shop and gave him the paper with the jihadist contact numbers in a sealed envelope, with instructions to give it to Michael if I wasn't back in a couple of hours. Then I called Michael.

"He wanted to cancel because of tooth pain," I told him.

"Please try to convince him," Michael answered. "I can offer him some Advil or Ambien."

Abu Jihad was surprised to see us, but he wasn't upset. He was tall and strong-looking with long hair, but on this day his face seemed a bit pale.

"Sheikh, I heard you wanted to cancel the interview because of a tooth problem?" I asked.

"Yes, I am sorry but I am in pain. Let's do it some other day."

I tried to explain that we had only a short time left in the country and that the interview with him was crucial. Without it, I told him, we wouldn't be able to tell the whole story.

He said he couldn't do it.

I couldn't believe that a mujahid who had fought alongside Zarqawi and spent years in prison was canceling the meeting because of a toothache.

Then a door opened and an older woman came into the room. She greeted Abu Jihad and asked how he was doing. Then she asked who I was.

"She is a visitor, Mother," Abu Jihad answered. His voice was much softer than before.

She hugged me and kissed my cheeks. "Welcome, my daughter. Where are you from, *habibti*, Morocco?" she asked, using the feminine form of the Arabic word for "beloved." She told me she loved Moroccan sweets. "But why are you looking so sad?"

I explained that I had come all the way from Europe to meet with her son, who was so important for this story, and my colleague had come from the United States. And now he wanted to cancel because his teeth hurt.

She began to scold him. "Son, this nice girl and her friend have come so far to see you. Of course you will meet with them, or I will curse the milk that I fed you from this breast." She pressed her right hand to her chest.

Abu Jihad jumped up and kissed his mother's head and hand. "Of course, Mother! As you wish!"

My source watched from a corner, trying not to laugh. I turned to Abu Jihad. "So, Sheikh, can I bring my colleague?"

"Yes, daughter, go and bring your colleague," his mother answered.

"I promise we will bring some medicine for your teeth as well, but I should go now, to bring him from Amman."

―――――

MICHAEL AND I often used a "good cop, bad cop" routine to throw our interview subjects off balance. They expected him to ask the tough questions. Instead, he played the friendly conciliator, while I raised thorny subjects like 9/11, militant infighting, or the documentary proof we needed to check the veracity of our sources. We felt they would be more forgiving with me, because I'm a woman and I speak Arabic, whereas Michael was an "infidel" who could easily be suspected of spying.

We took this approach with Abu Jihad. I asked about his affiliations with terrorist networks and whether he had been involved in funneling money to fighters, while Michael asked how his time in prison had affected him.

Abu Jihad really was the big boss people made him out to be. He knew everyone. We told him we wanted to meet the young men who'd gone to Iraq. Within an hour, he'd found one of them for us. Every time I feared he was losing interest, I'd ask after his mother and remind him how far Michael and I had come to talk to him.

Abu Jihad asked us to wait while he fetched the young man, who also spoke on the condition that his name and some personal details be withheld. We called him Abu Ibrahim—the name he would have used if he'd ever gotten to fight.

He spoke to us with some trepidation, often glancing at Abu Jihad, as if for permission.

"It's okay, you can tell them everything," Abu Jihad said. "They gave their word that they won't use our real names."

Abu Ibrahim was twenty-four and shy and lanky, with brown eyes. The oldest of the six friends who'd gone to Iraq, he wore white traditional clothes. As a teenager from a secular, middle-class family, he'd played billiards, listened to pop music, and had girlfriends. He had wanted to be a professional soccer player.

"I was just looking to have fun, but I was not alive," Abu Ibrahim said. "I was missing something. I didn't know what it was, but I felt it inside."

Abu Jihad and other more religious men reproached him: *Why are you not praying? Why not follow the rules of God?* Abu Ibrahim and the other young men started going to Abu Anas's mosque and watching videos like the ones Michael and I had seen. He considered his dead friends the lucky ones.

"I'm happy for them, but I cry for myself because I couldn't do it yet," he said. "I want to spread the roots of God on this earth and free the land of occupiers. I don't love anything in this world. What I care about is fighting." Zarqawi had been a hero, he told us, but it was his friends' departure that had convinced him to go to Iraq.

How he and the others got there was a story in itself. They worked with jihadist facilitators who functioned like travel agents, helping connect them to smugglers and giving them the address of a safe house in Iraq.

Abu Ibrahim spoke of his growing disaffection with his parents: "I started to tell them that God wants us to give up our lives for jihad. They didn't like it. They told me, 'You're still too young. Wait.' You know how mothers and fathers are. They didn't want to hear such things."

Carrying only a duffel filled with clothes, he paid eleven dollars for a seat in a shared cab to the Syrian border. The Jordanian border guards didn't ask many questions, he said, and neither did their Syrian counterparts. He showed us his passport, which confirmed he'd entered Syria the previous fall.

He broke after six days in a dark and drafty Syrian jail, telling officials how he'd made his way from a hotel in Damascus to the Iraqi border via bus. His plan had been to find a smuggler who he'd been told could spirit him across the border for $150. But the police dragged him off the bus for questioning, detaining him before he had the chance to find the man.

"Later, they put me in a cell with other prisoners and most of them had been less religious ones, so we, the religious ones, took one corner and we prayed and talked about the Koran," he said.

Three weeks later, the Syrians handed him over to Jordanian authorities. "I became much stronger," he said of his time in prison. "But most of the days I was very upset I didn't arrive, and I pray to God that he will get me what I wish to get."

Back in Zarqa, his parents told him it was enough. God didn't want him to go to Iraq, they said. He should stay home and get married. "It is hard to leave our families," Abu Ibrahim said. "But it is our duty, and if we don't defend our religion who should do it? The old people or the children?"

He had returned to something resembling a normal life, working with his brothers during the day and hanging out with like-minded friends at night. They would visit Islamic websites and talk about the news from Afghanistan, Somalia, and Iraq.

Asked to name his enemies, Abu Ibrahim said, "First, the Shia. Second, the Americans. Third, anywhere in the world where Islam is threatened."

————

THE DAY OUR story was published, when I was back home in Germany, I got a text message from one of the militants we had interviewed in Zarqa. "To the beautiful rose," it read in Arabic. "When I think of you and you are far away, my heart starts bleeding from the pain. The one who sees you once, he will always carry you in his heart."

I was sure he'd sent me the wrong message by mistake. It was embarrassing, so I decided to ignore it. Then a second message arrived. "Why can't I take you to my garden?"

I called him. "Sheikh, I am sorry," I said, "but I am getting some text messages from you, maybe by mistake?"

"Souad, no, I must admit, you are in my thoughts, you have entered my heart. It is a feeling so strong I can't hide it."

I thanked him for his honesty, but I reminded him that he had a beautiful wife and several children, adding, "May God always give them good health." I told him that I was going into a meeting and would have to call him back.

I hung up and called Michael in New York. When I told him about the texts, he started laughing. "You must let us know before it gets serious," he said, "so we can make plans for the wedding in Zarqa."

7

The Value of a Life

Algeria, 2008

In December 2007, militants staged twin suicide truck bombings in Algiers, outside a government building and the United Nations head-quarters, killing 41 and injuring 170. Al Qaeda in the Islamic Maghreb claimed responsibility for the attacks, the latest in a series of ambitious assaults against the government and Western interests in Algeria.

Islamist militants had been active in Algeria for decades, but their affiliation with global jihadist groups like Al Qaeda was relatively recent. A powerful local insurgent movement had existed in Algeria since 1830, when France invaded and colonized the North African country. The Algerians finally won their independence in 1962 after a brutal eight-year war that cost as many as three hundred thousand Algerian lives.

After more than twenty-five years of authoritarian socialism and increasing social unrest, an Islamist party known as the Front Islamique du Salut (FIS) swept the 1991 elections. To hold on to power, the secular Algerian military staged a coup, imposed martial law, and banned and repressed the FIS. In time, the most radical members of the FIS split off and formed the Armed Islamic Group (GIA), which pursued urban guer-rilla actions. At the heart of the GIA were some fifteen hundred Algerian Islamists who had returned home from the battlefields of Afghanistan.

The GIA went to war against the military government, aiming to end the secular state and establish Sharia law, a war that left more than a hundred thousand dead. But by the end of the decade the GIA had splintered; one of the branches, the Salafist Group for Call and Combat (GSPC), turned to kidnapping, smuggling, and human trafficking to bring in cash, but the GSPC soon found itself running low on money and weapons.

In 2004, a GSPC commander named Abdelmalek Droukdal became the group's emir. That fall, he got in touch with Abu Musab al-Zarqawi in Iraq. The Algerians needed support, Droukdal told him. In return, their organization would become an Al Qaeda franchise, operating under the distant leadership of Osama bin Laden. In 2006, the alliance between the GSPC and Al Qaeda became official. A year later, Droukdal announced the group was changing its name to Al Qaeda in the Islamic Maghreb, or AQIM.

This evolution had happened in plain sight, but no journalist had managed to talk to Droukdal or gain deep insight into what quickly became one of Al Qaeda's most powerful regional affiliates. I had been talking to one of Droukdal's deputies, who thought it might be possible for me to interview Droukdal if I came to Algeria. In the spring of 2008, a few months after the Algiers bombings, Michael Moss and I decided to make the trip together.

Michael learned about an American business delegation going to Algeria and asked the organizers if we could tag along. We were curious: Which politicians would the delegation meet? How would they handle security, given the recent attacks and kidnappings? The delegation also offered us some cover, a reason to be in the country so that we could learn more about the militants without arousing undue suspicion from intelligence agencies.

We arrived in Algiers near the end of May and checked into the hotel where the delegation was staying. The Americans were telecom and oil industry executives, most of whom had never been to Algeria before and knew little about its history or recent political upheaval. From their five-star hotel, the country looked peaceful and prosperous.

Two men in the group stood out. They said they ran an Internet company that specialized in telecommunications. It sounded a little vague, but we didn't inquire too deeply. They were tall, handsome, and fit; they spent a lot of time in the hotel gym, and one told me he had previously worked as a hand model. They sought out Michael and me, and sometimes joined us for dinner. The former hand model was especially charming and gentlemanly, opening doors for me and pulling out my chair when we ate together.

Things seemed normal, but I felt certain that we were being watched. I'd been to Algeria before, and I knew that there, as elsewhere in the region, intelligence services took a keen interest in foreign visitors, especially journalists. While reporting on Laid Saidi, the Algerian who had been held alongside Khaled el-Masri in Afghanistan, I'd spoken to Algerian human rights activists and lawyers who advised me never to leave anything in my hotel room. Even while you sleep, they told me, intelligence operatives come in and take things.

I always took precautions after that, and most of the time I carried everything with me. While I was sleeping, I slid my computer, phone, passport, a notebook full of contact numbers, and a flash drive under my pillows before turning in.

Michael and I tried to get rooms next door to each other, but this time, his was at the other end of the corridor. On our second night in the country, we said good night at about 11:00 p.m., and I fell into a sound sleep. Sometime later, I heard the door click open. A very small, soft light floated into the room. After a few seconds, the door closed again, very softly. Exhausted, I quickly fell back asleep. When I woke early the next morning, I thought I must have dreamed it. Then I noticed that the spare notebook I'd left on a table in my room was gone. Fortunately, I hadn't yet written anything in it. That night, before getting into bed, I stacked two chairs against the door.

We spent a few days in Algiers, talking to people about the security situation and joining the American delegation for meetings with Algerian businesspeople and government officials. At one of those gatherings, a government minister insisted that the country was ready for foreign tourism. "Take a car and go to Jijel, go to Boumerdès," he said. "It's very nice, and it's all very safe."

"The minister says we should go and take a look," I told Michael later. "So let's go."

We would travel with our driver and a coordinator from a major international nongovernmental organization, who asked us not to identify his employer. The coordinator, an Algerian, had agreed to take us to the area around Naciria, where AQIM had a presence. Algeria's wealth rarely trickled down, and the locals in Naciria felt forgotten by the central government, which they viewed as corrupt and punitive.

The morning began promisingly, when we managed to shake off the secret police, who had been following us since the day we'd landed in Algiers. These police weren't hard to spot. I'd tell our driver to go around a traffic circle three times, and if a car followed us around all three times, I knew we were being tailed.

On the way to the NGO compound, I told our driver to pull into a gas station. The car behind us passed by and made a U-turn farther down the road. The driver likely thought we would spend a few minutes getting gas. Instead, we quickly pulled out, leaving the other car behind. The police eventually found their way to the NGO compound and waited outside, but the place had two exits, and we left through a different gate than the one we'd come in.

Naciria was more than an hour north of the capital, in the direction of the mountains. I'd made contact with my source in AQIM, a commander in charge of the group's media operations, to let him know we'd be in the area, but we didn't schedule an appointment. If we met, it would be on short notice so as not to alert the authorities, who might be watching.

My source and I had devised what seemed, at the time, a novel and safe way to communicate. We avoided the phone completely. At first, we had been in touch by regular email. But at some point, worried about government surveillance, he and I had set up a joint email account using a German provider. We both had the log-in and password, which meant that we never had to send each other a message. Instead, as former CIA director David Petraeus and his mistress would do years later, we wrote emails and left them in the drafts folder, where each of us could log in and read them.

As an Algerian, our friend from the NGO felt a personal connection to the communities he helped, and he was outraged by the economic inequality in the area we were visiting. He told us that young Algerians particularly resented the government's penchant for importing Chinese workers instead of using local labor.

On the way to Naciria, we stopped to talk to some of his colleagues, who were handing out children's clothing and groceries to poor families. One of the recipients was a woman with a mentally challenged son about four or five years old. Her husband had died, and she said there were no services for her child and that she didn't get any support from the government. If it weren't for the NGO, she told us, she wouldn't be able to feed her children. Dilemmas like these, our guide told us, were part of what convinced boys from poor families to join AQIM. People had nothing, and they didn't trust the government to take care of them.

Our driver was a bit nervous about the trip to Naciria. He didn't ordinarily work with journalists but had recently lost his job, so he was helping us out. I told him to keep his ID cards and car registry documents ready in the well under the radio. If the police stopped us, he was to let me do the talking.

For security reasons and so as not to get our guide in trouble, we'd taken two cars. That way, if we wanted to stay on and do interviews after the NGO workers left, we wouldn't inconvenience them. Michael and I sat in the backseat of the first car, a white Renault, while our driver and the NGO coordinator sat in front. The VW bus behind us, packed with food and clothes, carried the Algerian woman and two Algerian men who had been handing out aid. They were locals who had worked with the organization for many years.

By then, it must have been about midday. We were driving toward Boumerdès when we saw a police checkpoint. An officer stopped us and asked our driver for his identity papers.

The driver opened the door and started to move his right hand down his back, as if he were reaching for something in his back pocket.

"Stop! Don't move!" the policeman yelled, pointing his AK-47 at the driver, his finger on the trigger.

"Please don't shoot!" I screamed. I turned to the driver. "You idiot, what are you doing with your hand?"

"I have the documents in my back pocket," he said.

"The idiot has the documents in his back pocket," I shouted to the policeman. Then I heard Michael say my name slowly in a worried voice. Turning toward him, I saw that his hands were raised and that another policeman was pointing an AK-47 at his head. To my right, yet another policeman was pointing an assault rifle at me. I also put my hands up and screamed at the driver, "You idiot! Didn't I tell you to keep them in front? Do you want to kill us?"

I knew we were in mortal danger. The police were nervous and trigger-happy. I screamed at the driver because I was scared but also because I suspected that if the police saw a man taking orders from a woman, they would know he wasn't a jihadi. I turned to the policemen and said, "It's okay, officers and friends! We aren't terrorists." They looked a little surprised, and I thought, *Yes, who the hell would say this to the police?* "This idiot driver has his documents in his back pocket, so please, if you need to see them, he has to reach behind him."

They finally allowed him to get out of the car and searched him while we waited. Armed police still surrounded us. Then they asked him to open the trunk. "These people in the car with you, are they foreigners?" the police asked.

"Yes, yes, they are foreigners," he replied.

"That's it, friend," I whispered to Michael. "We're done."

"You need to come to the police station," one of the cops said. He asked Michael to move over so he could sit in back with us.

One police car led the way and the other drove behind the second car in our convoy. I was more worried for the Algerians, our driver, and the NGO workers than for us.

"Do you speak English?" I asked the policeman sitting with us.

"No," he answered in Arabic.

I turned to Michael and told him in English that we would now be taken to the police station. Still speaking English, we agreed to try to ask as many questions of the police as possible while not revealing immediately that we were journalists. We also agreed that we would take full responsibility for keeping the locals out of trouble.

"So what were you guys doing here?" the police chief asked when we got to the station.

I said that we were traveling with this NGO, which was helping us to learn about its work and the area.

"Here? In this region? Are you out of your mind?"

I translated to Michael, who said, "Okay, keep asking them why."

"Why? What's wrong with this region?" I asked.

"Lady, this is Al Qaeda land. Don't you know we are having lots of attacks here?"

"Really? Who is attacking you?"

"Al Qaeda in the Islamic Maghreb. Droukdal and his people," the police chief said.

"You got Al Qaeda here?" I tried to play naïve.

"Yes, of course. You see these pictures here?" He turned around and motioned toward three pictures, each showing the face of a different man. "These are my men, who have been killed by Al Qaeda. But wait. First let me ask, who are you?"

He began with the Algerians, asking for their ID cards and affiliations. When he got to Michael, he asked me, "Is he American or what? And you?" I told him my name and said that I was a German citizen.

"Mukhnet?" he asked.

"No, no, Mekhennet."

"Yes, Mukhnet. Where does this name come from?"

I gave up trying to get him to pronounce my name correctly. When I told him I was Moroccan German, he turned to the Algerian NGO workers.

"Are you guys crazy or what, bringing a Moroccan woman and an American man to this area?" he asked.

I interrupted, trying to deflect his anger from the Algerians. "Sir, they didn't bring us. We asked them to take us. We wanted to see the region here and the work these NGOs are doing." I didn't lie, but of course also didn't tell him that we knew the region had suffered from terrorism.

"Wanted to see the region? And if anything happens to you guys? Lady, you don't know these people. They will kidnap you and force you to marry one of them and ask for ransom for the American, and then I will have his president and your king asking for my head."

We all started laughing.

"That's nothing to laugh about," he said in an angry voice. "Maybe I should take you guys downstairs and give you some chickpeas. Would you like to eat some chickpeas?"

The Algerian NGO workers grew very quiet and looked at the ground. I translated to Michael: "Wow, he asks if we want to eat chickpeas."

I turned to the police chief. I was excited about eating chickpeas, the way I knew them from my childhood in Morocco. My grandmother would sometimes cook chickpeas and add cumin and a bit of salt for me.

"That would be great," I said. "Do you make them with cumin?"

This time he was the one who burst out laughing, along with the other police.

I turned to our driver and the other Algerians and asked if they wanted chickpeas, too, but one of them whispered: " 'Chickpeas' is the code word here for beatings."

The police chief then asked who we worked for.

"We are journalists and we work for the New York Times," Michael said. When I began to translate, the chief interrupted me.

"Have I understood well? You are reporters for the New York Times?"

"Yes," Michael said.

The chief stood up. "I don't believe it. This would have been the perfect gift for these terrorists, kidnapping two journalists from an American media outlet."

He asked one of his officers to contact the Ministry of the Interior in Algiers and tell them where we were. Then he told us to go back to the capital. The police drove us to the edge of Naciria. From there, a dark blue Toyota tailed us all the way back to Algiers.

Several days earlier we'd submitted a request to extend our visas. I couldn't imagine our arrest would help. "I think the Algerians will throw us out of here," I told Michael.

To our great surprise, when we reached Algiers, we learned that the extensions had been granted. It didn't make sense.

We were still hoping to find a way to interview Droukdal in person. That evening, Michael called me in my room and said that I should come outside quickly and bring all my equipment. "Bring your phone and computer. We will need some time here."

We met on the hotel terrace. Michael told me that he had just received a phone call from our editors in New York. An FBI agent had come to the *New York Times* office and reported that there was a threat against Michael's life. The agent didn't get into specifics but said it was related to the work we were doing and came from somebody with ties to the militants.

"And what about me?" I asked. "We always work on these stories together, so if there is a threat against you, there must be one against my life as well."

Michael called the FBI agent in front of me, but the agent said there had been no threat against my life. He strongly advised Michael to get out of Algeria but said that I wouldn't have to leave.

"So we need to decide," Michael said. "I could leave, and you could stay and finish the job; or we both stay; or we both leave."

"This doesn't make any sense," I told him. "Why would they threaten you but not me? Both our names are at the top of these stories."

"Maybe it's one of these guys who wants to marry you and who is jealous," Michael said half-jokingly. But I didn't buy it.

We decided that I should reach out to some of the people we'd interviewed in the past to see if they knew anything. Had we upset the jihadists? But if we had, they would be after me as well.

I called Abu Jihad in Zarqa, using my satellite phone, and asked what was going on. I talked to Zarqawi's supporters in Jordan and the guys from the camps in Lebanon. "Do you have anything against my colleague?" I asked. They all said no.

Then I contacted my AQIM source through our email account. "We learned that there is a threat against my colleague's life," I wrote. "Do you have anything against him?"

"We have nothing against you or your colleague," he wrote back. "But you should leave the country for your own sake. Something is wrong here, and it's not coming from us."

I told Michael that I couldn't guarantee his safety if we stayed, and that I didn't want to stay either. "This stinks," I told him. "Let's get the hell out of this place."

We called our editors in New York, who told us there was an Alitalia flight leaving for Rome in three hours.

We ran back to our rooms, packed, and left Algeria. I spent the flight running through the list of people we had interviewed in my head. Who would have had a reason to threaten Michael? For days I wondered why this threat had surfaced on the same day Michael and I had been detained. Something was off, but we concentrated on finishing the story.

I was still determined to interview Droukdal and his group and also to give them the chance to answer some of the allegations against them.

"Are you and your colleague safe? Are you out of Algeria?" our contact person inside the group asked me in a draft message the next day.

"Yes we are," I wrote back. "Now how about we get you the questions for the head of your group and you guys send us back the answers, on your letterhead and with a recording of his voice?"

"I can't promise anything, but I can try."

Michael and I worked on a list of questions, and I sent them to my contact. "It is very important that we get the answers on tape so we can hear his voice," we told him in our message. We also wanted a statement from Droukdal on camera, with the date, which we would use for verification but wouldn't publish, and if possible the whole interview in writing.

Ten days later, I received a link to a Dropbox account. The link was valid for only an hour or two. When I clicked on it, I found the text of the interview, the voice recording, and the video clip we'd asked for. The group also sent us a message on stationery stamped with the Al Qaeda in the Islamic Maghreb letterhead, acknowledging that the group had received questions from the "honorable journalist Souad Mekhennet, who works for the *New York Times*."

Droukdal had answered all our questions. A university graduate who had studied mathematics, his voice was surprisingly soft. We worked some of what he said into an article and decided to publish the interview transcript as well.

After our story ran, AQIM continued to grow. The group was active in Mali, where a militant Islamist takeover of key cities would spur a French military intervention in 2013. Today, officials in Europe and the United States view it as one of the world's most dangerous terrorist outfits. Droukdal is still alive and still at the helm.

The reporting had been a success, but our experience in Algeria and the alleged threat against Michael's life hung over us like a shadow. We understood that if the threat was genuine, it could signal the end of our reporting on jihadists.

I checked with some of my intelligence sources to see if they knew anything. About two weeks after our story ran, I received a call from a European intelligence source. He said it was urgent, and he needed to see me. "It's related to the question you asked some weeks ago about your colleague," he said.

I talked to my editor Matt Purdy, and we decided that I should meet with the intelligence official. Two days later, at a small restaurant in the city where my source worked, he leaned across the table and whispered, "I just want you to know, in case you go back to North Africa, that you were followed from the beginning by a hit team."

"What do you mean? Whose hit team?"

"The CIA, NSA, you name it. They were all following you."

I thought it must be a joke, but his face was serious. "But why hit teams?" I responded. "And what's with that threat against my colleague's life?" I thought back on all the meetings we'd had at the U.S. embassy in Algiers, with the group of American businessmen who had traveled there. Which of them had been working for the intelligence services? I remembered the handsome American men from the little telecom company who had always tried to sit with us at dinner. But I still didn't understand. Why this ominous threat against Michael's life?

"They wanted your colleague to be out of the danger zone because he's American. They were thinking you would finish the job, so they would follow you."

I was stunned. Had these U.S. agencies been hoping I would lead them to Droukdal? If their goal was to kill him, would they have killed me, too? How far would they have gone to get to the leader of Al Qaeda in the Islamic Maghreb?

"Was my life in danger?" I asked.

The source nodded, then hedged. "Well, I don't know if they would have gone that far," he said. "But they were all over you in Algeria."

I knew that most European and U.S. intelligence agencies worked closely together. "That means you were, too," I said.

He was silent.

My own country had to be involved as well. Would the German government so willingly sacrifice one of its citizens in exchange for a counterterrorism victory? I didn't know the answer, but I was worried. Back home, I Googled the name of the company the two handsome Americans had said they owned and found a single, vague entry. I shut down the messaging system I'd established with my AQIM source in Algeria. I now think those online communications were what put me on the intelligence services' radar.

I went over everything again in my head. Did they really want Michael out because he was American, and was my life expendable because I wasn't? Did Germany consider me a second-class citizen because I was a Muslim and my parents were immigrants?

My jihadi sources often argued that in the calculus of the West, Muslim lives mattered less than Western ones. For a moment I asked myself if they were right and whether what had happened to me was proof. "Sympathy" would be too strong a word for what I was feeling, but I appreciated their anger and understood their point of view in a newly visceral way. I felt helpless and angry myself. It stank of hypocrisy, the same charge the jihadis leveled against Western societies all the time. They thought I would lead them to Droukdal. They wanted to use me as bait to capture or kill him. I would have been caught in the middle. Anything could have happened.

Algeria was the last reporting trip Michael and I took together. Because of the threat, he was pulled off the jihadist beat. He started working on food security, and in 2010 he won a Pulitzer Prize. "Look how often you and I risked our lives to bring those stories home, and to explain to people what was happening in the world, and we didn't win even one award," Michael said when I called to congratulate him. "I won the Pulitzer for stories about peanuts and meat."

I told my editors at the *Times* that I felt some intelligence services posed a greater threat to my safety than the jihadists did. A few months later, I met an American intelligence operative at a conference in an Arab country. I got the feeling that he knew more about me than I did about him. After we'd talked a few times, I asked if he knew anything about what had happened in Algeria.

"Look, there was a time when people had questions about you," he told me. "You had access to people who were on most-wanted lists and people wondered if you were a sympathizer. We later understood that you were doing it because you believed in journalism, but people wondered before, what's behind her drive to reach all these guys?" He confirmed that my family background and religion had led some to question my motives.

I began to be deeply worried that the way I was trying to do my job—not taking any side but speaking to all sides and challenging them all whenever I could—was becoming untenable for someone with my background. Could this kind of impartial journalism about jihadists and the War on Terror be safely practiced in the West only by someone whose parents had been born and raised there, rather than someone whose Muslim descent made her an object of special interest and suspicion? How much longer would I be able to do this kind of reporting?

These were dark thoughts that made me question the foundations and ultimate success of the West's supposed openness to outsiders and its commitment to freedom of speech and thought.

8

Guns and Roses

Pakistan, 2009

Working with American colleagues who were married with children had made me realize that I, too, wanted to find a partner and build a family—and definitely not with some jihadist sheikh looking for a second or third wife. After long, exhausting days in strange faraway places, I sometimes overheard my coworkers sharing their experiences with their spouses. Meanwhile, I was always trying to keep the truth about what I'd seen or heard or felt as vague as possible when I talked to my parents, my brother, and my sisters.

But finding a partner wasn't easy for me, as jihad followed me into my private life. After the Algeria debacle, I arranged to spend some time in New York, working out of the *Times* headquarters. I wanted to get to know my fellow reporters and editors better and improve my English, which was my fourth language after Arabic, German, and French.

My American friends seized the opportunity for matchmaking. Some arranged dinners to introduce me to "accomplished Arab Americans"; another signed me up for a website where I could supposedly meet Arab singles from around the world. All went well—until the men found out who I was and Googled my articles.

Some hated what I was doing and accused me of making Islam or

Arabs "look bad"; others sent messages full of compliments but noted that "what you are doing is so brave but also dangerous."

The man who wrote those words was an American-born engineer of Arab descent whom I'd met online. A friend had set up a profile for me, entering answers to questions about my preferences and whether I wanted to get married and have kids. (The answer to both was yes.)

There was no picture of me on my profile page, and I never sent my picture to anyone I met on the site. I wrote that I was of Arab-European descent and worked in media, without specifying where. I said I was independent and hardworking, that I liked to listen to music, that I liked long walks and art museums and went to the movies and read a lot, and that I was a very social person. When one man I met on the site learned who I was, he asked if by "social" I meant that I liked to meet jihadists.

Even before I got responses like that, I had mixed feelings about online dating. I didn't feel at home in that world, and separating the normal people from the nuts was time-consuming. But the friend who set up my profile told me that half her friends in America had met their partners online. "This is the new thing," she said. I thought it might be worth a try.

As with any dating site, some men were looking for a fling. I immediately deleted those messages. But some guys seemed more serious. An engineer I was talking to seemed well-mannered, friendly, and open-minded. He said he wanted an equal partnership. When I first told him I was a journalist, he seemed excited. He said he liked women with strong views, who were engaged in world events. He didn't mind a woman working or traveling, but when I finally told him my name (after chatting with him anonymously for nearly three months), he felt differently. Instead of the light conversation we'd shared before, his tone grew more stilted.

If I'd traveled the world to cover environmental issues or fashion, none of it would have been an issue. But this guy worked for the U.S. government. I interpreted his message as a way of saying good-bye. We dropped out of touch.

I never met the engineer in person, but I did have coffee with a wealthy Arab-American businessman whom I'd also first met online. He flew to

New York to meet me. On our way back to my office, a man accidentally bumped into me on the street. He said he was sorry, but the businessman was furious. "You should really apologize to her," he told the man. I assured him that everything was fine and that the man had already apologized. But I also thought, *I can speak for myself just fine.*

My colleague Michael Moss worried about me in his brotherly way. He and a *Times* researcher and friend convinced me to let them run background checks on the men who wanted to meet me, including the businessman. It turned out that he'd been arrested a couple of times for beating his ex-wife.

When he contacted me again online, I told him I didn't think we were a good fit. He seemed perplexed. "Why?" he wrote. "We had a nice coffee. I thought we had something." I told him I knew about the domestic violence arrests and asked him not to contact me again.

I felt I was wasting my time. Like most people, I wanted a steady and loving partner who understood me and appreciated my quirks. I knew that if I had children, my work might change, but I wanted to be with someone who would be proud of how I have built my career, not afraid or ashamed.

"What happened to all these people who say, 'Behind a strong man is a strong woman'?" I asked myself and all my girlfriends. "Where are they?"

My friend Mahvish pointed something out to me. "You're a badass in your job," she said, "but with guys, you're just too nice." I certainly felt pressure not to intimidate men with details about my day job. The fact is that many men have set ideas about women who work in the field I do. It was hard for the men I met to see me as anything but a thrill seeker or some kind of bizarre female action hero. Many were drawn to what they saw as the glamorous side of my work, but they were often surprised to learn that I also cooked, cleaned, and liked wearing nice clothes and going out with friends, or that I wanted to have children. It seemed impossible for them to hold all these ideas in their heads at once. The jihadis who said they wanted to marry me didn't get it, either. For them, I was little more than a curiosity.

As usual, work came to my rescue. In 2009, the *Times* sent me to Pak-

istan to look into the networks that had trained and helped the perpetrators of the attacks in Mumbai in November 2008, in which more than
160 people were killed at two luxury hotels, a train station, a Jewish center, and a hospital. The sole surviving shooter had given information to the
Indian police about the planning and coordination of the attacks that the
Times wanted to investigate.

I'd heard so much about Pakistan from prisoners and jihadists that I
was eager to explore it. But I had a lot to learn about the country and culture, which were very different from the Arab states I'd visited. This
time, I didn't speak the local languages, and I wasn't sure what to expect.
Pakistan is formally a democracy (albeit one that has had several extended
periods of military rule), but in recent decades Islamist groups have
grown more influential, establishing seminaries in which they promote
an ideological worldview. The seminaries, many of them cheap or free,
are often the best options for poor and working-class families to educate
their children. Meanwhile, the country's oligarchic power structure and
weak democratic institutions have helped strengthen Islamist movements.

One of my sources told me to look up a journalist named Jamal, who
had previously worked for Al Jazeera. Jamal had also covered the Taliban and Al Qaeda for several Arab papers. When I met him, he was living in Islamabad, where he ran a film and TV production company. He
became a trusted friend and a reliable adviser, and he helped connect me
to militants, civil society, and the Pakistani military and intelligence
services.

I would return to Pakistan nearly a dozen times over the next eighteen months for the *Times* and to make a documentary for the German
TV channel ZDF. On one of those trips, I managed to snag an interview
with a senior Taliban commander who belonged to the powerful Quetta
shura, led by the one-eyed Taliban leader Mullah Omar.

Like my meeting with the ISIS commander on the Turkish-Syrian
border several years later, the logistics of that meeting were complicated:
don't bring any recording devices; make sure no one follows you; once in
our car, you must take the battery out of your mobile. I was told that the
Taliban commander would choose the place. "It could be the last meal—
maybe a drone, maybe a special commando, you never know," the contact

man had told me. I waited for him to laugh after he had said it, but the expression on his face was serious. He ran his right hand through his black beard and said, "*Insha'Allah khair*"—God willing, all will be well.

My dinner date was a wanted man. He had to be extremely cautious, as did I. The meeting took place in Karachi, the city where the Jewish-American *Wall Street Journal* reporter Daniel Pearl had been kidnapped and killed in 2002. All my contact gave me was the name of a road and a description of the place where my car should stop and wait.

The Taliban commander had asked for the make, model, and color of the car, along with the plate number. My driver, Adnan, normally worked for tourists and visiting schoolteachers. When I handed him a sheet of paper with the names and phone numbers of two people and told him to call them if I didn't return in three hours, he blanched.

"I will stay here and wait for you," he insisted.

I told him that he should leave when the other car arrived. "No, no. I cannot leave you here alone. This is a side road leading to the highway," he said, pointing out the window. "And it is dark. You are crazy. This is dangerous."

Soon afterward, a car stopped behind us. The headlights were on and my phone was ringing. "I've got to go, Adnan," I said, climbing out of the car. "Please leave now."

I walked back to the other car, a new dark blue Mercedes with tinted windows. The door was opened for me and I got in. Inside, the Taliban commander was smiling. "Why is your car stopped?" he asked me in Arabic. "There is no need for your driver to wait. We'll take you back. Tell him to go."

As I phoned Adnan, all I could think about was that my editor at the *Times* was going to kick my butt if I got kidnapped by the Taliban so soon after my colleague David Rohde had escaped after more than seven months in Taliban captivity. That morning, Michael had sent me a link to the first part of Rohde's account of his imprisonment, which had just been published on the *Times* website. After hanging up with Adnan, I switched off the phone and took out the battery, as agreed. In the car I sat quietly, looking out the window and wondering if I'd made the wrong choice.

"Are you comfortable?" the commander asked. He must have noticed my nervousness. "Are you worried that some of your colleagues are going to ask how it is that you are meeting with us?"

This was insightful. Since my first days in Pakistan, some journalists had suspected that I might be a spy, and some militants had similar suspicions about me. I also knew from my time in Algeria that I could add several Western governments to that list. Someone in the Pakistani army spokesperson's office had told me he'd heard from some Arab reporters that I was Moroccan, and that in Morocco "there are a lot of Jews." They surmised that because I worked for American newspapers, I was also working for the CIA and Mossad. But most of my colleagues were simply worried about my safety. Western reporters in Pakistan, as in other conflict zones, are limited in their movements and access. The danger is great. Many news organizations depend on Pakistani stringers to cover everything outside the big cities.

I noticed that our driver seemed jumpy, his eyes moving erratically between the open road ahead and his rearview mirror. I tried to talk to him but he spoke neither English nor Arabic, and I don't speak Urdu or Pashto. Soon we had left the center of Karachi and were passing through neighborhoods with few lights. I stared out the window, trying to discern where we were going. I heard the sheikh open a bottle and start spraying something in the car. "Maybe the air is not good," he said. "You look very pale." The smell of roses and musk filled the car.

I couldn't believe it. I was worrying about whether I would survive, and this guy was spraying perfume. The night grew darker as we passed through the Karachi suburbs. Finally, the commander's assistant, who was sitting next to the driver, turned around and said in English, "Don't worry, we won't kidnap you this time. It's just that the sheikh would like to invite you for good barbecue, and the best places are by the highway." The assistant laughed and translated his words into Pashto for the driver, who started laughing as well.

It was after 11:00 p.m. when we arrived at the restaurant. The commander was skeptical of reporters, and he asked me many questions about my family, my goals, and my faith. I told him that my parents were Muslim and that I'd grown up in Europe. When he asked if I was married or had kids, I said no.

I, too, had a long list of questions, mainly about his thoughts on the new American president, Barack Obama, and the U.S. presence in Afghanistan.

"You know," he said, "Obama has no say in what his country does. It's the lobbies and other people. He has promised a lot, too much. But we are not expecting any changes."

I asked him what exactly he meant.

"If America and the West really want to have peace with the Muslim world, they have to change their global attitude and their arrogant way of pushing their interests. We don't see any changes. Obama is the same as Bush, only in black."

"Then what has to happen for peace?"

"We have nothing against the United States," he said. "We just don't like people telling us how to live." The West had forced the Taliban from power, but the commander believed that he and his comrades would retake Afghanistan.

I looked at the three men, all of whom sat across the table from me. "But what would that mean for women?" I asked. "For example, would I still be able to do my job if the Taliban were in power?"

The translator laughed, and soon the others joined him. The sheikh answered in Arabic. "Souad, choose the color of the burka, and no problem: you can go on with journalism." He was referring to the garment worn by many women in Afghanistan, and required under the Taliban, which covers the body from head to toe, including the face, leaving only a small latticework opening for the eyes.

"I don't like to wear the burka. The Koran doesn't tell a woman to cover her face."

"Yes, Souad, you are right. The Koran doesn't say that women have to wear the burka or cover their faces, but this is the tradition in some areas, and shouldn't it be up to the people to decide?"

"So then shouldn't the women decide if they want to wear the burka or not?" I countered. "Yet it seems you don't give them the option."

"Each finger on your hand is different," the commander said, smiling. "And it is the same with us. Not every Talib has the same opinion on how women should be. I personally like intelligent, strong women."

Soon the food appeared: grilled chicken, lamb kabobs, yogurt, rice with raisins, onion rings, potatoes, lentil daal, and greens. It was a feast, too much for four people.

I had been taking notes, but now the sheikh said, "Stop writing. It is time for the important questions now. Let's talk about life. You know, Sister Souad, I am also looking for a second wife. I've heard many good things about German women. I heard they read the wishes off their husband's lips. I think you are ready for this."

I immediately thought about the jihadist from Zarqa who had tried to woo me with text messages, or the time I'd unwittingly joked about marrying Shaker al-Abssi's son-in-law. This time I decided to play dumb. "I can't speak on their behalf because I'm not really German," I said in English. "My father is Moroccan and my mother is Turkish. But I think you've been reading fairy tales."

The sheikh listened to the translation. "Well yes, but there are also German women who have a Muslim background," he said.

"Sheikh, honestly, don't you think one woman is headache enough?"

"Yes, you're probably right. One is already headache enough," he said good-naturedly. "More wives, more headaches. It's good to have more children, though. Of course I would not take a second wife if my wife didn't give me the okay. But she would like to have someone else to help with the housework."

Great, I thought.

The commander, meanwhile, kept piling food onto my plate and his. "I want an intelligent wife," he continued. "The Prophet Muhammad had strong women, and a strong wife can make a strong leader."

I'll admit I was surprised to hear that.

"Let me ask you this," he continued. "How many people sleep around and are unmarried? Don't you think we are more honest? We don't just screw the girl. We marry her. We take care of her. We are not trying to hurt women. Allah frowns upon that. Souad, you should think about this. We have some very strong men in the leadership. They would love to get married to someone like you."

Again I dodged. My parents would have the last say, I said. It was an excuse that had always worked in the past.

All three men were working through their food, breaking pieces of bread and using them to scoop up the rice and meat. Though the sheikh said it wasn't as spicy as usual, I felt my tongue start to burn. I drank one glass of water after another, trying to put out the fire, and left most of the food on my plate. It was really delicious, I told them, but I had eaten already. Finally, the sheikh took my plate and finished my dinner. "That is a big honor," the translator noted.

"I do not eat off everyone's plate," the sheikh said. "Today we didn't invite you as a journalist. We invited you as someone we respect."

These shifts—from fear to familiarity, from the brink of disaster to a moment of warm acceptance as a human being, not as a potential enemy— were unnerving. After dinner, we stopped at a remote gas station along the highway. A man with a long beard approached on a motorcycle. He was carrying a gun and a bag covered with dark red flowers. For a second, I thought what a funny picture it would be: guns and roses.

The translator gave the bag to the Taliban commander, who handed it to me. "I cannot accept this," I said, wondering where the man on the motorcycle had come from and how long he had been waiting.

"You have to accept this, unless you want us to kidnap you," the commander said. Our journalistic code of ethics doesn't allow us to accept gifts, but there was no way my editor would punish me for taking this one.

"Thank you," I said, taking the bag from him. "And give my respect to your wife."

"Remember when you go back to Germany to look for a good candidate for me," he said with a slight smile.

Once back at the guesthouse in Karachi where I was staying, I called Adnan, who had been waiting frantically to find out if I was safe, and returned the calls of worried friends who hadn't been able to reach me. Then I went upstairs to my room and opened the bag. In it were perfumed oil and red and green decorative stones. I stared at the bag and tried to understand. I knew it was probably just exhaustion, but the whole evening was already beginning to seem like a dream—a strange, surreal dream. Yet when I awoke the next morning there they were: my gifts from the Taliban.

A month later, after a short break, I returned to Pakistan, this time to Islamabad, the capital. I contacted the Taliban commander, and he again mentioned that he was looking for a second wife. I told him about a dream I'd had of him with two lambs, and that it might mean his wife was pregnant with twins. He laughed and said that she was indeed pregnant, but that she wasn't having twins.

He asked if I thought the child would be a boy or a girl. I said a boy. He said that if he became a father of twin girls, he would name one after me. We laughed.

When we talked next, a few months later, he told me that his wife had indeed had twins. He sounded tired. "When you were a little baby, did you cry during the night and during the day?"

"I think I was a very nice baby," I said.

"How do you know?"

"I just know."

Later, he invited me to meet his wife and children. Proudly, he showed me his cache of U.S. Army boots, sunglasses, field beds, and Special Forces jackets, which he'd bought on the black market in Peshawar. "We are happy because we know that they cannot win the war," he said, standing amid his booty.

They gave me the baby who cried during the night to hold. She slept peacefully in my arms.

"She is crying all the night," the commander said. "She wants all the attention. I have named her Souad."

———

WHENEVER I GOT back to Islamabad after an excursion, I went to Jamal's office to catch up. One afternoon, after a trip to Quetta, a low-slung city near the Afghan border, I stopped by to say hello. Jamal had visitors, and he invited me to join them. I sat in a corner of the room sipping my tea and listened to one of the three men, who had come from Waziristan, a tribal region in northwestern Pakistan that had been a haven for the Taliban. The man introduced himself as Kareem Khan and said he was a journalist. He spoke Arabic and was cursing the United States. "The only choice one has is jihad against them, and to kill Americans," he said.

I had been listening for years to the same expressions of hatred, the same blame game that seemed to stretch from Pakistan to Iraq to Lebanon and Jordan. In fact, during my recent trip to Quetta, I'd met a group of Taliban fighters who told me they hated America because of its occupation of Afghanistan and its penchant for drone strikes in the Pakistani borderlands, especially places such as Waziristan.

"What would the Americans do if we went to the United States and told them how to live, or how not to?" one of the fighters had fulminated.

I reminded him that the United States invaded Afghanistan after the September 11 attacks.

"So, what, did Afghanistan attack the United States?"

"People who were trained in camps in Afghanistan did," I answered. "And the Taliban refused to hand over Osama bin Laden."

The men looked at me angrily and said something in Pashto that I couldn't understand. "Mullah Omar was very clear," one of the men told me. "He said, 'Show us the evidence that bin Laden was behind it; as long as there is no evidence, he will be a protected guest.' That's how our customs are."

I was about to challenge them further, but I sensed the spirit of the meeting had changed. While at first they had smiled a bit, their faces now looked stern. "If you were American, we would kidnap you," one finally said.

This time I didn't feel like backing off. "Why do you want to kill Americans?" I asked Khan.

He seemed surprised. "Because they are killing us with these drones. They killed some of my family members," he said, "and they had nothing to do with the Taliban." He told me he had lost his son and his brother in a drone strike that had also destroyed his house.

I knew, of course, that the United States was using drones to fight militancy in Waziristan and other areas in Pakistan. The CIA had been attacking the Pakistani border region with drones since 2004, hoping to kill Al Qaeda and Taliban fighters hiding there. But the bombs did not always hit their intended targets. It was horrible that innocent people were killed, and yet I felt I needed to somehow defend my American friends. I had editors and colleagues of all faiths who had supported me, even when they'd felt the sting of jihadi violence against their friends and in their own cities.

"Most Americans are not bad. They don't even know what happened to you and your family," I told him. "You cannot hold them all responsible for the actions of their government."

He disagreed. Americans surely knew that their government was killing "innocent people" like his relatives. I asked if he or his son or brother had ever belonged to the Taliban, Al Qaeda, or other militant groups. He said they hadn't and that many other innocents had been killed in drone strikes as well.

"This is the reason why many more people will now join the Taliban," he went on. "Because the Americans kill us. We have no choice but to fight back."

"Still, believe me, the majority of Americans don't know about what you are saying. Joining terrorist organizations is not a solution," I told him.

"You call them terrorists. What America is doing to us is terrorism as well! But Muslim lives don't matter to the West."

These were well-worn accusations, but I knew the reality was more complicated. I wanted him to know how many people in the United States were fighting injustice and had worked to help Khaled el-Masri and others who'd been treated unfairly. "I'm sure if people knew about what happened to your family and others, they would try to help," I told him.

"How would they help?" He looked as if he didn't believe a word I was saying.

I told him about the el-Masri case and how the *New York Times*, an American newspaper, had been the first to tell his story. Moreover, the editors had allowed me, a Muslim woman, to tell it, even though there'd been plenty of risks involved if I got it wrong. I told him about the reporting that other American papers, such as the *Washington Post*, had done on torture by the U.S. intelligence services and how many American lawyers had offered to help torture victims pro bono.

He listened carefully. "What is pro bono?"

I told him there were many lawyers who worked on such cases for no money because they objected to human rights violations. "I'm sure there are many lawyers in the United States who would help if they knew about how many civilians were killed in drone strikes," I told him. "Most Americans respect the rule of law."

He said he had to leave for his next meeting. I feared that he still believed fighting was the only choice. I wondered how we would ever break this cycle.

Weeks later, back in Germany, I came home from the gym one day and found my sister Hannan, with whom I share an apartment, watching the news. I'm not sure whether it was CNN or the BBC, but I remember what she said when I walked in: "You're just in time. They're about to interview someone who wants to sue the CIA for drone strikes in Waziristan."

I went to the kitchen to get a bottle of water, then hurried back to catch the interview. I swallowed a gulp of water, but when I saw the face of the man suing the CIA, I spit it all out.

"What's wrong?" Hannan asked. "You look like you've seen a ghost."

"I know that guy. I met him some weeks ago in Islamabad."

The TV reporter said that a Pakistani man named Kareem Khan had a list of all the innocents killed in U.S. drone strikes and that he planned to sue the U.S. government and the CIA.

"Didn't he tell you about his plans to sue?" my sister asked.

"No. I don't think he had any idea himself."

I called a colleague in the *Times* Washington bureau and told him about the conversation I'd had with Khan in Islamabad.

He burst out laughing. "It's very nice that you wanted to defend the people in the United States and our justice system," he said. He added that it was Khan's right to sue and that we should keep watching the story.

A couple of weeks after this, Khan's Pakistani lawyer filed a complaint that included the name of the CIA station chief in Pakistan. This was a jaw-dropping development, and it turned Khan's accusations into a major international incident. In a place like Pakistan, where the drone campaign had fueled anti-American sentiment, revealing the name of the CIA station chief put his life at risk. He was immediately withdrawn from the country. We soon learned that U.S. officials were blaming Pakistan's military intelligence agency, Inter-Services Intelligence (ISI), for Khan's lawsuit.

Some weeks later, when I was in Pakistan on another reporting trip, I requested a meeting with Ahmad Shuja Pasha, the head of the ISI. The agency's spokesman, Zafar Iqbal, always attended such meetings and took notes on the conversation. Journalists called Zafar "Mr. Ponytail" because he had one, making him a rarity among clean-cut Pakistani security men.

When I arrived at the ISI's offices, I greeted both men and observed that General Pasha looked very tired.

"General, how are things?" I asked.

"Well, if we speak about our relationship with the United States, it is very bad. Actually, I can't remember when it had been as bad as it is now."

"Really? Why?"

"We got used to them blaming us for the Taliban. We got used to them accusing us of supporting bin Laden. But now they're saying we told this farmer from Waziristan to sue them. And we really have nothing to do with it."

I started to feel very uncomfortable. "So is it that bad?"

"It's one of the worst situations between us, ever," he said. He shook his head, sat back, and sighed deeply. I could see the dark circles under his eyes. "I have no idea who told this guy to sue them, but it wasn't us."

"Yes, I believe you," I blurted out.

Zafar looked up from taking notes. "You believe us? You never believe us that easily. Why would you now?"

I decided to keep my mouth shut and suggested we move on to other topics.

After the meeting, Zafar walked me back to my car. "I don't know why," he said, "but I get the feeling you know more about this drone lawsuit than you're letting on."

I smiled and said good-bye.

— 9 —

Mukhabarat

Egypt, 2011

As the car entered the parking lot of the high-security intelligence facility on the outskirts of Cairo, I sent one last text message to my sister Hannan: "Don't let our parents know, switch off the TV, and call the numbers I gave you. Love you all."

The numbers I'd given her were for my bosses in New York, a friend who worked at the German foreign ministry, and some journalist colleagues. I knew that my phone would soon be taken away, and I was anxious about the worry and pain this would cause my family and friends.

There was a feeling of urgency and fear in the car. My colleague Nicholas Kulish and I were calling everyone we could think of: editors at the *New York Times*, the U.S. and German embassies in Cairo, various international organizations. Before we disappeared into what we feared would be a black hole, we wanted as many people as possible to know that we'd been arrested. A military officer had commandeered our car, and in the passenger seat our Egyptian driver dialed his brothers and friends, asking them to look out for his wife and kids. When he got his wife on the phone, she began to wail.

"It's your fault!" she told him. "Why did you work with these people?"

I could feel my heart beating faster and I could hear my pulse in my ears. It reminded me of Baghdad, after the hotel bombing near my guest-house, when I was thrown from my bed onto the ground: boom, boom, boom. *What will they do to us?* I wondered. *How far will they go?*

Now I had Bill Keller on the line. He was sitting with others around a speakerphone at the paper's headquarters in Manhattan. To help them figure out where we were being taken, we'd agreed that, under the cover of translating for Nick, I would try to describe what I was seeing for as long as I could.

It was getting dark. I looked out the window and talked about the shopping mall we were passing. I asked the soldier who was driving for the name of the neighborhood. At the checkpoint where we'd been stopped, a friendly Egyptian officer had told us there was nothing he could do for us except let us keep our phones. "You should call whoever you can," he told us. "You're going to the headquarters of the intelligence service, the Mukhabarat."

The car entered a compound with high walls and cars parked inside. I held the phone facing downward, making sure my hand didn't block the microphone. Our driver was trembling. "This is bad. This will end badly," he said, turning toward me. There was fear in his dark eyes.

"All will be good. Don't worry. We haven't done anything wrong," I told him, unsure if I was trying to calm him or myself.

"Please, do you know where we are?" I asked the soldier who was driving us. "Tell me, please."

He glanced into the rearview mirror. "Mukhabarat al-Jaish." Then he added in English, "army intelligence, high-level security."

I turned to Nick and spoke in a louder-than-normal voice, hoping the editors would hear. "So you heard, Nick. He said we are here at the army intelligence high-security facility."

The car stopped in front of an entrance where three men in plain-clothes waited. We all got out of the car. I tried to smile as I greeted the men in Arabic. In my head, I ran through some of the advice I had been given just three weeks earlier, when I took a course on surviving in war zones and hostage situations. One lesson stood out in my memory: *try to establish a personal rapport with your captors.*

Why wouldn't that work with intelligence officers? I wondered. But I was nervous and frightened. Instead of smiling back or saying hello, the men looked at us stonily. They turned to the officer who had driven us there: "Why are they not blindfolded? Why do they still have their phones?"

"Switch off the phone," one of them said in Arabic. I translated to Nick in a loud voice, again hoping the editors would hear. The man then looked angry and repeated in English, "I said you should switch off your phone."

"Me?" I answered. "Okay, I'll switch it off." I pushed the button. They took our phones and told us to walk into a building. Nick, our driver, and I followed one of the men while the other two officers walked behind us. From now on, we would be on our own.

———

IT WAS JANUARY 2011. A month earlier in Tunisia, a fruit seller had set himself on fire, sparking countrywide protests against poverty and economic inequality that led to the overthrow of the president, Zine el-Abidine Ben Ali. This marked the beginning of the wave of uprisings across the Middle East that would come to be known as the "Arab Spring."

Never would I have thought that Egypt would follow Tunisia. Nick and I had traveled there to do research for a book we were writing about one of the most-hunted Nazi war criminals, Dr. Aribert Heim, who had lived secretly in Cairo until his death in 1992.

While we were there, demonstrations gripped the country. Tens of thousands of people filled the streets calling for Egypt's president, Hosni Mubarak, to step down. After calling our editors at the *Times* and volunteering to cover the protests, we changed our plans and drove to Alexandria.

At first, the protests in Alexandria were relatively peaceful, but as the demonstrators' anger grew, some started throwing stones at the police, who responded with tear gas and, in some cases, live ammunition. Nick and I went to several hospitals to count the dead and injured, as frantic family members searched for relatives, wailing with grief when they found them. We also talked to the lawyers and activists who had been among the first to protest. At night, we drove to neighborhoods controlled by the Muslim Brotherhood, where clusters of young men manned checkpoints every few blocks.

Many Egyptians wanted free elections, but not everyone wanted Mubarak to go. Egyptian Christians, members of the Coptic Church, said things I'd heard before in Arab countries ruled by kings or autocrats: that even though these leaders were dictators, they sometimes protected members of vulnerable minority communities. These minorities did not want to take their chances with pure majority rule.

Nick and I were planning to write a story about the Copts and their apprehension about the protests. But the day we began our interviews, we heard there was another demonstration planned. When we arrived, we saw a two-man team from a German TV channel standing on a pickup truck filming the demonstrators. At this point in the protests, Egyptians would often gather in front of cameras and make a lot of noise, hoping to send a message to viewers across the globe. But the German TV reporter wasn't satisfied with the crowd's response; he wanted more. He raised his arms like a concert conductor, urging the men in the street to yell louder, while his colleague filmed them.

"Are you crazy?" I yelled at the TV crew in German. "Come down!" These crowds could be volatile, and riling them up seemed dangerous, not to mention unethical. As we moved through the crowd, I began to worry about Nick, who stood out as a foreigner because he is tall and blond. But Nick wasn't the problem—it was the Germans. I turned and saw people pointing at the TV team, and I heard men yelling, "Kill him! He filmed us! He's a Jew and a spy!"

Luckily, we'd brought along a large team. Nick and I had eight people with us: our driver, whom I'll call Z because naming him could endanger his family; seven Egyptian men who had formed neighborhood protection groups during the unrest in Alexandria; some of their friends joined us as well. It turned out to have been a prescient decision. I asked two of the Egyptians to stay close to Nick, while the other five and I walked back toward the TV crew. By the time we got there, the crowd at their feet had turned into an angry mob.

The Germans were trying to get away, but there was nowhere to go.

Just then, a man pulled up in a car. One of our Egyptian companions asked him to give us a ride. He agreed.

"Get the hell into the car!" I yelled at the TV guys in German. "These people will lynch you!"

They ran over and scrambled in, and I climbed in after them. Meanwhile, Nick had come over and was standing nearby. We both realized there was no room for him in the car. He gave a little wave, and I waved back, as if to say, "What can we do?" There was no chance; if he'd tried to get in, the doors would not have closed. Nick waved again, telling me to go on. I felt awful. I saw Nick turn back into the crowd and walk casually away. I hoped that the Egyptians I'd asked to stay with him would make sure he was safe, but I didn't know.

In the intervening seconds, one of the men in the crowd had reached through the driver's open window and grabbed the car keys out of the ignition. Now we were stranded, surrounded by angry men with knives, sticks, and machetes. The camera team was paralyzed. "What do you want?" I screamed at the mob.

"We want the camera, we want the pictures they took of us!" one man shouted. I looked out my window and saw that two men with knives were trying to slash our tires.

"There is no way out," our Egyptian driver said. He didn't know any of us but had stopped to help. Now this poor man was stuck with us, I thought. I told the cameraman to give me the memory card with the pictures he had taken. But the TV reporter refused.

I turned to him angrily. "Are you nuts or what? You want us to get killed for some pictures of protesters and your stand-up in front of the camera?"

The crowd outside our car was growing angrier. "Give me the memory card, NOW!" I shouted at the reporter and cameraman in German. Finally, the cameraman handed it over.

I opened my door and started screaming at the crowd in Arabic: "What's wrong with you people? What is it you want? You want the pictures?"

The Egyptians seemed to be in shock. They hadn't expected me to speak Arabic or to get out of the car. They started to back away. I hurled the memory card into the crowd, and the men in the street dashed to find it.

In the chaos, one of our friends from the local neighborhood watch group somehow managed to get our car keys back. The driver started the engine, but men packed the road ahead of us. "You have to drive now," I told him in Arabic. "Drive!" When he protested, I put my hands firmly on his shoulders and spoke in as even a voice as I could manage. "They'll move, just drive." He stepped on the gas and the men in front of us melted away.

We were all in shock. Back at our hotel, I greeted Nick with relief. One of our Egyptian neighborhood watchmen took me aside. "Are you aware there was a guy on your side of the car who had a knife?" he asked. "When you got back in the car, he was coming after you. If we hadn't held his hand, you would have had a knife in your back."

I was holding a glass of water and I saw that my hand was shaking. "Thank God they got what they wanted," I said.

"They didn't get what they wanted," the German TV reporter said with a smile. "We didn't give them the footage. We gave them an empty memory card."

I was furious. There were only two hotels in Alexandria where foreign journalists were staying: the Four Seasons and our place, the Cecil. We already had a security issue at the Cecil because an Al Jazeera crew was staying there and had been sighted filming stand-ups on their balcony. When the angry men we'd seen that day realized they'd been given the wrong memory card, I feared they would find out where we were staying and come after us.

We decided to get out of there. The next day, Nick and I headed back to Cairo, traveling in a convoy with the German TV team after they asked us not to leave them alone in Alexandria. When they ran out of space for their equipment in the trunk of their car, we even offered to let them stow some of their luggage in our trunk.

When we reached the edge of the capital, we were stopped at a checkpoint, one of many on the roads at that time. The men who ran them wore plainclothes and carried knives and sticks. It was impossible to know whether they worked for the government or some other group.

One of the men asked our driver for his identification papers and told him to open the trunk. Z had been growing more nervous the closer we got to Cairo; I played Arabic songs on my phone to calm him down. While we were sitting there, I saw the men at the checkpoint wave the Germans on. They sped past us toward Cairo, not even bothering to pull over and wait to see if we made it out all right.

When the men opened our trunk and saw a large bag with an orange microphone sticking out, they started screaming in Arabic, "These people are spies!"

"It's okay. We're not spies," I said, trying to calm them. "All is good."

One of the men had a gun in his hand. "We should kill them," he said. "They are spies."

"We're just journalists," I said. "It's all okay."

I had no idea what was going on, but then I remembered what was in our trunk: the gear belonging to the TV crew, including a satellite dish and a camera. Here was a woman of Arab descent with a German passport and a tall blond American in a car with a satellite dish and a camera. It didn't look good.

Two Egyptians got into the car. I thought they would take us to our hotel. In an attempt at friendliness, I offered them chocolate and muesli bars I had in my bag. "You're trying to help us, right?" They gave me strange looks, but they took the snacks.

The two guys sat in back and told our driver where to go. We stopped at a compound whose sign identified it as a lumber company. Later, the police told us that the station where they ordinarily worked had been set on fire by demonstrators. It drove home how tenuous the situation was in Egypt then. Back in Alexandria, we'd seen police stations with charred walls, broken windows, smashed computers, and piles of loose paper lying around.

The men took the TV crew's camera bag. I was told to get out of the car and follow them while Nick and our driver stayed behind. Inside, I saw some men in camouflage trousers and others in plainclothes with guns. We went upstairs to the roof, where a man in a suit was smoking a cigarette. He introduced himself as Captain Ehab. He asked about my background, and I told him who I was. I explained that the camera bag belonged to the German TV reporters who had been traveling with us, that they'd run out of space in their car and asked us to carry some of their gear.

Ehab seemed to believe me. He looked inside the bag and felt along the edges. Then he unzipped a pocket, reached in, and pulled out an envelope. I saw the faces of the two men who had been in the car with us turn serious. The envelope had a number written on it: 10,000. Inside, Ehab found ten thousand dollars in cash.

He raised a walkie-talkie to his lips: "Bring the American up."

"I could have believed you that you had nothing to do with them," he told us. "But in these days, who will leave ten thousand dollars with strangers?"

"We have a woman with a German passport of Arab origin and an American in a car with a camera, satellite equipment, and ten thousand dollars," he said. "This is very suspicious. I think they need to be checked."

He had to turn us over to the army, he said, but he would let us keep our phones. "Call as many people as you can," he said. The first person we called was a woman from the U.S. embassy, who urged Ehab to let us go. "You have to release these people," she told him. "They're journalists working for the *New York Times*." But Ehab wasn't the problem. He seemed as if he wanted to help us but said it was out of his hands.

He handed us off to his driver, who took us to an army base. We were relieved; the military was the closest thing Egypt had to a stabilizing force, and we thought we'd likely be released. The men at the base were very friendly, but then something changed. One of the leaders suddenly grew apologetic. "My heart goes out to you," he told me in Arabic. "I'm sorry." They put us back in the car, and my anxiety surged as we set off again, this time headed to the intelligence compound. On the way there Nick got Bill Keller and the other editors on the phone.

But now our phones were gone. We were sitting on plastic chairs inside this anonymous building, worrying about our families, worrying about what these intelligence people would do with us. "Maybe they will leave us here for weeks," our driver Z said. "Maybe they will torture us."

I was glad that he was saying these things in Arabic so Nick couldn't understand. I tried to soothe him, saying that we hadn't done anything wrong and would be out of here soon, but I was seriously worried.

We were taken to separate rooms, each with brown leather padded walls, to be interrogated individually. I ended up with the guy whom the others called "al-Pasha," which means "the boss" in Arabic.

Nick later told me that his interrogator spoke perfect English and said that he had lived in Florida and Texas. Between questions, he joked about the TV show *Friends*. Nick surmised that the interrogator, whom he found menacing, had learned his techniques in the United States. He would pretend to be nice for a minute, then say "We're friends. Aren't we friends?"

"Okay, if we're friends, can I leave?" Nick asked. "Can I have one of those cigarettes?"

"Maybe if I like the answers to your questions," the man replied.

"Who knows—maybe he's one of the guys who cooperated with the CIA in the War on Terror," I told Nick later. The Mukhabarat has had a long working relationship with American intelligence services.

My interrogation room was dim. The only light came from a lamp on the interrogator's table. He stared at me fixedly and smiled.

"Where are we?" I asked.

"You are nowhere."

He asked when we had arrived in Egypt and why we had come. To him, the timing was suspect. "You came right before all these events started," he said. "Why?"

At first, I tried to avoid telling him the real reason for our trip. When we'd reported previously on the Nazi doctor's links to Cairo for the *Times*, the Egyptians had not been pleased. We later learned that they'd interrogated everyone we'd talked to and even jailed some of our sources.

"We're working on a history-related book," I told him vaguely.

"On what topic?"

I suspected he already knew. "It's about a German man who lived in Cairo and died there," I said.

"What's so special about this man?"

"He was a Nazi who was living in Cairo."

He wrote something on the paper in front of him and looked up at me. "Yes, you are the woman who took his briefcase from Egypt to Germany," he said with a sarcastic smile. "This was very bad for my country."

I looked down. I'd smuggled Aribert Heim's briefcase out of Cairo in 2009, when we wrote our first story about him. It contained evidence of the life he'd built in Egypt: personal letters, medical reports, and other documents.

"Why are you holding us?" I asked.

"We have questions about your motives and who you are."

For some time, I'd been hearing what sounded like a man being beaten in a nearby room. Between his screams someone yelled, "You're a traitor working with foreigners!" I strained to catch the words. I knew that for the sake of our Egyptian driver, I had to be diplomatic.

My interrogator had been flipping through a file that lay open on his desk and making notes on a piece of paper. When he finished writing, he looked at me again. "We don't very often get women here, and not often such a nice-looking one as you." He didn't say anything else. The message was clear.

A few weeks earlier, I'd gone through a security training course for diplomats, aid workers, and journalists, taught by the German army. We'd been told to expect rape as a method to break and humiliate us. Until the moment my interrogator said that, I'd tried to hide my fear and nervousness. Now, for the first time, I felt that anything could happen.

He stood up. "I must go now," he said. "But some others will take very good care of you." The sarcastic smile flashed across his face again.

I was left alone in the room. A few minutes later, a man came in and said they would have to take me to another place. Playing for time, I asked if I could use the bathroom. He said it was across the hall and told me to go quickly. Other plainclothesmen stood in front of the interrogation room; one of them held a blindfold and handcuffs.

The bathroom was very dirty, but I thought it best to use it, since I didn't know when I'd get another chance. In the mirror above the filthy sink, I stared at my pale face and bloodshot eyes. I was worried they would separate me from Nick. *Whatever happens now, you will not allow them to break you,* I thought. *You won't break. It's your body, not your soul, Souad. You will not break.*

I opened the door. One of the men said they would have to blindfold me and take me somewhere else. "I'm not going without my colleague," I said in a loud voice, hoping that Nick would hear me.

"We need to go now," another man told me. I began to scream: "My name is Souad Mekhennet. I am a journalist. I will only go with my colleague Nicholas Kulish." My aim was to tell the other prisoners that I was here, or had been here. If I were to die or if anything else happened to me, I wanted to make sure someone would know my name.

One of the men began to tap his left foot impatiently. "Stop shouting, or we will need to use other methods," he said.

The door to an interrogation room opened, and an officer came out. "What is going on here?" he said. (I would learn later that this was Nick's room, and the officer was the chatty but creepy English speaker.)

"I don't want to leave without my colleague," I said.

"You need to go now," the officer responded. "We need this room for the next interrogation. Your colleague will come soon."

They blindfolded me and we started to walk. I heard the footsteps of several men. Two of them were holding me by my arms and shoulders, while another walked very close behind me. I heard a woman screaming. They led me toward the sound. I tried to stay calm and breathe. *Are they raping her? Will they rape me now too?* A door opened and we passed the screaming woman. I told myself again, *Whatever is happening now, it is only your body.* One of the men was breathing heavily into my ear. I could feel his breath on my neck, too, as if he were saying, *You're next.* I did my best to ignore it. *Don't break down. You will not break down.*

We walked further until a door was opened and I was taken inside. There they removed the blindfold. I stood in a small bare room with white walls and six orange plastic chairs. The tile floor was gray and dirty. A large clouded glass window let in a bit of light, but not much, since it was night. The room was very cold. A couple of moments later, Nick and Z were brought in.

"Did they beat you?" Nick and I asked Z after the men had left.

"No, I'm okay," he replied. So it wasn't his screams I had heard during my interrogation. They'd questioned him, he said, but he'd told them he was only the driver and didn't know much about what we were doing.

We compared notes on our interrogations and learned that the questions had been fairly mundane. They'd asked Z how long he'd been working with us, who had hired him, where we'd been, and whom we had met. Nick was asked about the reasons for our Egypt trip, who he worked for, and why we'd chosen to come when we did. As we talked, a picture came into focus. It seemed that our jailers thought that Nick and I were part of a possible conspiracy against Egypt, or could have been made to look that way. At the time, the Egyptian security services were accusing U.S. and European nongovernmental organizations and political groups of having orchestrated the protests, so the fact that Nick and I had arrived before the demonstrations, as well as the equipment and money found in the car, might indicate to some that we'd helped organize them. I already had a black mark against me for having smuggled out the Nazi briefcase. At the time, a few Egyptian media outlets had raised questions about my being a spy who was telling Dr. Heim's story as a way to damage Egypt's reputation. It sounded crazy, but from what we knew about how the Egyptian government thought and operated, it kind of made sense, in a warped kind of way.

At first, communication with our guards was relatively consistent; one of the nicer intelligence officers brought each of us a Pepsi and a small package of Oreos, saying, "Let me see what I can do for you." Later, he came back into the room, sat next to me, and told me that he loved Morocco. We started talking and it turned out that he had served at the Egyptian embassy in Rabat.

"Why did you get yourself into this situation?" he asked me.

"You guys brought us into this situation. We haven't done anything wrong."

He leaned close to my ear and whispered, "You should thank God that you ended up here. We know you. We know who you are. There are other places where they would just see you as a woman, do you understand?"

I begged them to release us, telling them I wasn't feeling well. They sent a doctor with a blood-pressure gauge. I remembered former detainees telling me that before the guards used electroshock, their jailers would bring a medic to examine them, to see how much torture they could survive.

"You need to be checked?" the doctor asked me, smiling.

"No, no. I think I'm okay," I replied.

We asked repeatedly to speak to our embassies or to the *Times*, but we were told to wait. After a while, some of the men we'd seen earlier came back to talk to us.

"We know you're just journalists," one of them said, "but we can't release you because it's very dark outside and it's very dangerous."

"Just give us our phones. We can call the U.S. embassy," I said. Our jailers refused.

The room was freezing cold, and it was difficult to sleep with only the hard plastic chairs to lie on. I thought about my past, about all that had gone wrong and all the things I wanted to do in my life. Maybe we would never get out of here. Maybe we would die here.

There is a saying that walls have ears. In rooms like this one, walls also have voices—voices that belong to the others who have been detained there. During our long night, I read Arabic graffiti written on those walls. "Allah, please release me from my pain," someone had scribbled. "Ahmad, 4.5.2010," another wall read.

I thought about whether I should leave my name behind. Maybe then at least people would know that we—that I—had been there. "Who knows what they'll do with us," Z told me, his whole body shaking. I asked if he was afraid, but he said he was freezing.

From time to time, we heard Egyptians being beaten and screaming after every blow. Someone, presumably an official, shouted in Arabic through the thuds and the cries that followed: "You are talking to journalists? You are talking badly about your country?" A voice answered, also in Arabic, begging for mercy: "You are committing a sin. You are committing a sin."

As the hours dragged on, the powerlessness and uncertainty became excruciating. I have no idea how anyone has the fortitude to survive weeks, months, or years in such limbo. We could hear protesters going past in the street, and we remembered the burned-out police stations we'd seen, as well as a Muslim Brotherhood member who told us he'd been in a prison that was set on fire and had nearly died. What would happen if a mob torched the intelligence facility where we were being held? We could easily burn or choke to death inside.

I looked at Nick and Z. We had all grown very silent, as if lost in ourselves; there was fear in this room, in all three of us. I thought about all the things I had saved on my devices. I knew they wouldn't be able to access the contacts list on my phone, as I had set up a special passcode to protect my information. Then I remembered something else. "Shit," I heard myself saying.

Nick looked up. "What?"

I explained that they had taken my Kindle, and that I had some books on it.

"So what? You've probably got stuff on Al Qaeda and the Taliban, but that's okay. You're a journalist."

I was thinking of something else. A friend had sent me a book that was supposed to help single women better understand men. I had just started reading it. I told Nick the title: *Why Men Love Bitches: From Doormat to Dreamgirl—A Woman's Guide to Holding Her Own in a Relationship.*

He burst out laughing. I translated the title for our driver, who also started laughing. I was glad that we had been able to break through the fear, at least for a few seconds. But before long, we heard the dim sounds of people screaming again.

The next morning a new officer appeared. He said his name was Marwan. He seemed angry with us, saying that he had enough problems to deal with, because there were "thousands of people under arrest just like you." Then he told us to come to the door and look out. We saw more than twenty people sitting in the hall outside our room, most blindfolded and handcuffed, several of them Caucasian. "We could be treating you a lot worse," Marwan told us.

Nearly twenty-four hours after we were first detained, Marwan said that we really would be released before long. Nick and I had agreed that we wouldn't leave without Z. They said we couldn't bring him. We said we had to bring him. They said Egyptians had to go through a different system. I knew we couldn't leave him behind.

"I will throw myself out of the window," Z told me in Arabic. "They will torture me to death and later bury my body in some mass grave." He was crying.

"He is Egyptian, he has to stay," Marwan told me.

"Marwan, to me the life of an Egyptian is worth as much as the life of an American or a German," I told him. "And I think you as an Egyptian should be happy to hear that."

He said that I was crazy. "You have to think about yourself, do you understand?" His voice was aggressive now.

In the moment, Nick and I came up with another idea. We took all our luggage—everything that had been in our trunk—and gave it to Z to hold. Bags hung from his shoulders and he held our suitcases in his hands. He looked as if he might collapse under the weight.

"He can't come!" Marwan repeated.

"Then you have to carry the bags," Nick told him.

Marwan looked at us in disbelief.

"Well, if you aren't carrying our bags, then you have to let him come," I said. "Are you going to drive us back to our hotel? Who is going to drive us?"

His expression turned to disgust, as if all these tasks were beneath his dignity. "Fine," Marwan grumbled. He confided his exhaustion to us. They had arrested so many people, he said—too many. He and his men were overwhelmed.

Soon afterward, some men came to get the three of us. They said they were taking us to the hotel where our colleagues were staying in downtown Cairo. We were brought out of our room but had to wait in the hallway as several people with jackets over their heads were led into the facility. Marwan and the man who told me how much he liked Morocco stood by the entrance as if waiting to say good-bye.

The evil-looking man who had interrogated Nick gave us back our phones and our other possessions, including my Kindle.

"There's one thing I want you to know," Nick's interrogator told him. "We still have complete control."

Nick smiled. "It sure doesn't seem like it out on the streets," he said.

"No, this is just for show. In reality, we are still in charge."

I turned to Marwan and the friendly man who liked Morocco. "We're going back to the hotel, right?" They stared at the ground and said nothing. The evil-looking man told Nick that we had to sign a paper saying we'd all been in good health when we left the facility.

"We can't do it till we get to the hotel," I protested. The man insisted. Finally, they brought us outside and turned us over to yet another set of guards. We were jubilant until I asked them to confirm that we were going to our hotel.

One of the men, who wore plainclothes over body armor and carried an assault rifle, told me we weren't.

"Where are we being taken?"

"You don't get to know that."

They put us into our car. Another guard, also armed with an assault rifle, said, "Put your heads down. Look down, and don't talk. If you look up, you will see something you don't ever want to see."

They left us for what felt like ten minutes. We heard ammunition clips being locked into place and duct tape being ripped. We all thought it was for our eyes and mouths.

"They will kill us, by Allah, they will kill us," Z started whispering. It sounded as if he was crying. "I can't stay in this car. I need to run away."

I was worried he would open the door and give them a reason to beat him up. "Don't," I whispered in Arabic. "Stay calm. Stay calm."

A man stuck his head in the driver's side window: "What did you do in Tahrir Square?" he asked our driver.

Z said we hadn't been there.

"So you're a traitor to your country."

"He is just a driver we hired, and we did not go to Tahrir Square," I said in Arabic.

I saw that Z was getting very nervous and had begun to cry. He said he couldn't take it anymore. He was hanging over the steering wheel, saying the *shahada*. "That's it, they're going to kill us," he said.

I didn't want to upset the men by talking, so I made small noises, trying to soothe Z. As I sat there with my head bowed, I switched on my phone and posted a message on Facebook to let people know that we were still being held. I asked my friends to contact whoever they could to help us.

The interrogator came around to my window, followed by two men who pointed handguns at my head. He repeatedly asked me if I was Moroccan. I insisted that I was a German citizen and kept telling them that we were journalists for the *New York Times*. The interrogator was holding a phone to his mouth, saying about Nick, "He's American. Did you hear it? Did you get it all?"

"You came here to make this country look bad," the interrogator told me.

"We came here to tell the truth," I answered. "We are professional journalists for the *New York Times*, and we have everything we need to prove that."

I remembered the names on the wall and was sorry that I had not left mine behind. The driver and Nick told me later that my voice was calm but strong during that interrogation in the car. Though the interrogator was screaming from time to time, I somehow appeared in control of my emotions. "Listen, even if you kill us, there are many others who will tell the story," I told him. "Even if we disappear, you cannot silence all the voices."

The interrogator was clearly relaying my answers to somebody else. He would lean down and speak to me, then step away and speak on a walkie-talkie, then come back and ask another question. "Why did you come when you did, right before all this trouble?" he asked.

I began to hear my inner voice. It was time to say good-bye to this world, time to say the words my parents and grandmother in Morocco had taught me as a child: *There is no God but God, and Muhammad is his prophet.* I heard myself whispering those words. This was the end. I felt oddly placid. I saw moments from my childhood and with friends and family playing in front of my eyes like scenes from a movie. *What are you leaving behind?* I asked myself. The answer made me sad. I had done some work I was proud of, but I wasn't leaving anything personal behind: no children, no partner. *Who's going to cry for you?* I thought.

One of the back doors opened and a man got in and sat next to Nick. Then a voice boomed into the car: "We will take you to another place now. Driver, you can look up and follow this other car. You two, don't look up and don't move. Mr. Muhammad will drive with you."

Z stared at the car ahead of us and drove. "They will dump us in the desert," he whispered.

Mr. Muhammad spoke into a walkie-talkie. Then he started to question me again. My throat was very dry and I could barely speak, but I answered his questions one after the other. This went on for about twenty minutes but it felt much longer.

Finally, Mr. Muhammad asked the driver to stop and wait. He got out of the car. My head was still bowed. "This is the end," I heard Z whispering in Arabic. Just then, Mr. Muhammad spoke to us through the driver's window. "You are free to leave. May Allah be with you."

I looked up and into Mr. Muhammad's face. He had green eyes and something friendly in his look. "What?" I asked him. "What did you say?"

"You can go. Go in peace." He walked away.

We were somewhere in Cairo, on a street lined with houses and shops. It was late afternoon. We parked the car, got out, and took a taxi to the hotel. In the cab the three of us hugged. The driver glanced at us in the rearview mirror, looking perplexed. I told him we were family who had just reunited after a long time apart.

I called my parents and told them I was okay, but I wasn't. We were all acting normal, but nothing was normal. We booked a hotel room for the driver and gave him some money. We hadn't eaten anything in more than twenty-four hours except the small package of Oreos we'd been given in detention, so we went to the hotel restaurant. I had just ordered spaghetti when my phone rang.

"Souad, listen, don't tell me where you are," said the voice of a journalist colleague in Cairo. "You should know the intelligence service is apparently calling hotels in Cairo and asking if you and your colleague are staying there. If I were you guys, I'd leave as soon as you can and go to a safe place."

We left our food untouched and called the German embassy. They sent a car to get us.

Nick and I left Egypt the next day, but only after we'd made sure Z was safe. The *Times* and German TV took care of him and his family, checking them into a hotel under a fake name.

Back in Germany, about three days later, I received an email from an address I didn't recognize.

"This is Marwan; we met in Egypt. I wanted to know if you are okay and let you know, I was impressed by you. Can we become friends on Facebook? I want to get to know you better."

It was Marwan, my jailer.

————

IT TOOK ME some time to get over the stress and trauma. I would often wake up in the middle of the night, sweating and screaming. I had to admit that while I was fine physically, my soul was not in a good place. I was afraid and didn't want to be afraid. If I felt fear, our jailers would win.

I took some time off from work and spent a week in Morocco. A friend had told me about a small hotel on top of a mountain outside Marrakech. It sounded like the right place for me. I needed to be alone; I needed to heal.

When my regular Moroccan driver, Abdelilah, picked me up from the airport in Casablanca to drive me to Imlil, I sat in silence in the backseat. Usually we chatted and laughed on the road, but this time we were both quiet. I wore my sunglasses and looked out the window.

As we drove, I thought about what had happened and what was coming next. Nick had been a great source of support. We both had to deal with what we had endured, and we hadn't finished the research for our book. Should we go back to Egypt? Was it worth it?

I thought about what might happen to the Middle East, and even Morocco. All these protests all of a sudden; all these protesters who wanted so many different things and had such high expectations. In Egypt, some asked for more rights; others said they wanted better jobs; others, better health care. I also met a group who said they wanted someone like Libya's president, Muammar Gaddafi, or former longtime Eygptian president Gamal Abdel Nasser in charge because they were "strong leaders."

I also wondered why the uprisings had come to be called the "Arab

Spring." Who had chosen that optimistic name? My thoughts went back to the Copts in Alexandria, and how one of our sources had whispered his fears that the Muslim Brotherhood would take over. He told us that we didn't understand how dangerous the Muslim Brotherhood was, especially for minorities like the Egyptian Christians. We were never able to write that story because we were detained.

I knew that sometimes democracy wasn't good for minorities. From my history lessons in school and in my research for the Nazi book, I'd read about how Hitler and his party had won power through elections and coalition politics. Why did people think that a voting system was protection against totalitarianism?

The hotel at the top of the mountain was reachable only on foot or on the back of a mule. I was too tired to walk and chose the mule. It was strange that although I didn't have much faith in people at that moment, I trusted this animal to carry me safely over the loose stones to the summit.

The people who ran the hotel asked what I wanted for lunch and dinner. Aside from me, the only other guests were a French couple. My room had a chair, a small table, and a bed with a couple of blankets—it was very cold in the mountains at night. There was an attached bathroom and a balcony with a dazzling view. A far-off mountain was covered in snow and ice, while the nearby peaks were brown and rocky. You could see people's houses in the village below. The air was clear and smelled of wood smoke. I heard a rooster crowing, but no cars.

For two days I left my room only to spend time alone on the hotel terrace, which also had a magnificent view of the region. I stared into the sky while drinking cups of sweet Moroccan mint tea.

Though I'd brought my Kindle with me, I hadn't switched it on since we'd been released from our detention in Egypt. Now I wanted to read one of the many books I'd downloaded. I charged the battery and turned it on. Then I noticed something odd. The Kindle said that I had made it to the end of *Why Men Love Bitches*, the book I'd mentioned to Nick, even though I had just started reading it when the intelligence service took my belongings.

There on the terrace, I burst out laughing so hard I cried. I pictured our interrogators going through the book all night, maybe expecting some juicy stories, only to find out that it was a book of advice for single women.

Nick and I returned to Cairo later that spring, two months after President Mubarak stepped down. Immigration took a long time checking my passport, but I was finally let in.

When I reached the friends' home where I was staying, I saw that I'd received an email from Marwan: "Hi. How are you? I'm also in Cairo." Was he tracking my movements? Was he trying to intimidate me? Did he think I would leave?

I didn't want to spend the rest of my trip wondering. I decided to take a drastic step.

A European source had given me the name of the coordinator for security and intelligence services at the Egyptian Foreign Ministry. He was one of the people who supposedly had connections to all the security services there. I decided to visit him.

In his office, I told him that, as he surely already knew, my colleague and I had been through a hellish experience in his country. "We came back because we need to finish the research for our book," I said. "We are not hiding anything. Everybody knows we are journalists, and everybody knew this last time we were here, too."

He nodded and asked if I wanted to smoke. I declined, but told him to go ahead. He lit a cigarette. I told him that I had received a message from my former jailer and wanted his guidance about what this could mean. He looked at me and smiled. "Maybe he just wanted to let you know that he and his friends are making sure you are safe," he said.

"Am I safe here? Are my colleague and I safe here, or will we be targeted by your services again?"

He finished his cigarette and stubbed it out in an ashtray. "I don't know many people who would have the guts to come here to me after an experience like the one you had."

He stood up and excused himself, saying he had to make a phone call.

After a few minutes, he reappeared. "You are most welcome in Egypt,

Miss Souad. Here is my mobile number. If you ever have any problems, call me."

Nick and I spent the next few weeks working. We finished our book research without any interference from the security services. I never heard from Marwan again.

10

This Is Not an Arab Spring

Germany and Tunisia, 2011

Along with the rest of the world, I spent the first half of 2011 watching the Middle East erupt. In January, a month after the Tunisian fruit seller, Tarek al-Tayeb Mohamed Bouazizi, set himself on fire, triggering nationwide protests, Tunisian president Zine el-Abidine Ben Ali resigned after twenty-three years in office. In February, shortly after Nick and I left Egypt, President Hosni Mubarak was deposed after thirty years in power. In Libya, Muammar Gaddafi was battling a vigorous armed opposition in a conflict that would engulf that country. And in Syria a movement to overthrow Bashar al-Assad was beginning. The international community pledged support to the rebel groups, and the whole region was flooded with weapons.

At the beginning, I'd shared in the general optimism I'd felt among the demonstrators, whose message was, "We want a change in our country, and this is why we are protesting." I understood their anger and their feeling that they needed to mobilize more people so that their voices and their message could be heard. For decades, the leaders of some of these countries had spoken out against monarchies, claiming to be republics or democracies. But while they might have technically been so, in reality small elites held all the power. Friends of the presidential family grew richer while others stayed poor. They might as well have been kingdoms. Moreover, some Arab leaders had underestimated the influence of social media in their countries. They did whatever they could to control the local press, but the growing availability of the Internet had given their people other sources of information and new ways to communicate.

As the revolutions unfolded, however, I grew increasingly troubled by the way the "Arab Spring" was being covered in the international press and what Western leaders were saying about it. People seemed to believe that the countries of the Middle East would now transform themselves overnight into open, Western-style democracies. In many cases, this was what the protesters said they wanted. But putting it into practice would be an immensely complicated decades-long project, which no one seemed to be talking about. I sensed that many in the West—and some in the Arab world as well—had given themselves over to magical thinking.

Sometime in late winter or early spring, I got an urgent-sounding text message from an imam in Berlin whom I'd known for a couple of years: "*Salam* Souad, can you call me? It's important."

"I see more and more young people inside my community who say they will go and fight jihad," he told me when I reached him.

"So what's new?" I responded. For more than a decade there had been a steady stream of young Muslim men seeking to fight in Afghanistan and the tribal areas of Pakistan, following the path of the September 11 attackers.

"They are not planning to go to Afghanistan or Pakistan," he answered. "They are talking about Libya or Syria."

"But who do they want to fight?" I asked him. "What jihad?"

"I don't know, but there is someone here you should meet. We call him Abu Maleeq. I think his real name is Denis, but people know him as the rapper Deso Dogg."

―――――

MY FIRST MEETING with Abu Maleeq was in a mosque outside the center of Berlin. The cabdriver pulled up in front of an old gray building that had once been a factory. Like most mosques in Europe, it didn't look impressive from the outside. In these places, Muslims would get together and establish an association, called a *Verein* in German. The building they rented or bought was officially the group's headquarters, and they would then convert part of it into prayer rooms. These buildings were called Hinterhofmoscheen in German, which can be translated to "back-yard mosques." They were usually not in the best neighborhoods, as had been the case in Hamburg, where the al-Quds mosque was in the red-light district. Some Muslims, especially younger ones, had told me they felt that the only place for mosques in Europe was in neighborhoods where no one else wanted to be. This did not bode well for long-term relationships between Muslim communities and the rest of European society.

The system of allowing anyone to establish an association to rent or buy property that could then be turned into a mosque was also potentially risky. I had met "imams" in some of these establishments who talked more about politics than religion. In fact, when I asked where they had received their Islamic training, some would stumble around and explain that they'd taken a course in Saudi Arabia or somewhere else, or that they were the oldest in their community, or that they were the only ones who spoke classical Arabic. Some of these imams had been brought in from other countries and were supervised from afar. In Germany's Turkish community, many mosques belong to an organization called the Turkish-Islamic Union for Religious Affairs. The Turkish ruling political party, the AKP, works through the union to influence what is taught in these mosques, from religion to political preferences.

It was different with the imam I knew in Berlin, who was young but had studied Islamic teachings in Europe and the Middle East. He had grown up in Germany, and he knew what he was talking about.

"He is in the office," the imam told me when I arrived. "He might not tell you immediately what he has on his mind, but maybe when he trusts you he will."

The man in the office stood up when I came in. "*As'salam alaikum*," he said.

My eyes went immediately to his hands, which were covered with tattoos. He noticed me looking and explained that they were from the days when he'd lived the life of an unbeliever.

"You mean when you were a rapper?"

He nodded.

The tattoo on his right hand said "STR8," and the one on his left, "Thug." He smiled and his white teeth showed. "You could say I was what people called a 'bad boy,'" he said. He looked at the tattoos and added, "Allah will erase them from me."

I asked how he had become Muslim.

"I was Muslim from the beginning," he replied. "But I had lost the right path until Allah brought me back."

Though he now went by Abu Maleeq, his birth name was Denis Mamadou Gerhard Cuspert. He told me that he'd been born in Berlin. His mother, a German, had raised him there with his stepfather, a former U.S. Army soldier. "My real father was from Ghana," he explained. "He dumped us when I was a baby. I had no idea that the American was in fact my stepfather until much later, when my grandmother told me."

His stepfather was strict with Denis and his brother. "We were constantly fighting, he and I, and I also began to do a lot of shit," he told me.

"What kind of shit?"

He smiled, again showing his teeth. "Well, the kind of shit you do when you end up in gangs in Berlin, street fights, drugs here and there, and some other stuff."

His mother and stepfather finally decided to send him to a facility for children with behavioral problems who had been part of gangs or had had trouble with the law. "That was kind of funny. I was already bad, and then they send me to a place where I met kids who were worse than me." He laughed. "So I learned some other things."

I wondered where all his anger came from as a child.

"Do you know how it felt to grow up as the only dark-skinned child in my neighborhood and school? I grew up with racism."

I didn't respond.

He paused and asked if I wanted a tea or coffee. I wondered if he was trying to change the subject. I pressed him.

"What was it like for you to grow up here?"

"It was very difficult," he said. Some teachers called him "Negro," and treated him and his Muslim friends badly.

It reminded me of my own experiences in kindergarten, with the teacher who always pointed out that the bad characters in the fairy tales "were all dark-haired, like you," and of the other children in Klettenberg-strasse who weren't allowed to play with us because we were children of guest workers and not really up to their "standards," or because my oldest sister was handicapped.

I could feel the pain in his voice when he talked, the sense of how difficult it was to be the outsider. Cuspert told me that he became increasingly interested in politics and what was happening in the world, an impulse to which I could also relate. "Maybe because of my own experience growing up here, I always felt I should support those who are weak, the underdogs," he said. I've often heard this argument from members of terrorist organizations. The problem is that if it's taken too far, "supporting underdogs" can easily turn into oppressing others.

That was why he took to the streets against what he called "unfair" American foreign policy around the time of the First Gulf War in the early 1990s. He grew up in a largely Muslim immigrant neighborhood in Berlin, where support for the Palestinian struggle mixed with general left-wing sentiments. Many of his neighbors saw America as the great evil. As a teenager, he told me, he'd even burned an American flag.

He said that from an early age, he'd trained himself in Thai boxing, tae kwon do, and Brazilian jujitsu. Social workers in Germany later sent him to a working farm in Namibia that aimed to put juvenile delinquents on a better path. The point of the place was to shock him and others out of their aggression and show them how good they had it back home. It was like going into the army, Cuspert said. They had to wake up at dawn to work on the farm, which grew vegetables and fruit and raised animals. It was a structured environment with strict discipline, but for Cuspert it was also the first time he lived in a mainly black community. He enjoyed the few weeks he spent there, but his behavior and worldview didn't change much.

In the 1990s, he found a new outlet for his anger when he started rapping under the name Deso Dogg, "Deso" being short for "Devil's Son." Cuspert felt that through music he would be able to reach hundreds or thousands of young people, air his political grievances, and speak frankly about social issues. He rapped about a stint in juvenile detention, racism, war, and occasionally religion. In 2003, as the United States prepared to invade Iraq, Cuspert and his stepfather engaged in endless political arguments.

"Were you doing all this to piss your stepfather off," I asked, "or because you really believed Saddam Hussein was innocent?"

He paused for a few seconds. "I think I wanted to piss my stepfather off, but I also was against this U.S. imperialism. They always think they can decide what should happen in other countries, and I didn't like it."

"But if I remember right, the Gulf states supported the U.S. intervention in 2003, because Saddam's army had entered Kuwait in 1990. Or at least they didn't object to the invasion."

He smiled. "Yes indeed, you are right. But those rulers are all in the pockets of America. They are all traitors, and so, God willing, soon they will all disappear."

His music career soared. In 2006, he toured with the American hip-hop artist DMX. Cuspert's most famous song, which begins, "Welcome to my world, full of hatred and blood," was featured in the 2010 German film *Civil Courage*. The video shows Cuspert engaged in the ritual washing that Muslims practice before prayers.

As his reputation grew, he gained fans. If he'd kept at it, he might have become as famous as Bushido, a half-German, half-Tunisian rapper who rose to prominence at about the same time and went on to fill stadiums and make millions. But after a bad car accident in 2010, Cuspert said that he began to feel that he'd been wasting his life in the pursuit of fame and recognition. He grew restless and started digging into his background. His biological father had been Muslim, but Cuspert had not been raised in the faith. Now he began to learn more about Islam, and in time he grew convinced that Allah had allowed him to survive the car accident so he could find a new path in life.

He stopped rapping. He now saw such music as *haram*: forbidden. Instead, he began singing the Islamic songs known as *nasheeds*, which often serve as sound tracks to videos issued by ISIS and other jihadi groups, and he turned his attention to fighting the United States and the West. He told me he'd reached out to a Taliban contact and sworn his allegiance to Mullah Omar, and that he began to follow the teachings of preachers such as Anwar al-Awlaki, the charismatic American-born inspiration to a generation of young jihadists, who would be killed in a U.S. drone strike in September 2011 after joining Al Qaeda in Yemen. He also listened to the speeches of Osama bin Laden, whom he saw not as a terrorist but as a Robin Hood type who'd left a comfortable life to help those less fortunate. When bin Laden was killed by U.S. Navy SEALs in May 2011, Cuspert would tell me he was happy the Al Qaeda leader had died a martyr.

I sensed that Cuspert was looking for answers, but I also knew that most imams, at least in Germany, wouldn't provide them. If he went to their mosques, started talking about politics, and asked what the religion would say about these matters, they'd have been inclined to turn him away out of concern that the intelligence services might shut them down. So instead of discussing his concerns, he began connecting with like-minded people online and grew even more radical.

While many in the West viewed the uprisings in Tunisia, Egypt, Libya, and elsewhere across the region as harbingers of democratic change, Cuspert saw them as an opportunity for anti-Western Islamists to gain power and operate more freely.

"What democracy?" he asked me. "This is not compatible with Islam, and all the people want Islam."

I asked where he had gotten the idea that Islam wasn't compatible with democracy. He smiled and answered that he had heard the sermon of a sheikh online—he refused to tell me the man's name—and then chatted with him about it. Cuspert seemed troubled about his own life, as well as what he saw as Western hegemony. His disaffection made him easy prey for jihadist recruiters, who knew exactly what to say to people like him. While three of the four September 11 pilots had been recruited and influenced by jihadi veterans or preachers, we were now dealing with a new, European-born generation of radicals, such as the Austrian Mohamed Mahmoud, whom Cuspert had also mentioned as an inspirational figure. Mahmoud not only spoke fluent German but also understood the language of youth, which made him even more compelling to Cuspert, who didn't speak Arabic at the time.

"But that's not what most of the people are marching for," I told him. I hadn't seen anyone demonstrating in favor of Sharia law.

He smiled again. "Don't think about what you see. The world will worry about what can't be seen now."

He told me he had been in touch with "brothers" in Tunisia who had been imprisoned because they were preaching about Islam. "Can you imagine?" he said. "They were jailed and tortured by people who also call themselves Muslims, but God gave them patience and they are free now, thanks to Allah."

And thanks to the Arab Spring, I thought. I asked Cuspert if he planned to go and fight.

"God willing, when my time comes, I will," he answered, adding only that he would do battle "in a country where they speak the language of the holy Koran."

This was the first of several conversations I had with Cuspert that spring. The more we spoke, the more I wondered if there was some kind of underground network of jihadists that was taking advantage of the Arab Spring. I wasn't sure how seriously to take what he was telling me, so I asked around.

"This guy is just a bigmouth. We don't think he matters," one security official told me. "You're wasting your time with him."

But I remained intrigued, especially by Cuspert's certainty.

These don't sound like radical ideas now, but at the time this wasn't the story that international news networks and major Western newspapers and magazines were telling. Instead, they carried report after report about the end of Islamism and the outbreak of democracy, as if a giant lightbulb had been switched on across the Middle East and North Africa. And while many liberals and young people in Tunisia, Syria, Egypt, and elsewhere wanted more rights and craved more progressive governments, journalists focused on these groups at the expense of other, more sinister forces. Readers and viewers were told that if they looked at Tahrir Square, they would understand what Egypt wanted. But Tahrir Square was not Egypt. Meanwhile, we ignored or failed to see people such as Cuspert and his friends—or we didn't want to see them because they didn't fit into the happy narrative of democratic progress.

Where were Al Qaeda and the Taliban in all this? Would some of those disenfranchised people who had once gravitated to Al Qaeda see

the Arab Spring as a better opportunity? I began to reach out to some of
my militant sources in Europe, North Africa, and the Middle East, and I
bought a new unregistered SIM card and a cheap phone to call the Taliban commander I'd had dinner with in Pakistan.

"I heard what happened to you in Egypt," he said. "Did they do anything to you? Torture or . . ." He stopped. "You know what I mean. Have
they touched your honor?"

I told him that no such thing happened, then asked how he'd found out.

He began to laugh. "Do you think we don't read the news?"

I asked if he was worried about losing his followers in the Arab Spring
countries. He was not. Instead, he praised the opposition forces for rising against "corrupt leaders." He added, "It's good that people will have
the power, because they will choose the right way, like we had under the
rule of the Taliban."

But that wasn't what I had seen on the banners the protesters carried.
Instead, people were asking for more rights, better living standards.

"That's not what the majority want," the commander told me. "People
want Sharia. They want no more Western interference and no puppets
in power." He knew this, he said, because some Taliban fighters came
from those countries. "Now they are back and make *dawah* and offer
their help to people there."

In Islamic practice, *dawah* means preaching and teaching. The men
the Taliban commander talked about were essentially jihadi recruiters.
"You will see," he told me. "Brothers from all over the world will travel to
those places and teach what was banned before, the right Islam."

I began to wonder if I should head to the Middle East to learn more.
Then a young Muslim man shot and killed two American airmen in
Frankfurt, wounding two others. The police said they had arrested the
killer, Arid Uka. I dove into reporting the story.

Uka was an ethnic Albanian who had been born in Kosovo and raised
in Frankfurt; his family and friends described him as a shy, calm twenty-
one-year-old who, along with his classmates, had won a government prize
in middle school for a project on how to prevent violence in society. His
parents were moderate Muslims, and they and his brothers told me they
didn't understand why he'd killed the Americans. But his older brother,

Hastrid, mentioned that Arid spent lots of time on the computer, "playing games, reading posts on Facebook, or watching movies on YouTube. Actually, recently he was listening also to *nasheeds* with some political messages in German."

I asked if he knew whose chants they were. He thought for a couple of seconds, and I could see he was trying to remember a name.

"It's this former rapper, something with like, 'Dog.'"

When I tried to call Cuspert, a message said his number was no longer in use. I reached out to the imam who had put us in touch and asked if he had the ex-rapper's new number.

"Sorry, I don't," he said. "Things have changed a lot, Souad. Abu Maleeq no longer comes to me. In fact, he called me a traitor because I told him his views were extreme and far from Islamic teachings."

He was hanging out with a different group now, the imam said. "He doesn't want to hear what the truth is. He just wants to hear what *his* truth is."

Since I didn't know how to reach Cuspert, I decided to dig into what he'd told me. I traveled to London to meet with three older militants originally from Egypt, Tunisia, and Libya. Two of them had fought the Soviets in Afghanistan in the 1980s and had witnessed the beginning of the era of global jihad; all had been members of domestic Islamist movements that had called for overthrowing the government and implementing a system based purely on Sharia law. As a result of their unpopular views, some of these men had been granted asylum in the United Kingdom, though they knew they were closely watched by British intelligence.

We met in a coffee shop in Knightsbridge, an area popular with rich Gulf Arabs. Although the men I met weren't wealthy, they told me they felt safer there because their ethnicity was less likely to draw attention. I had known the Egyptian and Tunisian men for some time, but was just meeting the Libyan. All three seemed happy with the developments in their native countries.

"The people have finally shown the world that they are fed up with the corrupt regimes," the Libyan said. He was very soft-spoken, and his dark brown eyes looked kind. "When people in Libya have the free choice, they will choose Sharia."

"What if they don't?" I asked.

"Everybody will chose the right way if they finally have the chance to see what the right way is," the Tunisian said. "And nothing can be better or more right than the law of Allah."

What would this mean for women in Tunisia? I asked. The country had long been very liberal and had granted women equal rights. Tunisia's first president, Habib Bourguiba, was seen as perhaps the most progressive leader in the Arab World in this regard. In the 1960s he introduced a series of reforms that included a ban on polygamy and guaranteed the rights of women to freely choose their husbands, to divorce while retaining primary custody of their children, and to obtain legal abortions. Bourguiba ultimately banned the veil, which he called an "odious rag." His approach came to be called *le féminisme bourguibien*.

To some Bourguiba was a hero for pushing these reforms through, while others, such as the man I was sitting with, called him a "dictator."

"This was by force," the Tunisian told me angrily. "Women had no choice. They were forced to give up Islam because of him and other traitors. We will liberate the Tunisian women."

"What about women who don't want to wear a head scarf?"

"Any woman who is really Muslim will be happy to cover her hair and face."

"The face too?" I blurted out.

If his wife and daughters, who had been born in the United Kingdom, wore the face-covering *niqab*, he told me, then surely a Muslim woman in an Arab country would do the same.

"But wearing hijab or *niqab* isn't what people are demanding in this Arab Spring," I answered.

"This is not an Arab Spring," the Egyptian interrupted. "This is a spring for Islam and Muslims."

He told me that many of his friends who had been freed from prison in Egypt were actively doing *dawah*. "This is a very good time for all the Muslim *ummah*," he said, referring to the Muslim people collectively. "We can now bring the right teaching of Islam into our countries, and soon the *ummah* all over the region will be stronger."

When we finished our tea and coffee, the Tunisian urged me to travel to the Tunisian-Libyan border region. "You will find some of my brothers there, helping refugees, *masha'Allah*. They have all been in prison for years." He gave me his wife's number in case I needed to be in touch.

As I walked back to my hotel, I passed groups of people who spoke the dialects of the Gulf region. Some carried Hermès purses and giant shopping bags from Harrods; others sped past in Rolls-Royces, Ferraris, and Maseratis. It struck me that they didn't seem concerned about—or even very aware of—the turmoil on the streets in some Arab countries. In that way and many others, they couldn't have been more different from the men I'd just met. I recalled something the Tunisian had said: "Egypt, Libya, Tunisia, and Syria won't be the only places. This is the beginning of an unstoppable wave. This will make things easier for the soldiers of Allah."

It sounded as if the Arab uprisings were about to become a new magnet for militants from all over the world, as Afghanistan and Pakistan had been in the fight against the Soviets. But I knew I'd have to visit some of those countries to find out for sure.

In August I flew to Tunisia, where the Ben Ali regime had given way to a Muslim Brotherhood–supported government. The head of the party, Rachid Ghannouchi, was viewed as a moderate Islamist and had spent more than twenty years in exile in the United Kingdom before returning to Tunisia in 2011. In Tunis, people seemed proud and euphoric. The Tunisians I spoke with were overwhelmingly optimistic, including Ahmad, the stringer I worked with there. Under Ben Ali, the country had been a police state. Intellectuals weren't allowed to write or say what they wanted. Now, Ahmad told me proudly, Tunisia would turn into a real democracy, with freedom of speech. Though that hadn't entirely happened yet, he felt that the new leadership was a step in the right direction in terms of fighting corruption and liberalizing the government.

At the Tunisian-Libyan border post at Ra's Ajdir, I found representatives from the Red Crescent, the United Nations, and other international aid organizations helping people who'd fled the fighting in Libya, including many Africans who had worked in that country. The United Arab Emirates, Morocco, and other nations had sent support as well. Some countries had set up camps for families and provided food, while Morocco had established a field hospital.

One tent in particular drew my attention. There, young men gave refugees bags with food and clothes, then sought to engage them in conversation about the true Islamic path.

Most of the men who worked in the tent wore the *gandoura*, a long dress common among North African men. Some had beards.

Were these the "brothers" that the Tunisian from London had mentioned? After greeting them politely, I asked if they belonged to any specific group or organization. "We are just here to help the refugees," one answered. He was cooking bean and vegetable soup on a large propane camp stove.

I asked what he did when he wasn't here.

"I just got out of prison. Since then I am helping here." He told me he'd been jailed for teaching the "true words of Islam."

Two other men were standing nearby, peeling carrots and potatoes for the soup. "Were you all also in prison?" I asked. They nodded. In the wake of the so-called Jasmine Revolution, hundreds of prisoners had been released in a general amnesty, including many jihadists. I asked about the name of their organization. Who was paying for all the vegetables in their soup and everything else they were giving to the refugees? They looked at each other. They had an emir, they told me, but weren't allowed to say anything more unless he ordered them to do so.

This surprised Ahmad. Like thousands of other young Tunisians, he'd taken to the streets and called for Ben Ali to leave. "Why do you need permission?" he asked. "We had a revolution. This is a free country now. You can speak freely. That's what we all risked our lives for."

But men like these evidently wanted something far different from what Ahmad and his friends had fought for. "I cannot speak without the approval of the emir," insisted one of the men, who said his name was Salah.

I thanked him and said I would be back. A group of refugees was waiting patiently for the soup to be ready. I left with Ahmad, who was still disturbed by what we'd just witnessed. Ahmad was Muslim, but very liberal and a committed feminist; he didn't like to see people mixing religion and politics, or trying to radicalize vulnerable refugees. He had different ambitions for his country.

As we walked to the car, I dug out my phone from my bag and dialed a UK cell number. The wife of the Tunisian I'd met in London picked up and handed him the phone.

"I am in Ra's Ajdir, and I think I found your brothers," I said. "One of them is named Salah, but he says he can't speak without the permission of his emir. Can you help?"

I heard laughter on the other end of the line. "*Insha'Allah*, God willing, all will be good," he answered. "I will try to reach his emir."

I thanked him and hung up.

"Who did you speak to?" Ahmad asked.

"That was the key to the emir," I replied.

Next, Ahmad and I went to a nearby Moroccan field hospital where we'd become friendly with some doctors. They would serve us fresh mint tea and share stories. Most of their patients suffered from diarrhea or skin rashes from sleeping in tents without much access to water and soap. From time to time, they also treated men with bullet wounds and women who had been raped in the camp. They said those cases were the hardest.

While we were talking to them, my phone rang. "You can go back to the tent," a woman on the other end of the line told me in Arabic. "Salah got instructions." Then the phone went dead.

Salah was inside with the two men we'd seen earlier and another man we hadn't met. I asked if he had any news from his emir.

"Yes, Sister Souad, he can speak to you," the new man answered. "The emir gave him permission."

I asked who he was, but he wouldn't give me his real name, instead calling himself Abu Khaled.

"Can I talk to the emir?" I asked.

"No, you can't, but he sends his regards."

"Can I talk to you?"

"No, you can't."

"Why not?"

"Because I haven't received the permission to speak, only Salah has."

"You seem to have tough rules in your group," I said. "Is the emir in Tunisia?"

He smiled. "My sister, you can try whatever way you like to get information out of me, but you won't succeed in what over fifteen years of prison and torture weren't able to do."

"Why were you in prison?"

"For preaching the right way of our religion."

He answered like so many others I had spoken to before and after him. What they often meant was that they had not only preached Islam, but also called for the toppling of regimes in the region, and in some cases for establishing a structure and rules based on Sharia as they interpreted it.

A few weeks earlier, Cuspert had told me about men like this. I wondered if there was a connection.

"Do you know Abu Maleeq from Germany? The one who sings hip-hop?"

"You mean the rapper?" Abu Khaled responded. Then his face suddenly changed, as if he knew he had said too much.

I tried to make him feel better, telling him he had nothing to worry about. I had already known that Abu Maleeq was in touch with them, that there was some kind of link, so technically he hadn't violated the order not to say anything.

I arranged to meet Salah that evening in a hotel in a nearby town to talk about his life and upbringing. I learned that he had come from a rural part of Tunisia. Born into a lower-middle-class family, he knew that even though he did well in school, he would have no chance to go to university. "I have eight brothers and sisters, and I am the oldest, so I had to start working to help my parents," he told me. He began selling drugs in a larger neighboring city and dreamed of going to Europe.

Then one day in 1999, when Salah was nineteen, he ran into another young man who had grown up in the same neighborhood. This man told Salah about a preacher who had fought in Afghanistan and Bosnia, and who had deeply influenced him. "I went with him and met this sheikh, who is today our emir," Salah said. "He told me that this life wasn't important, but the afterlife was, and that whatever I was doing today would count in the afterlife."

He stopped selling drugs and began to study with the sheikh. The man gave Salah and his other students a monthly salary so they could help their families.

The more time he spent with the group, the more he saw how "wrong" Tunisian and Western policies were. "No one cares about Muslim lives," he said, but he apparently believed his sheikh did. Salah's mentor planned to send him and others to Iraq in 2004 to fight alongside Abu Musab al-Zarqawi, but Tunisian authorities arrested them and charged them with being members of a terrorist organization. Salah and his friends were sentenced to fifteen to twenty years in prison.

"All for helping our sisters and brothers in Iraq," Salah said. The Tunisian security forces and prison guards tortured him and his comrades, even raping some of them, but he believed they had grown stronger in prison. I'd seen this before in other places. Militants were sent to prison and tortured, further radicalizing them. While there, they often met and connected with like-minded people who reinforced their views.

"And what now?"

"Now, Allah has freed us from the dog Ben Ali and the dogs of America in Tunisia. Next is Libya, then Algeria, then Morocco and all of the Islamic world."

He told me that some of his "brothers" had already traveled to Libya and were fighting there alongside Libyans against the Gaddafi regime. "We also send brothers to Syria," he said.

"And when the rulers are gone," I asked, "what is your aim?"

"The caliphate," he answered. I remembered my conversations with Shaker al-Abssi in Lebanon, who had given me the same answer several years before.

I flew back to Germany in mid-August. I called the imam in Berlin again and asked if he had heard anything from Cuspert.

"Yes, he is still here in Berlin," the imam answered. "He had to change his phone after the story broke about Arid Uka, but he asked me to give you his number."

I called right away. "I must see you," I told him.

He began to laugh. "Yes, I heard you met some of my brothers in North Africa."

11

Threats

Bahrain, Iran, and Germany, 2011–13

As protests erupted across the Middle East in the spring of 2011, one small country in particular drew my attention: Bahrain, an island emirate in the Arabian Gulf, off the coast of Saudi Arabia. The more time I spent there, the more convinced I became that Bahrain contained another clue to the true nature of the so-called Arab Spring. Much as Islamist groups were gaining ground under the banner of democracy in places such as Egypt and Libya, Bahrain was a shining example of the way religious and sectarian groups were hijacking old enmities for their own opportunistic ends. Only the players and the goals were slightly different in Bahrain. And Iran had a dog in the fight.

A former British protectorate, Bahrain gained independence in 1971 and quickly established itself as an important business and security partner to the United States and home to its Fifth Fleet. Prosperous and developed, it is also comparatively progressive for the Gulf region: in 2002, it became a constitutional monarchy, expanded suffrage to women, and allowed them to run for office. Two years later, the country named its first female minister, and in 2008 it appointed a Jewish woman, Houda Nonoo, as its ambassador to the United States. She is believed to be the first Jewish ambassador in the Arab world.

The main thing that sets Bahrain apart from its Arab Spring neighbors is its religious composition. Though there are no official or independent statistics, Bahrain is a Shia majority state that has long been ruled by a Sunni royal family, giving rise to decades of sporadic protests over sectarian discrimination. Iran also has a long-standing territorial interest in Bahrain. It officially renounced its claim to sovereignty over the island in 1970, when a UN report showed that the Bahrainis wanted independence, but that wasn't the end of the story.

Some Shia opposition figures who for decades had called for the overthrow of the royal family emerged as key leaders. While Western observers, diplomats, and journalists tended to see in Bahrain a nascent prodemocracy movement, some influential Shia religious leaders were also keen to convert a relatively progressive state into an Iranian-style Islamic republic. I saw how depressed some Shia women were in the more conservative parts of the country, wrapped in *chadors* with no right to divorce, even when their husbands abused them. The sectarian unrest and the push to make religion a bigger part of political and everyday life reminded me of what I'd seen in Iraq. The consequences, I knew, could be terrifying.

At some stage, the democracy protests were hijacked by people who had old arguments with the Bahraini state. This isn't to say there weren't Bahrainis who wanted more rights—there were. The government's crackdowns on protesters also entailed well-documented acts of torture, which were indefensible. But even if many Bahraini Shia felt discriminated against, it didn't follow that they wanted to live in a religious state run by Shia clerics.

The Shia opposition, while raising some legitimate concerns, could also be mercurial. In February, Crown Prince Salman bin Hamad bin Isa al-Khalifa met with representatives of Al Wefaq, the largest Shia political party, including its secretary-general, the cleric Sheikh Ali Salman. According to Salman's account, this meeting was held on the understanding that the crown prince was prepared to consider the significant demands for reform being expressed in the demonstrations. "During these discussions, which reportedly lasted for three hours, Al Wefaq voiced its reservations about the existing Constitution; expressed discontent with aspects of the government's performance, composition, and powers; and asked that demonstrators at a major traffic circle be allowed to remain there," it was later reported. "According to Al Wefaq's account of the meeting, despite having previously agreed to consider the significant reform demands, the Crown Prince stated that he was not mandated to reach an agreement on these issues. The Crown Prince suggested that the demonstrators move to a more secure location because the [Bahraini government] was concerned for their safety from possible attacks by vigilantes."

After six Bahraini protesters were killed in a three-day period, another meeting was arranged, but Ali Salman didn't show up. The crown prince waited all night. After this, the government concluded that the opposition didn't want a legitimate agreement, further damaging any trust between the parties. The chances for a fruitful dialogue vanished.

I traveled to Bahrain briefly in February 2011. I'd never been there, and I didn't know what to expect. I spent time at the funerals of protesters who had been killed in the demonstrations, including a teenage boy who had died of a head wound. The doctors told his family he'd been hit by a tear gas canister. The family thought it was intentional. The women screaming and beating themselves at his funeral reminded me of the mourning for Aquila al-Hashimi in Iraq. But what the women in Bahrain shouted was different from what the crowd in 2003 had said. The Bahraini women called for "death to the soldiers of Yazid and Muawiya," a reference to the Battle of Karbala in AD 680, when the soldiers of Yazid I, the Umayyad caliph, killed Hussein, the grandson of the Prophet Muhammad and the son of Ali, along with many relatives, including Hussein's infant son. The killings made Hussein a martyr and cemented the division between Sunni and Shia Muslims. The Shia consider themselves the loyal followers of Ali and commemorate the Battle of Karbala during the sacred month of Muharram with marches, tears, and self-flagellation.

I asked the grieving women who they were talking about. The police and security forces, they told me.

Like Bahrain's government, the country's security forces were mostly

Sunni, while the protesters were mostly Shia. But some Shia police told me they were constantly under attack from their own communities, and they showed me videos of burning cars to prove the point. Many Bahraini police were of Indian or Pakistani descent, exposing another rift between the native Bahrainis and these migrants (and their descendants), who were mainly Sunni but often lacked the benefits of citizenship and faced discrimination as "outsiders."

Later that year, I ran into my former *Washington Post* colleague Anthony Shadid at a conference in Qatar. Anthony had been a persistent and definitive voice on the Arab Spring, and he had been violently kidnapped in Libya while covering the revolt against Gaddafi. He shared my interest in Bahrain, and he urged me to go back.

But things were changing at the *Times*. In June, Bill Keller announced that he would step down as executive editor. Bill had always been a great supporter of the kind of investigative journalism I was doing, and of me personally. Along with my direct editors, he'd done much to help me in my years there.

The new leadership at the paper had different plans. In one conversation later that year, a high-level editor told me that because Osama bin Laden had been killed, terrorism was no longer a major threat. The Arab Spring was a game changer, he continued. He seemed to believe that the Islamists had been soundly defeated by the energy of youthful democracy activists. I tried to explain that my conversations with Cuspert and my time at the Tunisian-Libyan border had suggested that a new generation of jihadists was emerging. But this editor was sure the Middle East was changing and that there wouldn't be any space left for jihadists in this new world.

I was shocked by his assessment and worried that if we didn't cover these developments we'd be negligent, as we had been in the past. I remembered Maureen Fanning, the September 11 widow who had asked so movingly why no one had told her that so many people out there hated Americans. We couldn't afford to let readers like her down again.

At the same time, I couldn't help but wonder what these changes would mean for me as a freelance reporter working on contract. Was this the end of my career at the *New York Times*? My fears were soon borne out, as I found myself writing less for the flagship paper and more for the international edition, including a section called "The Female Factor."

There were many stories to tell about women in Bahrain. Of all the countries in the Gulf region, its society was the most open-minded. Women had more rights; they could drive and hold leadership positions. Women also played an important role in the protests there. I interviewed Rula al-Saffar, a forty-nine-year-old nurse who had been detained for five months. She described being blindfolded, threatened, and tortured with electric shocks. Her description took me back to my experience in the Egyptian prison. I remembered the screaming I'd heard when I was blindfolded. The truth was, I felt a deep sympathy for her. But when I asked her and others about the rules for medical personnel protesting during work time and challenged some of what they said, a woman serving as a minder from Wa'ad, one of the leading opposition groups, asked me, "Are you working for the other side or what?"

I soon learned that the minder's reaction wasn't unusual. The opposition, for all its merits, sought to impose a kind of thought orthodoxy on reporters writing about the uprising. The narrative was that the protests had been entirely peaceful and that no demonstrators had attacked police or anyone else. Yet I met Indian, Pakistani, and Bangladeshi workers who said they'd been attacked by protesters. Other people of Asian descent recounted that they had been refused treatment at hospitals. But when I raised this matter with opposition leaders, they seemed offended. Such stories were not part of their carefully crafted narrative.

Later, I spoke with Farida Ghulam, an education official whose husband, Ibrahim Sharif al-Sayed, was the general secretary of Wa'ad, whose formal name was the National Democratic Action Society. In 2011, al-Sayed was sentenced to five years in prison for allegedly planning to overthrow the government. Yet Ghulam mentioned that her son was studying at a university in Michigan on a scholarship from the crown prince's office.

"Does it mean your child's education is paid for by the royal family?" I asked.

She confirmed this. "But it's their right," she said of her son and his fellow scholarship students. "They worked hard for it."

"And how are you paying for his studies now?" I asked, assuming that the scholarship has been canceled once the father had been arrested.

"No, it's still going on," she said.

I added this to my growing pile of evidence that we in the West might be viewing the situation in Bahrain in overly black-and-white terms, given its complexity.

Meanwhile, it was time for me to look for a permanent professional home, and I started writing for *Der Spiegel* on contract, returning after an absence of nearly ten years. The magazine's editors were interested in the Bahrain story, and so in February 2012, a year after the uprising, I went back and dug deeper.

On that trip, a colleague and I interviewed the king, asking him about imprisoned activists and torture, as well as the human rights commission he had established, chaired by Mahmoud Cherif Bassiouni, an international law expert and human rights activist. The Bassiouni Commission was set up to investigate and report on alleged abuses, including accusations that security forces had tortured prisoners, and its report amounted to a stark indictment of the government's handling of the protests. It found that thirty-five people had died during demonstrations in 2011, including five security personnel, and that hundreds had been wounded. The government had arrested nearly three thousand people, seven hundred of whom remained behind bars.

I decided to confront the king directly on the subject of freedom of speech.

"Your Majesty," I asked, "what would happen if we were to shout 'Down with the king'?"

The king didn't seem offended. "They do shout it on the streets," he replied. "As I emphasized in my speech last year, this is not a reason to imprison someone. It's just a case of manners. But when they shout 'Down with the king and up with Khomeini,' that's a problem for national unity," he said, referring to the former Shia Ayatollah of Iran.

I found it notable that the king had made the reference to Khomeini, especially as Bassiouni and others did not report any Iranian involvement in the demonstrations. I wanted to see for myself and spend more time in the neighborhoods where the protesters came from. At a mosque in Diraz, where one of the most influential Shia clerics preached, large portraits of Ayatollahs Khomeini and Khamenei watched over the prayers. I began to wonder even more about the scale of Iran's involvement in the Bahraini opposition groups and demonstrations.

Some activist groups talked about "systematic" discrimination against Shia. My regular taxi driver, Abu Hussain, who lived in one of the Shia villages outside the capital, told me the same thing. He blamed the royal family directly. "First of all, why would they bring people to work from outside?" he said, trying to keep his voice level and friendly. "These people from Jordan, Syria, Pakistan, India, or Bangladesh."

I asked what jobs he was talking about.

"In offices, banks, or in the ministries. Why don't they take my children or the children of my neighbor? These jobs should be for real Bahrainis first."

"But maybe the other people are better qualified?" I suggested. Then I asked if he had a cleaning lady at home.

"Yes, of course," he answered.

"Where is she from?"

"Bangladesh."

"So Bahrainis should also do these kind of jobs, right? Your wife and daughters?"

"No, no, of course not. I would never allow them to do such work," he replied. He sounded shocked that I would consider such a thing. "This is beyond our honor. What would you say if I asked if you would do such work, or your mother?" He mentioned my mother because I'd told him she was a *sayyida*.

He certainly didn't expect to hear what came next. I told him that my mother had been a laundress and my father a cook. I explained how I had contributed to the family income since I was sixteen by working in bakeries, babysitting, cleaning floors and dishes, and cooking for and feeding elderly people in the church community where my mother worked. His face turned pale as he listened. "So when you say this is beyond your honor, it was not beyond mine, or my parents'," I said.

Abu Hussain raised his eyebrows in shock. He searched for words. "I am sorry," he finally said. "I didn't mean something bad."

On one of my visits, Abu Hussain took me to a house with a blue flag on top with "Al Wefaq" written on it. This was the office of Ali Salman.

The hall inside was filled with men. Soon, Salman descended the stairs. Though I'd seen him on TV and in magazines, I didn't immediately recognize him without his trademark white turban. Salman invited me into a separate office and asked someone to bring tea. I listened and noted down what he and his party demanded: more rights, a prime minister not named by the king but elected by the people, restricted citizenship for immigrants, and an end to discrimination against the Shia. Then he accused the government of giving Bahraini nationality to Sunni immigrants to change the country's demographics so that the Shia would no longer constitute a majority.

"Sheikh Ali," I said, "I thought you were asking for reforms for all Bahrainis, right? I thought you weren't just a party looking out for the rights of Shia."

He agreed that he and his party were defending the interests of all Bahrainis. But like Abu Hussain he mentioned the jobs that Pakistanis and Bangladeshis got before Bahrainis and insisted that Bahrainis should have priority when it came to employment.

"If people in Germany had followed your argument, neither my parents nor I would have gotten citizenship," I told him. I couldn't understand why granting citizenship to non-Shia would bother him so much if his party truly represented the interests of all Bahrainis. I acknowledged that I didn't live in the country and therefore might not have the full picture. When I had asked Abu Hussain in the car about some of the big business owners in Bahrain who were supposedly Shia, he had replied, "Well, these people are close to the system. That's why they were successful."

Then I asked Ali Salman about family law for Shia women. Bahrain technically has three courts: a civil court, a Sunni court, and a Shia court; it also has two sets of family laws, one for Sunnis and one for Shia. If a

Shia woman marries at a Shia court, she cannot get a divorce as easily, even if her husband beats her. Al Wefaq had argued against changing this. I told him I couldn't understand how he and his political party, which opposed discrimination so loudly, had voted to take away the rights of Shia women.

He said this was a religious matter, not a political one.

"But Sheikh Ali, if on one hand you argue that there shouldn't be any discrimination against anyone, how can you allow Shia women to be discriminated against?"

"That's not the most important thing, not even for Shia women," he said. "What is important is that the prime minister can be chosen by the people and doesn't stay in power for over forty years, like now." (The prime minister, Khalifa bin Salman al-Khalifa, was the uncle of the king and had been in office since 1970.) He didn't seem concerned about the growing influence of religious leaders in Bahrain.

I left the meeting with more questions than answers. I wondered if I was the only journalist working for a Western media organization who found Ali Salman's views questionable for someone who was widely considered a "democrat." Was the Bahraini opposition movement about democratic values, or was it simply about sectarian power? Ali Salman was a cleric as well as a political leader, and his religious authority added greatly to his power. I remembered how, after the fall of Saddam, whole neighborhoods in Baghdad had become sectarian enclaves as residents became more religiously observant, and how women—who had been more or less independent and had access to all kinds of jobs—were suddenly forced to cover up, to change their lives, and to give up most of their freedoms. There was something else Iraq had taught me. When there was a growing overlap between sectarianism and politics on one side of the divide, the other side would grow more extreme in response.

"Isn't he a great leader?" Abu Hussain asked when I got back into the car. "He would make a great prime minister, don't you think?"

I put on my big sunglasses. I'd hoped to avoid another political debate, but he'd asked for it. Besides, I thought Abu Hussain and men like him should be challenged from time to time. I told him about my experience in Iraq and that I didn't think religious or sectarian political parties or leaders like Ali Salman would work in multicultural and multiethnic countries. "It doesn't mean that there shouldn't be reforms or discussions about human rights," I told him, but I wasn't certain that Al Wefaq could gain the trust of all Bahrainis or would represent the interests of all.

"But that doesn't matter," Abu Hussain answered. "Democracy means that the majority will win and has the right to rule over the minority, like in the West."

But what about a constitution that protected the rights of other groups as well? My conversations with Al Wefaq members and Abu Hussain made it clear to me that while Bahrainis and Westerners both talked about "democracy," each side used the word to mean something different.

While the media and politicians concentrated mainly on Al Wefaq and the government, less was said about the unhealthy effect the conflict might have on Sunnis. One afternoon, I went to the small town of Busaiteen to interview four students I'd met at the University of Bahrain, along with their friends. They were all Sunni, and they were angry at their government and the West.

The government was "too soft on those Shia terrorists," a student named Adel told me. He called the protesters terrorists because they used Molotov cocktails and burned tires and had beaten up some of his fellow students.

I asked if he understood the Shias' demands for more rights.

"Look, we all know in the Gulf that people from the royal family have more privileges than others," his friend Muhammad answered. "It doesn't matter if you're Shia or Sunni."

"So then why are you unhappy about the protests?" I asked. "Aren't those some of the demands being made?"

They all shook their heads. "No, no, that's just an excuse to win the West over. What they really want is to turn Bahrain into a new Iraq," Adel said. "They want a sectarian war."

I asked why they were angry at the West.

"Because your governments are turning a blind eye to how radical and violent most of those people are," a student named Khaled said. "Instead, you're supporting them."

"What support do you mean?"

"All these comments from human rights organizations and politicians about how Shia protesters were treated. Why are there no such comments about the violence they are using? Aren't these double standards?"

Adel broke in: "To us and others here, this looks like a Western conspiracy to weaken Sunnis and give Iran more influence in the region," he said.

I spent almost two hours with them and could hear the anger and fear mixed into their arguments. I wondered how things were at the university, or if they had Shia friends.

"We never grew up asking if one was Shia or Sunni or Christian or whatever," Adel answered. Then he looked down and took a deep breath. "But now both sides keep to themselves."

"Why?"

"Because we don't trust each other anymore."

Since I had first come to Bahrain, most of the protesters had agreed on one demand: that the prime minister should step down. I asked his office for an interview but didn't expect much. Instead, I followed up with one of the Al Wefaq members I'd met several times before, at the Friday sermons in Diraz.

This man had become one of the most reliable sources I'd met in Bahrain. I often went to him to double-check information and for deeper discussions about where the country was going. He asked not to be named for various reasons. "Let's meet at Costa Coffee Shop on Boudaya Road," he said.

I thought I would visit some nearby villages before the meeting. I wore the sequined *abaya* I'd gotten in Zarqa over a T-shirt, jeans, and a black Pakistani scarf.

After Abu Hussain and I had finished our tour through the villages, he drove me to the coffee shop, a renowned opposition-group hangout.

"Why Costa Coffee Shop?" I asked my source when I met him there. He told me that the owner was a supporter of Al Wefaq and the protest movement.

"So does it mean you guys are boycotting other coffee shops? And vice versa?"

He confirmed that this was the situation.

"If you all hate each other so much, how will this country ever be one?" I asked him. "How will the wounds heal?"

"With time," he answered. *"Insha'Allah."*

I told him that this didn't seem to have worked in Iraq. "Now here, the sectarian divide is getting bigger," I said. "Don't people see what is going on in the region, more divisions everywhere?"

A group of men came over to greet my source. When they left, he told me that they were all working as stringers or translators for media outlets.

"Are they activists?" I asked.

"Yes, all supporters of the party and the protests, thank God," he answered.

"Are they also working with Western media?" I asked.

He nodded.

This was a shrewd move by the opposition, I thought. If the international press relied on stringers or translators who had already chosen a side, it would be easy to lose context.

Our coffees had just arrived when my phone rang. I recognized the number of the prime minister's media adviser.

I apologized and asked if I could take the call, saying it might be important. The media adviser asked where I was.

"I am at Costa Coffee Shop at . . . wait a second, what's this road called again?" I asked my source. He told me the name and I spoke after him.

"Costa Coffee? Boudaya Road? What are you doing there?" the media adviser asked. I could hear sarcasm in his voice.

I understood that this meeting point of opposition figures was known not only to the opposition but to the rest of the country as well.

"Well, it doesn't matter now," the media adviser said. "Do you have a car?"

"Yes. I've got my taxi with me."

"Okay. Come now to the prime minister's office. But now!"

"Why?"

"Didn't you say you wanted an interview with him? So come now. Your friends at Costa Coffee will surely wait for you."

My source began to giggle when he overheard where I was going. "So you are going to the prime minister's office? I won't ask specifically who you're going to see, but are you aware that you are in jeans and sneakers? I can't wait to read the interview." He laughed.

I looked down at my clothes. They were covered in dust. I'd just spent hours in the sun in villages with guys who had proudly shown me their Molotov cocktails.

In the car, I searched for whatever perfume, powder, or lip gloss I could find in my backpack. Abu Hussain was absorbed by his own problems. "And what shall I do?" he wailed.

"What do you mean?"

"What shall I do if they arrest you?"

"Arrest me? Why should they arrest me?"

"Well, he is the prime minister, and a very strong man. If you talk to him the way you did with Sheikh Ali or the way you do with me, they might arrest you."

"Abu Hussain, I think I've met more dangerous people than the prime minister."

Somebody was waiting at the gate for me. Abu Hussain said that he would wait close by and that I should call him when the meeting was over.

The man who accompanied me to the prime minister's office looked a little surprised when he saw my clothes. The media adviser waited in front of a door with some guards.

I apologized for my appearance. "It's not like you gave me any chance to get back to the hotel and get dressed," I told him.

"No worries, we won't take pictures of this meeting."

They'd scheduled fifteen minutes for the interview. The prime minister was very self-assured, with a proud, disciplined posture. I'd heard many people attack him, and I expected him to be arrogant and unlikable. Instead, he came across during the interview as serious and not afraid to engage in a tough discussion; he was respectful to me, but less so toward the protesters. He called the demonstrators "terrorists" supported by Iran and spoke about how the shah of Iran had once tried to lay claim to Bahrain. The prime minister himself had met with him and warned about interference. He said that Bahrain's main problem wasn't the Sunni-Shia divide, but an Arab-Persian split that had persisted for many years.

"This is all Iran's interference," he said, noting that his government had asked the Iranian ambassador to leave Bahrain.

I asked if he thought it was time for him to step down after all these years. His media adviser, seated behind him, blanched. The prime minister said that this was up to the king. "My duty was and remains to protect this country, and I will do this until the last day of my life. Believe me, if my position alone were the reason for the unrest, then I would have already stepped down from my office last year. But this is just a further excuse from the opposition."

I challenged him about the human rights abuses. He acknowledged that the government had made "mistakes" but said they would all be investigated. When we stood up to say good-bye, the media adviser didn't look happy. The prime minister, however, told me he'd enjoyed the "challenging debate."

I didn't depart with much optimism. The interviews with Ali Salman and the prime minister left the impression that these were two characters who weren't willing to compromise to find a solution.

At about the time of my interview, news broke that Abdulhadi al-Khawaja was on a hunger strike. Al-Khawaja, one of the presidents of the Bahrain Center for Human Rights, a nongovernmental organization, had recently been arrested for calling for the overthrow of the government.

Al-Khawaja has two daughters, Maryam and Zainab, who used social media as a platform for their activism, and they were frequent guests on international TV and radio programs throughout the uprising. The women were dual citizens of Bahrain and Denmark and had studied in the United States on scholarships. They spoke fluent English with American accents. They covered their hair with colored veils, wore jeans, and talked about democracy and human rights. They were ready-made media darlings with a touching narrative and the right cause.

Between trips to Bahrain, I had met with several intelligence sources from Europe and the United States, many of whom believed that al-Khawaja, the hunger striker, and his deputy and other leaders inside the opposition movement had ties to Hezbollah and the Iranian Revolutionary Guard, though there wasn't any clear evidence of direct Iranian involvement in the protests. A European intelligence official also linked Bahraini opposition figures to Ahmad Chalabi, the Shia activist who had helped lead the United States into war with Iraq.

I worried that this information might have been planted. "Is this coming from the Bahrainis? Or any other Arab service?" I asked.

"No, this is our own research," he said. "Bahrain is becoming a playground for Saudi Arabia and Iran."

I told him that what he was telling me was contrary to public opinion. "The Bahrain Center for Human Rights has received international awards even in Europe," I pointed out. "Those people are sitting on the boards of renowned international organizations, and you are saying they have ties to declared terrorist organizations and shady figures? How is this possible?"

It wasn't his job to explain politics, he said. He was just an intelligence official.

Online, I found an NPR piece reporting that Chalabi was supporting and advising the Bahraini opposition. The piece suggested that Chalabi was interested in Bahrain because it could become part of a "Shiite crescent" that included Iran and postwar Iraq. But Chalabi said that accusing him of sectarian aims was like "accusing Martin Luther King of being a racist. Is he a racist? He stood up for the rights of the blacks because they were oppressed as blacks. These people are oppressed as Shia. So when they stand up for their rights, it is not sectarianism, it is because they are oppressed as Shia."

But the focus right now was on al-Khawaja out of concern that he would die from his hunger strike. Through an intermediary, I requested an interview with his daughter Zainab. My meeting with her took place upstairs in the mall that housed the Costa Coffee Shop. The shopping center was owned by a prominent Shia supporter of the opposition, and on this day it was nearly empty; it had been a site of violent clashes and had lost business as a result. Zainab, then twenty-eight years old, was very articulate, but I had the distinct feeling she'd memorized her lines.

The conversation began cordially. She told me the same thing she'd told all the other media outlets about her father's situation. One could get the impression he might die at any minute.

I had watched many of the interviews she and her sister had given on networks such as CNN, the BBC, and Al Jazeera English. It sounded as if they were standing up for "peaceful protest" and nonviolent resistance, but they never denounced the protesters' violence, either in interviews or online.

In fact, the Bahrain Center for Human Rights didn't talk at all about how the protesters had assaulted Asian expatriates, or about the Sunni students from the University of Bahrain who had been attacked by demonstrators with iron sticks and had lain in pools of blood while others were still beating them, as had been documented in the Bassiouni report.

"Why is it that I don't read anything about those cases on your website?" I asked. Zainab called the violence "a reaction."

"We don't want peace over freedom," she told me. "We will choose freedom over peace. We will go on with our fight for self-determination and democracy. But if things continue the way they are, I expect the situation to become more violent."

"Are you calling for people to stop attacking police and to stop throwing stones and Molotov cocktails?"

"No, I will not stand against the victims' reaction. It really amazes me when people ask if I will condemn it. I will not." In a way, she reminded me of the ex-rapper Cuspert, who had also said that he was on the side of the underdog. Like him, she seemed to have taken that argument too far, to a point where she believed that only her views were legitimate.

I asked if she had any affiliation with Hezbollah or Chalabi, and if her father had told her about any military training he had received in Iran. She said she had never heard him talk about that; she believed this was something the government was saying about him.

Der Spiegel's policy on publishing a Q-and-A was that the interviewee had to authorize the transcript. I hated this rule. It ran counter to the principles I had learned working for the *Washington Post* and the *New York Times*, where this is not done. The rule at those papers was simply to record the interview. If the subject wanted, she could bring a recorder of her own, and if she had complaints, she could use her recording to support them.

When Zainab al-Khawaja saw the transcript, she called me. She said she felt I had tricked her. It was clearly not the kind of interview she had expected. But since it was exactly what she'd said, I didn't understand her surprise.

"It's my job to be critical of all sides," I told her. "I'm not an activist."

She asked what would happen if she objected to the interview. I told her that this was a decision for the editors, but that, for my part, I found it difficult to understand how someone who spent so much time promoting human rights and press freedom would now support what seemed like censorship to me.

She said she would get back to me.

My editor was also upset by the interview. He said it lacked empathy. "Her father is dying, and we are putting her in the hot seat," he told me. He decided to cut the interview severely. I sent Zainab the edited version, and she approved it.

Shortly thereafter, another story ran that drew the family's ire. The government had granted Frank Gardner, a veteran BBC Middle East correspondent, exclusive access to Abdulhadi al-Khawaja while he was in prison. Like everyone else, Gardner thought al-Khawaja was dying based on the interviews his family had been giving. On May 1, 2012, Gardner reported that he had visited al-Khawaja in the hospital.

"We went into the hospital room expecting to see a man at death's door, lying hooked up to drips," Gardner wrote to me recently in an email. "Instead Mr. al-Khawaja sprang up from doing his prayers and greeted us wearing a tracksuit. He seemed lively and alert, and we conducted a five-minute verbal interview before the Bahraini authorities closed it down and told us to leave."

Although al-Khawaja was thin, Gardner recalled, he "was clearly not at death's door, this was only a partial hunger strike. In fact, when the minders weren't looking, one of the hospital staff showed us a photo on his phone of Mr. al-Khawaja tucking into a sizable meal in his room."

Gardner's story contradicted the story that the family had been telling. Al-Khawaja's wife was especially furious. "She took to social media to accuse us of spouting whatever story the Bahraini authorities told us to write," Gardner recalled, noting that he had interviewed the wife and included her views in his story. "I found it depressing," he went on, "that a woman who we had devoted some considerable time to interviewing, letting her get her viewpoint across uninterrupted," should be so angry when things didn't go her way and, he said, "we didn't perpetuate a false myth."

I would get the answers to some of my questions about Iran's involvement in Bahrain more than two years later, when I was invited on a brief trip to Iran under the auspices of the Koerber Foundation, a German NGO whose work focuses on international dialogue for social change. The trip involved several days of roundtable discussions with Iranian officials. One night, we were invited to dinner at the German ambassador's residence, a beautiful villa with an amazing garden.

I was seated between high-level members of the Iranian and German Foreign Ministries. "You know that Bahrain used to be part of Persia?" the Iranian said. "It's very important to us." He went on to say that "the suffering of Bahrainis is of great concern to my countrymen and -women." And then he added that Iran had asked the Bahraini opposition to participate in elections some years earlier, a revelation that surprised the German diplomat seated on the other side of me.

"They would not have done it if we hadn't pushed them," the Iranian said.

"So they do actually have influence on the opposition?" the German diplomat whispered to me in German. "When the opposition visited us, they denied any links to Iran. Unbelievable."

The Iranian knew every main opposition member by name. He was "so glad," he said, that human rights organizations were following the abuses in Bahrain so closely. He also knew the al-Khawaja family and said they had many supporters in Iran, calling them "great fighters for human rights."

It was unsettling to hear him talk about human rights given the killing and imprisonment of protesters in Iran. I decided to press him on this point. "So when Assad or al-Maliki—both of whom, I believe, are backed by your country—commit human rights abuses, it doesn't seem to be such a big issue. Is it because they are mostly hurting Sunnis?" I asked. "But then, in the case of Bahrain, your newspapers are full of articles, and so are the Iranian-backed channels like Press TV."

He didn't answer me.

In the summer of 2012, things began to change at *Der Spiegel*. The people who had hired me got new jobs, and the man who had told me years earlier that I might be mistaken for a Taliban spy was promoted. I felt as if I was in the wrong movie. It sure wasn't *All the President's Men*.

I was grateful soon after to learn that I'd been awarded a fellowship at Harvard. I happily set off for Cambridge, where I spent a year researching long-term strategies of terrorist organizations since the outbreak of the so-called Arab Spring. I also worked with Nick Kulish to finish our book *The Eternal Nazi*, which was published in 2014.

But the truth was that I was in a deep crisis over my profession. Being a journalist of Muslim descent who helped track down the true story of a Nazi doctor accused of hideous crimes against the Jews made me fodder for rumors and accusations. The Arab Spring had also had a profound effect on what counted as international reporting, with one online outlet after another starting up. "Citizen journalism" seemed to be the new big thing, but I worried about what such activist reporting would do to what we call "truth." If readers and viewers got used to a kind of journalism that told them only one side of the story, how would their views of the world ever change?

What would people like Maureen Fanning say? Would someone else ask again why no one had reported that the Arab Spring was turning formerly stable countries into security threats? That in fact it was contributing to the sectarian rift that was increasingly dividing the Arab world? That some of those who claimed they were on the streets for democracy did not share the democratic values of the West?

Soon after finishing the fellowship in 2013, I was in Dubai having dinner with my brother and some friends when I received a call from my sister Hannan. I realized that she had tried several times before, but the restaurant was so loud that I hadn't heard the phone ringing.

"The special unit of the police was just here," she told me. "They said there is a threat against your life."

At first I thought it was a bad joke, but her voice sounded anxious.

"I swear I'm not joking. They said they have to speak to you immediately and left their number. You have to call them right away."

I couldn't understand what was happening. Who was threatening me and why?

I called the woman in charge of the German police branch that specialized in terrorism, and she explained that her colleagues from a different police branch and the intelligence services had asked her to immediately get in touch with me. "A very reliable source told us that there might be an imminent attempt to kidnap or even kill you. There is some talk about a Daniel Pearl scenario."

I was beside myself. "Who? Why? Where is this coming from?"

"I can't tell you much now, but it's related to the region you are in now. It has some jihadist connection to people you interviewed before."

"Could my family be in danger because of this?"

"It's best if you come back as soon as possible, and we can discuss this in person."

I tried to stay calm but I felt guilty that I might have put my family in danger. I also felt very alone.

I asked Hannan not to tell our parents anything. I flew back to Germany the next day and arranged to meet with the special branch people a day later.

The night before the meeting, I received an alert on Twitter. Maryam al-Khawaja had added my name to one of her tweets.

There was a link to an article she had coauthored for the magazine *Foreign Policy* that was a response to a piece I had written for the *Daily Beast* about Sameera Rajab, the Bahraini communications minister. Rajab was an unexpected character: a powerful Shia woman and mother of three with complicated family connections to the opposition. Al-Khawaja and her coauthor accused me of being a shill for the Bahraini government, using Rajab as an example of women's progress when she was the exception, not the rule. "Mekhennet fails to question any of

Rajab's official policy statements," they wrote. "She does not engage Rajab on her complicit role in the violations committed against Bahrainis. She misses the chance to do what journalists are meant to do. . . . Mekhennet's article on Rajab does not come as a surprise since her pieces on Bahrain have a precedence of uncritically embracing state narratives. This is certainly not lost on the Bahraini regime, which previously granted her an interview with the king, then several months later, an interview with Prime Minister Khalifa bin Salman al-Khalifa." Though I'm anything but a major player in Bahraini politics, the piece mentioned my name eight times. The authors had never bothered to ask for my side of the story.

Great. So now along with the jihadists, I have these other extremists attacking me, I thought. I wondered if this new threat had anything to do with these people in Bahrain. Sure enough, shortly afterward, one of my German intelligence sources called. "Did you see *Foreign Policy*?" he began. "You are mentioned by name, and they imply all kinds of things between the lines. This is not good, Ms. Mekhennet."

It wasn't as if I had told them to write this, I said. In fact, I'd had no prior knowledge of it.

I met with the police the next day. We were four people around a table. One of the men read from a file. He explained that apparently the German ex-rapper Cuspert, aka Deso Dogg, aka Abu Maleeq, and now known as Abu Talha al-Almani, had had a conversation with one of his comrades somewhere along the Turkish-Syrian border. "There was some talk about whether you were married or not," the German official said, looking down at his file. "And, well, apparently the plan was to get you to the Turkish-Syrian border region, supposedly for an exclusive interview."

His voice sounded as if he were just reading from some file, but it was my life he was talking about. "So basically," he continued, "if you went there for the interview, they would kidnap you and tell you to marry one of them or you would be beheaded, and a video would be made of this."

"They want to force me to marry one of them?" I said.

"That's what the threat says."

I was told not to travel to the border region, or anywhere nearby.

Since I didn't know who had reported the threat to the Germans, I decided to reach out to my contacts around the ex-rapper now calling himself Abu Talha.

"Maybe they were making some bad joke once about this, because Abu Talha asked if you had gotten married since you met last time, but there is nothing serious, by God," one of the jihadists told me. "Maybe some intelligence services want to silence you because you don't write the way they want? Arab Spring and so on."

I had reached the point where I didn't know whom to believe. Anyone might have taken what I wrote personally and decided to personally get back at me. I decided to take off for Morocco and spend a few days in the mountains. I needed a break.

The morning I was supposed to leave for the airport, I received a Facebook message: "*As'salam alaikum*, Sister Souad. I am supposed to send you regards from Abu Talha. He said he has no problem with you, what you heard is not true, and he wishes you all the best, *wa alaikum as 'salam*."

12

Boys for the Caliphate

Germany, 2013

In the fall of 2013, I was interviewing a Syrian refugee family in the Zaatari camp in Jordan when my phone vibrated in my bag. My voice mail picked up, and the buzzing stopped. Then it started again. On the screen, I saw an old friend's number blinking, followed by a text message: "Please call me back. It's urgent."

As soon as we were out of the camp, I returned the call.

"Souad, thank God you called back. We have a big catastrophe. You remember my nephew, Pero? He has left Germany with a group of people and gone to Syria."

I thought I had misheard her. "What are you saying? Pero?" I said, trying to piece it together. "Your Pero, who was giggling about the Miss Piggy cake we got some years ago for your birthday?"

I could hear her fighting back tears. "Yes, my Pero," my friend whispered. She asked me not to use her name or the names of her family members, so I'll call her Serce.

In my mind I played back a scene from eight years earlier, when we'd celebrated Serce's thirtieth birthday with her family, including Pero and his sisters. The highlight had been a specially made cake in the form of

Miss Piggy, because Serce had been a great fan of the Muppets as a kid. My friends and I got her the cake as a joke.

It was Pero, eight years old at the time, who had carried the cake into the room and giggled when his aunt kissed him. Now she was telling me that he'd begun to spend hours each day with a new group of friends his age. "He changed. He didn't go out much and started talking about religion," she said. I told her it was a typical pattern, one that had been described to me by many other parents whose children had left.

"What do you think is happening with him now?" she asked. "What will he do there?"

"Let's talk about it when we meet in person." I didn't want to tell her over the phone that Pero was probably on a journey to become a jihadist, that he was probably now in the midst of being indoctrinated, or that he might end up fighting and perhaps dying far from home, with boys he barely knew.

"Souad, my family and I, we want to speak to you. Please, can you come?"

On the flight to Germany, I thought about the thousands of other families who were also seeing their children head off to fight a war that had begun as part of the illusory Arab Spring.

Pero's family was devastated. I arranged to meet his parents, two sisters, and aunt at the boy's family home. His mother, Bagica, cried throughout the meeting, while his father, Mitko—Serce's brother—begged her to stop. They accused each other of not realizing soon enough what was happening to their son.

"Enough now!" Serce finally shouted. "You guys have to stop and think about helping Pero now."

"I have no idea why he would think that he has to go to Syria now. This is not our war," Mitko said. "And then all this talk about jihad? I don't understand."

What have we done wrong, the families of boys like Pero would often ask. Why my child? Many times, there was a deep-rooted conflict between the parents, or a conflict between the father and his sons. These were common problems in Muslim migrant families, including Pero's.

Pero was now sixteen. His family had emigrated from Macedonia before his birth, and they doted on him. Whenever I visited, his aunt would cuddle him or lightly squeeze his jaws, while his grandmother was always telling him to eat more of her beef stews and meatballs. They practiced a liberal form of Islam that included dancing and occasional drinking. They were hardworking, middle-class people. My friend Serce had run her own business for years. Bagica worked in a grocery store. Pero's father, Mitko, was the wild card. Serce had often told me that her brother had a temper. "I have done a lot of things wrong in the past," Mitko said. "I paid a heavy price and I have learned my lesson." He'd been arrested and convicted on a drug charge when Pero was a boy and had missed much of his son's childhood.

Bagica tried to stop crying. "What are they doing now with him there? Is he in danger?" she asked me.

"Can you tell me what happened?" I asked. "Please start from the beginning."

Bagica explained that on the night Pero left, he was supposed to sleep over at a friend's house. "He came to me, gave me a long hug, kissed me, and said he was going to a rally in the city center," she recalled, crying.

"What rally?" I asked.

"I don't know. Something about Syria. Some German preacher who he wanted to listen to—what was his name again?"

"Was it Pierre Vogel?" I asked. I had followed Vogel's activities for years. A former boxer, he had converted to Islam in 2001 and had become one of Germany's prominent self-proclaimed preachers. He liked to give public speeches in slang-laden, colloquial language that was especially attractive to young people and those who didn't know much about Islam. He was one of those people the German authorities kept an eye on, and I'd long wondered how people like him made a living and paid for rallies across Germany. Lately, he'd been talking a lot about the need to overthrow the government of Bashar al-Assad in Syria. While some German Salafists publicly encouraged young Muslims to join the fight against Assad, Pierre Vogel's position was contradictory, arguing at different times both for and against joining the fight, though he always called for donations to support Syrian groups.

This was the very man Pero had gone to hear, I learned. "He told me that he would come back the next day, but he didn't," Bagica said, bursting into tears again. The family tried to call him all day. They called his friends asking where he was, but no one knew.

The next morning, Bagica's cell phone rang. "It was Pero," she said. "I asked him where he was. He said, 'I'm in Syria.'"

Pero's sisters began to wail, and Mitko stood up to leave the room. I suspected he didn't want us to see that he was crying, too.

I asked if she'd heard any more from Pero.

"Yes. Sometimes he sends a message on WhatsApp."

"Do you know who he's with?"

"No. He only speaks about some emir who decides when he can use his phone."

"What do they do all day?" I asked.

"He said there was a sheikh who speaks to them about Islam, and they show them the videos and pictures of dead Syrians, you know, the people killed by what's-his-name . . ." Bagica trailed off.

"Assad?"

She nodded. She told me that they didn't often talk about politics or foreign affairs at home. But about five months earlier, Pero suddenly developed a keen interest in the Middle East. He also tried to grow a beard but only ended up with a soft fuzz on his chin.

He would meet with his friends every day to pray in mosques and study in small groups at somebody's home, Bagica said. They also set up stands in the city center, giving away Korans and inviting people to learn more about Islam.

I asked what they wanted me to do. "You know I am a journalist, not the police," I reminded them.

They told me they had gone to the police but were told they couldn't do much. "We can't just wait here and do nothing," Mitko said. "This is my child we're talking about."

"Did Pero say anything about returning to Germany?"

"No, but it seems the emir is always reading the messages before he sends them," Bagica said.

Of course he is, I thought. They didn't want recruits to disclose their exact location. I didn't know exactly where Pero was, either, but I knew time was short. Once the "religious teachings" were finished, his handlers would send him to a training camp, where he would be forced to choose whether to become a "fighter" or a suicide bomber, known as undertaking a "martyrdom operation."

I didn't want to tell his parents this, but I offered to write about their son's case, and in that capacity maybe I could ask authorities what they were planning to do or ask my own sources in the Turkish-Syrian border region and elsewhere if they'd heard anything about Pero's whereabouts.

"I saw you once wrote about this preacher who was doing some deradicalization work, the one who looks like Osama bin Laden," my friend Serce said. "Please can we get in touch with him? Maybe he can help."

I knew who she meant, and I couldn't help smiling. "You better not tell him he looks like bin Laden," I told her. I said that I couldn't give them his number without asking him, but I could give him their number if they wanted. They agreed.

Before I left, Mitko had a final request: "Souad, if we decide to go to the Turkish-Syrian border region, would you maybe go with us?"

I knew I couldn't. The German authorities had told me to stay away.

"Let me see," I said. I told him it would be up to my editors and that I would likely ask a second reporter to work with me on the piece. If there was a need to travel to the border and I couldn't go, maybe my colleague could.

As soon as I left their apartment, I sent a text message to Hesham Shashaa, who was also known as Abu Adam, the imam Serce mentioned. He was a onetime journalist who now traveled around the world preaching against militant groups and worked with the German authorities to persuade young people not to join. I'd profiled him several years earlier. He called the family right away.

My next call was to my former colleague Peter Finn, who was now the national security editor at the *Washington Post*. He was trying to get me to start writing regularly for the paper again, but I was still pitching stories one by one rather than working on contract. He agreed that I should do a story about Pero for the *Post*, but he told me, "You have to stay out of the Turkish-Syrian border region. There is no way I will let you travel

there now." In addition to the warning from the German intelligence services, U.S. officials had also picked up a possible threat against my life
from the border region, which they conveyed to a lawyer for the *New York
Times*, who passed the information on to me.

I told Peter that sources from the former rapper Abu Talha's group
had told me there was nothing to worry about.

"Okay, if they say so," he said. "But you are not going at this stage."

Peter put me in touch with Michael Birnbaum, the *Post*'s bureau chief
in Germany, who agreed to jump on the story as soon as possible. Abu
Adam also called and said he would visit the family the following day.
Michael and I arranged to meet him there.

In the meantime, I learned from German national security sources
that Pero had left for Turkey with twenty-two other young men, including at least four other teenagers. Like Pero, most had been born in Germany but came from immigrant families. "They took a cheap flight from
Frankfurt to Antalya, and most likely someone picked them up from
there and took them to Syria," one of my sources said.

I wasn't surprised to hear any of this, but never would I have thought
it would happen to someone I knew personally. I knew that parents and
other relatives often don't realize how serious these situations can be.
Their children's companions often instruct them not to trust their parents because they don't follow the "right interpretation" of Islam.

Now, in the midst of a destabilizing civil war, Syria had become lit-
tered with camps where militants trained young men like Pero from all
over the world. While his parents—like any other parents—were only
thinking about getting their son back, I wondered if he was already so
completely brainwashed that he might become a threat to the rest of his
family or the community if he returned.

Pero's mother told me that before he left he'd begun to talk about the
"anti-Muslim" rhetoric in Europe. "He said, 'This is not our country.
Many people in Europe, they hate Islam and Muslims,'" she told me.
Even though he was born in Germany, he'd begun to feel more alienated
the longer he spent with his new friends.

Michael and I showed up at Pero's family home the next day, at about
the same time Abu Adam arrived. Serce wasn't the first to think he

resembled Osama bin Laden; people had been saying that about him for years. Maybe it was his white clothes and checked *kaffiyah*, a traditional Islamic head scarf for men, or his long face and black and gray beard. He and I had spoken about his appearance before, and he said that it was crucial for the young men and women he was helping to see him as someone they could respect. "Imagine if I wore a suit and tie," he argued. "Do you think they would trust or listen to me?"

Abu Adam had four wives, but he never judged anyone else's lifestyle. Years ago, I'd visited his home and met his wives, who all told me they had married him of their own free will and that they felt like sisters.

At the time, I told them I didn't know how they could share the man each of them loved; by the end of my visit, after listening to the imam argue with his wives about whether their next vacation should be a trip to Spain (his choice) or to EuroDisney (the wives' pick, perhaps on account of their many children), I turned to him. "Actually, the question should also be, how are you handling this?" I asked.

"With a lot of patience," he answered, laughing.

Later, he and his wives sent me pictures from their vacation in southern Bavaria. I saw the four women dressed in black from head to toe, with their faces covered, on a sled sliding down a mountain.

Abu Adam had successfully deradicalized several people in different countries and had made plenty of enemies among jihadis. "There are many people who consider me a threat in their scheme," he told me. As a result, he always walked around with at least one acolyte as his bodyguard.

Pero's family repeated their story. Bagica cried again, while Mitko did most of the talking. Abu Adam listened and took notes.

"First when he began to go to the mosque every day, I was happy and also somehow proud," Mitko said. Then he turned to Abu Adam. "I'm being very honest with you. I am not the most religious person, you know. Okay, I pray sometimes, but not five times a day. So I was proud to see Pero's dedication. . . . I wanted my son to go the way of God. It's the best way. But not this."

Pero quickly grew more observant. At one point, he even told his father that he disapproved of him drinking alcohol and that he should be more religious. Since he left, his parents had kept in touch with him via his German prepaid cell phone. "I am making sure to add money, so we can speak to him," Mitko said. But Pero had less of a relationship with his father and kept in closer touch with his mother.

Mitko and Bagica were upset that the German authorities hadn't stopped their son and other minors from traveling. Why was it so easy for their son and his friends to get radicalized, and then sent to fight in Syria?

"Have you asked him to come back?" Abu Adam asked.

"Yes, I told him, 'I am not upset with you. Just come back home,'" Mitko said. His words had no apparent effect.

Mitko grew distraught as he repeated his shock that this had happened to his son here, in Germany, far from the war in his own native country and from conflicts in the Middle East. "I had no idea how to handle Pero's growing religiosity," Mitko said. "I thought it would be enough to make sure my children weren't lacking for money."

"I think his leader, this emir, is listening to every conversation we have with him, and they control him," Bagica said.

In the weeks before he had left, Pero constantly watched videos of alleged atrocities committed by the Assad regime. Pero told his parents that the world was at war with Islam.

"He mentioned that Syria was the latest example of this war and that it was the duty of Muslims to go and help other Muslims," Mitko said.

In one of their recent conversations, Pero had mentioned that the emir and others had told him about creating an Islamic state. His family didn't know what group he was with, but they mentioned one other teenager who had run away with their son, who had told his parents he was planning to join an Al Qaeda affiliate.

"One time I spoke to the emir, and he told me the best we could do for our son was to send him enough money to buy an AK-47 and a bulletproof vest," Mitko told us. "What kind of person would say this to the parents of a sixteen-year-old?"

I knew that this meant their boy had been chosen to become a fighter.

During one of his most recent calls, Pero had told his mother that he would pledge allegiance to a fighting group shortly after the Eid al-Adha holiday, just weeks away. They were running out of time.

Abu Adam suggested they reason with Pero, telling him that the Koran puts family obligations first and condemns violence. If that didn't work, maybe they could persuade him that his mother was sick, which she surely was from worry, so it wouldn't be a lie, and that he needed to come home, or at least to visit her in Turkey, rather than in Syria.

"It's not going to be as easy as, 'Oh, *habibi*,' and falling into each other's arms and then leaving," he told them, using the male form of the Arabic word for "darling."

Mitko and Bagica had already promised Pero a new start if he came home to Germany. "I told him, 'My son, just come home, all will be good. I promise I will be a better father.'" Mitko said, and I saw tears pooling in his eyes. "But this didn't change his mind."

Mitko had also tried telling Pero that his mother was seriously ill. That hadn't worked, either.

Then Abu Adam suggested another idea: "Kidnap him."

He advised the family what to tell Pero so that the emir wouldn't see any way out and would allow Pero to meet his mother one last time and get her blessing before he headed out to fight.

"Maybe this is our last chance," Bagica told me that evening. I stayed out of sight when she talked to Pero on Skype, in case the emir was with him. I listened to Pero's voice as he told his mother that she and his aunt would be picked up in Antakya and brought to see him in Syria.

Abu Adam had told them that Pero's emir might try to ask the women to cross the border for security reasons. "But don't agree to this," he told them. "You can tell him that under Islamic law, he has already committed a sin by leaving to fight jihad without his parents' permission. You are two women who cannot travel with strange men into Syria, and he as your son will have to come and see you."

Bagica told Pero exactly this. After speaking to another man who seemed to be in the room with him, Pero finally agreed. He also asked his mother to bring him warm socks, his leather jacket, T-shirts, and penicillin and other antibiotics.

"He looked very tired," Bagica said afterward. "He was wearing a T-shirt. And he wasn't alone."

"He might not come alone," Mitko said in a worried tone. "It might be a bit dangerous, but I can't stand here and watch as I lose my son."

I contacted Peter Finn and told him the family was getting ready for their trip to Antakya. "I still don't want to see you near the border at the moment," Peter told me. "We have to be careful."

I was disappointed not to be able to go with Pero's family to Turkey, but I kept in touch with Serce via text messages and phone calls. Mitko had a contact in the Turkish police, a family friend who put him in touch with the counterterrorism unit in the Turkish-Syrian border region.

Bagica stayed in contact with her son, telling him that only she and Serce were coming to see him. Unbeknownst to Pero, his father had flown to Turkey a few days earlier to meet the police in the border region.

Pero was supposed to meet Bagica and Serce at a hotel in Antakya. The plan was for him to spend a few hours with them and collect the clothes and other things he'd asked his mother to bring.

"Is he there, did he come?" I anxiously texted Serce from Germany while she and her sister-in-law waited in the hotel lobby.

"Not yet," she replied. He was already twenty minutes late.

Everyone was worried that Pero wouldn't come alone and that whoever might be with him would attack the family for trying to take him away. The police and Mitko were hiding in a car outside the hotel. The plan was for Turkish antiterrorism police to take Pero into custody, to make it seem that they had arrested him, and then drive Pero and his family to the airport so they could fly back to Germany the same day.

"I wrote him a message and asked, where are you? He just wrote back and said he was coming at 3 p.m.," Serce texted me.

At about 2:30 p.m. her time, she called to say that police officers in plainclothes had posted themselves inside the lobby and in cars parked at the exits. "This is like in a movie. I am so nervous, Souad! How do you do your job? I don't understand."

Thirty minutes later, I received a text from Serce: "He has sent a message to my sister-in-law. He asked where she was and said that he is coming."

I watched my phone nervously, unable to concentrate on anything else. Ten minutes later, another text arrived: "He is here, the police are with us, we are all crying, can't talk now but we are taking off to the police station now and then the airport. I will arrive tonight."

Pero had arrived alone, by bus, I learned later. Mitko, hiding with one of the police officers, had signaled that this was his son. Then the police got out of their cars, grabbed Pero by the arms, and brought him into the hotel, where his mother and aunt were waiting.

Serce later told us that even Mitko was crying when he saw Pero embracing his mother, the first time that Serce could remember having seen her brother weep.

"The little one was a bit shocked that he had been captured," she told me. He asked the police officers if he could pray before they took him, which they allowed him to do.

Serce showed Michael and me a video she had taken with her cell phone while they were driving to the airport with Pero. In it, a Turkish police officer turns around and speaks to Pero. "If you had stayed longer there, and you had taken the next step, you would have understood that you were on the wrong path," the officer says. "Be grateful to Allah that you got out now."

Pero says nothing.

"Who has the right to call for jihad? It's not so easy just to call for it. There are rules," the officer continues. "What is important is the family. Never leave them behind the way you did."

"I thought it was the right path," Pero says.

When Pero and his mother and aunt arrived at the airport in Frankfurt, he was arrested by German border police and taken to the main police headquarters in Frankfurt. That's where I met Serce, while she waited for her sister-in-law and nephew to come out.

Pero's family and Abu Adam worked on a program for him to reintegrate himself into German society. He was away from the group now, but the indoctrination had been very strong. "I told the family we must work a lot now, so he will not end up going back there," Abu Adam told me. "I am sure they will try to contact him and ask him to get back."

He was right. I'd seen other cases of people who had been caught on their way to join jihadist groups in Afghanistan, Somalia, or Yemen. They might not make it the first time, but they would often be contacted by their old circles and succeed with their journey on a second attempt. In fact, once they finally made it, they would enjoy even more respect because they hadn't stopped pursuing what they saw as the right path or the chance to die as martyrs. Pero's case was different; he wasn't truly convinced by the jihadist ideology but was more someone who followed orders. In fact, Pero thought he was saving "oppressed Muslim Syrians from being slaughtered by Assad." That was the story he had been told, and that was what he knew the duty of any Muslim man to be. There was still room to bring him back into society, but it would take a lot of effort, not only from his family but also from religious scholars who could explain to him that his friends or the "emir," as he called his group leader, had gotten the verses of the Koran out of context or explained them in a way that served their own objectives.

"We have to now wash his brain," Abu Adam continued. "It's dirty and we have to clean it."

Pero was lucky. He got out alive. Most of the others who had left with him did not.

Abu Adam and the family worked together for months to get Pero out of the circles he was in. They closed all his email accounts, changed his phone numbers, and shut down his Facebook page. Then there was the man Mitko suspected of making travel arrangements for his son and the other young men. Mitko had spoken to the police about this man. The police said they knew him and had him on their radar, but they didn't have enough evidence to put him behind bars.

Mitko wanted to make sure that this man, who was a German of Turkish descent, would stay away from his son, so he took matters into his own hands. "I went to his apartment," he told me, "and said to him, 'If you or any of your so-called brothers ever come close to my son again, I swear to God, your head will roll right in front of the feet of your emir. Do you understand?'"

The man nodded and Mitko left, satisfied that his message was received. The man and his associates never again got close to Pero or his family.

Pero finished school and cut off contact with his old friends. I saw him once on the street, about a year and a half later, holding hands with a young girl. Both wore jeans and trendy clothes, and the girl's hair flowed free, unburdened by a head scarf. He was laughing and joking. He reminded me once again of the little boy who had carried the Miss Piggy cake all those years earlier.

Some of his friends would later leave the group they'd been with in Syria and join a new one that called itself the Islamic State in Iraq and al-Sham, or ISIS, whose existence had been proclaimed the summer before. I learned that Abu Talha, the onetime rapper known as Deso Dogg, had also joined them.

13

Brides for the Caliphate

Germany and France, 2014–15

On January 7, 2015, Europe was hit. Two brothers, Chérif and Said Kouachi, carried out a deadly attack in central Paris on staffers at the French satirical magazine *Charlie Hebdo*, whose depictions of the Prophet Muhammad had enraged Islamists, murdering twelve people before being killed by police after a standoff in Dammartin-en-Goële, a town north of the French capital.

On January 9, another man, Amedy Coulibaly, assaulted a kosher supermarket in another part of Paris, killing five more people and taking fifteen others hostage. He was also ultimately shot dead by police.

France has been a target of religiously motivated terrorism for some time, and its own history of colonization and intervention in the Middle East and North Africa is characterized by violence. With its conquest of Algeria in the nineteenth century and its control of Syria and Lebanon after World War I, France came to be seen by many Muslims as arrogant and imperious. The long and bloody Algerian war of independence and the delayed reappraisal of France's role in it, which still has not been fully accepted by all parts of French society, further exacerbated hostility in the Muslim world. In 1983 the Lebanese militia Hezbollah bombed the French paratrooper barracks in Beirut, and in the 1990s the Algerian

Islamist terrorist group GIA hijacked a French plane and bombed Métro stations in Paris. Jewish institutions all over France, including schools, restaurants, and synagogues, have repeatedly been the targets of Islamist terror attacks.

Many French Muslims experienced one of France's colonial conflicts firsthand or through their family members' accounts. These communities have historically felt excluded from the full benefits of French society, not least because of their difficult economic situation. From the 1970s on, the *banlieues*, suburban high-rise estates originally a sign of the economic boom after World War II, were inhabited mostly by immigrants from North Africa. They have since become synonymous with high unemployment and weak social structures. Whoever could afford to leave, left. Today, the *banlieues* are still inhabited mainly by immigrants and their families, and they have often been the scene of antigovernment protests.

The Kouachi brothers claimed that they had committed the *Charlie Hebdo* attacks in the name of Al Qaeda in the Arabian Peninsula, while a video showed Coulibaly pledging allegiance to the Islamic State.

Like hundreds of journalists from all over the world, I headed to Paris to cover the attacks. I was particularly interested in the role of Coulibaly's wife, Hayat Boumeddiene. She had last been seen in a video on January 2, accompanied by another man with terrorist ties, at passport control at an Istanbul airport. Intelligence officials believed that she had since crossed into Syria and was living "under the protection of the caliphate." Photographs showing her years earlier in a bikini with Coulibaly made their way around the media, raising questions about how and why their lives had changed.

I had followed the phenomenon of women's radicalization for years, and I wondered if there were parallels between Boumeddiene's case and others. Years earlier, I'd met Fatiha al-Mejjati and Malika el-Aroud, two women who hadn't shown much interest in religion when they were young adults but who found their way to Islamic radicalism nevertheless.

These women had told me that their ways of living and their clothing choices had once been very Western—Malika had even had a daughter out of wedlock before finding her way to Islam. They said that their interest in religion was spurred by international political circumstances: the conflict between Palestinians and Israelis, the war in Iraq, the war in Chechnya. Both women would become catalysts for their husbands' radicalization.

The two women had never met in person, but their husbands would grow very close to Osama bin Laden in Afghanistan, where they all lived in the early 2000s.

I met Fatiha for the first time in Casablanca in 2007. Years earlier, she had been a teacher at a private school in Morocco, but when she grew interested in Islam her colleagues noticed changes; she stopped wearing skirts and began covering her hair. The director of the school urged her to reconsider, but she refused.

One of her male students, Abdulkarim al-Mejjati, was fascinated by her religious devotion. They began meeting to talk about Islam and politics. Al-Mejjati told Fatiha he wanted to marry her. She demurred, pointing out that he was younger than she.

"The Prophet Muhammad was also younger than his wife," al-Mejjati responded.

His wealthy family opposed the union, but al-Mejjati was determined. They married, and Fatiha gave birth to a son, whom they named Adam; two years later, they had another boy, Ilyas. Along the way, she and al-Mejjati grew even more radical, and in the spring of 2001 they moved to Afghanistan.

"It was the best times in my life, and I am praying to God that I will be living again under the flag of the Taliban," she told me, raising her hands as if in prayer.

From there, the family moved to Saudi Arabia. One day in 2005, while Fatiha was at the doctor's with Ilyas, Saudi antiterrorism police stormed their apartment and killed al-Mejjati and Adam, then ten years old. Saudi authorities suspected that bin Laden had sent al-Mejjati to lead an Al Qaeda offshoot and that he was planning attacks there.

Fatiha and eight-year-old Ilyas were arrested and held for months in a Saudi prison. Then they were repatriated to Morocco, where they spent a couple of months in a detention facility. Besides being interrogated about Afghanistan and her husband's contacts, she said, she could hear other detainees screaming, presumably under torture. Fatiha was not mistreated physically, but she said that her son had been psychically scarred for life.

I interviewed Fatiha after her release and spoke to her several other times as well. She said her views had not changed in prison; instead she became even more radical. When I saw her in 2011, she still spoke about jihad and the need to fight America and its allies, and she praised bin Laden, who had recently been killed. She referred to the Taliban leader Mullah Omar as "Emir al Mouminin," or "leader of the faithful," and told me she wished she could live "under an Islamic leader in a truly Islamic land."

In July 2014, she left Morocco for Syria and joined ISIS. She appeared in a few online videos and tweeted that she was planning a suicide attack. Then she disappeared. I heard that she had married an ISIS commander and that Ilyas had gone to work for the group's media division.

I met the other woman, Malika el-Aroud, in Brussels in 2008. At the time, she was a prominent Internet jihadist, encouraging men to fight and women to support them. I called her and asked if we could speak about her life and her role as a woman in the world of jihad.

During that first phone conversation she took notes. When I'd finished speaking, she asked for my name again. "You may call me back in two days," she said.

On that second call, her voice was much friendlier. "*Salam*, sister," she said warmly. "I spoke to the brothers from the Rafidain Center, and they said it's okay, I can talk to you."

I had no idea what she meant by the Rafidain Center. I thought it might be her mosque. I said I wanted to talk to her, but also to visit some of the places where she spent time. "Maybe we could go to the Rafidain Center," I suggested.

There was a long pause. "What?" she asked. She explained that she was talking about the people who translated Osama bin Laden's speeches online and that no one knew where they were.

Malika was born in northern Morocco but grew up in Belgium. As a child, she had rebelled against her religion. She married for the first time at eighteen, split up with her husband, and gave birth to a child on her own.

At a time when she was desperate and poor an imam helped her. She couldn't read Arabic, but she read the Koran in French and was drawn to a strict version of Islam. As she moved into more radical circles, she met and married a Tunisian fighter loyal to Osama bin Laden named Abdessater Dahmane.

From the beginning, Malika's religious fervor was mixed with a feeling of secular outrage. She felt the whole world was against Muslims. In 2001, like Fatiha, she moved with her husband to Afghanistan, where he trained in an Al Qaeda camp, and she lived in Jalalabad, in a compound with other foreign women.

Malika said the Taliban were a model Islamic government. Her only rebellion was against wearing the burka, the restrictive garment they forced on women, which she called "a plastic bag." As a foreigner, she was allowed to wear a long black veil instead. "Women didn't have problems under the Taliban," she told me. "They had security."

Her husband was one of two assassins ordered by bin Laden to kill the Northern Alliance leader Ahmed Shah Massoud on September 9, 2001, two days before the attacks on New York and Washington. Posing as Arab TV journalists who had come to interview the famed resistance leader, the men carried a camera packed with explosives. Dahmane survived the attack but was shot while trying to flee.

Malika was briefly detained by Massoud's followers. Frightened, she convinced Belgian authorities to arrange for her safe passage home after the United States began bombing Afghanistan in October 2001.

Back in Belgium, Malika was one of nearly two dozen defendants tried for complicity in the murder of Ahmed Shah Massoud. Wearing a black veil, she testified that she had been doing humanitarian work and was unaware of her husband's activities. In the end, there was not sufficient evidence to convict her.

Meanwhile, she rose in stature as the widow of a martyr. She told her story to a journalist who helped write her memoir, and she gained a reputation for urging others to jihad via the Internet. Online, she met Moez Garsallaoui, a Tunisian several years younger who had political refugee status in Switzerland. They married and moved to a small Swiss village, where they ran several pro–Al Qaeda websites and Internet forums that were monitored by Swiss authorities as part of the country's first Internet-related criminal case.

Swiss police raided their home and arrested them at dawn in April 2005. A source of mine who headed up the Special Forces unit said that her husband had rushed to the computer to delete incriminating material and that he'd begun trembling when they arrested him. Malika, meanwhile, was absolutely cool. Wearing pajamas, she demanded to be allowed to put on her hijab and cover her face. "She's quite a strong character," my source told me.

Malika later said that the Swiss police beat and blindfolded her husband and manhandled her while she was sleeping unveiled. Convicted in 2008 of promoting violence and supporting a criminal organization, she received a six-month suspended sentence.

Her husband, who was convicted of more serious charges, was released after just twenty-three days in prison. The Swiss authorities suspected he was recruiting to carry out attacks and that he had connections to terrorist groups operating in the tribal areas of Pakistan. By 2014, the authorities said that they had lost track of him after he was released from jail, and Malika wouldn't tell them where he was, saying only, "He is on a trip." Malika was eventually sentenced to an eight-year prison term in Belgium.

Now, following the *Charlie Hebdo* attacks in Paris, there was another woman of North African descent who was the widow of a "martyr" in a major international operation. I was now working on contract for the *Post*, and my colleague Michael Birnbaum and I began to dig into the life of twenty-six-year-old Hayat Boumeddiene. We visited the places where she or her family members had lived, and spoke to her relatives and friends. I also noted that French investigators had found a copy of Malika's memoir among the belongings in her apartment.

Along with our French stringer Cléophée Demoustier, Michael and I visited Villiers-sur-Marne, where Boumeddiene had grown up with her parents and siblings.

Most of the buildings there looked as if they'd needed maintenance ten years ago but had been abandoned. Graffiti covered the walls, and I heard children cursing each other in a mixture of Arabic and French as they stood around watching videos on their smartphones.

I had been to these suburbs several times before and was familiar with the contrast between the glamorous Paris portrayed in romantic Hollywood movies and the lives of the people in these buildings. Residents complained of racism, saying that when they applied for jobs, the combination of an Arabic-sounding name and their address would often make employers choose someone else. Some even told me they were considering changing their names to sound more French.

As my colleagues and I walked around the area where Boumeddiene had grown up, I couldn't help but wonder what would have become of me if I had come of age in a place like that. What would have become of anyone?

It wasn't an excuse for turning into a terrorist or a criminal. But growing up in a place like Villiers-sur-Marne can make it easy for youngsters to feel alienated. I remembered the mixture of anger and fear I felt as a teenager when I learned that the houses of Turkish migrants had been burned in Solingen and Mölln. Living in an affluent neighborhood such as Holzhausen had meant we weren't surrounded by other migrants who felt frustrated by persistent discrimination. I'd been inspired by the words my grandparents spoke to me as a child and the presence of my parents and my godparents, who constantly told me that if I worked hard I'd have a chance in life.

What encouragement did Hayat Boumeddiene have? And what about some of the teenagers and young men we saw now, standing around these public housing complexes? The place was not inviting. Many of the kitchens looked identical, with packages of vegetables or shelf-safe milk in the windows. African and Arabic music played through open windows, and people talked loudly inside the apartments. There was concrete everywhere, and no greenery or playgrounds. Small children didn't play here, it seemed, though we did see four guys standing in a circle in a shadowy corner, handling something we thought might be drugs. As we watched, an old man in a prayer cap passed, leaning on a stick.

Boumeddiene had grown up in one of these buildings. Her mother had died from a heart ailment when she was eight years old, family friends told us. "Her father had six children. He had to work and thought he had no other choice but to marry another woman," one of his friends said. It sounded like a convenient explanation for questionable behavior.

He remarried within a month of his first wife's death. But his new bride clashed with her stepchildren. "There was constant fighting at home," one of the family friends told us. "The father eventually took the side of his new wife."

For Boumeddiene and her siblings, that meant being thrown out of the house or given away. She was sent to a group home when she was thirteen. The family she stayed with came from the same Algerian city as her father.

Boumeddiene favored makeup and rambling phone calls with friends, said Omar, her foster brother, who spoke on the condition that his family's last name not be published. We met him in front of his parents' modest house. It was only a short distance from the tall gray towers of the *banlieues*, but in a much nicer neighborhood.

He said that his family was shocked when they learned that she might have been involved in her husband's plan. To Omar, it was as if they were speaking about a different person. "She was fragile and clearly shaken by her mother's death," he said. She wasn't often in touch with her father, who didn't seem very interested in her well-being.

"We introduced her to a very nice man in Algeria, but she didn't like him," Omar told us. When she turned eighteen, she moved to Paris, a long-cherished dream. Hungry for freedom and captivated by the idea of travel, she got a job selling sandwiches and coffee on a high-speed train. She loved to go out with friends and window shop. In 2007, a high school friend introduced Boumeddiene to one of her boyfriend's prison buddies, Amedy Coulibaly, who had just been released after serving time for armed robbery. Like her, he came from a migrant family and had been born in France.

Back at our hotel in Paris, we examined court documents we'd gathered from various sources, including a police interrogation of Boumeddiene in 2010, after Coulibaly was charged with trying to break a top militant out of a French jail. She said that neither she nor her husband had been very religious when they met, but they'd changed together.

She told the police about her difficult past and how Islam had answered all her questions and brought her peace. She had grown interested in the faith after she met Coulibaly, when she befriended the wives of some of his prison acquaintances, including the wife of one of the Kouachi brothers. Two years after they met, she and Coulibaly were married in a religious ceremony. (Such marriages are not recognized by French law.) Boumeddiene didn't attend, explaining that Islam doesn't require a woman to be present at her wedding. "My father stood in for me," she told police.

Boumeddiene quickly became more observant than her husband. He prayed at the mosque "on his own timetable," every three weeks or so. She, meanwhile, started wearing a full-face veil and quit her job as a cashier at a bakery. She also told police about the circles she and Coulibaly moved through, and how they grew close to Chérif Kouachi, the younger of the future *Charlie Hebdo* attackers.

Boumeddiene spoke of "innocent people massacred in Palestine, Iraq, Chechnya, Afghanistan, where Americans send bombs and all that—and they're not terrorists?" She continued: "When Americans kill innocent people, it's of course justifiable that men should take up arms to defend their wives and children."

At some point during this period, she reconnected with her father. But when I reached him in Algeria after the attacks, all I heard were accusations and excuses. "This girl didn't grow up in my house. She grew up in the house of nonbelievers. She made all these decisions on her own," he told me.

I was taken aback by his coarseness. "That's all you have to say?" I asked. It was.

I knew from my own experience how important it was to have a circle of family and friends who were there in moments of adolescent anger, when it was easy to listen to people who told us what we wanted to hear, namely that we were victims—and that all the millions of Muslims in the world were victims.

In October 2014, Boumeddiene and Coulibaly went on a pilgrimage to Mecca. I asked a Saudi intelligence official if he'd received any information or warnings from his French counterparts about Coulibaly's terrorism ties when he visited.

"No, we did not," he said, "and it's especially upsetting, because we had no options to decide if we wanted such a person in our country or to react accordingly and follow him so we could see if he was in touch with other people."

I asked one of my French sources why France hadn't shared its information with the Saudis. He told me that the government had hoped that Coulibaly and Boumeddiene "would leave Europe and not come back." This also helped to explain how so many people who were already well known to police and intelligence services made it to Syria and were now living and fighting there on behalf of the Islamic State.

In Boumeddiene's interrogation and according to her friends, she complained about Western policies toward Muslim countries and spoke of racism, discrimination, and the "evil done to innocents in occupied lands." Yet Boumeddiene had left the country of her birth and joined the so-called Islamic State, whose leaders forced their rules and "laws" upon millions of Syrians and Iraqis, who faced harsh measures when they didn't obey. As I'd seen over and again, people who see themselves as victims sometimes don't notice when they become oppressors.

SEVERAL OF MY sources in the Islamic State had told me that lots of women from Europe were contacting them, hoping to marry members of ISIS. To find out why, I'd started looking for such women. That's how I found Meryam, a young German convert to Islam. In 2014, one of Meryam's best friends got in touch and arranged for me to meet her in Berlin.

We agreed to meet at a subway station and go where we could speak freely. Meryam wore black gloves and a full Islamic veil, with only her green eyes and a slice of pale skin visible through the narrow slit. "Do you like chicken burgers?" she asked me. "It's halal, of course."

I followed her to a restaurant in a neighborhood where many Muslim families lived. The women in this neighborhood might wear hijab, but they also favored bright colors; no one was wearing the full veil. Meryam drew many looks, and she knew it. "Let them watch. I'm used to it. I don't care."

When we entered the restaurant, she greeted the cashier with "*As'salam alaikum*," but she spoke Arabic with a heavy German accent.

"Good day," he answered in German.

Meryam ordered a crunchy spicy chicken burger, fries, and a lemonade. "I don't drink Coca-Cola or Pepsi. That's all from *kuffar*," she told me.

In the women's and family section of the restaurant, she lifted her veil and I saw that her face was spotted with pimples, which made her look as if she was in the midst of puberty. I later learned she was eighteen. As we talked, it became clear that she had been so deeply indoctrinated that she saw the world entirely in black and white. She spent hours in front of the computer and on WhatsApp, chatting with her "brothers and sisters in Syria." They had answers to all the questions she was asking and sent her links to YouTube videos or pictures from the "caliphate." One of her friends, an Afghan girl, had already traveled to Syria and was living in a house with other single women, waiting to get married. Meryam told me that life in Germany was unbearable for her. She called the society "racist and lost." In her eyes, Islam and Muslims were the main targets of oppression and unfair treatment.

I asked her when and why she got interested in Islam.

"*Bismillah ar rahman ar Rahim*," she began, using an Arabic phrase that means "In the name of God, the most merciful and the most beneficent." It's often used by Muslims as an invocation to guarantee the truth of what they're about to say. "I was fourteen when I converted. A close Muslim friend was killed after a stabbing in the neighborhood, and then I went to his mosque, where the community had gathered to pray for him. That's when I began to be interested in Islam."

She liked the way that in Islam, families and members of the community were supposed to care for one another. People shared food and helped those in need, she said. She felt acceptance and warmth she hadn't felt in her own family in a long time. Her divorced parents were surprised but took no action to stop her conversion.

She says that she and other devout Muslims feel ostracized in German society. When she first started wearing a partial head covering, she said, she was already being turned down for jobs. When she started wearing the *niqab*, it became impossible to find work. At sixteen, she married for the first time. Her husband was a fellow convert, and they discussed going to Syria to live in the caliphate. Meryam said she believed it was her duty as a Muslim to live in an Islamic state, but her husband didn't want to. She said he wasn't a real man. She asked for a divorce, and she now had to wait a prescribed period of time before she could remarry.

Like Meryam, large numbers of Western jihadists have come from troubled or broken homes, where poverty, joblessness, and upheaval are the norm. She reminded me in that sense of Pero, whose parents' marriage had had problems and whose father had spent time in prison.

Meryam also had much in common with Hayat Boumeddiene. Like Boumeddiene's parents, Meryam's mother and father were divorced. Her father drank, and her mother didn't take much interest in Meryam or her other children. Growing up, Meryam had to care for her younger siblings.

In Europe, society is atomized. ISIS advertises its commitment to sisterhood, friends, and family, equality no matter where you come from— Arab, German, American, we're all Muslims. It represents a utopian vision that many European converts crave. Meryam longed for what she saw at her young friend's Muslim funeral: a broader, supportive community.

When I called Meryam's mother, she had only one question: "How much money are you paying her? We could give her story to a tabloid and get a couple hundred euros."

I told her I wasn't paying and that Meryam had agreed to talk to me.

It sounded as if Meryam, like Boumeddiene, wanted to fight those she saw as oppressors. And the roles seem very clear to her: "America, Europe, the Arab leaders" were all "taking from the oil and richness in the Islamic world and don't share with the poor." There was a "war against Islam," she said. To her, ISIS and Al Qaeda were heroic. She spoke about "Sheikh Osama" and "Sheikh Abu Musab," and now, finally, the caliphate.

"But there are lots of Islamic scholars who say this isn't the real caliphate and who have spoken up against ISIS," I countered. "What do you think about this?"

"Yes, I know," she answered. "I discussed it with the brothers and sisters online, and they explained to me that those scholars were all paid by the West and the rulers. They were all lying."

I asked her who those "brothers and sisters" were.

"They are in the caliphate. They said what we read and see here in the media is all wrong, and that life is very good there."

"What is missing in your life here?" I asked.

"I don't feel safe in Europe. All those right-wing parties, they hate Muslims."

"But if this is about safety, why would you go to Syria, where there is a war?"

"It is our duty to leave the land of the unbeliever, to go and live in the caliphate," she said. "Also, I want to get married to a real man, someone who is living his religion the right way and is willing to fight for it."

Various intelligence sources had told me that they saw a growing fascination with the idea of the caliphate among young people from Europe, including women. Meryam's plans to move to Syria were real, and she was already picturing her future there. The man she planned to wed was a Tunisian-born fighter for the Islamic State, she said. "He came to Europe with a group of other fighters of Yemeni and Chechen descent."

"How did they get here?" I asked.

"I don't know for sure, I think via Tunisia, but we don't speak about such things."

I thought she must be naïve not to understand the danger she faced, until she added, "I don't want to know these details. There are so many informants in the community, and intelligence services are listening to calls and reading messages, so when I don't know about things, I cannot speak about them." She smiled.

I wondered if it was her way of telling me that she wasn't as innocent as she seemed.

"What are they doing here?" I asked.

She said they sometimes went around and met with people, but he wouldn't tell her where and with whom. Meryam and her boyfriend once visited a mosque in Berlin called the House of Peace, where her betrothed was outraged by the imam's sermons against the Islamic State. "He said . . . these people are nonbelievers," Meryam told me.

I asked if she was in love with her future husband. "He is handsome, and he loves his religion," she began. "But it's very difficult to communicate because he speaks Arabic and French, and I only speak German and some English."

She would become his second wife. She worried she might be jealous.

"But you still would accept to become the second wife?"

"Yes. I believe I have found the right man." She grabbed a few French fries. "Don't you want to get married and have kids? Isn't something missing in your life now?"

I took a big bite of my chicken burger, not because I was hungry, but because I wanted a few seconds to think about how to answer.

"If your question is, do I want to get married and have children, well yes, that would be wonderful," I said. I thought that was the end of the conversation.

"Maybe I can ask my future husband if he knows one of the brothers there who is looking for another wife," she said, laughing.

I thanked her for the kind offer but told her it wasn't really for me. I did ask Meryam if I could meet her future husband, though. "Maybe we can have a coffee somewhere, or another of these chicken burgers?"

It seemed unlikely that he would agree, but I figured it was worth a try. She promised to ask him and get back to me.

My conversation with Meryam was in December 2014, just a month before the Paris attacks. I tried to get back in touch with her afterward, but her phone number had been disconnected.

She must have gone, I thought. I wondered if she and Hayat Boumeddiene would meet.

Meanwhile, one of Germany's best-known talk shows, *Günther Jauch*, named for its host, asked me to discuss the Paris attacks, cartoons about Muhammad, and what would come next. The invitation didn't thrill me. Yes, I was a professional journalist. Yes, I had covered extremism and the so-called War on Terror for many years. But I knew there was a big risk that I would be pushed into the role of "the Muslim" in a forum like this. Yet I accepted. Maybe this would be a good moment to build bridges, to explain and reach wise and moderate Muslims and others who could speak up, too, and contribute to a healthy debate.

The other guests were Germany's interior minister; the CEO of the Axel Springer publishing house; and a German journalist and former news presenter who had lived in France for many years. We debated freedom of the press, the reason why groups such as Al Qaeda and ISIS had called for the killing of cartoonists, and so on.

I made it very clear that killing journalists or cartoonists was unacceptable based on my understanding of Islam and my own principles, even if people disagreed with what somebody had drawn or written. Günther Jauch asked why such drawings didn't make it to the front page of the *New York Times* or the *Washington Post*. I explained that the leading American newspapers didn't publish satirical or otherwise offensive drawings that could spur hate against a particular race or religion.

I went on to tell the group that I'd recently been in the United States for book talks about *The Eternal Nazi*, and I related how some Holocaust survivors and members of the Jewish community said they'd been worried when they saw some of the drawings of the Prophet Muhammad that were published in Europe. "They said it reminded them of how the Nazis insulted Jews and Judaism. So maybe it would be important to have a discussion about when does freedom of speech end and hate speech begin?"

The moment I said this, Mathias Döpfner, the Axel Springer CEO, seemed to grow enraged. I waited until he finished and explained that he had misunderstood me. I wasn't saying that the *Charlie Hebdo* cartoons and Nazi propaganda were identical, only relaying what members of the Jewish community in the United States had said.

At the same time, I saw how highly emotional the situation had become. I tried to hide my discomfort, but when I reached for a glass of water, I felt my hand shake.

I tried to listen to my inner voice, which said, *keep calm*. I remembered my grandmother, who didn't shy away from uncomfortable confrontations and from speaking up. *We must show Muslim youth in this country that there are peaceful ways to disagree*, I told myself.

The discussion turned to questions of "Western values" and the rights that Europeans have enjoyed since the Enlightenment. I said that at some stage, it would be important that we as journalists not step into the trap of double standards. If we all agreed that there should be no restrictions on drawings, caricatures, or writing, we couldn't use different rules depending on what religion we were speaking about.

As an example, I mentioned the discussion around the so-called Muhammad cartoons that had been published in the Danish newspaper *Jyllands-Posten* ten years earlier. The cartoons grew notorious after they were reprinted in a Norwegian magazine, spurring outrage and protests across the Middle East. In January 2006, gunmen raided the European Union's office in Gaza, demanding an apology. *Jyllands-Posten* apologized, but newspapers in France, Germany, Italy, and Spain reprinted the cartoons as a mark of defiance. Danish and Norwegian embassies across the Middle East were attacked. That February, *Charlie Hebdo* reprinted the cartoons and was sued by Muslim groups for publicly insulting Islam, a claim that was later dismissed.

In 2008, several Danish papers, including *Jyllands-Posten*, reprinted one of the cartoons. Osama bin Laden responded with a video threatening revenge. In the years that followed, a Somali Muslim was jailed for entering the home of a Danish cartoonist with an ax and a knife, five men were arrested for allegedly planning a massacre at *Jyllands-Posten*, and *Charlie Hebdo*'s offices were burned and its website attacked after it published more Muhammad cartoons. In 2013, two years before the Paris attacks, the magazine was sued again by Muslim groups for inciting racial hatred.

What the whole world remembers are the pictures of violent protests in various countries, some radical groups calling for the killing of the cartoonists, and several Muslim countries boycotting Danish products. Politicians and journalists in Europe immediately spoke about freedom of speech, and for weeks and months there were debates about whether Muslims were capable of living in a democracy.

But the story of the "Muhammad cartoons" wasn't that simple. For an

earlier book, *Die Kinder des Dschidad* (*The Children of Jihad*), my coau-
thors and I had gone to Denmark and researched the whole story. We
learned that before the Muhammad cartoons were published, *Jyllands-
Posten* had refused to print cartoons depicting Jesus in a derogatory man-
ner because they believed those drawings would hurt readers' feelings.

I told this story to my fellow guests. Döpfner said he had never heard
this, and if it turned out to be true, it would indeed be a scandal. It
occurred to me that many people didn't seem to know even the basic
facts about these controversies. They didn't seem to understand that by
enforcing double standards and being unwilling to engage in an honest
and healthy discussion about ethics, freedom of speech, and hate speech,
the West would keep losing more young Europeans into the hands of
radicals who told them that the West was at war against Islam.

When I checked my email, Twitter, and Facebook accounts after the
debate, I found a few supportive messages from people who said they
were grateful that I'd stood my ground.

But there were many more attacks and threats. Some urged me to
"pack and go back to Turkey." I was called a "Muslim bitch" and a "whore."
A couple of people seemed especially upset about my "daring to contra-
dict a German man like Mr. Döpfner."

There were also two threats against my life. "We will get you," one
email read. It contained an attachment with drawings of knives and
guns. The other message called me an "enemy of the German race" and
said that I would soon be dealt with.

I spoke to one of my police sources about the emails. He told me to
keep an eye out for similar messages and cautioned me not to reveal my
home address. Even publicly identifying my home city could be dangerous, he told me.

The backlash after the TV roundtable followed me for some time. Two
journalist friends stopped speaking to me because they were upset by my
suggestion that we needed to talk as a society about where freedom
of speech ended and hate speech began. During a heated debate with
another journalist at a friend's dinner party, I asked why, if freedom of
speech was sacrosanct, I was being attacked and threatened simply for
saying what I thought.

"All those Muslims who are complaining about our freedom of speech or who feel offended by our cartoons and our values, they don't belong here and should just leave," she replied.

I told her that if she wanted to ban Muslims or other people from speaking freely and peacefully raising questions, it would be the beginning of the end for "freedom of speech." The whole time, I couldn't stop wondering where we were heading if even people who considered themselves liberal intellectuals were trying to ban speech that made them uncomfortable. "So does that mean the 'good and acceptable' Muslim has to shut up, not participate in intellectual debate, and shouldn't dare to disagree with the prevailing wisdom?" I asked. Or are people like me, who have lived here all our lives, to keep quiet, or else we will be seen as siding with Al Qaeda or ISIS? I didn't say this out loud, but it weighed on my mind.

I said that killing journalists or people who drew unpopular cartoons should never be an option. But I also asked if she was aware that there had been a time when Jews had been attacked in cartoons in Germany, too. Hadn't we been taught in school that something like that shouldn't happen again?

14

The Search for an Islamist Beatle, or Finding Jihadi John

Britain, 2014–15

The email from David Bradley arrived one day in October 2014. Bradley was the chairman of Atlantic Media in Washington, DC, the publisher of the *Atlantic* and several other U.S. media outlets. I didn't know him personally, but he was contacting me as part of a mission to free several journalists who had been kidnapped by ISIS.

"I'm raising a topic that may tax your sources unfairly," Bradley wrote. "I'm writing you to ask if you have any idea how I can open a back channel to the ISIS leadership."

Bradley's connection to the ISIS hostages had begun with James Foley, a freelance journalist from New Hampshire who had been kidnapped in Syria in November 2012. Bradley had gotten to know Foley's family a year earlier, when Foley had been held hostage in Libya. Bradley had helped free Foley along with another reporter, Clare Gillis, who was freelancing for the *Atlantic*.

This time, Foley had been captured in Syria while on assignment for the website GlobalPost, along with the photographer John Cantlie. Foley was moved often and tortured. By the spring of 2014, he and several other hostages had reportedly been moved to a prison on a mountain fifteen miles east of the Syrian city of Raqqa, which was now the capital of the Islamic State. The whole place was a heavily fortified military zone; by now its existence was an open secret. It was known locally as one of the three most important ISIS prisons in Raqqa Province. Even Amnesty International knew about it.

The U.S. military had raided the prison in July, but by then the hostages had been moved again. Foley's family received a final email from his captors in early August, and two weeks later he was beheaded; a video of his killing was posted to YouTube on August 19. In September, the group executed Steven Sotloff, another American journalist.

Now Bradley was directing his efforts toward freeing an American soldier turned humanitarian worker named Peter Kassig, who was still being held by the Islamic State. I spoke to Bradley and began looking for more information about Kassig and the circumstances of his captivity. Because he had been a soldier in the U.S. Army, I worried that he might be working for an intelligence agency and that he was only posing as an aid worker. But when I saw how easy it was to learn of his former military service online, I realized that was wrong. If he'd been undercover, there would have been more done to erase public information about his past.

Bradley told me that he had been in touch with some tribal chiefs in Iraq, but when I asked if he was in contact with anyone at ISIS, he said no. The tribal chiefs had access to parts of Iraq where ISIS was operating, but that was as close as they came to the terrorist group.

Peter Kassig had been raised in Indiana and had enlisted in the army as an infantryman in 2006. He served with the army's Seventy-Fifth Ranger Regiment, deploying to Iraq from April to July 2007, and was medically discharged later that year.

In March 2012, while on spring break from Butler University, he traveled to Lebanon to work as a volunteer emergency medical technician. Several months later, he founded Special Emergency Response and Assistance (SERA), an NGO devoted to providing emergency medical supplies for Syrians living in the conflict zone. In 2013, he moved SERA's base of operations to Gaziantep, Turkey. He was seized that October in eastern Syria, while traveling in an ambulance.

His family said that he'd developed a deep interest in Islam before his capture and had begun the conversion process to Islam the previous year. He had changed his name to Abdul-Rahman Kassig.

In addition to Foley and Sotloff, ISIS had also beheaded two British hostages, David Haines and Alan Henning. There was usually just a short period of time between the killings and when the videos appeared on the Internet, showing the victims dressed in orange jumpsuits that were supposed to look like those worn by prisoners at Guantánamo Bay and Abu Ghraib.

The same masked man always spoke first in the beheading videos, addressing President Obama directly and attacking him and his allies. He was known as Jihadi John, a name given to him by former hostages who reported that he and three other ISIS guards came from the United Kingdom. The hostages called them "the Beatles," and Jihadi John was their most prominent member.

Bradley's aim was to get Kassig out alive. I made a list of all the things I'd learned about Kassig. I Skyped with Bradley and asked if my information about his conversion was accurate. Bradley said it was, as far as he knew.

"This could be of huge help," I told him. I noted down some names on a piece of paper, sources of mine who were members and sympathizers of ISIS, the Taliban, Al Qaeda, and various go-betweens. I would contact them all to help free Kassig.

Even though ISIS had not recently had good relations with the Taliban and Al Qaeda, I knew that there were still links among them. Maybe Abu Bakr al-Baghdadi, the leader of ISIS, would think twice before killing a Muslim man whom other militants vouched for.

"Are you sure he is Muslim, and he was Muslim before he was taken?" one former bin Laden associate asked when I contacted him.

"Yes, Sheikh, he is Muslim and was before he was kidnapped," I answered, even though I felt a hostage's life shouldn't depend on whether he was Muslim. But it was the only obvious argument we had, one chance to avoid another beheading.

For a brief period, I checked in with Bradley and my sources almost daily. I heard that lots of people, including tribal chiefs from Iraq's Anbar Province, had been mobilized. Videos usually appeared a week to ten days apart. When no new one emerged, our hopes grew.

"Tell her the *shura* is discussing his case," ISIS commander Abu Yusaf told a contact, who relayed the message to me. The *shura* was a council that advised al-Baghdadi. In the end, it would be his decision to make. (Abu Yusaf was the commander I'd interviewed near the Turkish-Syrian border earlier that year, soon after the German intelligence services assured me that it was again safe for me to travel there.)

Then suddenly things changed. Media reports now said that Kassig and several other hostages had converted to Islam only after they were taken, to get better treatment from their captors. A short time later I received a message asking me to call the man who was acting as a go-between in relaying messages to and from Abu Yusaf.

"You saw the articles?" my contact said when I reached him. "You know what this means, right?"

"Maybe the articles are not accurate. Have you thought about this?"

"Souad, the people from the *shura* read as well. There were already some who had this suspicion, and now they say even the media is confirming it."

I felt helpless as I racked my brain for arguments to convince him otherwise.

"Please, what can we do? There must be something," I said.

"There is nothing. It's better for you to stop insisting; otherwise they will think you knew he was not Muslim and lied."

I went home with the devastating feeling that this was it for Kassig. I reached out to Bradley and asked if he had seen the reports. He had, and he was surprised. He told me he appreciated all the help, but he understood that this might jeopardize my relationship with my sources and said he wouldn't want to put me in that danger.

"I am very sorry," I told him, "and I am sorry for the family." In the days that followed, I scoured the Internet for any news or ISIS publications. I was hoping that Kassig might still have a chance.

On November 16, our hopes were dashed. A video appeared, showing ISIS executioners simultaneously beheading several Syrian pilots, followed by the man in black talking directly to Obama and the American people about Peter Kassig. It ended with a shot of Kassig's severed head on the ground between Jihadi John's legs.

It felt like a personal defeat. I stared at my laptop screen and asked the masked man, "Why are you doing this?" It was clear from the way he spoke English that he had either grown up in the United Kingdom or spent a lot of time there.

There he was, hiding behind his mask and taking someone else's life. I fervently hoped that one day his mask would be torn off and the world would learn his true identity.

———

ABOUT A WEEK after the massacre at *Charlie Hebdo*, while I was still in Paris, I got a call from Peter Finn. He wanted me to talk to another *Post* reporter, Adam Goldman, who was trying to identify the ISIS militants known to hostages as "the Beatles."

Adam's booming voice and thick New York accent reminded me of a character from a detective movie. He told me he'd heard that Jihadi John was of Yemeni descent, that his first name was Mohammed, and that he came from East London. He asked if I had good contacts in the Yemeni community in London. Not exactly, I told him, but I did have sources among radical Muslims there. I had reported in London and its suburbs after the transit attacks of 2005, and I'd interviewed Omar Bakri, a prominent British Islamist cleric, and some others who didn't often talk to reporters. I told Adam I'd ask around.

I made some calls, but no one wanted to talk on the phone, so I flew to London. Once there, I reached out to ISIS and Al Qaeda supporters, jihadi recruiters, and a handful of Bakri's former students. The identities of "the Beatles" was a hot topic around London, I learned. Some of my sources told me that even if they knew who the men were, they wouldn't tell me for fear of being punished as collaborators or supporters, since they hadn't shared their information with the police.

One of my sources was a bit older and lived outside the city. He had been involved with a couple of high-level Al Qaeda operatives and was seen as a sort of godfather by many radical young men in and around

London. The man said he'd heard rumors about Jihadi John, and he
thought he might have met him before he left to join ISIS.

"Is he Yemeni?" I asked.

There was silence, then laughter. "Who told you Yemeni?"

"So it isn't Mohammed from Yemen?"

"It is Mohammed, but not from Yemen."

"East London?"

"Not East. And I tell you, Souad, this man's story is different than
anything before. I can't say more than that."

He wouldn't tell me the man's surname or his country of origin. The
name "Mohammed" is as common as John, Paul, or George in London.

I called Adam. Was he sure that Jihadi John was Yemeni? That's what
his sources had told him, he said. I suggested we broaden our search. I
spent the next day in my hotel room, going over notes from my interview
with Abu Yusaf, especially the parts when he talked about the "brothers
from Britain." I also reviewed published interviews with released ISIS
hostages in which they spoke about "the Beatles" and learned that one
hostage reported that Jihadi John was obsessed with Somalia and would
show the captives videos about it. I had met one former French hostage
myself, and I pored over my notes from our conversation, looking for
clues. Finally I watched some of the terrible ISIS beheading videos again
and listened to what Jihadi John said and how he said it. Then I made
a list:

Mohammed
videos of Somalia
London (not East)
not Yemeni
The ISIS commander told me, "We have brothers from Britain of
various descents: Pakistani, Somali, Yemeni, and even Kuwaiti."
educated/university degree
deep hatred/personal vendetta

The last two items were based in part on instinct. In the ISIS videos,
Jihadi John sounded educated; Abu Yusaf had also told me about the

"brothers from Britain" with university degrees, and one of the freed hostages had said that his captors seemed well educated. "Deep hatred/personal vendetta" was a hunch based on Jihadi John's tone as he raged against British prime minister David Cameron, President Obama, and U.S. foreign policy. Something had angered him; the wound seemed personal.

I looked again at Abu Yusaf's words: *We have brothers from Britain of various descents: Pakistani, Somali, Yemeni, and even Kuwaiti.* I knew already from Adam's information that Jihadi John must be of Arab descent, so I crossed out "Pakistani" and "Somali." That left Kuwait as his most likely country of origin. I made a new list:

Mohammed
Kuwaiti
London
hatred/personal vendetta
educated/university degree
videos about Somalia

I set up another round of meetings, including one with a source linked to the Finsbury Park mosque in North London, a well-known center of jihadist recruiting. We met at 2:00 a.m. on the outskirts of the city. I took a taxi to a cabstand, paying in cash so the intelligence services, if they were watching, couldn't track my whereabouts too easily. My source picked me up there and drove me to a coffee shop owned by a friend. The place was closed at that hour, and it was just the three of us: my source and me sitting at a small table while the owner did paperwork at his desk in back.

My source was an ISIS sympathizer, and he knew people who had gone to fight in Somalia. Years before, he had been an acolyte of Abu Hamza al-Masri, the radical former imam at Finsbury Park, who was extradited to the United States in 2012, found guilty of terrorism, and sentenced to life in prison.

I asked if he knew anything about a Kuwaiti named Mohammed who had problems with the British authorities. He thought about it.

"Kuwaiti, Kuwaiti . . . yes! I remember there had been a Mohammed who got into trouble in Tanzania."

"What trouble?"

"I don't remember. It was related to Somalia, I think."

I tried to keep my cool.

"Do you know his full name?"

"Why are you so interested in him?"

I didn't tell him that I suspected this man might be Jihadi John. Instead, I said that I was trying find out if this Mohammed had gone to Syria.

"I'll see what I can do for you," he said, "but it will take some days."

He dropped me off at the same cabstand. It was almost 4:00 a.m. when I finally made it back to my hotel in central London.

I decided that I had to get in touch with a senior Islamic State official I'd known for years, the man who had helped arrange my meeting with Abu Yusaf. After that story ran, he'd asked somebody to deliver a message to me: *Salam. The Turks were pissed about your story; intel is asking about you. Don't come to the border region again, and don't reach out to me unless it's an emergency.*

This is an emergency, I thought. But to make contact with him, I had to go back to Germany, where I had a secure, if circuitous, way of reaching him. I would observe a strict protocol we'd developed years earlier to avoid detection by intelligence agencies or militants, who might punish him for talking to me.

First, I had to talk to a woman who was living in northern Germany. I called her and took a train north to speak to her in person. I told her I needed to talk to my source. She knew it had to be important and agreed to pass on the message to him. She also gave me an unregistered SIM card, which I would put into one of four old Nokia phones that I kept for communicating with people like him. Unlike smartphones, these primitive devices were hard for authorities to track.

A few days later, I got a text message from the woman I'd visited: "Will you be jogging at 4:00 p.m. tomorrow?"

"Yes," I replied.

I'm not really a jogger. This was a code: whenever my source set a time for an appointment, I would double the number; if he said "p.m.," that really meant "a.m.," and vice versa. At 8 a.m., according to the text, I should leave my apartment, turn on my old Nokia, put in the SIM card she'd given me, and wait for my source to call.

A short while before the appointed time, wearing sneakers, a black pullover, and a warm jacket, I walked to a park near my apartment. The winter sky was blue and the air was chilly. I'd left my smartphones at home and carried only the old Nokia in my jacket pocket. Although we'd arranged the call, there was no guarantee it would happen. I strolled through the park, feeling antsy. I'd likely have just a few minutes on the phone with him; it was a onetime shot. He might tell me what I wanted to know or he might say nothing. He might tell me never to call him again.

The phone rang. I fumbled to answer it.

"*As'salam alaikum*. How are you?" he asked in Arabic.

"I'm okay. And you?"

"All well. But what is urgent? What disaster are you working on this time?" He was laughing.

I started laughing too, relieved that he was in a joking mood. "Tell me about Mohammed from Kuwait, the man in black."

Silence.

"Are you there?" I asked.

"Yes, I'm here." His tone was serious. "Who told you?"

"Told me what?"

"That he is Kuwaiti and that his name is Mohammed?"

"I can't tell you," I said. "You know I can't."

There was another silence.

"Interesting," he said after a while. "So I assume the British dogs are spreading these rumors to get their lies out and hide the truth about him?"

"What do you mean?" I asked. "What lies? What truth?"

Silence again.

I decided to take a risk. "Do you mean the Somalia story?"

"So they told you about the Somalia story?" he asked. "Dogs! I knew it. They're trying to create their own narrative."

Walking through the park with my headphones on, I opened my small black notepad and wrote "Somalia."

"So tell me the true story then," I said.

"He had suffered a lot. The British intelligence was after him and closed many doors to him. It's too long a story to tell over the phone now."

"I need to know the truth. How else can I write it?"

His tone grew serious again. "Listen, you know I admire your guts and honesty, but be careful. You've upset some people in Turkey." He meant the intelligence services and government officials. "The man you are touching now, if you don't write the narrative the Brits dictate, that will piss them off as well. No more shopping at Harrods." He started laughing again.

I told him I didn't have much time for Harrods anyway and that he shouldn't worry.

"What do you want?" he asked.

"I want the truth. But I need his full name to get the right information about what you said happened to him." Another silence. "Listen, the story will come out soon, anyway. So help me get it right."

"You're crazy, but okay. I need to get back to you. Keep walking for a few more minutes."

The line went dead. I walked around the park, pulling my jacket tight against the wind. I felt this was my best shot at getting Jihadi John's name. Just then, my phone buzzed, and a text message appeared on the screen in English: "Go to London, Emwazi had tried to solve his problems with help of a group, ask CAGE. Delete this message and throw away this SIM now. *Wa'alaikum as' salam.*" I could barely believe it. For the first time, I had a possible last name for Jihadi John, the masked man, casually dropped in a text.

I looked around to see if anyone was watching, then noted down the information, took the SIM card out, and threw it away. Back home, I called Peter and Adam and said I might have something but needed to get back to the United Kingdom. I also shared the new information with both of them, using an encrypted messaging program. My next call was to CAGE, a British advocacy group that campaigns against rendition, unlawful detention, and other government abuses in the name of fighting terrorism. I had been in contact with the group before, while working on other stories. I said I wanted to talk to them about a case they'd worked on.

"What case are you talking about?" the CAGE staffer asked.

"Is there a case of a man called Mohammed Emwazi?" I asked. "It might be related to Somalia."

The man said he would check the files. He called me back soon after. Yes, he said, they had worked on a case involving a man of that name a couple of years ago. He invited me to come to London to discuss it with Asim Qureshi, the research director of CAGE. I booked a flight.

I had spoken to Qureshi before. He's a lawyer who has worked on cases involving detainees in Guantánamo and secret prisons around the world. British-born but of Pakistani descent, he speaks with a fine English accent, drinks his black tea with milk, and enjoys scones with clotted cream. Yet he'd told me that some people doubted he was truly British because of the nature of his work.

Founded in 2003 as Cageprisoners.com, CAGE has built a track record as an advocacy group for Muslim prisoners. It was among the groups pointing out alleged torture in Guantánamo, and in the past decade and a half many who didn't trust other organizations have come to CAGE with stories of mistreatment and injustice. That's partly because CAGE doesn't shy away from speaking to young men like Emwazi, who have been in trouble with police in terror-related cases.

In fact, CAGE itself has had problems with the British authorities. Since March 2014, the group has been operating without a bank account and, according to its website, is "under constant pressure and scrutiny from politicians and various government agencies. Despite these difficulties, *alhamdulillah* we have been able to work on major cases of significance in the War on Terror and continue to advocate for due process and the rule of law."

Qureshi and I met at a coffee shop close to CAGE's office. He explained that the group had been in touch in the past with somebody called Mohammed Emwazi, who had been in trouble with British authorities. "But this case was many years ago. Why are you interested in it now?" he asked.

I didn't want to tell him about my suspicions, given that so far I had only one source. But I needed to collect as much information as possible, and I wanted to be as truthful as I could. "I'm looking into a case that's related to Syria, and his name came up," I said. This was true. I asked if CAGE had any contacts for his family.

He shook his head. "We haven't been in touch with this man in years." Qureshi added that he'd had to go back through the archives to refresh his memory of Emwazi's case.

"Why don't you start from the beginning," I said.

"That's actually what I told him, when he came to the office the first time, why don't you start from the beginning," Qureshi recalled. He said that Emwazi was a British citizen whose family had come from Kuwait. "They were Bidoon," Qureshi told me, "so they weren't seen as full Kuwaitis." When the British ended the protectorate in 1961, about a third of the Kuwaiti population were denied citizenship; Emwazi's family belonged to this group.

He had gone to a sort of charter school called Quintin Kynaston, in the tony London neighborhood of St. John's Wood. The school drew students from all over the city, including many from poor and immigrant families. Two other boys who had gone there had also become Islamist fighters.

Emwazi's trouble with the law began when he and two friends were arrested in Tanzania in May 2009. My ears perked up when I heard that. I was looking for clues that might confirm that Jihadi John was obsessed with Somalia, and I knew that Tanzania was a frequent stop on the way to Somalia at that time.

According to Emwazi's account, the local police detained them when they landed in Dar es Salaam. He told CAGE they'd been threatened and, at some stage, mistreated by the Tanzanian police, who suspected that the three planned to travel to Somalia. He told CAGE they were on their way to go on safari before beginning university or getting married.

He and his companions flew back to Amsterdam, where they'd changed planes on the way to Tanzania. "He said that an MI5 officer interrogated him there, together with a supposedly Dutch intelligence officer," Qureshi said. MI5 is Britain's domestic intelligence service.

The MI5 officer, too, believed Emwazi and his friends had been on their way to Somalia to join al-Shabab, a militant group allied with Al Qaeda that operates in the southern and central parts of the country. Emwazi denied the accusations and claimed that MI5 agents had tried to recruit him.

Emwazi and his friends were allowed to return to Britain, but he said that he and his family subsequently felt "under pressure" from MI5. In the fall of 2009, he again met with Qureshi, talking about visits from MI5 agents, calls to his home, and strange cars following him. Finally, he and his family decided it would be better for him to return to Kuwait.

"Mohammed was quite incensed," Qureshi said. He felt "that he had been very unfairly treated."

In Kuwait, Emwazi got a job at a computer company, according to emails he wrote to CAGE. He came back to London at least twice. "He wanted to get married to a woman in Kuwait and settle there," Qureshi said. "The second time, he came back to finalize the wedding planning with his parents."

In June 2010, Emwazi emailed CAGE to say that British counterterrorism officials had detained him again during that visit to London, searched his belongings, and fingerprinted him. When he and his father went to the airport the next day, the airlines said he was on a list and refused to let him board a flight back to Kuwait.

I asked Qureshi if I could read this part of the email myself.

"I had a job waiting for me and marriage to get started," Emwazi wrote, but now he felt "like a prisoner, only not in a cage, in London. A person imprisoned & controlled by security service men, stopping me from living my new life in my birthplace & country, Kuwait."

I was surprised by the language in the email, which was very thoughtful. These were the words of someone who sounded emotional and slightly desperate. It wasn't how I envisioned the person I'd seen in videos cutting off journalists' heads. While reading his letter, I tried to picture the man in the black mask as its author. "What does he look like?" I asked. "Do you have a photograph?"

"No, we don't," Qureshi answered, but he described Emwazi as tall and good-looking with brownish skin and the fine features common in the Gulf. When he came to the CAGE offices, he brought sweets. Qureshi said he was very polite and grateful for their support and advice.

I had already typed his name into Google when I'd heard it from the ISIS source for the first time, but there had been no pictures. Either he was never very fond of social media or someone had cleaned up after him.

Qureshi said he'd last heard from Emwazi in January 2012, when Emwazi sent an email seeking more advice.

"No more emails or calls?"

"No, nothing from him," Qureshi said.

"Do you know if he is still in the United Kingdom or if he has left the country?" I tried to avoid the word "Syria."

"No, we don't know," Qureshi said, adding that he had emailed Emwazi in 2014 to check in, but there was no response.

I thanked Qureshi for his time and said I would be in touch again soon.

When I stepped out of the coffee shop, I felt as if I were carrying a weight. I was almost certain that Mohammed Emwazi was indeed Jihadi John. At the hotel, I went through all my notes from the conversations I'd had so far, and then watched some of the videos I'd downloaded on the *Post* server, because downloading certain violent online content was forbidden by Britain's Terrorism Act of 2006. I wasn't sure how the authorities would react to this Emwazi story, but I planned to leave the United Kingdom before it was published.

As I watched the videos, I tried to find one that offered a clearer view of his eyes. I took a screenshot and filmed some of the video clips on my phone.

But so far I had only one source, the senior ISIS official. I needed more. On one of my unregistered phones and SIM cards, I called my source in the United Kingdom who had already indicated that he knew something.

"I'm here in London," I told him. "I need to have tea with you."

"You are welcome," he said.

I had to travel outside the city to meet him, and he warned me that he had time for only one cup of tea.

"It's okay, this won't take much time. You just have to tell me is Mohammed Emwazi this man?" I showed him the screenshot I'd taken of Jihadi John.

He looked at the photograph and then looked at me.

"Wait, we haven't even ordered the tea yet," he said, beginning to laugh.

We asked for tea, switched off our phones, and put them a few meters away from us, next to speakers blaring a mix of Hindi and Arabic music.

"You look tired. Are you not sleeping much?" he asked me. I acknowledged that this story wasn't giving me much time to sleep.

"You know, one day a couple of months ago, a young man whom I had met on different occasions came to me and said he believed his friend was the man in black," he finally began. "He said that from the voice and the body language and the eyes, he felt that this was someone he used to know, and he was the one who mentioned something about Somalia and other stories."

I began to tremble. Maybe it was because I was exhausted, or because I felt we were very close to getting a second source.

"Did he tell you the name of his friend?" I asked.

"Yes. It was the name you mentioned, Mohammed Emwazi."

He asked me to keep his comments off the record, given the sensitivity of the case, but promised to put me in touch with Emwazi's friend. He picked up his phone, dialed a number, and spoke to the man, trying to convince him to meet me. He even handed me the phone so we could say *Salam* and I could hear his voice.

"I'd like to meet you," I told him, but he didn't agree then and there.

"I will give him the number for your unregistered phone," my source said after they hung up.

"Where does he live? In London?"

He confirmed this but said he couldn't tell me more and that he had to leave. I took a train back to central London, checking often to see if anybody was following me.

As soon as I got to the hotel, I sent an encrypted message to Adam and Peter and gave them what I had so far. I also told them that I still had to meet with more sources and asked that nobody mention my name anywhere as the person who was on the ground for the *Post* in London.

Once I had met Emwazi's friend, I'd have to go back to CAGE and confront them with our findings. I worried about someone trying to destroy my notes, so I took pictures of each page of my notebook and sent them to Peter and Adam.

"Did you get them?" I asked.

"Yes, but don't worry, no one will ever be able to read your handwriting," Adam said with a laugh.

It was clear that the *Post* would have to confront American and British authorities with our findings before we could publish the story. But first I hoped Emwazi's friend would agree to meet me.

Finally, at about 8:00 p.m., I received a message on my unregistered phone from an unknown number: "*Salam*. I am the friend of Mohammed. I can meet you in one hour. Please come to the following address; you will be picked up from a different car then."

So he knew I would most likely come by taxi and didn't want anyone to know where we were going. After he sent the message, I received a call from the man I'd had tea with.

"Did the friend contact you?" he asked.

"Yes, he just did."

"I thought since you weren't sleeping much these days, you wouldn't mind to meet in the evening, it's better for him," he said, giggling. He assured me I would be safe.

I had known this source for many years, and he had always helped me and been very particular about my safety, so I was not as nervous as I might have been about meeting someone I didn't know alone in the middle of the night.

The place he wanted me to go to was almost an hour away by car. The address was a pub. When we got there, I double-checked it with the driver to make sure we were in the right place.

"Yes, my dear," he said in his proper British accent. He sounded like the butler from *Downton Abbey*.

It was surreal to be meeting Jihadi John's friend at a pub, even if it was just the pickup point. I'd gone through the dance of being dropped somewhere and then picked up to go somewhere else many times before, but I didn't know what to expect this time. Could this person really be the second source I was looking for?

"Get out of the taxi, I can see you," a new message on my phone read.

After my taxi had left, a car on the opposite side of the road turned on its lights, and I saw a man in the driver's seat winking me in.

"I am Mohammed's friend," he said. I recognized his voice from earlier on the phone. He was in his late twenties but asked that I not reveal any further details about him.

Before I got in, I asked him for the *kunya*, or fighting name, of the man who had called me earlier and who had put us in contact. I wanted to be 100 percent sure that this was the right man.

He knew the answer. I got into the car.

He said that he would prefer if we could walk a little, even though by now it was dark. He stopped in a residential area where streetlights shone into the car. When we got out, he asked for my mobile phones. I hesitated at first because I'd planned to show him the video clip of Jihadi John, but then I remembered that I had some magazine and newspaper clips in my bag with pictures of the ISIS executioner, so I switched off the phones and left them in the trunk of his car.

We started walking toward a park nearby, which was really just a small grassy area with a bench. He took a tissue from his jacket pocket and wiped the bench. By the light of a streetlamp, I showed him the clips and photographs of Jihadi John.

"Is this your friend?"

"Yes, I am very sure it's him. It's my friend Mohammed Emwazi."

Then he told me the same basic story I'd heard from Asim Qureshi. I asked how he knew Jihadi John was Emwazi, or vice versa.

"There is another friend of ours, he is there as well," the man said, and then he stopped for a moment. "When the first video came out showing him with this journalist, our friend contacted me and said I should watch it and that it was our friend Mohammed there."

He said that parts of the video had been shown on the news and that he'd watched it again and again. He believed that the voice and the eyes were indeed Emwazi's.

He never went to the police because he feared getting in trouble. "I recognized his voice and the eyes, but the person I saw in the video is not the Mohammed who used to be my friend."

"Why do you think he became who he has become?"

"I don't know what he might have seen there in Syria the last few years. Maybe this changed him."

"But wasn't he always interested in going to fight? Wasn't he planning to travel to Somalia, and that's how he got into trouble?" I asked.

"He was interested in what happened in the Muslim world, including Somalia, and he felt the West was following unfair policies and double standards," the man told me. But he didn't understand how his old friend could cut off the heads of journalists and aid workers. "This is very difficult for me to swallow. I am asking myself the whole time, *why Mohammed?*"

I asked if he had a photo of his friend, but he said he didn't. We walked back to the car, and he offered to drive me to a cabstand a bit closer to the city.

Back at the hotel, Adam, Peter, and I got on Skype, and I told them that we now had a second source: a friend of Emwazi's who said he was Jihadi John.

"I guess we will have to contact British authorities now," Peter said. He said he would speak to the *Post*'s top editors and let me know about next steps.

"I know it's quite late where you are and it's been a long day, but could you stay up so we can update you on what we are doing?" Peter asked.

I told him that I wouldn't be able to sleep now anyway. The adrenaline was unbelievable. I understood that we had the name of one of the most wanted men in the world, but I wasn't sure that British authorities wanted the full story out. Maybe I was being paranoid, but I wondered if MI5 would storm my hotel to try to get our information.

Adam pointed out that as soon as we contacted British authorities, the story might break anytime. "But let me check it with my sources here in the United States first," he said. "Well, actually, if we ask the Americans for reaction, it's very likely they will immediately tell the Brits." He had a couple of trusted sources in the United States he could at least ask off the record, he said.

We agreed to regroup via Skype within the next few hours. I typed up my notes and took a quick shower. I realized that I hadn't eaten since breakfast, so I called the night porter at the little bed and breakfast where I was staying and asked if he had anything warm to eat.

"I am afraid all I could offer you is a cheese sandwich and a banana," he said. I told him that would be okay, and I ordered a pot of chamomile tea as well.

I played some music on my cell phone to calm myself down. I was especially worried about the British authorities leaking our story to British news organizations. The night porter arrived with the sandwich, banana, and chamomile tea on a wooden tray.

"I'm sorry we don't have any warm food to offer you, but I found some crisps and shortbread," he said, setting the tray down on the table.

There go my good intentions for better nutrition, I told myself. I was in the midst of tipping the porter when I received a Skype call from Peter.

"There is an update. Adam told his source what we found out, and after some back and forth he said we wouldn't be wrong if we wrote that it was Emwazi." I had pushed my earbuds deep into my ears so as not to miss any of what he said.

Even though I already had two sources, having someone from the U.S. or British government confirm or at least not disavow our findings was very important.

"Adam's source was quite shocked when he heard what we had found out," Peter continued. "At first he didn't want to say anything, but when we told him we had two sources, he at least didn't deny it."

Hearing this, I was in shock myself. "We'll now reach out officially to U.S. authorities and also the United Kingdom, so you may want to tell CAGE as well," Peter said.

I told him I would and that I would also try to make contact with Emwazi's family.

He agreed. "Now, get something to eat and get some sleep. We have some intense days ahead."

After we hung up, I sent a message to the CAGE people asking if we could meet. I told them it was very important and that soon there could be something breaking in the media. I wanted them to read the message first thing in the morning and get back to me right away. I drank the cup of chamomile tea and fell into a deep sleep, leaving the cheese sandwich and the rest of the food on the tray untouched.

The next morning, Asim Qureshi called and said he could pass by my hotel, as he had something to do in the neighborhood. When he arrived, I told him what we had learned: that the Mohammed Emwazi who had reached out to him some years ago was Jihadi John. He seemed astonished. I told him that now we were also reaching out to British authorities and that he should be prepared for a big reaction.

I showed him a video of Jihadi John and made him listen to the jihadist's words. "What do you think has happened to him?" I asked Qureshi.

He said he couldn't answer that question. "This is a young man who was ready to exhaust every single kind of avenue within the machinery of the state to bring a change for his personal situation," Qureshi said. Ultimately, Emwazi felt "actions were taken to criminalize him, and he had no way to do something against these actions."

I'd found an address for Emwazi's family on the Internet. "I think they should know that this might break soon," I told Qureshi. "I'd like to give them a chance to react beforehand."

He said he understood but that he couldn't help me get in touch with them. Emwazi's friend confirmed the address I had, but he too said he wouldn't be able to help me connect with them.

After Qureshi left, I went back to my computer and saw an update from Adam: "The Brits are upset. They are scheduled to have a conversation with our bosses." He meant the Post's executive editor, Marty Baron; the national editors; and Peter. "We didn't tell them that you are the reporter on the ground, but be aware there might be more eyes on you soon."

He added that they wanted to pull the story together as quickly as possible and that I should write my part and send it to him. I sat in the room for hours, noting down everything I had and wondering what the conversation with the editors would lead to.

I then left the hotel, taking all my notes and my computer with me. I walked to the main road, watching my surroundings and trying to figure out if anyone was following me. I stopped a taxi and gave the driver the address of Emwazi's family.

The Emwazi family lived in a largely well-to-do West London neighborhood called Ladbroke Grove, in a semidetached house on a diverse block, nothing like the *banlieues* I'd explored outside Paris. There was no light on in the house, and, when I knocked, no answer. It was early afternoon. A neighbor who looked Southeast Asian came out to collect a package from a delivery service. I asked if she knew the Emwazis.

She said not much, that everyone here kept to themselves. But she mentioned that she hadn't seen them in some days.

I thanked her and spent a few minutes in front of the house. How much pain had Mohammed Emwazi brought to various families, including his own? His friend had told me that the family had done everything to give Mohammed an excellent education. His sisters had gone to school, too, and at least one had been to university. He had grown up very differently from the Kouachi brothers or Hayat Boumeddiene. But I had no idea what might have gone on in his family as long as I couldn't speak to them.

My phone rang. It was Peter. "Any luck with the family?"

I told him there was no one at the house. He asked me to let him know when I could Skype, as there was some news.

Back at the hotel, he filled me in. "There was a conversation with the British authorities. They still didn't want to give any comment, but they asked us not to publish the story."

"Why?" I asked.

"They said this could endanger the life of John Cantlie, the hostage. What do you say? Could this endanger his life? The editors would like to hear your opinion."

This was something I hadn't expected. I was still upset that we hadn't succeeded in the Kassig case, and now this.

"Please give me a few hours," I told Peter. "I can't give you a clear answer now."

There was one person I did want to ask: Emwazi's friend. I was able to arrange another meeting with him and my old source at the coffee shop with the Indian and Arabic music outside London.

"You look even worse than the last time," my source said when I arrived. Emwazi's friend was already sitting there and drinking a juice cocktail.

"Well, it's not like I'm on honeymoon."

"I pray for the day you will call me from your honeymoon," he answered and opened his hands as if he were praying.

We all started laughing. I told him that I hadn't laughed in days. I had indeed been very exhausted, and my stomach ached from the tension.

I asked both of them if they thought Cantlie's life might be in danger if we published the story. The two men looked at each other.

"No, I don't think so," Emwazi's friend said.

Both told me that a critical but fair article would not lead to the killing of the hostage. "It would be worse if it would be a one-sided British propaganda piece," the friend said.

I told him that he had to be aware that our article would of course be critical and mention all the killing for which Emwazi was responsible. He said that this was clear, but they were sure it would be fair. When I asked if there was any chance I might get a short interview with Emwazi, the friend shook his head.

"No chance. ISIS has him on lockdown," my source said. "They seem to know something might come out soon."

I got back to the hotel and reached Peter. I said I'd spoken to some people who knew the "subject" and that they didn't think it would have an effect on the British hostage.

"Okay, I'll let the editors know." I later learned from Peter that U.S. officials were also skeptical of the British argument that Cantlie would be endangered by the story's publication.

In the meantime, Adam and I wrote messages back and forth regarding the article and various revisions. Hours passed before Peter called me back on Skype.

He said the paper had told the British authorities that we would go ahead with the piece. They had asked for forty-eight hours to inform all the families involved, both Emwazi's and those of the hostages and victims. "We agreed to do this," he said.

But a couple of hours later, I received a message from Adam. It seemed that someone very high up at the BBC had called the *Post* and said they'd heard we were planning to reveal the identity of Jihadi John.

"Does this means the Brits are playing games with us?" I asked. "Are they trying to stop us from writing about the case with the argument that it would endanger the hostage, so they can leak things to the BBC?"

I endured another sleepless night. The next day I got an encrypted message from one of the people I'd talked to in London: "Souad, something weird is going on. Some BBC and ITV people are asking about the guy."

"How detailed?" I asked.

"They go around in the community and ask about the guy and know his name."

Now I was getting angry. It looked to me as if British authorities were trying to trick us. First, they had used Cantlie's safety as an argument to delay us. Then they'd said they had to inform the families and take precautions. Now it looked like they were leaking all kinds of information to the BBC and ITV, so that a British news organization would break the story.

We had worked so hard to get this information carefully and ethically, and now we might get beaten on the story anyway. I called Peter and told him what I'd just heard.

"Don't you think we should reconsider the forty-eight hours?" I asked. There were still twenty-four hours left on the clock, and a lot could happen. He said that the *Post* would honor the agreement for the sake of the families, but that if I heard that someone was about to break the story we would go ahead.

Something else had been occupying my mind. A friend who worked for an Arab newspaper called me that night. He said a friend from the BBC had told him that the *Post* would publish the name of Jihadi John the next morning. He'd assumed I was somehow involved. "Do you think it's wise to put your name on that story?" he asked.

I'd been wondering the same thing. How would the notorious ISIS executioner react to seeing his real name, Mohammed Emwazi, in print? And how would the Islamic State respond to the knowledge that a Muslim woman had unmasked him? Would it make a video broadcasting

my face to the world and accuse me of being the enemy or a spokesperson for the intelligence services?

I didn't seriously consider taking my name off the story, but I did
some risk assessment and damage control. I'd done what I could to make
sure that Emwazi's friends knew we had reported the story fairly. Through
the person I'd met in the park, we gave Emwazi's mother and siblings,
who were still in London, a chance to speak, which they declined.

I had my own reasons for acknowledging my role in the story. I
wanted to send a message to Jihadi John and others like him: we will tell
the world who you are and stop you from spreading fear—and a Muslim
journalist, a woman, has the power to do this.

In the end, we broke the story with the BBC snapping at our heels. I
was proud of our achievement, but it also had a personal resonance. I was
sending a message to those in the West who blame every Muslim and
Islam.

15

Terror Comes Home

Austria, France, and Belgium, 2015–16

The train stations in Austria were packed with people when I arrived in September 2015 to cover the refugee crisis that was paralyzing swaths of Europe. In some corners, food stands and kitchens had been set up; elsewhere, there were field beds for the newly arrived crowds to nap on. Helpers from many backgrounds and all corners of Austrian society had come to support the needs of the refugees, who were streaming in from Syria, Iraq, and Afghanistan, but also from other places, as I soon learned. Many journalists were covering the story. As I read German media accounts and listened to the politicians talk, I sensed a completely uncritical euphoria about the newly arrived foreigners.

Wir schaffen das—translated variously as "We'll manage it" or "We can do it"—was German chancellor Angela Merkel's slogan, a way to encourage Germans to take an optimistic view of the refugees' arrival. This upbeat, determined spirit was echoed in news articles and TV programs. I shared the hope that these refugees fleeing horrific circumstances in their home countries would be accepted and find peace in Germany and other countries. But I also knew this would be a perfect opportunity for all kinds of jihadi groups to send recruits to Europe, where they could operate as sleeper cells.

In the train stations of Austria, I began to see signs that this was already happening. Merkel had spoken of the magnitude of the refugee crisis and the need to temporarily open Germany's borders to families fleeing war. But in some parts of the world, her speech wasn't fully translated or was shared in fragments on social media. It was interpreted by many as an open invitation—a onetime shot at a new life in Europe. People from all over North Africa, the Middle East, and even South Asia flew to Turkey, destroyed their passports, and joined the flood of refugees. The numbers were so large that European authorities didn't have time to set up a comprehensive system of translators and others who could verify people's identities or at least confirm that they were really Syrian or fleeing severe conflict.

While wandering through the train stations in Vienna, I heard many different dialects of Arabic: Algerian, Moroccan, Tunisian, Egyptian, Yemeni. I also heard Farsi, Urdu, and Hindi.

I met a tall man in his late twenties named Hamza. He confessed that he was from Algeria and told me that he'd spent half his life in prison there for selling drugs and attempted murder. He said that the wave of refugees had offered an ideal cover for people like him to slip into Europe. Hamza wore jeans and a T-shirt and smiled a lot, thrilled to have made it this far. He had a group of friends with him who didn't look like they wanted to work as cooks or cleaners. Maybe I was being uncharitable, but to me they looked like trouble.

"We flew to Istanbul and then took a bus to Izmir," Hamza told me. "There we destroyed our passports and just mixed with the Syrian refugees. We then took a boat from Izmir to Greece. From there to Macedonia, Serbia, Hungary, and now we are in Vienna." He said that he had seen many other North Africans arriving to join the refugees, and he introduced me to some of his Algerian friends.

Portions of several major train stations in Vienna had been converted into makeshift campsites for refugees. In these enclosed areas, the smell of sweat and food mixed with urine and feces—some of the children and others had been unable to use toilets during their long trips from Turkey and beyond and had relieved themselves in their clothes or used other methods. I saw people with skin diseases and lice. People who had a bit of money told me they'd hired cabs or buses to speed their journey, while others walked. Some had been on the road for a week or more. In addition to the cots and food stations, local volunteers who spoke Arabic were on hand to help the travelers.

While walking around the stations, I noticed that most of the refugees were men. Many told me they'd come from Damascus, though they didn't have the lighter olive skin tones common in Syria; instead, they looked more North African, with curlier hair and darker skin and eyes. When I asked which part of the city, they walked away.

An Austrian security official told me that there were thriving black markets for Syrian passports in Croatia, Serbia, Hungary, and Austria, in addition to Turkey. But most of these people had arrived in Vienna without ever having shown a passport or document to officials, as long as they traveled in a stream of asylum seekers. Authorities along the way might have asked for names and countries of origin, but they weren't scrutinizing documents. Opportunists could easily pass through borders simply by claiming to be Syrian, without offering any proof.

But when I heard Syrian and Iraqi dialects, I stopped to listen. There were enough pretenders that the true Syrians began to complain about the false Syrians, saying that opportunists such as Hamza would quickly wear out their welcome, if they hadn't already.

"Look at these people, what are they doing here?" a sixty-two-year-old Syrian named Mustafa asked me. He was lean and his black hair was streaked with gray; he'd traveled to Austria with his son and a group of other Syrians and was now waiting to buy a train ticket to Germany. "We are the ones who are fleeing from war and slaughter, and now these men are taking away our space." He had paused to help a woman who had fainted, giving a group of Afghans the opportunity to cut ahead of him in line.

Real Syrians, too, often had no documents, so it was hard to verify what they said. When I talked to a few of those carrying Syrian documents, I learned that they had been living in refugee camps in Jordan, Turkey, or Lebanon and had seized the opportunity to come to Europe, mainly for economic reasons.

People told me they believed that in Germany they would get furnished apartments, cars, money for each child, and health care, as well as the chance to open their own businesses. Some young adults asked me about the universities, and whether tuition was free.

I sympathized with their wish for a better life. Many had been through traumatic situations, and suffering was written on their faces. But some of these conversations tried my patience. When I asked, here and there, if they would agree to work for the benefits they received, I sometimes heard answers like, "I don't want my wife or daughter to work."

"Cleaning houses or washing dishes?" one Syrian woman said incredulously. "No, that's not for me." She was in her late twenties and said she had been a teacher in Syria. I thought back to my conversation with Abu Hussain, my driver in Bahrain, who'd expressed similar horror at the notion of members of his family having to take menial jobs.

I also wondered about the idea some German politicians were spreading that most of the people who were coming were highly educated and had professional backgrounds. "Educationally, they are the flower of their country," read an article produced by the UN High Commissioner for Refugees, referring to the Syrian refugees arriving in Europe. "Eighty-six percent say they have secondary school or university education." That wasn't what I saw in the train stations. Most of the Syrians I met were farmers or laborers. They didn't speak any other language than Arabic and hadn't spent much time in school. That wasn't a problem in itself, but politicians and the media were telling a very different story, suggesting that the influx of new refugees would fill a growing gap in Germany's aging workforce, reducing unemployment and helping to propel the economy.

I also met some migrants who said they'd lived under ISIS and liked it. My colleague William Booth and I chatted with one young man who said he had come from the so-called caliphate. "It's good to live under Islamic law," he told us. Bill and I traded looks. Why, then, had he chosen to leave? we asked. "Because of the job opportunities," he said, adding that he was still in touch with people back home.

Bill and I spent hours roaming around the train stations, trying to speak to as many people as possible. In the city's main train station, Wien

Hauptbahnhof, we found a group of Iraqi men who were sitting cross-legged on a blanket near a staircase.

I knew they were Iraqi from their accents. Iraqis comprised one of the largest groups among the refugees. One of the men showed another his smartphone. "*Illa tahin*," he said. "This is what we have to do with all of them."

Illa tahin means "grind them to dust" in Arabic. It was the slogan of a Shia commander named Ayyub al-Rubaie, who went by the nom de guerre Abu Azrael. He made news in August 2015 when a video circulated on the Internet showing him slicing flesh from the burned body of an alleged ISIS fighter. "ISIS, this will be your fate, we will cut you like *shwarma*," he said in the video. A number of Shia militias aligned with the Iraqi government have been accused of atrocities and serious human rights violations against Sunnis in Iraq as part of their broader war against ISIS.

The men were just about to dig into white plastic plates of rice, chicken, and salads they'd gotten from one of the aid stations. I walked up to them.

"*As'salam alaikum*," I said.

They looked up in surprise. "By God, I didn't think you understood Arabic," one told me. "I thought maybe you were Indian or Pakistani."

I explained who I was and asked where they were from. They looked nervously at each other. One claimed he was from Mosul and that they had fled ISIS.

"Your dialect reminds me of the way they speak in the South," I told him. "Like in Basra or Umm Qasr."

"You know Basra?" one asked.

I nodded and told them that I'd spent several months in Iraq in 2003. "So where are you really from?" I asked.

Two of the older men in the group took me aside and began to tell a story that I knew was still not true, a convoluted tale about having lived in Mosul recently. But at least they confirmed they were from the South and were Shia.

After listening for a while, I looked one directly in the eye. "Could it be that you guys were members of the Iraqi army or some militias?"

One of the men put his index finger to his lips, signaling that I should not mention this too loudly.

"Why?" I asked.

"Because members of other groups are here as well."

A different group of men claimed to have just escaped from Fallujah. One had a fresh bullet wound. When I asked what they did for a living, one answered "army." His friend gave him an angry look and corrected him. "We're all drivers," the friend said.

After a couple of days of reporting, I was certain that many security challenges lay ahead. Meanwhile, Islamophobia was on the rise in many countries, and my European Muslim friends and I got the feeling that parts of the Muslim community were also growing more religiously conservative, even extremist. The two trends were intertwined and inseparable. The more alienated Muslims felt in Europe, I thought, the more separate they actually became, embedding themselves ever deeper in the faith and community the majority culture was criticizing. I remembered how, when I was fifteen or sixteen and enraged by racism and violence against Muslims in Germany, I wanted to wear the hijab as a sign of protest. My parents talked to me. "You're angry," they said, explaining that fury wasn't a good reason to adopt a religious practice.

Now there was a large group of people coming to Europe who had not been through rigorous security screenings. There was also the question of what they expected from their new lives and what they would do if those expectations were not met.

On Friday, November 13, a series of attacks rocked Paris and a northern suburb, Saint-Denis. Eleven men, including some who had fought in Syria and at least two Iraqis who had used falsified Syrian passports to blend in with the wave of refugees arriving in Europe, attacked the Stade de France, the Bataclan theater, and a handful of restaurants and bars, killing 130 people.

Most of the plotters were the sons of Moroccan migrants in Belgium or France, and I yearned to know what had led to their radicalization. Most of the attackers had long been known to French police for crimes such as drug dealing and robbery. In short, they were petty gangsters.

I grew especially interested in Abdelhamid Abaaoud, one of the ringleaders. He was among the attackers who had spent time fighting in Syria but had made it back to Europe, even though they were wanted by authorities. Abaaoud had grown up in Brussels' Molenbeek neighborhood, the oldest son of Moroccan immigrants. By his late teens, Abaaoud had been expelled from school, had become involved in neighborhood gangs, and had embarked on a life of small-time crime. Between 2006 and 2012 he served a number of brief jail terms for misdemeanors. When he got out for the last time, his father later told investigators, Abaaoud had changed. He grew a beard, stopped hanging out with his neighborhood friends, and promised his father he'd never go back to prison.

Instead, he traveled to Egypt to study Arabic, and then to Syria, where he told friends back home that he "wanted to help the innocents." In late 2013, he was spotted in Molenbeek. Belgian authorities were watching him, but a few months later he returned to Syria and what he called the "caliphate," taking his thirteen-year-old brother with him.

I wondered what might have happened, not only to him but inside his family as well. After the Paris attacks, I spent some time in Molenbeek, and from the outside it sounded as if Abaaoud had had plenty of opportunities to forge a life for himself. His father owned a business that imported items from Morocco to sell and was not in bad financial shape. Abaaoud had gone to a private school. But there were problems in his parents' marriage. Abaaoud was closer to his mother than to his father. According to intelligence sources, Abaaoud was frustrated and angered by how his father lived his life and by the constant fights at home.

Molenbeek didn't look like the *banlieues* I had visited in France. There weren't any gray high-rise buildings, and the shops and coffeehouses reminded me of Morocco. But the *Post*'s Belgian stringer Annabell Van den Berghe told me how difficult it was to get information; the people in Molenbeek didn't like to speak to reporters. And while it might not have looked as dismal as the *banlieues*, Molenbeek had many similar problems. The unemployment rate was about 30 percent, and in some areas even higher; there was a high percentage of foreign-born individuals; and many people lived in poverty. Radical Islam and sectarian conflicts also thrived. Some deplored the influence of Saudi, Kuwaiti, and Qatari religious organizations, claiming that they financially supported radical Sunni Islam in the area.

On our first visit, Annabell and I tried to get a feel for the people and the area, so we looked for a busy coffee shop. When we found one and went in, we realized the only people inside were men. They looked just as surprised to see two female visitors.

"*As'salam alaikum*," I said. It was a greeting but also a signal that I shared their cultural background. "*Wa'alaikum as'salam*," a few replied.

I tried to break the ice with the serious-looking waiter, asking in Moroccan Arabic if they had some Moroccan pancakes or *sfinj*, a kind of Moroccan doughnut. He must have been in his twenties, the same age as most of the attackers, and he began to laugh. "I wish I did," he said. "I can offer you baguette or croissants."

"How about Moroccan tea?"

"That I can do."

The TV was on, and a group of men was following a soccer match. When the waiter brought the tea, I told him that I was a journalist and asked him if he knew any of the men who had been involved in "what happened in Paris."

"I have only seen them when they used to live here and would stop by for a coffee, or on the streets, but I wasn't friends with them," he said.

I asked if he had any idea where they hung out, but he said he didn't.

Annabell and I waited for customers who might have been in the same age group as Abdelhamid Abaaoud or Salah Abdeslam, another suspect in the French attacks, both of whom were on the run. Finally, a younger man came in and ordered a coffee and a croissant. I looked at the waiter and pointed with my eyes to the customer who had just ordered. The waiter nodded, and I understood that the young man might know something.

When I approached him, he told me that he and Abaaoud used to hang out sometimes but that they hadn't been in touch for a long time. "All this that happened is very bad for all of us, everybody will think we in Molenbeek are all dangerous," he told me.

He gave me one tip: he suggested I go to a sandwich place not far from the coffee shop. "They used to spend a lot of time there, and you'll find more of their friends," he said.

Annabell and I made our way to the sandwich shop, where two very well-built men who looked like brothers worked side by side. They had several customers, and they all seemed to know one another.

One tall young man in jeans, a sweatshirt, and a dark blue jacket looked at me. I looked back at him and smiled. He smiled back, took his sandwich, and went outside. He looked the way I imagined a friend of Abaaoud and Abdeslam might, with an air of gangster cool. My instincts told me to follow him.

"Excuse me, please," I said outside. *"As'salam alaikum."*

He stopped walking and turned around. *"Wa'alaikum as'salam. Oui, mademoiselles?"* he answered.

I told him that I was a journalist and explained I was there to learn more about Molenbeek. I went on, trying to find a diplomatic way of getting at what I really wanted to ask, when he stated the question for me.

"So you want to ask questions about those who did the attacks in Paris and whether I knew them?" he asked in Moroccan Arabic.

"Yes."

He told me that he had known Abaaoud, Abdeslam, and others who had left for Syria. "Do you know that we usually don't like to speak to journalists here?" he asked. "Recently a camera team was hit with stones. But since you are of Moroccan descent and don't work for one of the lying tabloids, we can have a coffee at least."

We went to a nearby bar, where the waitress greeted him warmly and he called her by her first name. He was evidently a regular. The room was cloudy with cigarette smoke. Even though it was about 1:30 p.m., most of the customers were drinking beer or other alcoholic drinks.

He saw my look of surprise. "This place is okay. I feel safe speaking to you here. Most of the people here don't speak Arabic, so we can speak freely." We sat next to each other on a wooden bench, with Annabell sitting across from us. (She remained mostly silent during the conversation, as she did not understand the Moroccan dialect.) He agreed to speak only if I promised not to mention his real name. He said I could call him "Farid," his grandfather's name.

Farid told me he'd been born in Belgium to Moroccan parents who had moved to Brussels in their youth. His father worked in the coal mines, while his mother stayed home to care for the children. He said that he had spent several years in prison for taking part in robberies, selling guns, and other crimes.

"I was born here in this neighborhood, like Abdelhamid and Salah," he said. "We were all friends."

Farid was tall, with fair skin and dark brown eyes. He had a nice smile, which he flashed a few times, but he was angry, too. He spoke as if he didn't feel accepted anywhere. "When you do something great, the Belgians will say you are Belgian and the Moroccans will say you are Moroccan," he said. "But if you do something bad, the Belgians will say you are Moroccan and the Moroccans will say you are Belgian."

It's a paradox many of us in the second generation of Muslim immigrants to Europe have felt. I had called the Moroccan embassy in Brussels after the attacks and asked if they had anybody who was dealing with the Moroccan community or challenges faced by second-generation immigrants. "These terrorists, they weren't Moroccan," the person at the embassy told me. "They were French or Belgian citizens."

I said that I understood this, but that they were still somehow attached to Morocco through their parents, some of whom had homes and businesses in their country of origin. He was adamant that this wasn't a Moroccan problem.

Farid explained that people such as Abaaoud, Abdeslam, and he despised Belgium or France as much as they did Morocco. He said that they had often discussed questions of identity, home, and relationships with their families.

"They all treat us bad. In fact, the people in Morocco and other Arab countries will treat the white man or woman better than they will treat people like you and me," he said. Farid recalled colonial times, and how France and other European powers never discussed "the crimes they have committed in those countries." His father and his friends had worked very hard and helped to build Belgium, but they hadn't made enough money for a decent living, he said. "My parents are getting eight hundred euros and have to pay rent and all other things. After working over thirty-five years in a job Belgians didn't want to do, that's all my father gets." He told me that he'd sworn he wouldn't let the Belgians take advantage of him.

I agreed that our parents' generation had mainly worked in physically demanding jobs in Europe. "But what would they have done if they'd stayed in Morocco?" I asked.

"Nothing, of course. What could they have done in Morocco? In Morocco, you become something only if you come from one of those famous and very rich families. Don't you think I'm right?"

The more I listened, the more it sounded as if he saw himself as everyone's victim. I told him that I share certain frustrations about Morocco, that I had not come from one of those famous and very rich families, as he called them, and that I also felt that sometimes I wasn't fully accepted by one side or the other. But that wasn't a reason to join ISIS.

"You mean the *dawla*?" he asked, using an Arabic word favored by ISIS sympathizers that means "the state." "The caliphate?"

I nodded. He seemed familiar with the ideology.

"I admire al-Baghdadi and all the brothers there, they are real good Muslims," he said. "They are finally the ones who show these pigs in the West that Muslims are no longer victims."

I needed to challenge his victimization narrative. I told him that from my understanding, Abdeslam and Abaaoud had dealt drugs and committed robberies. How did this fit into his idea of being a good and innocent Muslim?

"This society deserves it," he shot back. "They are all racist, and people like us have no other choice. If you apply for a job and your address says Molenbeek and your name is Arabic, you won't get it." It was the same complaint I had heard in the *banlieues* outside Paris.

I asked Farid whether he'd gone to school.

"Until the tenth grade, and then I left," he said.

It seemed to me that he liked to argue and debate, but he hadn't considered studying and finishing school as a way to improve his life.

"Studying? For what? To become a cabdriver?" he scoffed.

I looked at him. "You can always find some reason not to try to achieve something."

He looked at me in surprise. "Don't you believe me? You think I am lying?" he asked.

I tried to lower the temperature. I told him I just wanted to understand why he didn't think he had a choice in life. Abaaoud and Abdeslam had had a choice as well.

He said he understood what I meant, but that most of the parents in this area didn't understand their children well and didn't care much about how they were doing in school. As I'd realized when I got to know more about Abaaoud's troubled family, sending your son to private school doesn't make you a good parent. Farid and Abaaoud, like many children of Muslim migrants in Europe, had grown up in an awkward situation. They'd been born into European society, but they saw their parents invest all their money in trying to build a reputation back home. Farid told me that he, Abaaoud, and their friends and families were forced to live on a pittance most of the year, only to see their parents lavish gifts on friends and relatives in their native countries. The kids didn't know if they were Belgian, French, or Moroccan, and the parents didn't care if their children integrated. They cared about making money and building businesses, but especially about becoming somebody in the eyes of people back home. The drive to prove they had succeeded was so powerful that it overwhelmed everything else. "It was the same for all of us," Farid told me. "We lived here like shit, and all they cared about was what people thought in Morocco, and how they could show them that they'd made it."

Perhaps as a result, Farid had been drawn to easy money. He carried a big roll of fifty-euro bills, and I understood that even though he was out of prison, he wasn't working in a kitchen or supermarket. "If nobody believes that you can become something and if you grow up in a neighborhood like Molenbeek, it's very hard to believe in yourself and see yourself in a different life than the one I'm living now."

When he heard about the Paris attacks, he'd celebrated, he told me. He felt that France and all of Europe had been taught a lesson as well, because most of the attackers were French and Belgian citizens. "They paid them back for treating Muslims like shit for decades," he said.

I asked what he thought about the fact that most Muslims didn't share his views and that many had even spoken up against terrorism and these attacks.

"Those are people from our parents' generation, but this is not the real

Islam," he answered. His words echoed what I'd heard from so many others. The former rapper Abu Talha had also told me that most first-generation Muslim immigrants in Europe were only living the Islam they had learned from their home countries.

It didn't make sense to argue with Farid, I realized. His worldview was set.

When I asked the waitress for the bill, Farid said he would like to pay for our drinks. I told him that there was no need, but he insisted, saying that since he had a gun on him we had no other choice. He smiled and winked.

"You have a gun?" I whispered.

"That's normal here. I have a gun and a knife on me. You never know."

We said good-bye and left, and I wondered what might have been done to deter Farid from criminality and, one day, possibly terrorism. The roles of parents, friends, community leaders, teachers, and youth workers seemed crucial. Beyond that, of course, there was the general mind-set that confronted young Muslims as they came of age in Europe. Farid believed he wasn't accepted by Belgian society, so he saw no problem with stealing from or even killing Belgians and other Europeans. It was as if they weren't real. Each side had succeeded in dehumanizing the other.

I tried to get in touch with Abdelhamid Abaaoud's parents. His father had told a respected member of the community that he would speak to me, and I was given his phone number. But a few days before we were supposed to meet, he told me that a newspaper had offered him a lot of money for the story of his son and that I could match it if I wanted to.

I told him that we never paid for information, adding that I was surprised to hear and see how after all that had happened he seemed more interested in money than in helping the world see his son as a human being, rather than simply as a deranged killer.

French police found and killed Abaaoud five days after the Paris attacks, during a raid on an apartment in Saint-Denis. The big question on everyone's mind was how they had learned where he was hiding. In a press conference on the day Abaaoud was killed, Paris prosecutor François Molins said that the police had been led to him by a crucial source, but he declined to give details.

I later learned that, after the attacks, Abaaoud had reached out to a cousin living in Paris named Hasna Aitboulahcen, asking for help. She did not let him down. In fact, she was one of two people killed alongside Abaaoud in Saint-Denis. As a result, her name was in the media for days, and photographs circulated on social media, supposedly showing her bathing (they later turned out to be pictures of somebody else). Some even suspected that she had become the "first female suicide bomber in Europe."

The attacks in Paris reignited a debate about the place of Islam in Europe, along with increased fears about the possibility that Muslim women could turn into suicide bombers or participate in plots to kill and terrorize people. Once again, I read editorials in many European newspapers asking why Muslims weren't doing more to fight terrorism. People wondered if the Paris attackers had had some kind of protection system within the Muslim communities in Belgium and France that could have helped them operate without the police finding out.

In a batch of investigative files, I learned of a woman who apparently had informed the police about Abaaoud's return to Europe, and specifically to France. The more my colleague Greg Miller and I went through the documents, the more it looked like this woman—we called her Sonia—had played a crucial and largely unknown role. For me, one detail about her stood out: she appeared to have been Muslim.

I reached out to various sources and asked if they could tell me more about the true story of how Abaaoud was found.

"There was this one woman, but she is now under police protection," a French government source told me, but he refused to tell me anything about her background.

"Was she a Muslim woman?"

"Why would that be important to know?" he asked. "I don't think her religion is important here."

I asked why, in that case, it was always so important to mention the religion of the terrorists, or of people like Hasna Aitboulahcen. "If a Muslim woman has helped find Abaaoud and prevented further attacks, I believe it should be known to the world," I argued.

He said he couldn't say any more because she was under police protection. I then reached out to Sonia through an email address in the documents. To my surprise, she wrote back, sending me a phone number.

"I responded to you because I saw you are Muslim yourself," she said when I called her. I told her we knew she was under police protection and didn't want to endanger her, but that we believed her role was important and wanted to explain it to the world.

This story felt especially personal to me. Just as I'd felt an obligation to tell Westerners what some Muslims really thought of them after I met Maureen Fanning, I now felt obligated to tell the story of a Muslim woman who had risked her life to make her fellow Europeans safer.

Sonia was living under police protection in Paris, but that didn't mean much. She hadn't been given a new name, and although she'd been relocated to a different apartment, there were no police standing guard outside. She was forty-two years old, the mother of several teenagers, and she was living in fear that she'd be killed for ratting out Abaaoud. Even so, she was not sorry about having done it, because she felt that he and the other Paris attackers didn't share her religion or her morality.

Sonia and her husband, who asked not to be identified, met me at a restaurant in central Paris. I brought along the *Post*'s local translator, Virgile Demoustier, because Sonia had told me that she wanted to tell some of her story in French. I speak the language, but this was such a sensitive interview that I wanted a native speaker by my side.

We also didn't know at that time how the French would react to our publishing Sonia's story. Over dinner and in a long interview afterward at my hotel, I learned that Sonia had been forbidden to talk to the press. Later, we asked a spokesperson from the prosecutor's office what would happen if a news organization published an interview with her. "Whoever speaks to her and publishes her story, even without her name, will face consequences," the spokesperson told us. After much debate, we decided to go ahead, figuring it was unlikely that the French would actually try to prosecute the *Washington Post*. As it turned out, we were right.

Sonia was French, but of Algerian descent. Born and raised in the Vosges region of France, she had grown up in a secular family. "We were born Muslims and we will die Muslims, but nonpracticing," she said. "Our father never told us when to pray or what to wear."

She moved to the Paris area in 2010 and met Hasna Aitboulahcen in a nightclub a year later. Aitboulahcen was nineteen or twenty at the time, and Sonia described her as "a disaster! She was like a bum . . . very skinny, with pimples on her face, greasy hair, a real mess." The young woman's father had gone to Morocco without leaving her the keys to his apartment, and she was living on the street, carrying her belongings in a plastic bag. She asked Sonia to help her for a month. "I cooked her lunch, showed her where the shower was, took her dirty clothes to clean them, and gave her my daughter's clean clothes to wear in the meantime. I gave her cream to clean her face. She wasn't well, you could tell. There was a lost look in her eyes. She felt embarrassed and ashamed. She told me her story."

Aitboulahcen and her three siblings had an abusive mother who hit them and denied them food. They were placed in foster care as children. Aitboulahcen stayed with the foster family until she turned seventeen and reunited with her father, who had moved on and remarried his first wife.

I asked Sonia why she'd taken in a complete stranger.

"I've always sheltered the homeless, the poor, those who are in need," she replied.

"People of North African descent?"

"People from any origin. The human being is not meant to live outside in the streets. The human being needs a roof over his head and food on his plate. As I always said: if I were rich, I'd shelter all the homeless."

Sonia became a kind of surrogate mother to Aitboulahcen. The month turned into years, as Aitboulahcen moved into Sonia's apartment and became part of her family. There were problems: Aitboulahcen sometimes behaved wildly, and she struggled with various chemical dependencies.

"She lived with me from 2011 to 2014, on and off," Sonia told me. "She would run away for two weeks, come back [for] a month, over and over again. She took a lot of drugs, mostly cocaine, and drank too much."

But Aitboulahcen could also be charming and lovable. She washed dishes, expressed genuine gratitude for her adopted family, and told engaging stories about her nights out in Paris. "She would always make us laugh," Sonia said.

In 2014 and 2015, Aitboulahcen lived with a man from the Comoros Islands, a drug dealer who beat her, and whom she believed she would marry. At about the same time, at Sonia's suggestion, she reunited with her mother, but the results weren't happy. She learned that her brother was a Salafist Muslim, and she became captivated by Islam. She began wearing the *niqab*, the full veil that leaves only the eyes uncovered.

"I told her on WhatsApp that she'd end up in prison if she kept on wearing it," Sonia said. "She even made videos saying she wanted to go to Syria."

Aitboulahcen also had begun "chatting with someone in Syria" on WhatsApp, according to transcripts of Sonia's conversation with French police after the Paris attacks. Aitboulahcen was too cautious to name the recipient of her feverish texts, but it was almost certainly her cousin Abaaoud, given that he was in Syria at the time and the two are believed to have been close.

Although they didn't grow up in the same city, a strange sense of romance bound them together. Aitboulahcen told friends she would marry Abaaoud, who was two years older than she. She may have had a reason to think so—or it may have been all in her head.

In the summer of 2015, Aitboulahcen traveled to Morocco, apparently to marry a Salafi man who would take her to Syria. She spent several months there but returned to Paris that fall to finalize some documents related to her citizenship at the Moroccan embassy.

"When she came back to me, I told her to take her *niqab* off. God never asked for this," Sonia said. "When she told me their plan was to go to Syria, I told her that what she was doing was crazy. 'You're going to get raped if you go there,' I said."

But Aitboulahcen had grown fascinated by Hayat Boumeddiene, the wife of the kosher supermarket shooter Amedy Coulibaly. Boumeddiene was "her role model," Sonia told me. When the Paris attacks happened, Aitboulahcen didn't respond with sorrow or outrage. Instead, she asked Sonia to straighten her hair so that she could go out.

"They're all unbelievers," she said of the victims, Sonia recalled. "Nothing can happen to me."

She remained casual and seemingly unaffected until Sunday evening,

November 15, when she and members of her surrogate family returned home after a walk through Saint-Denis. Then Aitboulahcen's cell phone lit up. The number on the screen started with the country code for Belgium.

But Aitboulahcen did not recognize the number, Sonia recalled, and didn't believe the man on the other end of the line when he said he was calling on behalf of her cousin. She hung up. But the phone rang again.

"I'm not going to explain everything: you saw what happened on TV," the caller said. She was then instructed to find a hiding place for her cousin, "for no more than a day or two."

A switch seemed to flip in Aitboulahcen's mind. She began to believe that this might really be someone calling on behalf of her cousin, and Sonia said she seemed thrilled. "Tell me what I have to do," Aitboulahcen said eagerly.

Sonia later told police that at the time even Aitboulahcen was unsure which cousin needed her help. Both women wondered if it was actually Abaaoud's younger brother—the one he'd kidnapped and taken to Syria several years earlier. The boy was thought to be dead, but in the chaos of the caliphate anything was possible.

"She hung up and told me her little cousin from Syria was here, sixteen-year-old Younes," Sonia said. "I told her we were going to get him but that if he was injured we would take him to the hospital. And that if he'd done something wrong, I'd take him to the cops. . . . I said to myself, *I can't leave a sixteen-year-old outside in the cold. I have a son the same age.*"

That night, they drove to the address Aitboulahcen had been given. Abdelhamid Abaaoud stepped from the shadows into a dim streetlight. "This is when I recognized him," Sonia told authorities. Earlier, Aitboulahcen had shown Sonia and her family a video of Abaaoud in Syria, dragging corpses tied to the back of a truck.

 Abaaoud told Aitboulahcen that he would give her five thousand euros to help him find a hiding place for forty-eight hours and to pay for new suits and shoes for himself and an associate, who stayed out of sight.

Her anger exceeding her apprehension, Sonia asked Abaaoud whether he was involved in the attacks and why he would be willing to kill so many innocent people.

"He said we were lost sheep and that he wanted to blow us all up," Sonia recalled. He added that many other Islamic State acolytes had come back to Europe with him and that the Paris attacks were "nothing compared to what was going to happen for the holidays."

As the three walked toward the car, Abaaoud seemed exceedingly nervous. Sonia's husband—a stranger to Abaaoud—was in the driver's seat. It looked to them as if Abaaoud was reaching for a weapon. Abaaoud opened the car door and climbed into the back, but the group made it only 150 yards before he suddenly asked them to stop and let him out.

The women and Sonia's husband drove off, and Aitboulahcen's phone rang again. "You can tell the little couple that if they talk my brothers will take care of them," the caller said. When Aitboulahcen laughingly told Sonia and her husband about it, Sonia's husband slapped her in the face. He later told me he was so upset and angry that she'd put them in danger that he couldn't control himself.

That night, Sonia said, she kept pouring wine for Aitboulahcen "to get her drunk so that she would call the police." But the ruse didn't work, and the others in the house were too paralyzed to make a move themselves.

"I was scared because I thought if the terrorists knew I'd come forward they'd kill me," Sonia said.

The next day, when Aitboulahcen left the house, Sonia called the French equivalent of 911. Records indicate that it took more than three hours for the critical tip to prompt a return call from France's elite counterterrorism squad. She spent much of that evening giving the authorities a detailed account of the meeting with Abaaoud. When she got home, a curious Aitboulahcen asked where Sonia had gone. To dinner and a movie, her friend replied.

For the next twenty-four hours, Abaaoud remained at large. Aitboulahcen, meanwhile, bought the shoes and suits her cousin wanted.

As she left home on Tuesday night, "it seemed like she was saying good-bye," Sonia recalled. "She told me that she loved me, that I'd been a great mother to her, that I would go to heaven."

Trying to act normally, Sonia asked Aitboulahcen if she could pick her up later that night. Aitboulahcen gave Sonia the address, which she quickly passed on to the authorities.

Until we published our story in the *Post* in April 2016, the public had no idea that the critical tip in the hunt for Abaaoud came from a Muslim woman who now fears she is a target of the Islamic State.

Video of the Saint-Denis raid includes a female voice pleading to be let out, saying, "I want to leave," followed by an explosion so powerful it sent debris into the street. At first, French authorities said that Aitboulahcen had detonated a suicide bomb as police closed in, but they later conceded this was not the case. Sonia suspected that she played a role in forcing police to alter that account by calling them and threatening to go public with her role and her interactions with investigators.

"I heard of Hasna's death on TV," Sonia said. "I was devastated. I miss her."

Sonia and her husband felt somehow responsible for Aitboulahcen's death. "I had told the police not to harm Hasna," she said. "They should have allowed her to leave, she wanted to leave the apartment. You can hear it in the video."

"What really gets on my nerves is how people now speak badly about Muslims, though it was me, a Muslim woman, who helped the authorities to find Abaaoud," Sonia said. "There could have been more attacks otherwise."

Sonia believes that people like Abdelhamid Abaaoud drift into the arms of ISIS not because of Islam but because of their broken families and the racism they face in Europe. "I told him, 'You have killed innocent people. Islam does not allow this,'" she said, opening her dark brown eyes wide. "This is also the reason why I decided to call the police and tell them where he was. He had killed innocent people, and he was going to kill more."

The Deepest Cut

Germany and Morocco, 2016

My bags were almost packed, and the cabdriver was on his way to pick me up. I was headed to Morocco, where I planned to travel with my parents, visit relatives, and maybe do a little research into my family history. I had already postponed the trip once, a week earlier, when news broke of an attempted coup in Turkey, and I flew there to cover it and the mass arrests that resulted. I needed a vacation. Now, it seemed, I was finally on my way.

At about 6:00 p.m., as I tossed a few final items into my suitcase, I heard a news update on TV: shots had been fired near the Olympia shopping center in Munich. A few minutes later, my sister Hannan got a call from an aunt who lives there. "Your cousin's wife works in the H&M store in that mall," she said. Our relatives in Munich were calling around desperately, trying to figure out what was going on.

I sent a message to my editors at the *Post*, letting them know there had been a shooting and that German TV was already suggesting a possible jihadist connection. It had been a bad summer in Europe—the Bastille Day attack in Nice had happened just a week earlier—and we all immediately wondered whether ISIS was involved.

I dialed my cousin's wife, Sabiha, the one who worked at the H&M

store, and amazingly I reached her. "I'm okay," she told me. She'd seen the shooter, whom she described as dark-haired and olive-skinned. "He started shooting and we locked the doors and took people away from windows." Now she, her coworkers, and their customers had crowded into the back of the store, waiting for word from the police.

We were relieved to learn that she was safe. Then Peter Finn called. It turned out that the *Post*'s regular correspondent was away; Peter wanted me to change my travel plans and head to Munich. The city is nearly 250 miles from Frankfurt, but we agreed I should go by taxi, as we expected train and air service to be shut down. Fighting off disappointment, I grabbed a few things out of my suitcase and threw them into an overnight bag. "Forget the airport," I told the cabdriver. "We're going to Munich."

On the road, Hannan called with more news. Another cousin's son, fourteen-year-old Can, was missing. I called his father, my cousin Hassan, to ask what had happened.

"He went with his best friend to the Olympia shopping center, and now we can't reach him," Hassan said.

I told him to keep calm and that there were many different reasons why Can might not be able to answer his phone. I asked for the boy's phone number, hoping that one of my police sources might be able to use it to locate him via GPS. I also double-checked that Can had his wallet on him. I knew there was a lot of confusion and that the Munich police were nervous about the possibility of multiple shooters, so I wanted to make sure they could easily identify him if they needed to. Can, whose name is pronounced *Jan,* is of Turkish descent, and although he looks more Italian than Middle Eastern, I worried that anyone with dark hair and Mediterranean looks might be mistaken for the shooter or one of his accomplices.

Hassan told me that he and his wife, Sibel, were headed to the shopping center to look for their son. When we hung up, I texted a longtime police source in Munich to let him know that one of my relatives was missing and that the family would be very grateful for information. "Please could you give me an update? Or is there somebody I could call?" I wrote.

He called me back and asked who Can was to me and where he had been. Somewhere near the shopping mall, I told him.

"Okay, I'll see what I can do," he said. "Contact me when you reach Munich."

While riding in the car, I called every source I could think of, trying to pin down the basics. Was there one shooter or more than one? How many people had been killed or injured? The scene was cloudy with rumors.

When my cabdriver and I reached the Munich hotel where I'd booked a room, we saw a crowd of people standing outside looking for taxis. Because of the specter of multiple shooters, the police had banned taxis from operating in the city; it was now 11:00 p.m., and people were anxiously trying to get home. One woman was standing near the entrance to the hotel, shouting into her phone, "The city is on lockdown, probably because some shitty Muslim wanted to kill unbelievers again."

I glanced at my driver, Malek, a Muslim of Pakistani descent whom I often called when I needed a ride to the airport. He must have seen the mix of anger and shock on my face. Malek parked and I grabbed my bag and climbed out of the car. As I passed the woman with the phone, I couldn't resist setting her straight. "First of all, not every Muslim is shitty and wants to kill 'unbelievers,'" I told her. "Secondly, we don't know who's behind this yet." She just looked at me, her mouth open.

"Don't worry about it," said Malek, who had come in with me because he needed to use the bathroom.

"No, we need to worry about these things," I said, but I didn't know why I'd spoken to her like that. It must have been some kind of reflex. I chalked it up to being worried about my relatives, especially Can. The latest report was that as many as eight people had been killed. I called Hassan, who said they still hadn't heard anything about their son. I could tell he was trying to stay calm, but his voice was strained.

"Is it true that eight people died?" I texted my police source. "Can we meet?"

"Not yet," came the response.

We picked up my aunt Emel and her son, then drove to a stadium near the shopping center where the police had asked families waiting for information about missing loved ones to gather. In happier times, soccer tournaments were held there, but now the cavernous space was mostly empty. We roamed around for a while looking for the meeting point, which turned out to be a big hall stacked with benches where spectators ordinarily watched sporting events. Aid workers from the Red Cross and Caritas, along with volunteers, had set out food and drinks for the waiting families. They kept lists of who was missing and who was waiting, but they didn't have much information. Mostly, they tried to make sure people didn't get too upset or dehydrated.

Every once in a while, a bus would arrive full of people who had been rescued from the Olympia shopping center. With each arriving bus, my spirits wilted a little more. *It's really late,* I thought. *Why isn't he on one of these buses? He should be here.* I tried to console myself with the idea that he might have been injured and taken to a hospital and that in the confusion they'd forgotten to tell us, but I had a funny feeling in the pit of my stomach. We watched people step off buses into the joyful embrace of their families and happily make their way home.

I texted my police source again but got no answer. When I called, he didn't pick up. Something felt wrong. My pulse quickened. Why wasn't he getting back to me?

Hassan's wife, Sibel, was pale. We embraced. "Have you heard anything new?" she asked, her tone pleading. I told her I hadn't. "There were many more people here, but their family members were already brought in by bus, and they went home," Sibel told me. "I don't understand why my son isn't here yet."

Hassan hugged me and whispered in my ear, "One of the people said there is only one more bus coming. I'm praying to God he's on it."

Hassan's brothers had arrived with their children. Some of the younger ones were monitoring social media on their phones, looking for the latest news and updates from friends. A blond woman, one of the volunteers, approached Sibel. "He's on the next bus, right?" Sibel begged.

The woman nodded. I could see hope returning to Sibel's face. "*Alhamdulillah*, Can is coming on the next bus," she told us.

"Somebody posted on Facebook that Can is injured!" someone shouted. "They said he is alive and in the hospital."

Hassan and Sibel asked one of the volunteers to take them to the hospital mentioned in the Facebook message. The rest of us, including Can's brother and grandmother, stayed at the stadium, waiting for news.

I looked at my phone, hoping for a message from my source that would tell me not to worry, that Can was all right, just slightly injured. But there was no message, and my increasingly desperate calls continued to go unanswered. *By now,* I thought, *they probably have a list of the dead.* Someone from Caritas told me the police were organizing a press conference.

At about 1:00 a.m., half a dozen plainclothes police came into the hall. They had grim looks on their faces and papers in their hands. They seemed to be bearing news, but they also looked weighted down, as if whatever they carried was heavy. My stomach began to churn. "How many families are you going to talk to?" I overheard one asking another. A blue-eyed officer with dark grayish hair glanced down at the papers and asked one of the volunteers to point out various people. He seemed to be looking for certain families. I walked up to him.

"I'm sorry, but are you one of the police officers from the crisis center?"

"Yes," he answered.

"We have a family member missing. Please, can you tell us anything?"

He folded the paper he was holding and opened a notebook. "Please give me your name, address, and who is the missing family member."

My voice shook as I recited the details. "For full disclosure, you should know I am also a journalist working for the *Washington Post*," I told him. "But I'm not asking you these questions as a reporter. I'm asking as a member of the family."

He said he understood and asked me to wait while he spoke to someone on his cell phone. My aunt had come to stand next to me, and I pressed her hand while watching the policeman's face and trying to read his lips as he spoke softly into the phone a few feet away.

He stared at the ground, and as the conversation continued, he bowed his head further. Finally, he hung up and walked over to us. "Where are Can's parents?" he asked.

"They went to look for their child in the hospital," I said.

"Aside from you, are there any other family members here?"

I motioned to my aunt and told him there were others, too. Including family and friends, there were sixteen of us. "Why, do you know anything?"

He looked at me for a few seconds, then leaned closer and whispered, "I think we need to go to a private room."

"Oh, God, please, no." The words slipped out, because I knew what going to a private room meant. I felt my knees weaken.

He closed his eyes as if trying to push the moment away. "Please stay calm, gather whoever is here, and let's all go to another room."

We were directed down a flight of stairs into a locker room. The police officer with the blue eyes and one of his female colleagues entered through a separate door. I heard them say something about "McDonald's" and "shooting" and that they'd found a tall, slim young man whose wallet had an ID card with the name Can Leyla.

"This young man wouldn't have made it into the hospital," the male police officer said. "I am sorry."

"What are you saying?" Can's twenty-one-year-old brother, Ferid, stood up. "You are talking about my brother? Are you saying Can is dead?"

"I am sorry. Your brother is dead."

"The boy was just fourteen years old," Ferid said. "How is this possible? There must be a mistake."

It was only later that I heard the whole story and was able to make sense of it. An eighteen-year-old German-Iranian student named David Sonboly had opened fire at the McDonald's across from the Olympia shopping center, killing five people inside, including Can. Outside, on Hanauer Strasse, Sonboly shot and killed two pedestrians, then walked to a nearby electronics store, where he shot and killed another person before crossing the street and entering the shopping mall. Moving from the ground floor through the parking garage, he killed one more person and discharged seventeen rounds into a parked vehicle. Shortly after 6:00 p.m., Sonboly was seen on the parking garage rooftop, where a man living in a neighboring apartment building yelled at him. At least two bystanders filmed this episode on their phones. The police shot at Sonboly, causing him to run through a grassy area leading onto Hencky-strasse, where he hid in the stairwell of an apartment building. When he stepped out, the police confronted him, and Sonboly shot himself in the head.

The whole thing took several hours. When it was done, ten people were dead, most between fourteen and twenty years old; the exception was a forty-five-year-old Turkish mother of two. Although many were German citizens, all were of foreign descent: Turkish, Romanian, Hungarian, or Kosovan. Thirty-six others were injured, ten seriously.

The locker room filled with screaming. "Oh, my God, how can we tell his parents?" my aunt cried. "They won't survive this." We were both weeping. I had no idea how or what to tell them. It was unthinkable.

The police officer walked over to me. "I need to ask you to call the parents and tell them to come back, but you must stay calm. I don't want them to hear about this until we have them in a safe place."

I was in tears and shaking. *But my pain doesn't matter*, I thought. We had to do what we could to help Can's parents and brother. "I will try," I answered in a broken voice. I went upstairs, where it was quieter, and dialed Hassan's phone. He picked up after two rings.

"Yes, Souad?"

"Hassan? Where are you?" I tried to keep my voice even.

"On the bus. We wanted to go to another hospital and look for Can."

"No, please can you and Sibel come back here? The police just came, and they want to speak to the families."

"The police? Do they want to speak to us alone?"

I knew I had to speak carefully. I didn't want them to figure out what happened while they were out in the city, away from the rest of the family. "No, no, they want to speak to families in general, make some announcements," I lied. "But they are waiting until everybody is here so they don't have to say it twice."

To calm myself, I made a fist, clenching my thumb between the other fingers. A police officer standing nearby laid her hand on my shoulder.

"Ah, okay, we're coming back," Hassan said.

As we waited for them in the locker room, I thought about Hassan and Sibel, and the horror and pain that lay ahead for them. I didn't know how I would be able to look at them when they walked in. Some of Can's cousins asked to wait outside. The police, fearing that Can's parents would see their red eyes and damp faces, advised against it. But the young people insisted.

A few minutes later, one of the cousins returned, shouting, "Come up, hurry, Sibel is screaming and breaking down! She just learned Can is dead!"

We all ran upstairs, where a crowd of anxious people, many also awaiting news of their loved ones, stood watching Sibel and Hassan. Sibel was lying on the ground, pulling her hair. Hassan walked around shouting and screaming Can's name over and over. Apparently one of the female volunteers had told Sibel "I'm sorry" as she and Hassan climbed off the bus.

"Noooo, noooo, my son is not dead!" she screamed, beating her hands against her head. "Can!" Hassan, meanwhile, screamed and sobbed in his brother's arms. Sibel began biting herself. "Kill me now," she said. "Just kill me. Why would somebody take my beautiful son? He hasn't done anything."

Hassan just sat there, crying. He tried to hold her. "Don't touch me!" she yelled. "Just bring me my son." She begged God to take her life and bring Can back. "Please, you are all lying to me, my son is not dead," she said. "No, no, my son is not dead. They said he will come on the bus." She cried and screamed his name again.

This went on for what seemed like an eternity. Then I heard another man and woman screaming nearby and knew that some other family had just learned their own bitter news.

Somehow, we found our way back to Hassan and Sibel's apartment, where we stared helplessly at pictures of Can hanging on the walls. Sibel was screaming and beating herself. It was as if she were trying to wake herself up from a nightmare. Hassan went into the bedroom, closed the door, and cried.

"Souad, my son is not dead—right, Souad? Can is coming back?" Sibel cried. "Please tell me you all lied to me. Please, Souad."

I held her. "Sibel, I wish we had lied." I felt weak and useless as she shouted and screamed. Then we heard shouting from the house next door, whose balcony was only a few feet away. Another father and mother were screaming for their son.

"Who are they?" I asked my aunt.

"They are the parents of Selçuk Kiliç, Can's best friend. They grew up together."

I learned that Can and Selçuk, who was fifteen, had been like brothers. Both families were Muslim, but Can was Shia, and Selçuk Sunni. For hours, two families and their friends mourned the loss of boys who'd shared everything. Hassan and Sibel's apartment filled with relatives and friends. Whenever the doorbell rang, Sibel asked if it was Can coming back.

At 5:00 a.m., I called a taxi and went back to my hotel. I wore my big sunglasses to hide my eyes. I'd told my parents and siblings, as well as my editors, as soon as we'd heard. I had come to cover a story, and now I was crying for a family member. In my hotel room, I called my police source. This time he picked up.

"You saw my message?" I told him in a low, tired voice. "The boy is dead."

"I can't tell you how sorry I am. I got a list with the victims' names around midnight and was on my way to a briefing."

I held the phone closer to my ear so as not to miss a word.

"When I saw the name Can Leyla, I was in shock," he said.

I felt tears flood my eyes. "Why? Can you tell me why he killed Can?" I whispered. "I need to know, please."

We agreed to meet soon. I hung up and pressed my face into the pillow, shouting and sobbing as I hadn't been able to do while caring for Hassan and Sibel.

I stayed in Munich to help out, going to Hassan and Sibel's house every day to grieve with them and other relatives and friends. A few days later, a police officer from the crisis center called. "We are finished with the autopsy and would like to organize for the family to say good-bye." He asked if someone would come to see Can and decide where and how he should be buried. They invited a family representative to come to the funeral home where the body was being kept to prepare it for a viewing.

"Do the parents want flowers? Some would like to see their son wearing something special. All this could be taken care of before the parents will see him," he said, "but somebody will have to come for that."

Hassan and Sibel's two-bedroom apartment was still packed with relatives and friends, but everybody seemed overwhelmed. When I told Hassan what the police had said, he begged me to go and see Can's body. Sibel's cousin's roommate Kader, a medical doctor by training, said she would come with me.

I asked Hassan if he wanted Can to wear something special. He requested that Can be dressed in the shirt of his favorite soccer team, Fenerbahçe Istanbul, whose colors were blue and yellow. I took the shirt, and Kader and I drove to the funeral home, stopping on the way to buy two big bouquets of yellow and blue roses. Inside, we saw a white coffin. The undertaker, who happened to be Turkish, said we should let him know when we wanted him to open it. I didn't say a word and wondered if maybe there had been some misunderstanding, and this might not be Can. I found myself hoping the coffin held someone else.

"Are you all right?" I heard Kader asking. "Are you ready?"

"I am ready."

It was Can, all right. I looked at his face, the cold, pale skin and long eyelashes. His mouth and eyes were half open, as if he were surprised. "I'm sorry," I whispered. They'd dressed him in a long white tunic and put a white bow tie around his neck, presumably to hide the incision made there during the autopsy. His feet were bare.

We struggled to lift him, to get the soccer jersey on. He was heavy and stiff-limbed, and I found myself wondering if we might hurt him. They had given me gloves, but I could feel his skin through the plastic. He was very cold. He had grown a lot since I'd last seen him six years earlier, I thought. Our families weren't especially close. I remembered him as a child, but the body in the coffin belonged to a young man. Kader and I stood still for a few seconds. The last faint hope that there might have been some kind of misunderstanding was gone.

"My God, Can, what has he done to you?" I whispered. I began to pray in Arabic. I remembered all the people I'd interviewed who had lost loved ones in wars or attacks and all the times I'd had to meet with parents who had lost their children. I remembered Anas in Iraq, and being at the

family's home a day after he was shot. I remembered how Nicholas Kulish and I had counted the bodies of dead protesters in Alexandria. But
this time I wasn't covering a story, I didn't have that wall to protect me.
In fact, I wondered if I'd ever really been able to build that wall. As Kader
and I climbed the stairs to Hassan and Sibel's apartment to tell them how
their son looked, I felt the pain of all those parents coursing through me.

"How does my boy look?" Sibel asked.

I didn't know what to say. "He looks very peaceful," Kader finally
answered. We'd been told that his parents should see him alone first,
along with his brother, Ferid. We told the rest of the extended family to
wait. But Sibel drove with Kader and me, and we got a little lost on the
way to the funeral home. By the time we arrived, Hassan and a swarm of
uncles and cousins were already inside. Sibel screamed at the sight of
Can's cousins standing over her son, kissing him good-bye. When she
reached the coffin, she just stared. "Was I a bad mother, that's why he left
me so early?" she asked, touching his skin. "My beautiful son. He's freezing." She stroked his eyebrows, recalling that he'd always complained
that he didn't like their shape.

Watching her, I was filled with anger and guilt. Anger because it
seemed we hadn't learned much from the suffering of the past fifteen
years. Guilt because it was part of my job to give people clear information that could help dispel racism and fight violence, and I, along with
other journalists, had clearly failed. This shooter stood for all those
people I'd come across who killed because they had created their own
ideologies of hatred and, in their sick minds, a justification for taking
other people's lives.

As it turned out, David Sonboly wasn't an Islamist; he was deeply
troubled and subscribed to a more familiar ideology. It was no coinci-
dence that the shooting had taken place on July 22, the fifth anniversary
of the attack by Anders Behring Breivik, a right-wing Norwegian terrorist who blew up a van in Oslo and then fatally shot sixty-nine participants
at a Workers' Youth League summer camp on a nearby island. Born on
Adolf Hitler's birthday with the name Ali (he'd changed it to David when
he turned eighteen), he was a dual citizen of Germany and Iran whose
parents had immigrated in the 1990s as asylum seekers. Before he became

a mass killer, he was known to the police as a victim of petty crime: he'd been beaten up by other kids, and he'd been a victim of theft. Reportedly bullied at school, he was receiving psychiatric care and taking antidepressants to cope with anxiety and social phobia. In 2015, Sonboly spent two months in a hospital and subsequently attended diagnostic sessions at a youth psychiatric clinic. According to my police source, Sonboly had walked around for fifty minutes inside the McDonald's before killing Can, Selçuk, and the other young victims. The police believe he was targeting young, handsome "cool kids" of foreign origin, the kind of boys he'd hoped but failed to be himself.

In his room at his parents' home in a middle-class Munich neighborhood, the police found books and news clippings on school shootings, among them a book called *Rampage in the Head: Why Students Kill*. Investigators also discovered photographs taken at the school in Winnenden, Germany, where seventeen-year-old Tim Kretschmer killed fifteen people in 2009 before taking his own life. Sonboly had killed his victims with a Glock pistol purchased illegally on the so-called dark web.

They said that Sonboly had struggled for years with psychological problems, but at that moment I didn't care. He had killed Can and Selçuk, two boys of different sects whose lives had argued powerfully against the set narrative that Sunni and Shia cannot live peacefully together.

Later, I sat alone at a table in my hotel's rooftop restaurant, surrounded by people enjoying the sunset. Can's killing brought back memories of terrible violence, and the scars from those old wounds began to hurt again. What happened to him had made it clearer than ever how easy it was to die before you'd led the life you hoped for. I also couldn't help being haunted by the life Hassan and Sibel had led. They'd found each other and raised a family, but one of their children had been taken from them in this unimaginable way.

I flew to Casablanca two days later and met my parents. For the first time, we traveled together to the area where my grandfather used to have his lands, in al-Haouz and on the road to Khenifra. I also went back to my grandmother's house in Meknes, to revisit the window where I used to sit and watch people outside. There was the corner where my grandmother and I used to sleep on a blanket. I remembered how I sat at the doorstep with my grandparents listening to my grandfather talk about his past and how much he regretted that he couldn't read or write. Storytellers are powerful, he told me. They explain the world. They write history.

My parents and I visited my grandparents' graves and prayed over them. I wondered what they would have said if they could have seen that their granddaughter was now reporting and writing about the world and that she was doing so because of what they had taught her. I wondered what advice they would give me now. Were the pain, the worries, the threats to my family and me worth whatever I was gaining? Was my work making a difference? I missed my grandmother's loud laughter and her gift for healing and strengthening. I could have used some of that now.

I looked at my parents, the Sunni-Shia couple who had endured so much yet hadn't let it divide them. They'd decided decades earlier to take a stand for their love and against the hatred. They had worked to plant the seed inside us, their children. Now I could tell they were worried about me. They knew I didn't tell them much about what I saw and did on my journeys.

I also spent some of the Morocco trip alone at the little hotel in the mountains, thinking about the hatred we're fighting. I was born with the Arab-Israeli conflict already under way, at a moment when Iran was establishing itself as an Islamic republic, awakening a new competition in the Middle East. In the Middle East, many of those who had sought peace were dead, and the ones still alive were so deeply wounded that they would probably never forgive the other side. They say children inherit the hatred of their parents. My grandfather was bitter, but my grandmother was resilient. I inherited hope from my Moroccan grandparents, along with the will to understand.

Why do they hate us so much? The question that had pushed me all these years to cross borders rang in my ears. Since 9/11, I had scoured the world for answers, hoping that knowledge and understanding would lead people to do what they could to prevent more hatred, more killing.

But some people in Western countries don't see the hazards of setting standards for others, as if our way is the right way and the only way. This is the same argument ISIS makes. Meanwhile, in our democracies, secret detention centers, torture, and mass government surveillance have violated what we call our core values. Our governments have faced no consequences for these transgressions. People such as Khaled el-Masri are too weak to hold the United States accountable for ruining their lives.

Is democracy really what we want, or do we instead seek to promote the values we hold dear: the equality of men and women, the rights of minorities to survive and thrive, the freedom to speak our minds and practice whatever faith we choose? Instead of talking about the need for a voting system, we should seek to adhere to a code of universal values.

At the same time, a dialogue is overdue within Islam, and within Muslim societies, about what can and cannot be justified by our faith. Religion doesn't radicalize people; people radicalize religion. In Mecca, where I recently made the *umra* pilgrimage, women are not supposed to cover their faces, and there is no separation of the sexes. How can we argue that a woman should cover her face and be separated from men when it doesn't even happen in the holiest place in Islam? Opportunists have created their own ideology within Islam, and this is profoundly dangerous. If no one is willing to speak up for what the religion actually requires, anyone can use it for his own ends.

Way back in 1979, the year after I was born, the ruling family in Saudi Arabia allowed religious leaders to blackmail them because the monarchs needed those clerics' support before sending in armed soldiers to end the siege of Mecca and guarantee loyalty to the crown. The clash between secular power and faith radicalized many Muslims in Saudi Arabia and beyond. My generation had to grapple with the consequences of leaders in the West, Arab countries, and Asia who believed they could fight their enemies—the Soviets in the Cold War—by encouraging "jihad" against them. It was a failed strategy.

If Middle Eastern leaders got their act together and stopped fueling a senseless sectarian conflict—always in the name of a religion whose true character is apparently impossible to agree upon—the next generation in that region would have a chance to grow up learning about history, medicine, and mathematics instead of running from bullets and bombs, fleeing their homes, and living in refugee camps or on the street.

Iran and Saudi Arabia, in particular, must stop their quiet war, and

along with it the radicalization of their youth in the name of hollow ideologies. Western politicians sold the Iran nuclear deal as a big achievement, saying it would support the reformists within the country. But Iran
is a state with many different players. My colleague Jason Rezaian at the
Washington Post became a victim of what some call "the deep state."
While Iranian officials claim they want to coexist peacefully with their
neighbors, increasing Iranian interference in Arab countries is no longer
a secret. Iranian-sponsored Shia militias in Iraq and Syria are only one
example.

I've often asked preachers or imams who abuse religion for their
political ambitions why they do it. Many have told me they believe it's
what Islam requires. Others said they know what's best for the *ummah*.
Most people argue this is how the Prophet Muhammad would have
wanted it to be. But they're talking about one of my forefathers. Why
should they be the ones to decide what Muhammad wanted or how he
saw the world?

While I've carried the pain of the discrimination I faced as the
daughter of Muslim guest workers in Germany, I'm still very grateful for
the chance I had to get a good education, and thankful for the wonderful
people who pushed me and convinced me not to give up. Yet when I visit
countries in the Middle East, I feel the pain of laborers from Southeast
Asia or the Philippines. No matter if their employers are Sunni, Shia, or
of some other religious background, these workers are often treated
badly and barely have any rights. The fact is that many Arab states har-
bor some version of entrenched racism.

The rise of groups such as Al Qaeda and ISIS is not the problem of
any one specific country or group. It is the result of many mistakes. There
are the political leaders who too often look for short-term solutions.
There is the "enemy of my enemy is my friend" thinking that has led to
arming more militias in Syria and Iraq. But the history of Western
involvement in Afghanistan and Pakistan should have taught us all that
the one you train and arm today may turn against you tomorrow. Empow-
ering militias can lead to the destruction of nation-states as we know
them today. I grew up among different religions and in different worlds, and
in the spirit that civilized people don't clash, even if they have different

opinions or orientations. The world is full of those who offer easy answers in challenging times. They know how to play with the fear and hopelessness of the disenfranchised. In a paradoxical way, all those who preach hatred against the possibility of peaceful coexistence are benefiting from each other.

The world is not facing a clash of civilizations or cultures, but a clash between those who want to build bridges and those who would rather see the world in polarities, who are working hard to spread hatred and divide us. While the work of the bridge builders is certainly difficult, there are people in every generation who live their beliefs and who are willing and able to seek out common ground. I was lucky enough to have the examples of my parents and grandparents to show me what is possible.

Who sets the rules for everyone else? This isn't just a problem for the Muslim world; it is also a problem for the West. You cannot expect tolerance if you're not willing to give it to others. The minute somebody says I'm right, you're wrong, is the minute we give up the space for conversation. This has happened too often. It is still happening.

Over the years, my work had made me a target of various forms of hatred, from Germany, the land of my birth, to Iraq and Pakistan, among Muslims and Christians alike. These days, people expect a reporter to take sides. But that's not my job. It is difficult to stand in the middle, but I believe losing the ability to listen is far more destructive.

If I've learned anything, it's this: a mother's screams over the body of her murdered child sound the same, no matter if she is black, brown, or white; Muslim, Jewish, or Christian; Shia or Sunni.

We will all be buried in the same ground.

NOTES

PROLOGUE: MEETING ISIS

4   "If the U.S. hits us with flowers": Anthony Faiola and Souad Mekhennet, "In Turkey, a Late Crackdown on Islamic Fighters," *Washington Post*, August 14, 2014.

1: STRANGER IN A STRANGE LAND

8   on the first day of the Islamic year 1400: Information in these paragraphs for the most part is from Yaroslav Trofimov's superb *The Siege of Mecca: The 1979 Uprising at Islam's Holiest Shrine* (New York: Anchor Books, 2008).

8   a group of armed religious extremists: "While the [Saudi Interior Ministry] statement did not specify the nationality of the attackers or mention casualties, unconfirmed reports from other Arab sources indicated the invaders were followers of Iran's Ayatollah Ruhollah Khomeini and said the takeover resulted in casualties when the attackers clashed with Saudi authorities." Edward Cody, "Armed Men Seize Mecca's Great Mosque," *Washington Post*, November 21, 1979.

8   German companies were recruiting workers: The Federal Republic of Germany (FRG) concluded various recruitment agreements with: Italy (1955), Spain (1960), Greece (1960), Turkey (1961), Morocco (1963), South Korea (1963), Portugal (1964), Tunisia (1965), and the then Yugoslavia (1968). The number of recruitments decreased during the economic recession of 1966–67

and then came to a complete halt in 1973 due to the economic impact of the oil crisis. The former German Democratic Republic (GDR) employed so-called contract laborers from Hungary, Vietnam, Cuba, Mozambique, Poland, and Angola.

9 the 1972 Olympic Games in Munich: David Binder, "Munich Police Ordered 5 to Ambush 8 Terrorists," *New York Times*, September 8, 1972.

10 Baader-Meinhof included the children of German intellectuals: Stefan Aust and Anthea Bell, *Baader-Meinhof: The Inside Story of the RAF* (New York: Oxford University Press, 2009).

13 a dynasty of *sharifs*: "Sharif." In *The Oxford Dictionary of Islam*, edited by John L. Esposito, Oxford Islamic Studies Online, http://www.oxfordislamic studies.com/article/opr/t125/e2173.

14 some Shia see Aisha more critically: Nabia Abbott, "Women and the State in Early Islam," *Journal of Near Eastern Studies* 1, no. 1 (1942): 106–26.

26 They didn't realize that a quiet battle was beginning: "But with the benefit of hindsight it is painfully clear: the countdown to September 11, to the terror-ist bombings in London and Madrid, and to the grisly Islamist violence ravaging Afghanistan and Iraq all began on that warm November morning, in the shade of the Kaaba." Trofimov, *Siege of Mecca*, p. 7.

28 xenophobic riots broke out in Hoyerswerda: Stephen Kinzer, "A Wave of Attacks on Foreigners Stirs Shock in Germany," *New York Times*, October 1, 1991.

29 The attackers called the fire department: Marc Fisher, "2 Neo-Nazis Confess in Death of 3 Turks," *Washington Post*, December 2, 1992.

29 another Turkish guest worker, Durmus Genc: Mevlüde and Durmus Genc emigrated from Turkey in the early 1970s. Bundeszentrale für politische Bil-dung, "Hintergrund aktuell: 20 Jahre Brandanschlag in Solingen," August 25, 2013, http://www.bpb.de/politik/hintergrund-aktuell/161980/brandanschlag -in-solingen-28-05-2013.

29 Genc's two daughters and two granddaughters: Terrence Petty, "Five Turks Killed in Arson Attack," Associated Press, May 29, 1993.

2: THE HAMBURG CELL

47 *Der Spiegel* was Germany's most famous weekly magazine: Christoph Gun-kel, "50th Anniversary of the 'SPIEGEL Affair': A Watershed Moment for West German Democracy," *Spiegel Online*, September 21, 2012.

50 The case involved five Algerians: Four were convicted in March 2003; the fifth was dropped from the case in August 2002 due to lack of evidence. "Four Convicted of Strasbourg Bomb Plot," *Guardian*, March 10, 2003, https://www .theguardian.com/world/2003/mar/10/germany.france; Peter Finn and Erik

Schelzig, "Algerian Accused in Bombing Plot Ejected by Judge; Defendant Disrupts Trial in Germany," *Washington Post*, April 17, 2002.

51 "Hamburg's Cauldron of Terror": Peter Finn, "Hamburg's Cauldron of Terror," *Washington Post*, September 11, 2002.

54 Al-Janabi's alarming claims: Vice Admiral L. E. Jacoby, Director, Defense Intelligence Agency, Info Memo, Subject: CURVEBALL Background, January 14, 2005. National Security Archive, http://nsarchive.gwu.edu/NSAEBB /NSAEBB534-DIA-Declassified-Sourcebook/documents/DIA-36.pdf.

54 the Bush administration ignored the warnings: Professor Friedbert Pflüger was interviewed for a public broadcast documentary by the German *Norddeutscher Rundfunk* (NDR), 2010: "Die Lügen vom Dienst: Der BND und der Irakkrieg" (The Lies of the Service: The BND and the Iraq War), http://www .daserste.de/information/reportage-dokumentation/dokus/videos/die -luegen-vom-dienst-der-bnd-und-der-irakkrieg-100.html.

54 Powell spoke of the "sinister nexus": Weeks after Powell's presentation, UN weapons inspectors investigated a facility in Djerf al-Nadaf, Iraq, finding a concrete wall where Curveball reported mobile weapons production trailers would enter and leave the installation. Inspectors found that the wall must have already existed for quite some time, making trailer movement impossible. Only in March 2004 did the CIA gain access to Curveball. He was questioned directly for the first time and confronted with satellite imagery that contradicted his claims about large trailers moving through the facility in Djerf al-Nadaf. The CIA and DIA officially declared Curveball a fabricator. George Tenet later resigned as the director of the CIA.

3: A COUNTRY WITH A DIVIDED SOUL

61 The historic roots of the religious Sunni-Shia conflict: Heinz Halm, *Der Schiitische Islam: Von der Religion zur Revolution* (Munich: C. H. Beck, 1994), p. 16.

61 their own religious practices and sources: The Shia themselves are also divided in subsects, the Shia of the twelve, Ithna Ashariyya, being the biggest. In referring to "Shia" in this book, I generally refer to the practices of the Ithna Ashariyya. *Oxford Islamic Studies*, "Shii Islam," accessed November 25, 2016, http://www.oxfordislamicstudies.com/article/opr/t125/e2189.

64 the Americans had arrested him: Vernon Loeb and John Mintz, "Iraqi Who Might Have Met with 9/11 Hijacker Is Captured; New Focus Is Put on Iraq's Alleged Links to al-Qaeda," *Washington Post*, July 9, 2003.

68 he'd lived in Iran and Syria: "Maliki Gives Up Fight to Remain Iraqi Prime Minister," Radio Free Europe, August 14, 2014.

68 Iran continued to provide political, financial, and military support: Kenneth

Katzman, "Iran's Activities and Influence in Iraq," Congressional Research Service (CRS) Report for Congress, June 4, 2009.

70   Another *Post* reporter, Kevin Sullivan, joined me: Kevin Sullivan and Rajiv Chandrasekaran, "The Doorbell Rang and 'There They Were'; Hussein Sons Came to House to Hide," *Washington Post*, July 24, 2003.

76   his role as a respected religious leader: Anthony Shadid, "Cleric Mourned by Huge Crowds," *Washington Post*, September 1, 2003.

76   claimed responsibility for the attack: Laura Smith, "Timeline: Abu Musab al-Zarqawi, *Guardian*, June 8, 2006, https://www.theguardian.com/world/2006/jun/08/iraq.alqaida1.

76   Najaf, one of the holiest places on earth for Shia: Halm, *Der Schiitische Islam*; Hussain Abdul-Hussain, "Hezbollah: "A State within a State," Hudson Institute, May 21, 2009, http://www.hudson.org/content/researchattachments/attachment/1312/abdul_hussain_vol8.pdf; August R. Norton, *Hezbollah: A Short History* (Princeton, NJ: Princeton University Press, 2009); Ian Rutledge, *Enemies of the Euphrat: The Battle for Iraq, 1914–1921* (London: Saqi Books, 2015).

80   one of only three women on the Iraqi Governing Council: Vivienne Walt, "Iraqi Official Dies; Bomb Hits NBC Hotel," *Boston Globe*, September 26, 2003.

81   al-Hashimi had been shot in the stomach and leg: E. A. Torriero and Bill Glauber, "Wounded Official Dies; 8 Soldiers Injured As 2 Bombs Hit Military Convoy," *Chicago Tribune*, September 26, 2003.

82   an explosion at the hotel where the NBC crews stayed: "Bomb Explodes at Baghdad Hotel Housing NBC Offices," Associated Press, September 25, 2003.

4: A CALL FROM KHALED EL-MASRI

84   U.S. soldiers torturing and humiliating Iraqi prisoners in Abu Ghraib: "Chronology of Abu Ghraib," *Washington Post*, February 17, 2006.

84   what its leaders called "the shadows": "Vice President Cheney on NBC's *Meet the Press*," transcript of an interview with Vice President Cheney conducted by Tim Russert, *Washington Post*, September 16, 2001.

85   deeply involved in water security issues: He was even once appointed by the UN secretary-general as chairman of the advisory board on water and sanitation (UNSGAB): https://sustainabledevelopment.un.org/topics/water/unsgab/board.

85   "My name is Khaled el-Masri": "Khaled el-Masri," *The Rendition Project*, https://www.therenditionproject.org.uk/prisoners/khaled-elmasri.html. With links to additional source material.

86   "They asked a lot of questions": Don Van Natta Jr. and Souad Mekhennet, "German's Claim of Kidnapping Brings Investigation of U.S. Link," *New York Times*, January 9, 2005.

86   Al Haramain was an Islamic charity: In June 2008, Al Haramain Islamic
     Foundation (AHIF) was designated by the U.S. Department of the Treasury
     "for having provided financial and material support to al-Qaida, as well as a
     wide range of designated terrorists and terrorist organizations," https://www
     .treasury.gov/press-center/press-releases/Pages/hp1043.aspx. Already in 2004,
     the Treasury Department designated the U.S.-based branch of AHIF over
     links to terrorists, https://www.treasury.gov/press-center/press-releases/Pages
     /js1895.aspx. The AHIF later sued the U.S. government for infringing its con-
     stitutional rights and won a partial summary judgment. This ruling was
     reversed on appeal, and the case was dismissed.

87   the Macedonian authorities turned him over: "He was then transferred by
     armed officers in plainclothes to the Skopski Merak hotel in Skopje, where he
     was detained for 23 days, guarded at all hours by rotating shifts of armed
     Macedonian officers." "El-Masri v. Macedonia," Open Society Foundations,
     last updated January 23, 2013, https://www.opensocietyfoundations.org
     /litigation/el-masri-v-macedonia.

88   "outside of the legal process": Jane Mayer, *The Dark Side: The Inside Story of
     How the War on Terror Turned into a War on American Ideals* (New York:
     Anchor Books, 2009), p. 102.

88   Maher Arar, a Canadian born in Syria: "Maher Arar," *The Rendition Proj-
     ect,* https://www.therenditionproject.org.uk/prisoners/arar.html; Commis-
     sion of Inquiry into the Actions of Canadian Officials in Relation to Maher
     Arar, "Report of the Events Relating to Maher Arar," September 2006, http://
     publications.gc.ca/site/eng/9.688875/publication.html; "Rendition to Torture:
     The Case of Maher Arar," Joint Hearing of the Committees on Foreign Affairs
     and the Judiciary, https://fas.org/irp/congress/2007_hr/arar.pdf.

88   an Australian man named Mamdouh Habib: "Mamdouh Ahmed Habib,"
     The Rendition Project, https://www.therenditionproject.org.uk/prisoners
     /mamdouh-habib.html; U.S. Department of Defense, "JTF-GTMO Detainee
     Assessment: Mamdouh Habib," http://projects.nytimes.com/guantanamo/
     detainees/661-mamdouh-ibrahim-ahmed-habib/documents/11.

91   Ramzi bin al-Shibh and a future 9/11 hijacker, Marwan al-Shehhi: Accord-
     ing to the 9/11 Commission Report, it was Binalshib (transliteration used
     in the report) and Shehhi who were approached by Khalid al-Masri, not
     Binalshib and Atta. The paragraph reads: "The available evidence indicates
     that in 1999, Atta, Binalshib, Shehhi, and Jarrah decided to fight in Chech-
     nya against the Russians. According to Binalshib, a chance meeting on a train
     in Germany caused the group to travel to Afghanistan instead. An individ-
     ual named Khalid al-Masri approached Binalshib and Shehhi (because they
     were Arabs with beards, Binalshib thinks) and struck up a conversation about
     jihad in Chechnya. When they later called Masri and expressed interest in
     going to Chechnya, he told them to contact Abu Musab in Duisburg,

Germany. Abu Musab turned out to be Mohamedou Ould Slahi, a significant al-Qaeda operative, who, even then, was well known to U.S. and German intelligence, though neither government apparently knew he was operating in Germany in late 1999. When telephoned by Binalshib and Shehhi, Slahi reportedly invited these promising recruits to come see him in Duisburg." Thomas H. Kean and Lee Hamilton, *The 9/11 Commission Report: Final Report of the National Commission on Terrorist Attacks Upon the United States* (Washington, DC: National Commission on Terrorist Attacks upon the United States, 2004), p. 165.

92 recruited to commit the September 11 attacks: Kean and Hamilton, *9/11 Commission Report*, pp. 165–66.

93 When I saw the story online: Van Natta and Mekhennet, "German's Claim of Kidnapping."

93 the Germans publicly admitted that they had mishandled el-Masri's case: Souad Mekhennet and Craig S. Smith, "German Spy Agency Admits Mishandling Abduction Case," *New York Times*, June 2, 2006.

94 Skopje to Baghdad to Kabul: "No public record states how Mr. Masri was taken to Afghanistan. But flight data shows a Boeing Business Jet operated by Aero Contractors and owned by Premier Executive Transport Services, one of the C.I.A.-linked shell companies, flew from Skopje, Macedonia, to Baghdad and on to Kabul on Jan. 24, 2004, the day after Mr. Masri's passport was marked with a Macedonian exit stamp." Scott Shane, Stephen Grey, and Margot Williams, "C.I.A. Expanding Terror Battle Under Guise of Charter Flights," *New York Times*, May 31, 2005.

94 The man, Laid Saidi: Craig S. Smith and Souad Mekhennet, "Algerian Tells of Dark Term in US Hands," *New York Times*, July 7, 2006; "Laid Saidi," *The Rendition Project*, https://www.therenditionproject.org.uk/prisoners/saidi .html.

98 "The Director strongly believes that mistakes should be expected": U.S. Senate Select Committee on Intelligence, *The Senate Intelligence Committee Report on Torture: Committee Study of the Central Intelligence Agency's Detention and Interrogation Program* (New York: Melville House, 2014), pp. 118–19.

98 "This Report concludes that there was an insufficient basis": CIA Office of Inspector General, "Report of Investigation: The Rendition and Detention of German Citizen Khalid al-Masri," July 16, 2007, https://www.thetorturedata base.org/document/report-investigation-rendition-and-detention-german -citizen-khalid-al-masri, p. 5.

99 The unanswered questions were frustrating: Both "Khalid 'Abd al Razzaq al-Masri" (#98) and "Laid Ben Dohman Saidi" (#57) are on the list of 119 names of people detained by the CIA in the Senate's report on torture. Khaled el-Masri's name is still misspelled as Khalid al-Masri in the report. Saidi's name

is bolded as one of those "subjected to the CIA's enhanced interrogation techniques." El-Masri's is not. U.S. Senate Select Committee on Intelligence, *The Senate Intelligence Committee Report on Torture: Committee Study of the Central Intelligence Agency's Detention and Interrogation Program*, Appendix 2: CIA Detainees from 2002 to 2006, Errata, February 6, 2015, http://www.feinstein.senate.gov/public/_cache/files/5/8/5871bb22-f4fb-4ec4-b419-99babb2eca3d/2CE49560261479702BE070249CACE775.errata.pdf.

100 "People in the West are the last ones in the world": Souad Mekhennet, "A German Man Held Captive in the CIA's Secret Prisons Gives First Interview in 8 Years," *Washington Post*, September 16, 2015.

5: EVEN IF I DIE TODAY OR TOMORROW

101 the bombings in Madrid: Victoria Burnett, "Conviction and Key Acquittals End Madrid Bomb Trial," *New York Times*, November 1, 2007.

101 bombs exploded on three underground trains and a bus in London: "Report of the Official Account of the Bombings in London on 7th July 2005," May 11, 2006, p. 13, https://www.gov.uk/government/publications/report-of-the-official-account-of-the-bombings-in-london-on-7th-july-2005.

102 A Palestinian born in the West Bank: Justin Salhani, "Forgotten but Not Gone: Fatah al-Islam Still a Factor in Lebanon," *Daily Star* (Lebanon), December 6, 2014.

102 he'd given up his medical studies: Andrew Wander, "Fatah al-Islam Says Leader Was Killed or Captured in Syria," *Daily Star* (Lebanon), December 11, 2008.

102 He later staged attacks on Israel: "Abssi denied accusations by Syrian interior minister Bassam Abdel Majid that the Palestinian militant has been jailed in Syria because of links with al-Qaeda and for planning terrorist attacks. 'I was jailed in Syria, but not over links with al-Qaeda as he has claimed,' Abssi said. 'I was jailed because I was accused of having planned to carry out an operation in the [Syrian] Golan [territory occupied by Israel], as well as of having carried and smuggled arms into Palestine [Israel],' he said." "Fatah al-Islam Chief Denies Al-Qaeda Link," Agence France-Presse, March 16, 2007.

102 From 2002 to 2005, the Syrians imprisoned him: Much of the account of Shaker al-Abssi draws on reporting done by the author in collaboration with Michael Moss for the following articles: Souad Mekhennet and Michael Moss, "In Lebanon Camp, a New Face of Jihad Vows Attacks on U.S.," *New York Times*, March 16, 2007; Michael Moss and Souad Mekhennet, "Jihad Leader in Lebanon May Be Alive," *New York Times*, September 11, 2007.

103 inspired by the 1979 siege of Mecca: Trofimov, *Siege of Mecca*, pp. 248–50.

103 "Salafism" derives from the Arabic expression: While this definition of Salafism is appealing to many Muslims, especially conservative ones, and does not

necessarily oppose a secular state or society, Salafists in the contemporary understanding of the term oppose any new interpretations of holy scripture as well as democracy as a form of government. However, not all contemporary Salafists are political; some try to practice Islam as "purely" as possible only for themselves. Others are political but refuse violence to achieve their aims or only legitimize it under specific circumstances. But there are also the "terrorist Salafists" or Jihadi-Salafists, who call for violence and revolution to fight unbelievers and establish a theocratic Islamic state. See Rashid Dar and Shadi Hamid, "Islamism, Salafism and Jihadism: A Primer," *Brookings*, July 15, 2016, https://www.brookings.edu/blog/markaz/2016/07/15/islamism -salafism-and-jihadism-a-primer/; Guido Steinberg, "Wer sind die Salaf-isten?" Deutsches Institut für Internationale Politik und Sicherheit, May 2012, https://www.swp-berlin.org/fileadmin/contents/products/aktuell /2012A28_sbg.pdf; Quintan Wiktoriowicz, "Anatomy of the Salafi Movement," *Studies in Conflict & Terrorism* 29 (2006): 207–39, http://www.clagsbor ough.uk/anatomy_of_the_salafi_movement.pdf.

103   imprisoned for plotting attacks in Jordan in 1994: Joby Warrick, *Black Flags: The Rise of ISIS* (New York: Doubleday, 2015), pp. 55–56; "The Islamic State," Mapping Militant Organizations, Stanford University, May 15, 2015, http:// web.stanford.edu/group/mappingmilitants/cgi-bin/groups/view/1?highlight =zarqawi.

103   Zarqawi also hated the Shia and saw them as rivals: Ibid.

103   Colin Powell named him in the speech to the United Nations: "U.S. Secretary of State Colin Powell Addresses the U.N. Security Council," February 5, 2003, http://georgewbush-whitehouse.archives.gov/news/releases/2003/02 /20030205-1.html.

104   Al Qaeda in Iraq set off bombs in three Amman hotels: Jonathan Finer and Naseer Mehdawi, "Bombings Kill over 50 at 3 Hotels in Jordan; Coordinated Attack in Amman Linked to Zarqawi's Network," *Washington Post*, November 10, 2005.

104   Atiyah Abd al-Rahman, wrote that Zarqawi: Warrick, *Black Flags*, p. 201. See also letter from Atiyah Abd al-Rahman to Abu Musab al-Zarqawi, late 2005, translation provided by the Combating Terrorism Center at West Point, https://www.ctc.usma.edu/posts/atiyahs-letter-to-zarqawi-english-transla tion-2.

104   the Askari mosque in Samarra: This is where the tenth and eleventh Shia imams are buried and where, according to some Shia, the twelfth imam went into hiding. Imranali Panjwani, "The Compartmentalisation of Holy Figures: A Case Study of the Heritage of the Samarran Shi'i Imams," *World Journal of Islamic History and Civilization* 1, no. 1 (2011): 15–26, http://idosi.org/wjihc /wjihc1(1)11/2.pdf.

104   Zarqawi celebrated by starring in a video: Warrick, *Black Flags*, pp. 201–5.

105   just in time to watch Zarqawi die: Ibid., p. 217.

105   the 2002 assassination of the American diplomat Laurence Foley: Neil Mac-
      Farquhar, "Threats and Responses: Attack on US Diplomat; American Envoy
      Killed in Jordan," *New York Times*, October 29, 2002.

106   the country's fifteen-year civil war: BBC News, Lebanon profile timeline,
      August 10, 2016, http://www.bbc.com/news/world-middle-east-14649284.

106   One of the September 11 hijackers came from Lebanon: "Born on May 11,
      1975, in Mazraa, Lebanon, Ziad Jarrah came from an affluent family and
      attended private, Christian schools." Kean and Hamilton, *9/11 Commission
      Report*, p. 163.

106   planting bombs on German trains: "Lebanese Jailed for 12 Years for Germany
      Attack Plot," Agence France-Presse, December 18, 2007.

106   plotting to blow up the train tunnels connecting New York City and New
      Jersey: "Lebanon: 2-Year Sentence in Plot to Blow Up Hudson River Tunnels,"
      Associated Press, February 17, 2012.

108   Lebanese authorities had limited access to this camp: From http://www
      .unrwa.org/where-we-work/lebanon: "The Nahr al-Bared camp was set up by
      the Red Cross in 1949 to care for refugees from northern Palestine. UNRWA
      has been taking care of the camp and its inhabitants since 1950. According
      to a 38-year-old agreement, the Palestinians in the Lebanese camps control
      their own affairs, and the Lebanese Army is forbidden from entering the
      camps." "Background: Palestinian Refugee Camp Nahr al-Bared," Deutsche
      Presse-Agentur, May 21, 2007.

110   semiautonomous ministates within Lebanon: "The Cairo Agreement of 1969
      put the camps under control of the Palestine Liberation Organization (PLO),
      and banned Lebanese security forces from entering. Although the Lebanese
      government withdrew from the Cairo Agreement in the late 1980s and the-
      oretically reclaimed its rule over the camps, the state has refrained from
      exercising its authority. Politically, the camps have been ruled by popular
      committees, while security committees have been serving as an internal
      police force. When in 2006 Fatah al-Islam trickled into Nahr al-Bared, how-
      ever, the camp only had a weak popular committee and no functioning secu-
      rity committee. The Palestinian parties were divided, and consequently failed
      to push the well-armed Islamist group out of the camp, effectively allowing
      it to take over," https://electronicintifada.net/content/lebanon-tightens-control
      -over-palestinian-refugee-camps/8632.

120   two commuter buses had been bombed in Lebanon: Iman Azzi, "Routine
      Commute Turns Deadly as Bombers Target Civilians," *Daily Star* (Lebanon),
      February 14, 2007.

6: THE LOST BOYS OF ZARQA

123 In Zarqa, Jordan: Much of the account of Zarqa draws on reporting done by the author in collaboration with Michael Moss for the following articles: Souad Mekhennet and Michael Moss, "In Jihadist Haven, a Goal: To Kill and Die in Iraq," *New York Times*, May 4, 2007; Michael Moss and Souad Mekhennet, "The Guidebook for Taking a Life," *New York Times*, June 10, 2007.

7: THE VALUE OF A LIFE

143 cost as many as three hundred thousand Algerian lives: Helen Chapin Metz, *Algeria: A Country Study* (Washington, DC: Federal Research Division, Library of Congress, 1994), p. 34.

143 formed the Armed Islamic Group: Ibid., pp. 37–38.

144 kidnapping, smuggling, and human trafficking: Christopher S. Chivvis and Andrew Liepman, "North Africa's Menace: AQIM's Evolution and the U.S. Policy Response," RAND Corporation, 2013.

144 an Al Qaeda franchise: Souad Mekhennet, Michael Moss, Eric Schmitt, Elaine Sciolino, and Margot Williams, "Ragtag Insurgency Gains a Lifeline from Al Qaeda," *New York Times*, July 1, 2008; Camille Tawil, "New Strategies in al-Qaeda's Battle for Algeria," *Terrorism Monitor*, Jamestown Foundation, July 27, 2009, https://jamestown.org/program/new-strategies-in-al-qaedas -battle-for-algeria/.

144 changing its name to Al Qaeda in the Islamic Maghreb: "In a statement dated 13 September 2006, Droukdel announced the official alliance of GSPC with Al-Qaida (QDe.004) and pledged allegiance to Usama bin Laden (deceased). In a statement dated 24 January 2007, he announced that as a consequence of its merging with Al-Qaida, and after consulting Usama bin Laden, GSPC changed its name to the Organization of Al-Qaida in the Islamic Maghreb. In a July 2008 interview with the *New York Times*, Droukdel again claimed responsibility for having GSPC officially join Al-Qaida and acknowledged the role played by Ahmad Fadil Nazal al-Khalayleh a.k.a. Abu Musab al-Zarqawi (deceased) in the first phases of the merging process," United Nations Security Council Subsidiary Organs, "Narrative Summaries of Reasons for Listing: Abdelmalek Droukdel," https://www.un.org/sc/suborg/en/sanctions /1267.

146 the area around Naciria: Naciria is a town and commune in Boumerdès Province, east of Algiers.

152 decided to publish the interview transcript as well: "An Interview with Abdelmalek Droukdal," *New York Times*, July 1, 2008.

8: GUNS AND ROSES

160 the first part of Rohde's account: David Rohde, "Held by the Taliban: Part One: 7 Months, 10 Days in Captivity," *New York Times*, October 17, 2009. See also "Times Reporter Escapes Taliban After 7 Months," *New York Times*, June 21, 2009, and David Rohde and Kristen Mulvihill, *A Rope and a Prayer: A Kidnapping from Two Sides* (New York: Viking, 2010).

165 said he was a journalist: "Among them was Kareem Khan, a 50-year-old from Machikhel, North Waziristan, who works as a journalist with an Arab TV channel." Andrew Buncombe and Issam Ahmed, "Protests Grow as Civilian Toll of Obama's Drone War on Terrorism Is Laid Bare," *Independent*, March 3, 2012. See also "Kareem Khan," Reprieve, http://www.reprieve.org.uk/case -study/kareem-khan.

166 he had lost his son and his brother in a drone strike: "Pakistani Tribesman to Sue CIA Over Drone Strike Deaths," Agence France-Presse, November 29, 2010.

166 attacking the Pakistani border region with drones since 2004: "The Bush Years: Pakistan Strikes 2004–2009." Bureau of Investigative Journalism, August 10, 2011, https://www.thebureauinvestigates.com/2011/08/10/the-bush -years-2004-2009/#B1.

168 the name of the CIA station chief in Pakistan: Declan Walsh, "CIA Chief in Pakistan Leaves after Drone Trial Blows His Cover," *Guardian*, December 17, 2010.

168 U.S. officials were blaming Pakistan's military intelligence agency: Alex Rodriguez, "CIA Identity Breach Stirs Mistrust with Pakistan," *Los Angeles Times*, December 19, 2010; see also Sabrina Toppa, "Pakistan Edges Closer to Charging CIA Over Drone Strikes," *Time*, April 16, 2015.

9: MUKHABARAT

170 As the car entered the parking lot: Much of the account of the author's expe- riences in Egypt draws on recollections from the author and her colleague Nicholas Kulish, and the following article: Souad Mekhennet and Nicholas Kulish, "2 Detained Reporters Saw Police's Methods," *New York Times*, Feb- ruary 4, 2011.

172 would come to be known as the "Arab Spring": Joshua Keating, "Who First Used the Term Arab Spring?" *Foreign Policy*, November 4, 2011, http:// foreignpolicy.com/2011/11/04/who-first-used-the-term-arab-spring/.

176 "These people are spies!": Souad Mekhennet and Nicholas Kulish, "Blood on the Nile: An Encounter with Egypt's Secret Police at the Height of the Crisis," *New York Times*, February 6, 2011.

10: THIS IS NOT AN ARAB SPRING

193   "people know him as the rapper Deso Dogg": Much of the account of Denis
       Cuspert (aka Deso Dogg, Abu Maleek, and later Abu Talha) draws on report-
       ing done by the author in collaboration with Anthony Faiola for the follow-
       ing articles: Souad Mekhennet, "German Officials Alarmed by Ex-Rapper's
       New Message: Jihad," *New York Times*, September 1, 2011; Anthony Faiola
       and Souad Mekhennet, "Battle with the Islamic State for the Minds of Young
       Muslims," *Washington Post*, December 19, 2014; and Anthony Faiola and
       Souad Mekhennet, "From Hip-Hop to Jihad, How the Islamic State Became
       a Magnet for Converts," *Washington Post*, May 6, 2015.

196   "Deso" being short for "Devil's Son": Sarah Kaplan, "'Jihad Is a Lot of Fun,'
       Deso Dogg, a German Rapper Turned Islamic State Pitchman Said. Now He's
       Reportedly Dead from U.S. Air Strike," *Washington Post*, October 30, 2015.

196   a stint in juvenile detention: Cuspert was convicted for property crime and
       bodily harm, unauthorized possession of weapons, and narcotics-related
       offenses. He spent terms in prison more than once. According to the State
       Office for the Protection of the Constitution (Berlin), he used the "street cred-
       ibility" gained in prison for his later rap music career. See Senatsverwaltung
       für Inneres und Sport Berlin, "Denis Cuspert—eine jihadistische Karriere,"
       September 2014, pp. 8–9, http://www.berlin.de/sen/inneres/verfassungsschutz
       /publikationen/lage-und-wahlanalysen/lageanalyse_denis_cuspert.pdf.

200   shot and killed two American airmen in Frankfurt: Souad Mekhennet,
       "Frankfurt Attack Mystifies Suspect's Family," *New York Times*, March 8,
       2011; Jack Ewing, "Man Charged in Germany in Killing of U.S. Airmen," *New
       York Times*, July 7, 2011.

202   *le féminisme bourguibien*: Samar El-Masri, "Tunisian Women at a Crossroads:
       Cooptation or Autonomy?" *Middle East Policy* 22, no. 2 (Summer 2015),
       http://www.mepc.org/journal/middle-east-policy-archives/tunisian-women
       -crossroads-cooptation-or-autonomy.

204   including many jihadists: Haim Malka and Margo Balboni, "Violence in
       Tunisia: Analyzing Terrorism and Political Violence after the Revolution,"
       Center for Strategic and International Studies, June 2016, http://foreignfighters
       .csis.org/tunisia/violence-in-tunisia.html.

11: THREATS

208   the first Jewish ambassador in the Arab world: Julia Duin, "Bahrain Protests
       Have Complicated Job for Houda Nonoo, First Jewish Ambassador from an
       Arab Nation," *Washington Post Magazine*, May 26, 2012; "Bahrain Profile—
       Timeline," BBC News, September 1, 2016, http://www.bbc.com/news/world-
       middle-east-14541322.

209 could also be mercurial: Bahrain Independent Commission of Inquiry, "The Report of the Bahrain Independent Commission of Inquiry," November 23, 2011 (final revision of December 10, 2011), pp. 72–73, http://www.bici.org.bh /BICIreportEN.pdf.

210 "was concerned for their safety": Ibid.

210 After six Bahraini protesters were killed: Ibid., pp. 228–32.

210 The crown prince waited all night: Ibid., p. 80.

210 The chances for a fruitful dialogue vanished: The commission concluded, "If HRH the Crown Prince's initiative to hold a national dialogue at the time had been accepted, it could have paved the way for significant constitutional and political reform in Bahrain." Ibid., p. 169.

211 Bill Keller announced that he would step down: Jeremy W. Peters, "Abramson Named Executive Editor at The Times," *New York Times*, June 2, 2011. Keller announced his resignation in June 2011 and stepped down in September.

212 blindfolded, threatened, and tortured with electric shocks: Page 292 of "The Report of the Bahrain Independent Commission of Inquiry" describes the findings of torture: "1213. The medical experts noted that 33 detainees had significant physical marks or symptoms, which the detainees alleged had been caused by mistreatment. The experts identified 19 different methods of mistreatment. The most common were beatings, forced standing for prolonged periods, use of excessively tight handcuffs, exposure to extreme temperatures, head traumas and the use of electric shocks. The experts concluded that physical findings on 32 detainees were highly consistent with mistreatment and traumatic events. The experts also concluded that 15 detainees had significant psychological symptoms or impairments as a result of the alleged mistreatment. Of these 15 detainees, 13 required follow-up treatment. The experts also concluded that the physical findings on 34 detainees were highly consistent with beatings and blunt trauma. In addition, the physical findings on 19 detainees were highly consistent with and even virtually diagnostic of injuries caused by firearms. The physical findings on 22 detainees were highly consistent with the use of painful handcuffs, while the physical findings on 20 other detainees were highly consistent with exposure to extreme temperatures. The experts also found in a number of cases that scars on different parts of the body were consistent with a sound bomb injury as described by the detainee, but these scars were non-specific (i.e., could be produced by different causes). Three cases were highly consistent with cigarette burn scars on different parts of the body."

212 who said they'd been attacked by protesters: See page 373 of "The Report of the Bahrain Independent Commission of Inquiry": "1525. The Commission found sufficient evidence to establish that some expatriates, in particular South Asian workers, were the targets of attacks during the events of February/March 2011. The Commission finds that four expatriates were killed by

mob attacks during the events and many were injured. 1526. Pakistanis, in particular, were the target of attacks owing to their membership of some of them in the BDF and police force. Various neighbourhoods where expatriates live in Bahrain were the subject of sporadic attacks. The attacks on expatriates created an environment of fear, resulting in many of them leaving their homes and living in shelters. Other foreign nationals relayed to the Commission that they feared leaving their homes, attending services at their places of worship, or going to work. This caused many foreign nationals economic loss because they were fearful of returning to work and opening their businesses. The attacks on South Asian expatriates also resulted in hundreds of Bangladeshis, Pakistanis and Indians fleeing the country."

212   on a scholarship from the crown prince's office: Souad Mekhennet, "Bahrain Women Take Pride in Vital Protest Role," *New York Times*, December 20, 2011.

213   thirty-five people had died: "The Report of the Bahrain Independent Commission of Inquiry," p. 219.

213   "They do shout it on the streets": "SPIEGEL Interview with the King of Bahrain 'Arab Spring? That's the Business of Other Countries,'" *Spiegel Online*, February 13, 2012, http://www.spiegel.de/international/world/spiegel -interview-with-the-king-of-bahrain-arab-spring-that-s-the-business-of- other-countries-a-814915.html. Interview conducted by Alexander Smoltczyk and Souad Mekhennet.

221   the government had made "mistakes": "Interview with Bahrain's Prime Minster: The Opposition 'Are Terrorizing the Rest of This Country,'" *Spiegel Online*, April 27, 2012, http://www.spiegel.de/international/world/interview- bahraini-prime-minister-prince-khalifa-bin-salman-al-khalifa-a-830045. html. Interview conducted by Souad Mekhennet in Bahrain.

222   "accusing Martin Luther King of being a racist": Kelly McEvers, "Iraq's Chalabi Advises Protesters Abroad," NPR, April 11, 2011, http://www.npr.org/2011 /04/11/135324059/iraqs-chalabi-advises-protesters-abroad.

223   "No, I will not stand against the victims' reaction": "Interview with Bahraini Opposition Activist: Regime Using Formula One Race to 'Trick the World,'" *Spiegel Online*, April 20, 2012, http://www.spiegel.de/international/world /interview-with-bahraini-human-rights-activist-zainab-al-khawaja-a -828407.html. Interview conducted by Souad Mekhennet.

224   "another story ran that drew the family's ire: Frank Gardner, "Bahrain Activist Khawaja to Continue Hunger Strike," BBC News, May 1, 2012, http:// www.bbc.com/news/world-middle-east-17908449.

227   "Mekhennet fails to question any of Rajab's official policy statements": Samia Errazzouki and Maryam al-Khawaja, "Beware of the Middle East's Fake Feminists," *Foreign Policy*, October 22, 2013, http://foreignpolicy.com/2013/10/22 /beware-of-the-middle-easts-fake-feminists/.

12: BOYS FOR THE CALIPHATE

230 "We have a big catastrophe": Michael Birnbaum and Souad Mekhennet, "As Son Heads to Syrian Front, Family in Germany Plots Kidnapping to Bring Him Back," *Washington Post*, November 11, 2013.

231 Pero's family was devastated: Ibid.

232 While some German Salafists: Marwan Abou Tamm et al., "Kontinuierlicher Wandel. Organisation und Anwerbungspraxis der salafistischen Bewegung," HSFK-Report Nr. 2, 2016, http://www.hsfk.de/fileadmin/HSFK/hsfk_publika tionen/report_022016.pdf.

232 he always called for donations: Jörg Diehl et al., "Glaubenskrieger: Taxi in den Dschihad," *Der Spiegel* 43 (2013): 36–39.

234 I'd profiled him several years earlier: Souad Mekhennet, "Munich Imam Strives to Dilute the Elixir of Radical Islam for Some Young People," *New York Times*, May 17, 2010.

13: BRIDES FOR THE CALIPHATE

243 Hezbollah bombed the French paratrooper barracks: Richard Ernsberger Jr., "1983 Beirut Barracks Bombing: 'The BLT Building Is Gone!'" HistoryNet, October 27, 2016, http://www.historynet.com/1983-beirut-bombing-the-blt -building-is-gone.htm.

244 they have often been the scene of antigovernment protests: Katrin Sold, "Ein unvollendeter Aufarbeitungsprozess: Der Algerienkrieg im kollek- tiven Gedächtnis Frankreichs," Bundeszentrale für politische Bildung, Janu- ary 21, 2013, http://www.bpb.de/internationales/europa/frankreich/152531 /algerienkrieg; Simone Gnade, "Problemgebiet Banlieue: Konflikte und Ausgrenzung in französischen Vorstädten," Bundeszentrale für poli- tische Bildung, January 21, 2013, http://www.bpb.de/internationales/europa /frankreich/152511/problemgebiet-banlieue; ABC News, "Paris Attacks: A History of Terror Attacks in Modern France," November 14, 2015, http:// www.abc.net.au/news/2015-11-14/history-of-terror-attacks-in-modern -france/6940960; John R. Bowen. "Three Reasons France Became a Target for Jihad," *Time*, January 8, 2015.

245 "It was the best times in my life": Souad Mekhennet, "Divining the Future in Morocco," *New York Times*, May 10, 2011.

246 "under an Islamic leader in a truly Islamic land": Ibid.

246 "Maybe we could go to the Rafidain Center": "Rafidain" is Mesopotamia/Iraq, i.e., "land of the two rivers." Elaine Sciolino and Souad Mekhennet, "Al Qaeda Warrior Uses Internet to Rally Women," *New York Times*, May 28, 2008.

247 Malika was one of nearly two dozen defendants: Ibid.

248 an eight-year prison term: "El-Aroud Loses Appeal against Eight-Year 'Jihad' Sentence," Agence France-Presse, December 1, 2010.

250 She was sent to a group home: Michael Birnbaum and Souad Mekhennet, "Hayat Boumeddiene, Wife of Paris Attacker, Becomes France's Most-Wanted Woman," *Washington Post*, February 2, 2015.

251 she and Coulibaly were married in a religious ceremony: Michael Birnbaum and Souad Mekhennet, "The Woman on the Run," *Washington Post*, February 3, 2015.

251 "My father stood in for me": François Labrouillère and Aurélie Raya, "Le destin monstrueux d'un couple ordinaire," *Paris Match*, January 30, 2015, http://www.parismatch.com/Actu/Societe/Hayat-Boumeddiene-et-Amedy-Coulibaly-Le-destin-monstrueux-d-un-couple-ordinaire-700346.

252 a pilgrimage to Mecca: Ibid.

252 "evil done to innocents in occupied lands": Ibid.

252 That's how I found Meryam: Faiola and Mekhennet, "Battle with the Islamic State."

258 In 2008, several Danish papers: "Prophet Mohammed Cartoons Controversy: Timeline," *Telegraph*, May 4, 2015, http://www.telegraph.co.uk/news/world news/europe/france/11341599/Prophet-Muhammad-cartoons-controversy-timeline.html.

259 For an earlier book, *Die Kinder des Dschidad*: Souad Mekhennet, Claudia Sautter, and Michael Hanfeld, *Die Kinder des Dschihad: Die neue Generation des islamistischen Terrors in Europa* (Munich: Piper, 2008).

14: THE SEARCH FOR AN ISLAMIST BEATLE, OR FINDING JIHADI JOHN

261 a prison on a mountain fifteen miles east of the Syrian city of Raqqa: James Harkin, "The Fight to Save James Foley," *Daily Telegraph*, October 31, 2015.

262 he founded Special Emergency Response and Assistance (SERA): "SERA is focused on the distribution of aid materials to populations with an acute and immediate need. We administer aid in the form of food and cooking materials, medical supplies, and clothing." Nick Schwellenbach, "An Army Ranger Helps Syrian Refugees," *Time*, January 8, 2013.

263 he'd developed a deep interest in Islam: Adam Goldman, "Islamic State Beheads Aid Worker from United States," *Washington Post*, November 17, 2014.

265 It ended with a shot of Kassig's severed head: SITE Intelligence Group, "IS Beheads Peter Kassig, Challenges U.S. to Send Ground Troops," November 16, 2014, https://news.siteintelgroup.com/Jihadist-News/is-beheads-peter-kassig-challenges-u-s-to-send-ground-troops.html.

271 He's a lawyer who has worked on cases involving detainees: Ben Hayes and

Asim Qureshi, "'We Are Completely Independent': The Home Office, Breakthrough Media and the PREVENT Counter Narrative Industry," CAGE Advocacy UK, 2016, p. 3, http://cage.ngo/wp-content/uploads/2016/05/CAGE _WACI.pdf.

271   "under constant pressure and scrutiny": Kevin Rawlinson, "Charities Sever Ties with Pressure Group Cage over Mohammed Emwazi Links," *Guardian*, March 6, 2015.

272   "They were Bidoon": Sebastian Kohn, "Stateless in Kuwait: Who Are the Bidoon?," Open Society Foundations, March 24, 2011, https://www.opensociety foundations.org/voices/stateless-kuwait-who-are-bidoon; see also abstract of Marie Brokstad Lund-Johansen, "Fighting for Citizenship in Kuwait," master's thesis, University of Oslo, 2014, https://www.duo.uio.no/handle/10852/43302.

272   charter school called Quintin Kynaston: Tim Ross, Robert Mendick, and Edward Malnick, "Ministers Order Inquiry into Jihadi John's School," *Telegraph*, February 28, 2015, http://www.telegraph.co.uk/news/uknews/terrorism -in-the-uk/11442434/Ministers-order-inquiry-into-Jihadi-Johns-school .html; Nile Rice, "What Going to School with Jihadi John Taught Me About Radicalization," *Vice*, March 17, 2015, http://www.vice.com/read/quintin -kynaston-jihadi-john-531.

273   "I had a job waiting for me and marriage to get started," Emwazi wrote: "The Emwazi Emails: CAGE Releases Its Correspondences with Emwazi in Full," CAGE, February 28, 2015, https://cage.ngo/uncategorized/emwazi-emails -cage-releases-its-correspondences-emwazi-full/.

274   forbidden by Britain's Terrorism Act of 2006: Souad Mekhennet and Dexter Filkins, "British Law against Glorifying Terrorism Has Not Silenced Calls to Kill for Islam," *New York Times*, August 1, 2006.

281   Ladbroke Grove: Colin Freeman, "Ladbroke Grove Connection—the Wealthy West London District that Bred Jihadi John," *Telegraph*, February 15, 2015, http://www.telegraph.co.uk/news/worldnews/islamic-state/11438534 /Ladbroke-Grove-connection-the-wealthy-west-London-district-that-bred -Jihadi-John.html. Robert Mendick, "Jihadi John: From Ordinary Schoolboy to World's Most Wanted Man," *Telegraph*, February 26, 2015, http://www .telegraph.co.uk/news/worldnews/islamic-state/11438545/Jihadi-John-From -ordinary-schoolboy-to-worlds-most-wanted-man.html.

15: TERROR COMES HOME

286   In the train stations of Austria: Much of the account of the refugees in Vienna draws on reporting done by the author in collaboration with William Booth for the following article: Souad Mekhennet and William Booth, "Migrants Are Disguising Themselves as Syrians to Enter Europe," *Washington Post*, September 23, 2015.

288 "Educationally, they are the flower of their country": United Nations High Commissioner for Refugees, "Syrian Refugee Arrivals in Greece, April–September 2015," https://data2.unhcr.org/en/documents/download/46542.

288 new refugees would fill a growing gap: Tina Bellon and Caroline Copley, "In Aging Germany, Refugees Seen as Tomorrow's Skilled Workers," Reuters, September 10, 2015.

289 a Shia commander named Ayyub al-Rubaie: "Abu Azrael: No Safe Place for ISIL in Iraq," All Iraq News Agency (AIN), March 18, 2015.

289 "ISIS, this will be your fate": Robert Verkaik, "'We Will Cut You like Shawarma,'" MailOnline, August 28, 2015.

289 accused of atrocities and serious human rights violations: "Iraq: Possible War Crimes by Shia Militia," Human Rights Watch, January 31, 2016, https://www.hrw.org/news/2016/01/31/iraq-possible-war-crimes-shia-militia.

290 Abdelhamid Abaaoud, one of the ringleaders: Much of the account of Abaaoud's background and activities draws on reporting done by the author in collaboration with Anthony Faiola for the following articles: Anthony Faiola and Souad Mekhennet, "'He Is a Barbaric Man'—the Belgian Who May Be Behind the Paris Attacks," Washington Post, November 16, 2015; and Anthony Faiola and Souad Mekhennet, "The Islamic State Creates a New Type of Jihadist: Part Terrorist, Part Gangster," Washington Post, December 20, 2015.

291 the influence of Saudi, Kuwaiti, and Qatari religious organizations: Bruce Riedel, "Saudi Arabia Is Part of the Problem and Part of the Solution to Global Jihad," Brookings, November 20, 2015, https://www.brookings.edu/blog/markaz/2015/11/20/saudi-arabia-is-part-of-the-problem-and-part-of-the-solution-to-global-jihad/; Nikolaj Nielsen, "Bearded Infidels in the EU Capital," EUobserver, February 1, 2016, https://euobserver.com/investigations/131883.

297 His worldview was set: Anthony Faiola and Souad Mekhennet, "Jihadists Adding Crime to the Mix," Washington Post, December 21, 2015.

297 led to him by a crucial source: Greg Miller and Souad Mekhennet, "Friendship Led Police to Paris Ringleader," Washington Post, April 11, 2016.

298 a cousin living in Paris named Hasna Aitboulahcen: Much of the account of Hasna's experiences and those of the woman called Sonia draws on reporting done by the author in collaboration with Greg Miller for the following article: Greg Miller and Souad Mekhennet, "One Woman Helped the Mastermind of the Paris Attacks. The Other Turned Him In," Washington Post, April 10, 2016.

EPILOGUE: THE DEEPEST CUT

311   The whole thing took several hours: "Münchener Amokläufer wollte keine
      weiteren Menschen töten," *Zeit Online*, August 17, 2016, http://www.zeit.de
      /gesellschaft/zeitgeschehen/2016-08/lka-amoklauf-muenchen-taeter-ende
      -toetung-selbstmord; "Täter erschoss 9 Menschen. Das sind die Opfer des
      Amoklaufs von München," *Focus Online*, July 23, 2016, http://www.focus.de
      /politik/deutschland/taeter-erschoss-9-menschen-das-sind-die-opfer-des
      -amoklaufs-von-muenchen_id_5756199.html.

316   purchased illegally on the so-called dark web: Jana Illhardt and Matthias
      Maus, "David S. hat seine Tat ein Jahr lang geplant," *Der Tagesspiegel*, July 24,
      2016, http://www.tagesspiegel.de/politik/wer-war-der-amokschuetze-david-s
      -hat-seine-tat-ein-jahr-lang-geplant/13918328.html; Lars Langenau, "Ein Täter,
      58 Kugeln—der Amoklauf von München," *Süddeutsche Zeitung*, July 24,
      2016, http://www.sueddeutsche.de/panorama/amoklauf-in-muenchen-ein
      -taeter-kugeln-1.3093354.

318   the *umra* pilgrimage: Contrary to the *hajj* pilgrimage to Mecca, which every
      Muslim should undertake once, as it is one of the five pillars of Islam, and
      which has to take place in the first days of the twelfth month of the Islamic
      calendar (Dhu'l-Hijja), the *umra* can be undertaken at any time of the year.

ACKNOWLEDGMENTS

This book would not have been possible without many people's support, advice, and labor.

I cannot thank Vanessa Gezari and Margot Williams enough for their crucial impact, support, and contributions. They are wonderful friends and became the godmothers of this project.

Peter Finn is not only one of the most talented editors at the *Washington Post*, he was also very helpful in the writing and editing process of this book. I owe Peter the greatest thanks for introducing me to the world of U.S. journalism when I started this journey, and he has since become a trusted adviser and friend.

My friend and former *New York Times* editor Christine Kay helped me develop the idea of this book and has since been a source of inspiration and support.

Michael Moss is not only one of the most talented reporters but he has also been a source of support through all these years, and his family has always welcomed me with warmth at their home.

I am also thankful to Julie Tate, Charlotte Wiemann, and Stefan Pauly for their extraordinary work as fact-checkers and researchers. They have been a great source of enthusiasm and worked on this project with an unstoppable spirit.

Many important characters and sources who appear in this book and helped me with information and access cannot be named. They are spread across five continents and couldn't be more different from one another. They have trusted me with their opinions and stories, and this book could not have been written without their assistance.

I was helped immensely throughout this writing process by the support and encouragement of a number of friends, especially Antje and Robert Ehrt (my godparents), Laila Alaoui, Loulwa Bakr, Steffen Burkhardt, Michel Friedman, Lama Hourani, Adam Hunter, Ali Ibrahim, Lonnie Isabel, Ryan Nibblins, Claudia Sautter, Baerbel Schaefer, Soraya Sebti, and Dina Shoman. They have cheerfully served as editors and sounding boards as well as indispensable sources of strength and steadiness.

My friend Nicholas Kulish—also my coauthor on *The Eternal Nazi*—offered suggestions and support that were invaluable.

My *Washington Post* colleagues and friends Joby Warrick, Greg Miller, and Anthony Faiola helped with their suggestions and edits to shape the book.

I could not have attempted this book without the generous support of my employer, the *Washington Post,* and so many *Post* colleagues and friends. I am especially indebted to Marty Baron, Cameron Barr, Tracy Grant, and Scott Wilson for their kindness in allowing me to pursue this project. I am also grateful to Michael Birnbaum, William Booth, Karen DeYoung, Thomas Gibbons-Neff, Adam Goldman, Anne Hull, David Ignatius, Doug Jehl, Carol Morello, Ellen Nakashima, Missy Ryan, Anthony Shadid, Mary Beth Sheridan, Kevin Sullivan, Griff Witte, and Jia Lynn Yang.

Special thanks to some family friends and colleagues for their help and insights throughout the years, among them Abdulla Alkhan, Silvia Console Battilana, Raymond Bonner, Martin Bussmann, Desmond Butler, John Crewdson, Inge Feldhusen, Judith Fessler, Marcie Goldstein, Christian Haenel, Michael Hanfeld, Ingeborg Hensel, Almut Hielscher, Jason Isaacson, Yaakov Katz, Vivian Kervick, Renate Lehnert, Moulay Tayyib Mdghri-Alaoui, his wife Aisha and daughter Leila, Guy Raz, Majda and Boris Ruge, Steven Sokol, Yaroslav Trofimov, and Ivan Vatchkov. I thank Ann Marie Lipinski and Stefanie Friedhoff for their kind support during my Nieman Fellowship, where I had the chance to work with amazing writing teachers like Anne Bernays and Paige Williams.

My New America Foundation fellowship gave me freedom to report and write this book for some time without distractions. I would like to thank especially Peter Bergen for his help and friendship.

Thanks also to the Johns Hopkins University School of Advanced International Studies, the Weatherhead Center at Harvard University, and the Geneva Center for Security Policy, for their access to valuable information. Special thanks as well to Professors Carla Adams, Vali Nasr, and Karl Kaiser.

At ZDF, I would like to thank Elmar Thevessen and Claus Kleber for their support.

The former executive editor of the *New York Times* Bill Keller provided the backing and support that allowed me to gain a foothold in American journalism.

At the *New York Times*, I was lucky to work with some amazing editors like Matt Purdy during my time at the Investigative Unit. I also had the honor to work with some very talented colleagues, and I can't thank them enough for their insight, among them Richard Bernstein, Chris Chivers, Bryan Denton, Steven Erlanger, Carlotta Gall, Mike Kamber, Mark Landler, Mark Mazzetti, Jehad Nga, Richard Oppel, Monique and Lonnie Schlein, Eric Schmitt, Elaine Sciolino, Alison Smale, Craig Smith, Marion Underhill, and Don Van Natta.

A very special thanks goes to all the fantastic local reporters whose help and input have been crucial in so many projects throughout the years: Fakhr al Ayoubi, Said Chitour, Jamal Ismail, Ranya Kadri, Leena Saidi, Marwan Shada, Ahmad Zouhir, and others who cannot be named here due to possible threats to their lives.

Some people have helped to provide spaces where I was able to work on this book in my free time: special thanks to Abdelilah al Aouni, Samy Boukhaled, Kamal Bouskri, and Malek Houssein.

I am ever grateful to my literary agent, Gail Ross, for her suggestions, spirit, faith in this project, and advice, and to the entire staff of the Ross Yoon Literary Agency for logistical support.

I'm indebted as well to the people at Henry Holt and Company, including Leslie Brandon, Patricia Eisemann, Fiona Lowenstein, Devon Mazzone, Maggie Richards, and Stephen Rubin.

And I'm profoundly thankful for the assistance of my remarkably talented editor Paul Golob, who saw potential in my book proposal. Any successes in these pages are a tribute to his strong ideas, peerless editing skills, and patience.

Finally, and most important, I would like to express my love and deepest gratitude to my parents, Aydanur and Boujema, and my siblings, Fatma, Hannan, and Hicham. None of this book would have been possible without all of them. And not one day passes where I don't remember my grandparents, who have influenced my life so much and are no longer with us.

INDEX

ABOUT THE AUTHOR

SOUAD MEKHENNET is a national security correspondent for the *Washington Post*, and she has reported on terrorism for *The New York Times* and other news organizations. She is the coauthor of three previous books and was named a Young Global Leader by the World Economic Forum. She was a Nieman Fellow at Harvard University and has also held fellowships at the Johns Hopkins School of Advanced International Studies and the Geneva Centre for Security Policy.